Work Time Regulation as a Sustainable Full-Employment Strategy

Robert LaJeunesse looks beyond the twentieth-century arguments for shortening the work week. He writes a careful, convincing critique of traditional full-employment policies in advocacy of an alternative macroeconomic paradigm. In focusing on the effort bargain, the author advocates a policy of work time regulation that is not only appropriate for a twenty-first-century post-industrial economy, but speaks to concerns about balancing work and family, environmental sustainability, stabilizing incomes and prices, and social and economic well-being.

Through its unique conceptualization of employment relations as a social effort bargain, this book proposes that governments can achieve egalitarian and sustainable macroeconomic objectives by regulating work hours. Equally important to achieving sustainable full employment and price stability, work time regulation offers the capability for citizens living in an age of abundance to define themselves as something other than paid employees. Work time reform represents a first step in a process of enlightenment in which workers will create an identity through the whole of their relationships at work, home, community, and at play. There is certainly a role for government in fostering the pursuit of "loftier ideals" subsequent to a redistribution of work time, but the first precondition for enhanced human development is greater socioeconomic participation, which means more paid work for some and less for others.

In addition to students and researchers in economics, sociology, and political science, this book will be of interest to policymakers, policy analysts, labour unionists, environmentalists, and other social reformers.

Robert M. LaJeunesse is a senior lecturer in Economics at the University of Newcastle, Australia.

Routledge Frontiers of Political Economy

Work Time Regulation as a Sustainable Full Employment Strategy

The social effort bargain

Robert M. LaJeunesse

Routledge
Taylor & Francis Group

LONDON AND NEW YORK

First published 2009
by Routledge
2 Park Square, Milton Park, Abingdon, Oxon OX14 4RN

Simultaneously published in the USA and Canada
by Routledge
270 Madison Avenue, New York, NY 10016

Routledge is an imprint of the Taylor & Francis Group, an informa business

© 2009 Robert M. LaJeunesse

Typeset in Times New Roman by
Taylor & Francis Books
Printed and bound in Great Britain by
TJ Digital Ltd, Padstow, Cornwall

British Library Cataloguing in Publication Data
A catalogue record for this book is available from the British Library

Library of Congress Cataloging in Publication Data
LaJeunesse, Robert.
Work time regulation as a sustainable full employment strategy : the social effort bargain / Robert LaJeunesse.
    p. cm.
1. Hours of labor. 2. Labor. I. Title.
    HD5106.L29 2009
    331.25'7–dc22
                    2008043530

ISBN 978-0-415-46057-6 (hbk)
ISBN 978-0-203-87953-5 (ebk)

To Oscar Francis LaJeunesse (1915–2007) – who taught me
how to pluck and while the hour, the day, the season,
and the year virtuously and well.

Contents

Charts, tables and figures

Charts

Table

Figure

Acknowledgements

I would like to express my profound gratitude to Dr. James Ronald Stanfield for cultivating my interest in social inquiry and introducing me to the Institutionalist methods, tools, and thought process necessary to contemplate improvements and alternatives to our social predicament. In addition to the many heterodox labor economists who have influenced my thinking on work time issues, I am grateful to Deborah Figart, Bruce Philp, and John King, who have taken the time to make constructive theoretical and compositional suggestions specific to this manuscript.

My thinking on the role of work time regulation has been sharpened by many discussions and debates with associates of the Centre of Full-Employment and Equity at the University of Newcastle, including William F. Mitchell, L. Randall Wray, Martin Watts, James Juniper, and Victor Quick. (Acknowledging their contribution to the development of my ideas on work time regulation in no way suggests their endorsement of the policies and programs proffered on these pages.)

I am also thankful for the collegial research support of IGR-IAE de Rennes at the Université de Rennes, during my study leave in Rennes, France. Special thanks are owed to David Alias, Gwenaelle Poilpot-Rocaboy, and Yvon Rocaboy. Invaluable translation assistance was provided by Marléne Maillez.

Finally, I am supremely grateful for the loving and selfless support of my wife and family, particularly 6-year-old Harmony who routinely cautioned me about the hypocrisy of working long hours in advocacy of work time reduction.

Introduction

"The full employment policy by means of investment is only one particular application of an intellectual theorem. You can produce the result as well by consuming more or working less. Personally I regard the investment policy as first aid ... Less work is ultimate solution ... How you mix up the three ingredients of a cure is a matter of taste and experience, i.e., of morals and knowledge."

Letter from JM Keynes to T.S. Eliot dated April 5, 1945 (Keynes 1980: 384)

Labor economists of all persuasions are increasingly recognizing that employment relationships can be characterized as an effort bargain. Whether the analysis takes the form of gift exchanges, efficiency wages, or the economics of agency and signaling, the outcome hinges on the level of effort elicited from employees. Although these research streams have only recently found a footing in the mainstream economics profession, the importance of the effort bargain has long been espoused by Marxist and Institutionalist economists. Marx distinguished between labor and labor power over 200 years ago, and Institutionalist thinkers, such as Clark Kerr, Lloyd Reynolds, and John Dunlop, began articulating an efficiency wage theory as early as the 1950s.

Recognition of labor relations as an effort bargain has become vitally important to private and social productivity improvements in a post-industrial economy in which few workers directly produce tangible outputs. Moreover, as workers in advanced countries begin to place less emphasis on future wage increases—realizing rapidly diminishing returns when trying to "buy happiness"—employment negotiations will need to focus more attention on working conditions than wages. Work time is one condition of work that has been relatively unexplored as part of the effort bargain. Since the social division of labor determines both the magnitude of productivity gains and how those dividends are shared, it represents a profoundly important social compromise. The central premise of this book is that in a post-industrial, climate-constrained world of material abundance, employers, governments, workers and other concerned social parties will need to be increasingly experimental in terms of work time organization and regulation in order to promote greater socioeconomic participation in a manner that is socially and environmentally sustainable. That is, employment relations should be conceptualized as a *social* effort bargain to be regulated in the public interest.

Throughout the history of capitalism, a variety of methods and tactics have been used in an attempt to achieve greater harmony in the social effort bargain. Welfare capitalists attempted to buy the loyalty of the worker. When that failed, behavioral scientists (like Frederick Taylor) sought non-material motivations to increase productivity. Using notions such as "employee participation," theorists hoped that the social pressure of work groups could substitute for the missing loyalty to management. However, the human relations approach to greater employee participation was widely recognized as pre-emptive action against unions and the productivity-enhancing exit/voice option that they provide their members. Presently, the search continues for a suitable social balance in the effort bargain. As Thompson (1983: 151) writes, "methods of increasing productivity largely fall within a spectrum that ranges from directly controlling the worker to attempting to gain some sort of voluntary commitment to production goals through earning their gratitude and loyalty or helping to make work more pleasant." Both common sense and the emerging evidence from work time experiments (featured in Chapter 5) suggest that an effective way of making work more pleasant and productive is to make it less extensive for any one individual.

The boundaries within which the social effort bargain takes place greatly influence the potential outcomes. For example, if long hours are the only option on offer, workers will adjust their effort accordingly and private productivity rates will suffer. Long hours and low productivity growth rates will then create negative externalities for society as overworked parents, citizens, and volunteers will be less effective in their non-paid, but fundamentally important, social tasks as well. Alternatively, if the negotiation zone is limited to moderate hours that are deemed to be socially and environmentally sustainable, both private and social productivity rates could burgeon. Since the social effort bargain has a vital impact on living standards and well-being, the State has a justifiable interest in promoting an outcome that reflects a collective settlement between employers, employees, families, communities, and future generations. Given the profound ramifications of the social effort bargain, this book addresses the potential for the regulation of work hours to achieve the widely held macroeconomic objectives of full employment, price stability, and adequate growth in a socially and environmentally sustainable manner.

In post-industrial societies, work time is no longer governed by the exigencies of the factory system. The vast majority of the labor force engages in non-mechanical work that can be performed at different times and with varying degrees of proficiency. The diversity of average annual work hours across Organization for Economic Co-operation and Development (OECD) countries, suggests that a great variety of work time regimes are capable of propelling the industrial system. As indicated in Chart i.1, many workers, particularly in English-speaking, Anglo-Saxon countries, tend to work 30 to 40 percent more hours than workers in Scandinavian and Central European countries. In some cases the longer hours translate into greater gross domestic product and higher output per *worker*, but this tends to occur at a diminishing rate with each additional *hour* of work. Annual reports from the International Labour Organization regularly observe that labor productivity per *hour* is routinely higher in short-hours countries like Germany and France than in countries where workers log nearly 30 percent more hours per year (Boules and Cette 2005).

Many advanced economies are also characterized by growing labor market inequities fueled by a polarization of work hours around a rather stable average workweek. Citing a deteriorating link between aggregate income and well-being and a limited ability for the ecosystem to absorb more industrial waste, an expanding group of social scientists has begun to challenge contemporary growth patterns. Moreover, the track record of traditional macroeconomic policies shows little promise of ever vanquishing the twin problems of unemployment and inflation. In wealthy countries, therefore, the efficacy and desirability of traditional demand stimulus (Keynesian) policies to address an underutilization of labor is suspect. A growing chorus of social critics is recognizing that stimulating greater throughput may marginally tighten labor markets, but it also results in longer hours for the already overworked and greater degradation of a fragile environment. This discourse therefore contends that conventional full-employment policies result in a mal-distribution of work time and a treadmill pattern of

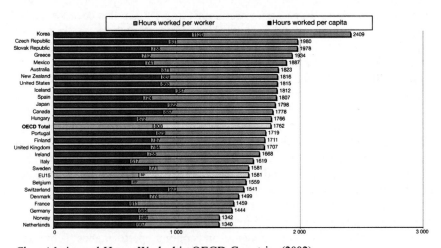

Chart i.1 Annual Hours Worked in OECD Countries (2002)
Source: OECD Annual Hours and Productivity databases
Population and employment-weighted OECD average of total hours per capita and hours per worker for the countries shown - StatLink: http://dx.doi.org/10.1787/174615513635

consumption that is socially and environmentally unsustainable. As such, the lodestar of employment policy in post-industrial societies should be the enhancement of socioeconomic participation, which entails more remunerative work for some, but less for others.

Given the failure of conventional macroeconomic policy to address the socioeconomic and environmental exigencies of post-industrial economies, reform of the social division of labor represents one of the most important public policy issues of our time. This book proposes an alternative distribution of labor as a means of affording individuals a more sustainable engagement in both the paid workforce and the third sector—the realm of activity conducted independently of the market and the public sector. The narrative maintains that a policy of work time regulation is a superior way of achieving greater socioeconomic participation than competing full-employment plans—such as job or income guarantees—that rely on greater economic growth and the creation of more employment hours in the aggregate. Since a truly sustainable employment policy will need to alter the existing distribution of social labors as well as the social psychology of economic gain, an hours-based regulation of the labor market is the most appropriate way to promote greater harmony between lives and livelihoods.

Although numerous social scientists have marshaled the "well-being" and "environmental" critiques of the sustainability of market capitalism to advocate for work time reduction, this thesis builds on that logic by showing that work time reform under a desideratum of improved socioeconomic participation is consistent with sustainable macroeconomic policy objectives. Significant space is devoted to the development and critique of the political economy of working time as macroeconomic imperialism has been known to trump progressive social and ecological concerns throughout the history of capitalism. Greater social inclusion through work time reform will only come to fruition if the vested social partners of market-based societies are convinced that a reformation and regulation of our social labors will result in broad-based socioeconomic improvements. Given the current social psyche, such persuasion must begin with the ubiquitous macroeconomic concerns that permeate the lives of all citizens before the social, philosophical, psychological, ethical and ecological arguments in favor of work time reform can have their full and rightful influence. Thus the salient contribution of this work is the exposition and advocacy of the macroeconomic possibilities of work time regulation.

Experiments with work time reduction and work sharing suggest that a comprehensive work time regulation regime could have substantial employment effects and a stabilizing influence on economic performance. Moreover, hours regulation that linked future labor productivity increases to work time reduction could be viewed as an egalitarian incomes policy designed to stabilize prices, equitably reward the working class (which has been deprived of their fair share of productivity dividends since the late 1960s), and curtail the most neurotic aspects of the "work and spend" culture. It is important to note that hours *regulation* does not always entail a *reduction* of hours. Although the secular trend would be towards shorter average workweeks, extraordinary conditions may arise in which society would choose to postpone hours reduction or even increase average workweeks.

As traditional work becomes more scarce and material goods more abundant, social scientists will be forced to rethink the role of remunerative employment in post-industrial economies. Intent on expanding participation levels in highly productive market democracies, policymakers will have to make important decisions in striking a balance among several competing social pressures. Should public policy encourage more private jobs and throughput, grant individuals access to participatory income, expand public sector employment, regulate work time with an eye towards payroll expansion, or pursue a hybrid combination of these policies? Although there may be great merit in pursuing a suite of labor market policies, this research endeavors to show that a policy of work time regulation offers the best chance of achieving the objective of enhanced socioeconomic participation in an environmental and socially sustainable manner than any one of the competing policies on its own.[1]

In order to understand the current infatuation with paid work, the first chapter features a historical account of the sociology of work and the ascendancy of economic gain as a societal foundation under capitalism. Such background knowledge reveals that the capitalistic method of social organization may be a more ephemeral and contrived structure than is commonly perceived. Rather than markets growing spontaneously out of natural human interaction, the factitious market system was established through the conscious actions of powerful individuals and institutions. The historical investigation of the market system implicates the economics profession in legitimizing and propagating a social system based on acquisitive behavior with little regard to side effects, alternatives, or long-run consequences.

The second chapter features radical critiques of the market-based economic system that encourages the idolatry of economic growth and paid work. Although focused on the labor market, the chapter features broad economic critiques of the underlying assumptions of the neoclassical paradigm in an attempt to subvert the growth and work fetish. In particular the assumptions of insatiability and scarcity are challenged as false representations of human behavior, and revealed as inappropriate in governing our social division of labor. Dismissal of these crucial assumptions challenges the sovereignty of consumption and the primacy of production. After investigating some of the many critiques of economic growth, including the burgeoning literature on the disconnect between national income and well-being, the chapter examines the future of paid work in post-industrial societies. The discussion suggests that the dynamic nature of technological development will force any employment program to incorporate a secular decline in working hours as the amount of traditional "work" that needs to be performed will be curtailed by technological imperative.

Guided by the desideratum of greater socioeconomic participation, Chapter 3 then examines the effectiveness and feasibility of work time regulation to achieve widely held macroeconomic objectives vis-à-vis two of the leading models of labor market intervention—job and income guarantees. Admittedly, this comparative analysis is highly dependent on the state of economic development within a country because a chief virtue of work time regulation is its ability to serve as a break on the neurotic "work and spend" cycle that is the source of many social and environmental costs in wealthy nations today. It follows then that regulating work time with an eye toward greater socioeconomic participation is most relevant to advanced, post-industrial economies. Indeed, full-employment policies designed to generate more industrial output and more aggregate hours of work may be more appropriate for developing and transitional economies that have yet to experience the "paradox of abundance." But for a growing number of advanced economies, a better distribution of socially necessary labor offers genuine and sustainable social benefits that dwarf those that could be achieved via the threadbare employment policies of the industrial era. The macroeconomic discussion in Chapter 3 further shows that work time regulation can provide superior price stability as it is essentially an incomes policy that grants future productivity dividends in the form of leisure time rather than money. The price stability achieved through work time regulation has the potential to make the federal financing of private payroll expansion a more politically palatable social policy than full-employment plans that rely on the stimulation of aggregate demand and the direct employment of the jobless.

Chapter 4 examines the social and environmental costs associated with current industrial and labor market arrangements in capitalist societies. The issue of climate-constrained growth is addressed from the Institutionalist perspective, which emphasizes an alternative definition of abundance and the dynamism of technology. Although the environmental threats of conducting "business as usual" in the developed world are now well known, Chapter 4 briefly summarizes the issue of ecological damage through a "labor market lens" to illustrate the exigency of revisionist thinking regarding the social division of labor in the developed world. The chapter then investigates the social costs of long hours related to physical and psychological health as well as costs associated with parental neglect. As workers are often the first to become cognizant of the physical and social costs of long hours, an assessment of desired work hours relative to actual hours is offered as an indictment of the labor-leisure choice model and a rationale for government intervention in socializing the effort bargain surrounding work time determination.

Chapter 5 addresses the macroeconomic arguments (such as the "lump-of-labor-fallacy") that often forestall progressive socioeconomic policies out of fear of economic contraction and job loss. After dispelling this major obstacle to work time regulation, the chapter examines past work time reduction experiments to assess the potential for a more comprehensive work time regulation scheme to create jobs and improve social productivity in a sustainable manner. The investigation provides useful insight into the appropriate design of hours regulation, which varies slightly with the democratically determined objectives of the social effort bargain.

Chapter 6 offers a collection of policies that long-hours countries could implement in an effort to improve the accountability, equity, and transparency of the social effort bargain. Social and ecological imperatives suggest that public policy in general should seek to: improve the distribution of our social labor, diminish the importance of paid work, reform consumption patterns, achieve stable and sustainable economic output levels, and encourage individual activity that is autonomous from the market system. Although it sounds ambitious, when coupled with other modest socioeconomic (education and taxation) reforms, comprehensive work time regulation is capable of yielding substantial improvements over existing macroeconomic policies and practices and launch society on a path toward a more rewarding and sustainable balance between lives and livelihoods.

1   The Origins of the Work and Growth Fetish

"If a man will not work, neither shall he eat."

John Calvin quoting St. Paul

"To become a fully functional adult male, one prerequisite is essential: a job."

US President's Commission Report, 1964

In contemplating an alternative social system of accumulation and social division of labor, a firm understanding of the history and development of contemporary market economies is imperative. This chapter therefore investigates the historical development of the idolatry of paid work. As an important corollary, it also references the social acceptance of the pursuit of economic gain and the acquisition of private property. It begins with the social and religious origins of private property and the work ethic and concludes by examining the role of the discipline of economics in re-enforcing the work fetish through its ethnocentric promotion of "economic man."

The religious and social genesis of private property and the work ethic

As children of the Reformation we have been conditioned to celebrate the work ethic. Yet, the moral sanctioning of assiduous work habits is by no means universal or time-honored. It was only after the Reformation in the sixteenth and seventeenth centuries that hard work began to reflect good character and strong morals. It was soon imbued with religious virtue by Judeo–Christian teachings that promised or signaled eternal salvation through hard work. By the time the religious virtue of hard work began to wane, the work fetish was well established in societal norms, policies and institutions. It continues to exact a prodigious influence on the social structure of accumulation and distribution.

Past civilizations have taken a much more ambivalent or even condescending view of work and acquisitive behavior than modern market economies. Valuing freedom above material attainments, ancient Grecian society attached no moral value to work, with the Greek philosophers often disparaging it (Tilgher 1931). For the Greeks, work was little more than a curse, with their word for it—ponos—having the same Latin root as sorrow. We find the same burdensome meaning in the English words: toil, fatigue, travail, and labor. This toil was the heavy price exacted by the gods for the goods of life, according to Xenophon. Tilgher (1977: 4) writes that most Greek thinkers "deplore the mechanical arts as brutalizing the mind till it is unfit for thinking of truth, for practicing virtue." Such sentiment is consistent with the admonition of the Delphic Oracle of "nothing to excess." The Greeks attempted to fashion a social ethos around the knowledge that happiness could only be achieved by successfully balancing the pursuit of material and spiritual needs.

Aristotle and Plato both viewed work as interfering with the duties of citizens and distracting them from more lofty pursuits like politics, art, and philosophy. Spiegel (1991: 7) writes, "The Greeks were politically minded to an excess, and much of what otherwise might have been their working life was spent in political activities often required by the institution of direct democracy." Such sentiment is reflected in Plato's prohibition of private property. In his second and third approximations, Plato contends that the soldiers and philosophers should be freed from the burdens of private property, manual labor and family in order to devote their lives to their natural calling-fighting or ruling. This meant that members of the upper class would possess no private property and live communally. As such they would be freed from the humdrum of daily toil and the pursuit of wealth: "that mortal dross which has been the source of many unholy deeds" (Plato from Speigel 1991: 17).

Placing more emphasis on self-sufficiency, Aristotle argued in favor of private property on efficiency grounds but also because it afforded the expression of temperance and liberality. In addition to the obligation of liberality to one's fellow citizens, Aristotle argued that acquisitiveness should be limited by encouraging both "natural exchange" and justice in exchange, or reciprocity. The desire for natural exchange (or use-value) emanates from natural wants, as opposed to those desires driven by monetary gain (Chrematistics). When exchange takes place, the notion of reciprocity should be in force to maintain equity. Reciprocity in exchange meant that the goods exchanged must somehow be equal when measured by a common yardstick. The strictures that Aristotle placed on private property suggest that he was very concerned about the prospect of acquisitive behavior threatening the stability of society. In sum, work for the Greeks was a necessary activity that needed to be performed for the sustenance and progress of the city-state, but was in no way glorified into something larger.

Perhaps the earliest example of work being imbued with spiritual undertones comes from Hebrew religious doctrine. Hebrew thought held that work was the duty of mankind to absolve the race from the original sin committed by the forefathers. Work was more than a natural or "blind tragic necessity" as it was for the Greeks (Tilgher 1977: 11). In the Talmud it is written that, "man does not find his food like other animals and birds but must earn it, that is due to sin." Work is accepted by the Hebrews as a penalty, an expiation, through which man can atone for sin and regain original spiritual purity. Work thusly assumes a religious virtuosity under Hebrew doctrine.

The Hebrew notion of the "virtue" of work is limited however to man's worldly existence. The divine activity which created life had nothing in common with man's earthly condition. The sanctity of the Sabbath, with its prohibition of work, is reflective of the superior divine existence. Tilgher (1977: 13) writes that, "for the Hebrew thinker, man's task is to lead the world, troubled and disturbed by man's abuse of his liberty, back to the cosmic unity and harmony which reigned when man was first brought into being by divine activity." Work is clearly a consequence of man's transgressions on earth and not a natural or divine affliction. In Hebrew thought, work becomes the continuous process of restoring the original harmony that existed when man was first brought into being by divine action.[1] "To work is to cooperate with God in the great purpose of the world's salvation (Tilgher 1977: 16)."

Yet, Hebrew thought did not counter the penalty of work with an acquisitive existence. Hebrew religious doctrine identified the rich as the wicked and the poor as the holy and righteous. Contrary to contemporary social attitudes, early Judeo–Christian teachings placed little emphasis on production and material pursuits. There was no need in the Kingdom of God for hoards of worldly possessions. The Bible teaches that Jesus' followers relinquished their occupations and possessions (Matthew 4: 18–22). Biblical references to the indifference of work abound, including the parable of the laborers in the vineyard, who receive the same pay for differing hours of work and Jesus' admonition of Martha, who is absorbed in work rather than his sermon.

When it comes to the accretion of wealth as opposed to manual labors, the bible's lessons turn from indifference to hostility and disapproval. The Sermon on the Mount admonished that treasure is not to be stored up on earth but in heaven (Matthew 6: 19–20). When a wealthy young man queries Jesus about the path to perfection, he is advised to sell his personal property and give the money to the poor (Matthew 19: 21 and Mark 10: 21). Moreover, the Bible is replete with anti-acquisitive aphorisms: "No one can serve two masters ... You cannot serve God and Mammon (Matthew 6: 24)," "It is easier for a camel to go through the eye of a needle than for a rich man to enter the Kingdom of God (Mark 10: 23–32)." Beder (2000: 12) concludes that "Early Christian, Hebrew, Roman and Greek philosophy all contain the idea that humans once lived in a golden age, communally and in harmony, sharing all that they had, and that the struggle for individual possessions spoiled that harmony and created conflict between humans." It would be the height of naïveté to deny that these societies were not racked by other economic and social conflicts, but the salient point is that the prevailing moral philosophy in pre-capitalist cultures attempted to minimize economic opportunism and invidious wealth distinctions.

The early "fathers of the church" generally persisted along these acetic lines with Basil (c. 330–79) making egalitarian pronouncements that "whoever loves his neighbor as himself, will possess no more than his neighbor."

Gradually, however, fault lines developed in the interpretation of the Bible that led to an expanded role for private property and the eponymic work habits associated with John Calvin. Writing in Athens around the end of the second century, Clement of Alexandria began preaching an allegorical interpretation of the Bible as an alternative to the literal interpretation (Spiegel 1991). As such, the rich young man that was advised in Mark 10: 21 to sell all of his possessions is now counseled to "cast from his mind all attachment to and longing for wealth." In Clement's analysis, Jesus was preaching a purging of the soul rather than explicit corporeal acts. Clement went on to parrot many of Aristotle's arguments for private property, in particular the religious virtuosity of practicing liberality, charity, and munificence. Clement redefines wealth as a gift from God designed to enhance human welfare. The doctrine that wealth was a tool that could be used either righteously or diabolically marked an attitudinal shift that would eventually achieve great prominence in Western civilization.

The rise of the Puritanical labor process: Aquinas, Luther, and Calvin

The writings of Saint Thomas Aquinas were pivotal in advancing the social acceptance of private property and acquisitive behavior. In his synthesis of Christian doctrine and Aristotelian beliefs, Aquinas places private property in harmony with the laws of nature. Like Aristotle, Aquinas displayed no preference for an egalitarian distribution of wealth, only that wealth be regulated by the government and shared with others by the owner. Profit, in itself, was neither reprehensible nor praiseworthy but morally neutral. Yet Aquinas still held reservations about the corrosive potential of wealth accretion and argued that those wishing to lead a life of moral rectitude should limit themselves to communal property.

Although Aristotle, Aquinas, and later, Augustine, made great strides in redeeming the image of the businessmen or merchant, it was not until the sixteenth century that profit-making and diligent work behavior would acquire significant moral virtue. Like Aquinas, Martin Luther served as a halfway house toward the market mentality through his promotion of assiduous work habits. Early promotion of the market mentality was forced to advance in a measured and slow progression as the denizens of medieval society did not aspire to amass ever-increasing wealth, or to work with growing intensity and efficiency. Influenced by such medieval mores, Luther espoused hard work but favored those activities with a tangible bias. Agriculture, fishing, and artisan or manual toil were superior forms of work, where banking and trade (or speculation) were sinful. Bernstein (1997: 35) aptly summarizes Luther's confliction:

> His medieval perspective led him to approve of traditional toil in the field or workshop, but compelled him to oppose the new capitalist

"spirit" that seemed to undermine all that he cherished. His particular dislike of merchants and bankers stemmed from their desire to be successful in this world, to 'climb out of the place where God had put them'.

While Luther blessed the sweaty brow of labor, he worried about the power and influence of the growing business establishment. Luther, like so many to follow, was impaled on the horns of the progress paradox, encouraging a devotion to work while proscribing wanton desires to amass wealth and improve one's station in life. Luther's faithful were to engage in sustained and sedulous work, while abstaining from the lust for acquisition and gain. Trade was permitted provided it was confined to the exchange of necessities and that the seller demanded no more than would compensate him for his labor and risk. Work was benevolent, but it had to be practiced under a moral asceticism that denied the ambitious the full fruits of their labor. The collection of interest on money lent was also anathema to Luther, even though significant concessions had been made by the canonists on the issue of usury. Luther maintained that "the greatest misfortune of the German nation is easily the traffic in interest ... the devil invented it, and the Pope, by giving his sanction to it, has done untold evil throughout the world (Tawney 1937: 104)." Given Luther's reserved embrace of the market mentality, business interests would have to look to John Calvin and his puritan successors for a broader social acceptance of economic gain.

In the late 1500s, French Theologian John Calvin resuscitated the ancient doctrine of predestination in a form opposed to that of free will, meaning that the souls of the righteous are preordained to be saved while others are abandoned. Calvin also diminished the role of priests and the Church hierarchy from the relationship between individuals and their "Creator," leaving the individual alone before God. This autonomy was of little use on judgment day, however, as God's benediction was predestined. Assiduous work and benevolent behavior would not change one's fate, but people who were blessed were known to engage in such behavior. Oddly enough, for Protestants the virtue of hard work was not the golden key to heavenly salvation, but merely a signal of one's preordained status. Good deeds were not a way of attaining salvation, but they were indispensable as proof that salvation had been attained. Thus, people intent on convincing others, or themselves, of their "chosen status" had to devote the utmost diligence to their labors.

Under Calvinism, sedulous work effort not only promised pecuniary awards but the outward appearance of salvation. Beder (2000: 15) points out that this differed from Catholic doctrine, "unlike Catholics, Calvinists could not be forgiven for occasional lapses; rather, such lapses were a sign that a person was not one of the elect." Protestant preachers in both Europe and America frequently made work the preferred topic of their sermons and the importance of work remained a keystone of many Christian teachings well into the eighteenth century (Bernstein 1997).

Calvin's emphasis on self-control and methodical behavior helped prepare a generation of workers for toil in an industrial setting. Attention to detail and attendance during afternoon nap times or saints' days was critical for the success of the workshops, factories, and counting houses of the new era. Calvin thusly acted as an important bridge between medieval life and modern capitalistic notions of work. Tawney (1937: 120) writes that "it is not wholly fanciful to say that, on a narrower stage but with no less formidable weapons, Calvin did for the bourgeoisie of the sixteenth century what Marx did for the proletariat of the nineteenth."

Time was now viewed as a precious commodity because it made possible the production of other commodities. Efficient use of the commodity of time was aided by the widespread use of clocks and watches—known to the Kabyle people of Algeria as the "devil's mill" (Thompson 1967: 89). The very analogy of a precision time piece was used to reinforce the concept of proficient labor. Baxter (quoted in Bernstein 1997: 79) writes that lives "should be ... as parts of a clock or other engine, which must be all conjunct, and each rightly placed." With the introduction of time measurement and Puritan views, there was to be little rest in the world. Mumford (1934: 14) opines that "the clock, not the steam engine [was] the key machine of the industrial age." Leisurely agrarian rhythms—that once afforded Spanish workers 5 months' annual leave for religious holidays and festivals and French workers in excess of 100 days for saints' days—rapidly gave way to the exactitude of the clock and the religious opprobrium of idleness (Reid 1996). Hunnicutt (1988) observes that before "struggling about time" workers "struggled against time" to protect their diurnal activities and rhythms from the sterility of the clock. Prior to the industrial age, Hunnicutt (1988: 46) writes, "bursts of concentrated work alternated with long periods of milling about. Moreover, skilled artisans enjoyed considerable control over their trades. Not only were they able to set their schedules and control their work rhythms; they had the chance to perfect traditional skills and designs and often incorporated their own creative ideas into their work." With the rise of mass production, the "time-frame" supplanted the "task" as the focal point of production. As church and school fell in line with industry's time requirements, workers grudgingly accepted the new time disciplines. Punctuality and diligence became central aspects of individual, social, and moral life. Anthony (1977: 44) writes:

> Work had every advantage. It was good itself. It satisfied the selfish economic interest of the growing number of small employers or self-employed. It was a social duty, it contributed to social order in society and to moral worth in the individual. It contributed to a good reputation among one's fellows and to an assured position in the eyes of God.

Such religious values gave work and profit-making a quiet nudge forward, offering a philosophy that shaped Anglo-Saxon work values for generations to come.

The vilification of vagrancy and the spread of Social Darwinism

The antithesis of hard work—unemployment or idleness—attracted severe odium in the wake of the Protestant Reformation. Unemployment became a badge of moral degradation and humiliation. This societal contempt and disdain for the poor broke with early Christian attitudes toward the downtrodden, which viewed pauperism as an opportunity for those more fortunate to provide succor. Beder (2000: 16) writes, "whereas beggars had been tolerated in medieval society as a natural part of the normal God-given order, even glorified because of the opportunity they gave Catholics to do good deeds, they were despicable to Protestant society." In the Protestant paradigm idleness was a sin and the destitute were seen as being responsible for their state through their own wickedness. Consequently, charity and alms—incumbent upon the wealthy in early Christian times—should not extend to those who were able to work for themselves. Calvin complained that there is "nothing more disgraceful than a lazy good-for-nothing who is of no use either to himself or to others but seems to have been born only to eat and drink (from Bernstein 1997: 56)."

It should be noted that Europe at the time was experiencing rapid social, economic, and technological change that resulted in the displacement of workers from a variety of backgrounds. Events in sixteenth- and seventeenth-century Europe, such as increasing life-expectancy, population growth, the enclosure movement, and the beginning of the Industrial Revolution, placed tremendous pressure on workers and swelled the ranks of the "drones" loathed by the Protestants. Yet, there was little recognition from the Protestants that the circumstances of the condemned mendicants and vagrants were beyond their control.

Many of the tramps and beggars imprisoned for being idle were displaced by the enclosure movement or by the depression of the 1590s. While the earliest enclosures dated back to the Statutes of 1235 and 1285, it was those of the Tudor era which first appropriated large tracts of land in England. By 1500, significant acreage had been enclosed, including much of Essex and Kent. Men and women accustomed to agrarian life found themselves subject to pressures they could neither understand nor control. Sixteenth-century England was a period of inordinate economic disruption caused by an agrarian revolution, a waning manorial system, a waxing industrial system, and a rapid spread of commerce. The economic stress generated a large class of wandering laborers. The upheaval led members of the ruling elite and the middle class on a campaign of stereotyping the poor, which largely persists in modern political discourse.

This condescending opinion of the indigent eventually permeated the public view and policies of sixteenth-century England. Feagin (1975) chronicles British policies that resulted in beggars and vagrants being whipped, forced into compulsory service or put in prison. The British Beggars Act of 1536 allowed for even harsher corporeal punishment. If whipping did not provide sufficient motivation, a part of one ear could be severed. In 1547, the Duke of Somerset permitted the enactment of laws that required healthy vagrants to be branded with the letter "V" (Bernstein 1997). Although the practice was short-lived, similar treatment resurfaced in the 1603 Poor Law which stated that "incorrigible rogues" should be branded on the shoulder with a large "R" (Garraty 1978). Thus, discipline and order became the Puritan watchwords of the late sixteenth century and significant resources were devoted to the task. In the Middlesex Quarter Sessions Court, whipping and branding proceeded at a rate of one person per day in the autumn of 1590 (Hill 1991). These accounts prompted Robert Allen to testimony in 1603 that, "Men are so busy in examining the poor about their estate ... that they can find no leisure to open their purses or relieve their wants (from George and George 1961)."

In 1531, English law attempted to favor the "deserving" poor by granting licenses to beg; the unlicensed were forced to work, whipped or sent back to where they came. Sidney and Beatrice Webb (1963: 351–52) illustrate how the stereotyping was given the imprimatur of public policy, "the Vagrancy Act of 1597 systematically enumerated those considered to be vagrants; the list encompassed certain types of wandering laborers seeking higher wages, fortune-tellers, peddlers, actors, and a number of other categories of the poor." Such laws remained in effect until the eighteenth century and provided a legal framework to punish those considered to be economically or politically threatening to the English ruling class. Thus the concern of the ruling class was not so much to fulfill a Christian duty, but to maintain order in a system increasingly dependent on private property.

A demeaning attitude towards the poor was apparent in Continental Europe as well, where the first workhouses were established in Amsterdam in 1596 to teach work skills and the value of hard work to the indigent population. The English Poor Laws of 1597 and 1601 drew upon the Dutch practice and made apprentices of poor children and institutionalized their parents in workhouses. Feagin (1975: 57) writes that, "in a Protestant country becoming industrialized, the deification of profit-making and hard work led many to advocate forced employment for the unemployed poor." Workhouses thus became a standard way of dealing with destitution and unemployment; they were cheaper than paying relief, imposed work and unpleasant living conditions on the poor and ensured that welfare was not an attractive alternative to any low-paid work in the private sector.

By the eighteenth century, the number of workhouses increased to around 2000 in Europe, incarcerating tens of thousands of people (Feagin 1975; Bernstein 1997). Despite high structural unemployment, the workhouse conditions were intentionally harsh—indicative of public opinion that "those who really wanted alternative work could find it." The workhouses thus represented public sector employment at its worst, becoming general shelters for the poor, healthy and infirm alike. Although most institutions were economic and social failures, some entrepreneurs set up their own workhouses in a futile effort to take advantage of the cheap forced labor (Feagin 1975).

Despite the passage of the Poor Laws and other legislation that codified the attacks of the affluent on the downtrodden, the scourge of poverty persisted. The problem of penury continued to be viewed as an individual affliction, both in cause and in cure. The structure of the economy and the societal flaws that led to unemployment were not circumspect. By sharpening the distinction between the "deserving" and "undeserving" poor, Protestant society tolerated destitution as a natural part of the social order, denying that poverty revealed defects in the social system. Bernstein (1997: 106) comments on the policy changes and frustrations of the time:

> Earlier Stuart efforts to reduce joblessness by controlling the use of new machines or prevailing on employers to keep unneeded personnel on the payroll were set aside in the floodtide of laissez-faire enthusiasm toward the end of the seventeenth century. By the end of the Stuart reign unemployment and poverty had become established in the public mind as the outcomes of idleness ... Attempts to return vagrants to their home parish did not have the desired effect, workhouses that meted out harsh labor along with beds and meals also failed to push the idle to work ... So serious was the concern over vagrancy that both James I and John Donne suggested the idle be sent to Virginia.

Although the overwhelming majority of European immigrants to the American colonies were of middle-class standing and ventured aboard of their own accord, a large portion were castaways of European society. Dunn (1984) estimates that 50,000 vagabonds, convicts, and political prisoners were sent to North America between 1607 and 1775. Scores could be found among the debtor colonies of Georgia or the felons exiled to Maryland. Poor economic conditions in the early and mid-seventeenth century combined with the Thirty Years War and the promise of economic mobility in the New World drove many laborers from England and Germany to set out for North America between 1630 and 1660. In addition to liberal land terms and religious freedom, many immigrants were lured by higher wages and the hope of economic improvement in a new productive economy.

Many immigrants needed to sell them themselves into indentured servitude to finance the expensive travel to the new world. To a large degree, indenture servitude represented an extension of the Puritan existence that prevailed in Europe. Work and living conditions were so harsh for indentured servants that an estimated 40 percent never survived the bondage to realize their freedom toll. Wealthier workers—those able to pledge some combination of cash and credit for their passage—were able to immigrate as redemptioners and negotiate shorter terms of indenture. Simmons (1976: 184) estimates that about two-thirds of the 65,000 to 75,000 Germans who came to Philadelphia from 1727 to 1776 were redemptioners. It is immensely telling that prior to the Declaration of Independence large numbers of immigrants were legally committed to exploitive work before even setting foot in the American colonies.

Prevailing European attitudes regarding the poor washed ashore in North America with the relatively affluent European settlers that preceded the indentured servants and redemptioners. The British elite not only viewed the colonies as a Mercantilist mother load of raw materials but also as a repository for its increasingly vexatious riffraff. John Locke and John Donne both publicly endorsed the notion of settling undesirables in Virginia as a way to "sweep your streets, and wash your doors from idle persons (Garraty 1978: 37)." A popular Puritan poem of the time, Good News from New-England, suggested that those with small earnings should "Venter to this new-found world, and make amends for all (Innes 1988: 6)."

As in Europe, idleness was ferociously attacked and proscribed by law in early America. On both sides of the Atlantic, poverty was thought to be a character flaw rather than an imperfection of the social system. Colonial responses to unemployment and mendicancy were descendent from the inauspicious approaches taken in Britain. The pilgrims and Puritans of North America also established workhouses and almshouses in many seaports to inculcate a work ethic among the flood of immigrants. Conditions in the establishments were designed to be harsh and to instill improved behavior and work habits. Meanwhile preachers, such as Cotton Mather, kept up the assault on the poor and denigrated the unemployed with statements like, "let them starve." Oberholzer (1959) reports that the Boston First Church records show that in 1657 the Puritan clergy excommunicated a woman who insisted that Christ told her "to remain idle"—which, in fact, he does in the "admonition of Martha."

The attitude of religious leaders filtered into social values and public policy. As in Europe, public whippings were used to deter idleness. Morris (1946) argues that whippings and fines were commonplace in Massachusetts, Connecticut, and Rhode Island. In 1648, idleness was actually made a legal offense in Massachusetts (Labaree 1979). In 1723, legislation in Virginia directed that the English Poor Law of 1601 be used against vagabonds found to be "loitering" and failing to maintain themselves (Morris 1946). By 1770, the leaders in Fairfield, Connecticut began prosecuting idle strangers and pushing vagrants out of town. In New Jersey, the English practice of requiring paupers to wear a large red or blue "P" on the right shoulder was used to stigmatize the unemployed in hope that work would become a preferable alternative (Bernstein 1997). Generally, only children younger than 8 years, the aged, and the ill were exempt from paid labor. With no monarchy in America, this public zeal for work resulted in a high labor force participation rate and one of the smallest leisure classes in early modern history (Bernstein 1997).

Despite the use of workhouses, almshouses, religious condemnation, and legal prohibition of vagrancy, poverty and unemployment persisted in early America. The moral indignation of idleness and the distaste for giving succor to the undeserving poor that pervaded the colonial ethos would influence American policies for centuries to come. As Bernstein (1997: 139) points out, Americans would come no closer to a solution for unemployment "in the self-fulfillment world of the 1990s than they were in the more Calvinistic ethos of the 1690s."

While unemployment and indigence became a sign of moral opprobrium, wealth came to signify God's benediction. American Protestants and the Puritans took Aristotle's and Aquinas' defense of private property to new heights and provided a major societal foothold for the rise of capitalism in Western society. With the spread of Protestant thought, the robber barons of the Gilded Age were able to shed the guilt of profiteering that inhibited medieval merchants and early industrial capitalists. The nineteenth century became the pantheon of the self-made man in which entrepreneurship and the accretion of wealth was glorified from the pulpit to the political platform. The Protestant doctrine was strategically commingled with social Darwinism to celebrate successful businesspersons as "the very pinnacle of morality itself since they testified to the bourgeois virtues of thrift, diligence, hard work, dedication, and persistence (Marshall 1982: 124)." In the Puritan doctrine, extracting the greatest possible gain from work was viewed as one's moral obligation. Profits reflected God's benediction and an approval of one's work. Yet, for Puritans the obligation for liberality and charity was still pressing so that the pursuit of wealth was awkwardly conflated with the abstinence and austerity of asceticism.

The reverence of a Spartan existence encouraged capitalists to reinvest their profits to create yet more capital. Capitalists, and particularly American capitalists, were no longer seeking to trade and barter to satisfy consumer needs or achieve personal success and independence, but for the pursuit of profit and business expansion as ends alone. The importance of this defining feature of Puritanism to the development of capitalism led Bertrand Russell (1935: 119) to observe that, "the Puritan habit of postponing pleasures to the next life undoubtedly facilitated the accumulation of capital required for industrialism."

Indeed a unique and defining feature of modern capitalism is its substantial reinvestment of the social surplus. Although past societies have accumulated vast accretions of wealth—as manifest in public works such as the Great Wall of China, the pyramids of Egypt, and the temples of the Incas and Aztecs—capitalism has tended to devote a far greater share of its surplus to continual accumulation of material wealth. Heilbroner and Singer (1998: 5) write:

> Under capitalism the accumulation of society's wealth is put to a use not found in prior societies. *Wealth is used to create still more wealth [sic]*. The primary purpose of capitalist accumulation is not consumption for the upper classes or public monuments, but the creation of capital – wealth-in-general, produced for the sake of producing still more wealth-in-general.

This feature of capitalism would have been foreign to past societies uninitiated to the moral sanction of work and private property. Profits may have been pursued in earlier societies, but without the ardor that guides modern capitalism. Stanfield (1986: 60) explains, "the motive for gain, the calculated pursuit of individual economic interest, may well be ubiquitous in human history but its historical maturity or predominant social position occurs only in market capitalism because it is there instituted as the principal incentive to economic activity." When coupled with the exponential growth of technological development, the capitalistic heuristic of churning a large portion of the social surplus back into production has yielded three centuries of unprecedented economic growth. According to Marx, a societal maturation into and beyond industrial capitalism was a necessary phase in the evolution to a superior social system of accumulation. Experiencing a stint with industrialization afforded society the material productivity and technological know-how needed to sustain an alternative social arrangement.

Few luminaries were more successful at "instituting" the morality of parsimony and economic gain into the social structure of America than Benjamin Franklin. Consider one of Franklin's most famous admonitions, "Remember that time is money. He that can earn ten schillings a day by his labour, and goes abroad, or sits idle, one half of the day, though he spends but sixpence during his diversion or idleness, ought not to reckon that [as] the only expense; he has really spent, or rather thrown away, five shillings besides." Loathing alcohol's deleterious effects on trade, Franklin also castigated the wastage of "Saint Monday"—the feudal penchant for a 3-day weekend involving bacchanalian festivals. In his 1753 pamphlet on *The Value of a Child*, Franklin cautioned that "idleness is a sort of non-existence" (Bernstein 1997: 132). In pre-capitalist societies, Franklin's Puritanical sentiments would have been considered a form of debased avarice, but after the Reformation, they became a guiding social ethos in the Anglo-Saxon world.

The writings of Franklin, Alger, Emerson, and Longfellow all celebrated a farm-boy frugality and reinforced the notion of upward mobility as a reality for multitudes of workers. Any lingering Christian compulsions toward liberality of charity were diluted by the gospel of self-help and the growing acceptance of Social Darwinism. By the late nineteenth century, conservative Darwinism was standard fare in thousands of American pulpits, universities, and newspaper editorial offices. Science was thusly commingled with religion to legitimize the primacy of individualism and indifference to the structural origins of poverty. Bremner (1956: 16) sums up the nineteenth-century view of the poor that largely persists today:

> Indigence was simply the punishment dealt out to the improvident by their own lack of industry and efficiency ... Poverty is unnecessary (for Americans), but the varying ability and virtue of men make its presence inevitable; this is a desirable state of affairs, since without the fear of want the masses would not work and there would be no incentive for the able to demonstrate their superiority; where it exists, poverty is usually a temporary problem and, both in its cause and cure, it is always an individual matter.

Many of America's most prominent Protestants methodically forged an ethos of hard work upon the anvil of religion. With the conflation of religion and social Darwinism, they asserted that success was dependent on earlier sacrifice and the character lessons cultivated from poverty. In a Sunday school lecture, John D. Rockefeller likened the sacrifices to the pruning of a rose bush:

> The growth of a large business is merely the survival of the fittest ... The American Beauty rose can be produced in the splendor and fragrance which bring cheer to its beholder only by sacrificing the early buds which grow up around it. This is not an evil tendency in business. It is merely the working-out of a law of nature and a law of God.
>
> Hofstadter (1955: 45)

Andrew Carnegie (1933) referred to such sacrifices and deprivations as the "school of poverty." To his mind, the existence of poverty in society was healthy because the greatest men of the human race had been molded by the lessons of poverty. Since the co-existence of wealth and poverty were grounded in the natural order of things for Carnegie, it is no surprise that little of his initial almsgiving took the form of direct relief for the poor, although many have since benefited indirectly.

When coupled with the frontier conditions that celebrated a "rugged individualism," Social Darwinism elevated self-reliance and hard work to new heights. A.C. Bedford, a prominent Standard Oil executive of the 1920s, told his employees that work was more important than love, learning, religion and patriotism, for none of them could exist without paid work. The manufacturer H.C. Atkins strongly opposed the shortened 5-day week for fear it would elevate leisure above work, a sentiment echoed by the National Association of Manufacturers' President, John E. Edgerton (Prothro 1954). The persuasiveness of this pro-work campaign was manifest in the belief system of industrial workers. Pipedream or not, the optimism of improved economic status was widespread during the Industrial Revolution. Alfred Chandler (1977: 121) uses the analogy of there being "a baton [and top hat] in every toolkit" when describing the deluded optimism of eighteenth-century workers in America.

Beder (2005) argues that the "success" ethic that emerged from the Gilded Age has been reinforced by a "responsibility" ethic, which encourages hard work as a sign of being personally and socially responsible. Sustaining one's self and family through paid work gives workers the moral satisfaction of contributing to society and allows them to avoid the stigmatism of relying on the public purse. Beder further suggests that part of the anger and indignation directed at those that do not contribute through paid work stems from jealousy. The envy derives from the fact that "we don't really like working ourselves (Beder 2005)."

Having acquired moral and social sanction for its rapid expansion, capitalism became methodical, calculating and self-serving in its encroachment upon competing social values. The moral authority given to the capitalist way of life allowed for the promotion and protection of private property through public policies that perpetuated the Protestant moral code. Calvinistic beliefs were given great currency by those possessing disparate political power and financial clout within industrial societies. Many of Calvin's ardent followers had a vested interest in the virtues of diligence, thrift, and pecuniary gain. As Bernstien (1997: 60) notes, "it is no accident that these urban merchants, bankers, and artisans were among the earliest and most fervent supporters of Calvinism … They found in this faith a reinforcing rationale for their belief in hard work and enterprise." Although the capitalist class would become much more sophisticated and diverse in selling the work ethic and capitalistic ethos, the bestowing of religious virtue on the concept of economic gain was a critical cornerstone in the construction of capitalist society.

Following the greater social acceptance of the market economy, the Protestant church was eventually joined by other mainstream religions in preaching the work ethic. The World Council of Churches has issued multiple resolutions on the importance of work (Beder 2000). There have also been various Papal Encyclicals trumpeting the value of work, such as John Paul II's 1981 "Laborem Exercens (On Human Work)." Similar developments have led McCann (1995: 78) to conclude that the work ethic is "now more honored, ironically enough, in Catholic social teaching than it is among mainline Protestants."

Once the capitalist ethos was set into motion, it was difficult to resist. The pursuit of profits for the sake of profits created a prisoner's dilemma for less-acquisitive traders. The reward to size created by economies of scale meant that all competitors had to clamor for greater sales. A leisurely or relaxed way of trading became a relict of the past as business owners everywhere were forced to compete with ever-expanding entrepreneurs or to liquidate to the new captains of industry. Money-making and economic mobility became a central motivation for paid work in America, eventually overshadowing the religious virtues of work. Bernstein (1997: 125) writes that "the secular calling had become widely accepted among Anglicans, Congregationalists, and Quakers in the middle colonies and New England, and while still important to a shirking coterie, the old religious prohibitions against excessive wealth and worldliness were giving ground to the desire for a better life through profitable work." Indeed this new economic order in which each person would be obliged to fend for themselves and abandon old communitarian values worried many religious leaders. Despite lingering concerns about social stability, the American populace apprehensively came to accept economic individualism as a social convention. Yet, a fundamental ambivalence between individualistic gain and social or communitarian values continues to torment the post-industrial American conscience.

Ideologies are often governed by the same laws of inertia as objects; once set into motion, they tend to persist. Thus a critical lesson to be drawn from the short history of capitalism is that dominant beliefs and ideas about the virtue of work and self-help have not gained ascendancy on their own accord. Wolfe (1973: 171) avers that the ideological propagation of capitalist beliefs has been "consciously and subconsciously disseminated through the means of mental production, i.e., the press, the schools, the churches, the state, etc." Prevailing attitudes have been reinforced by advertising campaigns for many decades now, a major function of which is to maintain allegiance to the capitalist system and its core values. Moreover, a plethora of television and media outlets reinforce competitive and individualistic values from an early age. Many mainstream newspapers and book publishers further cement these dominate values, as do private associations such as veterans' groups, unions, and other profession associations. Also important is the acceptance of the ideology among ordinary citizens whereby those who have gained economically—often those with the smallest advantages—vigorously support dominant individualistic views out of fear of losing their marginal benefits. Feagin (1975: 131) writes, "particularly important too is a kind of self-repression among ordinary citizens whereby those who have gained economically—no matter how small the gain may be—vigorously support dominant individualistic views out of fear of losing what hey have gained." Zinn (1999) likewise argues that the acceptance of the capitalist system has been expanded by the exaggeration of such fears.

Through a variety of means, the work fetish has instilled a moral dimension to work, which is reinforced by a society that values diligence and enterprise expressed through paid employment. Work has become a virtuous, dignified, and socially redeeming activity, and being employed is highly respected irrespective of the financial or social status of the individual. Contemporary societies still cultivate a moral desire for work, which leaves workers with conflicting desires. Noon and Blyton (1997) juxtapose survey results that indicate economic need as the reason why the majority of workers engage in paid employment with other results in which the majority of workers would continue to work even if there was no economic compulsion to do so. Clearly, the work ethic is deeply engrained in our collective psyche and will require a gradual and concerted process of erosion if we are intent on liberating ourselves from its influence.

The role of economics in cementing the market form and the work fetish

If the vested interests of the business class could use the institution of religion in their favor, scarcely few other social institutions could be expected to remain immune to the market imperative and the infiltration of the work ethic. As the religious underpinnings of capitalism yielded some ground to a utilitarian "worldview," the work ethic was affirmed by other means. Many secular institutions have since played a surrogate role in preaching the virtues of work and economic gain. Bleakley (1983: 81) comments on the lasting influence of the idolatry of work, "the identification of labour and enterprise with some sort of higher service remains with us—less God-centered, but still associated with notions of 'good behaviour.' Our major political, industrial and cultural institutions are permeated with the work ethic—party leaders preach the message; unions and management display solidarity on the issue." The social paean to economic gain can be heard in the utterances of labor leaders, business executives, government officials, academicians, and the media, constantly shaping our social consciousness.[2]

Although the selling of the work ethic has been convoluted, multifaceted and multidisciplinary, the economics profession has played a central role in the social transformation to a market society. A great deal of the social and political fixation on the "market myth" finds its justification and sustenance in the discipline of economics. Mainstream economic theory has been vital to the institutional fixation on the market form because it provides a logical—albeit methodologically, empirically and historically flawed—expression of economistic behavior. Given that the structure of economic organization concatenates most other social policies, economics can be viewed as the keystone of social inquiry. Schumacher (1974: 33) writes that "economics plays a central role in shaping the activities of the modern world, inasmuch as it supplies the criteria of what is 'economic' and what is 'uneconomic', and there is no other set of criteria that exercises a greater influence over the actions of individuals and groups as well as over those of governments." Keynes (1936) famously spoke to the profundity of economics when he wrote that "the ideas of economists and political philosophers, both when they are right and when they are wrong, are more powerful than is commonly understood. Indeed the world is ruled by little else. Practical men, who believe themselves to be quite exempt from any intellectual influence, are usually the slaves of some defunct economist." From an environmental perspective, Sachs (1998: 104) writes, "economic institutions are the most powerful forces across the world, so the necessary changes can only be introduced with their support." Given the preponderant influence of mainstream economic ideology and analysis, the remainder of this chapter will be devoted to understanding the role of formal economic analysis in fashioning the market mentality and its attendant fetish for paid work.

A closer look at the major stages of development of Western economic thought provides a deeper understanding of how formal economic analysis has contributed to the idolatry of paid work through the pursuit of self-interested economic gain. The origins of the "formal" study of economics roughly coincide with the genesis of market society. In relative terms, the discipline of economics is quite young; the publication of Adam Smith's *Wealth of Nations* in 1776 is commonly accepted as the birth of the formal study. This in not to say that topical economic debates were uncommon before Smith, as suggested by earlier references to the Greek philosophers and church scholars, but like the market itself, the discipline had not garnered the attention it has had since the late eighteenth century. The political influence of the market mentality emerged quickly during the Mercantilist era, as governments were preoccupied with maximizing the putative wealth of the nation through advantageous terms of exchange. With great deft and dispatch, Adam Smith redefined the notion of national wealth, while fortifying the role of self-interested exchange. In the liberal era that followed, the consciousness of the economy was shifted to the micro level and infused with the motive of self-gain. Thus, as Smith's invisible hand replaced the hands of the aristocracy and the deity, social provisioning was to be achieved automatically in the new competitive milieu.

Characteristics of a market society began to emerge in the sixteenth century. Stanfield (1986: 106) comments on its growth:

> The sixteenth century witnessed a dramatic growth in the scope and strength of market forces. This engendered in the next century a profound crisis in the meaning and guiding principles of everyday British life. From the crisis emerged the market mentality which reached its mature intellectual expression in classical economics and its institutional, practical fruition in the nineteenth century.

Historically, the "economy" is stripped of the anonymity in which it was located in early society. Stanfield (1986: 32) cautions that "the pursuit of gain through exchange is an institutionally-enforced pattern of behavior which must be analyzed as a result rather than as antecedent of the historical process."

Many of the earliest economic writers were men with vested commercial interests. Aptly named the Mercantilists, the subject matter of their "pamphlets" was largely practical and parochial. The Mercantilist writers were aware of the possible conflict between their own interests and those of society as they tried to follow the narrow path of acceptable commerce outlined for them by the religious leaders of the Middle Ages. Adam Smith would later characterize the system as a fraud foisted on the public by the business class. In *The Wealth of Nations*, Smith (1776: 558) wrote that under mercantilism "the interested sophistry of merchants and manufacturers confounded the common sense of mankind."

The prevailing wisdom of the mercantilist era was that a nation's prosperity would rise and fall based on the specie or bullion it held in its Treasury. It is important to note that when precious metals become the measure of wealth, economic expansion becomes a zero-sum game in which one nation gains at the expense of another. Since one way to acquire gold and specie was through trade, production and parsimony become virtuous practices under Mercantilism. The thinking was aptly described by the Mercantilist writer Thomas Mun, "the ordinary means to increase our wealth and treasure is by foreign trade, wherein we must ever observe this rule: to sell more to strangers yearly than we consume of theirs in value (cited in Muchmore 1970)." Since the extraction of precious metals proved difficult, Mercantilism amounted to a national call to arms to produce more throughput. Idle land, labor and resources (including money) needed to be urgently pressed into action in order to either eliminate the need for imports or to produce exportable goods. In addition to the impetus of production, frugality was also promoted as a way to reduce imports and leave more goods available for exports. In a pivotal departure from history, Mercantilism no longer preached parsimony out of a moral or ethical code, but rather for improvement of the trade balance.

With its emphasis on the aggrandizement of bullion through production and export, mercantilism fostered a great deal of conflict between private and public interests. Governments of the period granted monopoly status to those engaged with external trade while those entities that produced for domestic markets were largely ignored. Consequently, the fortunes of the former swelled relative to the latter. Yet, the average working-class consumer was likely the biggest loser under a system that considered production, and not consumption, the ultimate purpose of commerce. Workers were pressed into production at low wages that kept costs down and domestic consumption low. This mistreatment of working-class consumers rankled Adam Smith so thoroughly that he devoted roughly 200 pages of the *Wealth of Nations* to subverting the Mercantilist system. In stark contrast with Mercantilism, Smith (1776: 28) argued that, "consumption is the sole end and purpose of all production."

Mercantilist thinking developed against a background of rivalry and warfare among the great nations of Europe, which were incessantly at war between 1600 and 1667. The rise of Mercantilist thought thus parallels the rise of the British Empire over its erstwhile economic superiors, the Spanish Armada, the Dutch, and the French. The competitive mentality and the view of economic development being a zero-sum game that emerged under Mercantilism are of particular relevance to the development of the work fetish. The notion of economic growth being a cutthroat competition at the expense of one's adversary left an indelible mark on the Anglo-European psyche that later influenced attitudes toward trade, production, industrial policy, and work. According to Spiegel (1991: 98) Mercantilism came to be known as "a bundle of ideas and an exercise in statecraft." Although the Mercantilist system illustrated the effectiveness and expediency of statecraft, it also provided lasting evidence of the ruinous impact of poorly conceived economic policy. Astute students of economy history and thought will find many vestiges of Mercantilist thinking in contemporary economic policies relating to international trade, monetary theory (e.g. the quantity theory of money), industrial policy, and labor markets. With respect to the latter, a lingering Mercantilist mentality may explain some of the urgency placed on throughput maximization and international competitiveness in many modern labor market policies.

One of Smith's chief objectives in writing *The Wealth of Nations* was dispelling the Mercantilist notion of national wealth. By locating the wealth of a nation with the individual, Smith was most interested in reducing the influence of the monopoly trader. But in so doing, Smith also diminished the institutional role of the state, the church, and the community. Adam Smith's masterful synthesis of the erstwhile sporadic economic thought sowed the seeds for the development of hedonistic man and the market mentality. Yet, much of Smith's work has been bowdlerized by what Polanyi referred to as an ethnocentric interpretation of capitalism. Many of Smith's reservations concerning the social impacts of commoditization and free competition— such as the stultifying effect of an overly minute division of labor or the bargaining imbalance between master and worker—have been given relatively little shrift by economists. Despite Smith's misgivings, the notion of a self-interested economic agent satisfying an inveterate and insatiable need to exchange for gain has been accepted as an accurate depiction of human nature and a justification for the market form.

The world of Adam Smith was a Newtonian one and he accepted the social order of his day as being naturally self-equilibrating. Social forms in the eighteenth century were viewed as fixed within limits set by natural order. The universe was analogous to the workings of a clock, well organized and mechanically ordered. The advancement of humankind could be attained by an objective scrutiny of the mechanical universe which would uncover the great principles by which social relations were guided. By comprehending these principles, Hamilton (1970: 30) writes, "man would be able to conform to them and thus would enhance his contentment and happiness on earth … Misery and despair, the product of man's ignorance, which was also the source of his folly in flaunting these immutable natural principles, could be banished from the world." Smith's price theory is a paragon example of Newtonian thinking. According to Smith (1776: 55), "there is in every society or neighborhood an ordinary or average rate of wages and profit and this rate is naturally regulated." Prices are seen as gravitating around a natural point, occasionally repelled from the point, but always being forced back to it by the pull of a natural self-interest. Although the explanation of competitive prices has been sophisticated with 200 years of refinement, it is still fundamentally dependent on Newtonian principles. It bears mention that change, to the Classical economist, meant a quantitative change in output triggered by a change in price. Thus, the orthodox economic system established by Smith was Newtonian in outlook, particularly in its acceptance of a mechanical, rather than an evolutionary, concept of change.

Smith's followers, men like Malthus and Ricardo, further solidified the ubiquity of calculative, gain-oriented economic behavior, overshadowing the other mainsprings of human action. A vital step in the economistic transformation entailed the commodification of traditional social ties linking man to nature. New social linkages formed under a system of commodity production depended on an economic rational that afforded property rights to land and labor akin to other commodities. For Karl Polanyi (1944), the treatment of land, labor and money as "fictitious commodities" was a crucial stage in economic matters engulfing social relations. Commodity production is the specialized production of objects for sale on the market, with marketability being the sine qua non of production. The commoditization of the labor market required dissolution of historical relationships between man, society and natural subsistence. As Stanfield (1986: 113) writes, "work as the meaningful relation to the natural environment, work as a cement binding a way of life, work as the source of an individual's social and self-image, all of these and more are cast aside by the commodity fiction of labor."

The classical economists deftly intertwined "natural law" with their ethnocentric view of human relations in market societies. Stanfield (1986) cites Malthus' population doctrine as telling evidence of the market mentality pervading one of the most fundamental of all human relations and functions-procreation. Stanfield (1986: 77) explains:

> For Malthus the right to engage in this human activity is to be determined by one's position in the market. Neither a man nor his children have a right to subsistence unless his labour will fairly purchase it in the market. Malthus refers to this explicitly as a law of nature, which society cannot abrogate without dire consequences. This is in sharp contrast to the traditional economy in which, short of general famine, belonging to a group guarantees the individual his subsistence.

For Malthus, and the majority of economists since, economic function and success dictate social status rather than social status dictating economic position (Stanfield 1986). The classical economists employed a natural law philosophy to support the claim that market capitalism is historically and consistently the social formation most compatible with invariant human nature—atomistic exchange for gain (Stanfield 1986). Doubtless, the appeal to natural law has contributed to the permanence and prevalence of the economistic view. The acceptance of unbridled personal gain also established a sturdy foundation for a lasting commitment to economic efficiency. The ethos of efficiency was socially constructed, congruent with the belief that individuals should acquire as much wealth as possible. Princen (2005: 55) comments on the seductive appeal of efficiency to those shackled by parochialism in pre-capitalist societies, "although developed by economists as an analytic device, the concept had everything an aspiring modern could want: a scientific aura, an association with business and wealth, and a code of conduct all its own – efficiency."

Debates on the prospect of abundance during the Classical period

A frequent debate among the Classical thinkers that is relevant to the establishment of a work fetish was whether growing material abundance would lead to a satiation of needs and an age of leisure or an inflammation of emulative desires and a highly materialistic society. Emerging material abundance either held the promise of a great awakening for workers and a new social hierarchy or a work-driven society based on false needs. Many of the early Enlightenment thinkers viewed the demand for leisure as unlimited while the quest for goods was relatively finite. Others suggested that Aristotle's notion of "natural needs" could not be relied upon to yield a communal and rational use of free time and that material pursuits would carry the day. The optimistic twist on this view was that prosperity represented a choice between the anarchy of undisciplined free time or the constant growth of material well-being through greater work and consumption. From either perspective, the prospect of extensive freedom from work was a normative, moral issue as much as it was an economic concern. Conflict over the implications of abundance is apparent in the works of writers in the Classical period.

Rousseau offered some of the earliest insight on the matter. For Rousseau, misery was caused by a need for things. In his "republic" he offered an alternative to the endless expansion of the market. He envisioned a timeless community of self-sufficiency and self-imposed simplicity. David Hume, on the other hand, justified emulative consumption as a means of assuring economic progress. Yet, recognizing the potential neurosis of unrestrained vanity, he promoted equally a stoic hero of self-control and self-fulfillment.

A similar moral conflict was apparent in the political discourse of Revolutionary America as exemplified in the Federalist Papers and a series of debates between Alexander Hamilton and Thomas Jefferson. Jefferson initially favored a country of self-sufficient farmers that would trade only for those few necessities they could not produce themselves. According to Jefferson, no man could be truly free if they were dependant on another for their livelihood. Wage labor was a form of dependency that contradicted the very republican principles of liberty upon which the country was founded. Jefferson also had a great affinity for the land and the natural rhythms of life. In *Notes on Virginia*, Jefferson (1785: Query XIX) wrote, "Those who labor on the earth are the chosen people of God, if ever He had a chosen people." As with Rousseau, simple agrarian life possessed moral virtue for Jefferson.

By contrast, Hamilton envisioned America as an agricultural and industrial behemoth—a strong, prosperous, diversified economy conducive to political independence. As Secretary of the US Treasury, he advocated the use of federal government spending to leverage national finances, subsidize manufacturing and agriculture, promote technology and knowledge, and equalize trade barriers in an effort to achieve the greatest economic progress possible. Clearly, Hamilton was little bothered by the seamy side of economic progress that was endemic to the factory towns of Great Britain— Colonial America's erstwhile tyrant.

Interestingly, their contemporary, Benjamin Franklin, would also come to struggle with the moral issue of work later in his life. In his autobiography, Franklin offered a compromise in the form of an early retirement from an otherwise business-like life. This strategy divorced money-making from a retirement of true leisure in which one might redeem one's self. Relying on personal forgiveness or healing to recover from a life of self-interested behavior shows that Franklin was ambivalent about the true virtues of his puritanical preaching.

It should be noted that the early social observers were contemplating a society on the verge of an Industrial Revolution and did not have the advantage of future social critics of witnessing the munificence of industrialization. Some of those that did experience the initial fecundity of the industrial age—men like Marx, Mill, and Veblen—came to view the highly productive aspects of industrial society as a source of hope and optimism. For John Stuart Mill, the coming abundance represented the vanquishing of the politics of scarcity and the opportunity to build a democracy of abundance and leisure. Questioning the cultural or institutional restrictions to human fulfillment, Mill held the view that the so-called economic problem might someday be solved if only humanity is capable of recognizing its solution. Indeed, Mill's "daydream" of the stationary state envisioned a new collective value set that placed less value on quantitative economic progress. Mill's (1929: 751) stationary state was one in which, "while no one is poor, no one desires to be richer, nor has any reason to fear being thrust back by the efforts of others to push themselves forward."

Over 150 years ago Mill (1929: 748) was skeptical that more industrial throughput and a growing economy could serve as an effective unction for Britain's transitional pains, loathing the "trampling, crushing, elbowing, and treading on each other's heels." He suspected that nineteenth-century consumption patterns were increasingly driven by social comparisons. Mill (1929: 748) laments, "I know not why it should be a matter of congratulation that persons who are already richer than anyone needs to be, should have doubled their means of consuming things which give little or no pleasure except as representative wealth." Thus, over a century and a half ago, Mill suggested that the key to improved economic and social well-being was not necessarily more throughput but rather a better distribution of income and resources. "It is only in the backward countries of world that increased production is still an important object: in those most advanced, what is economically needed is a better distribution (Mill 1929: 749)."

Mill's time-honored insight is of great relevance to current employment policy debates as traditional Keynesian solutions that rely on a stimulation of aggregate demand have failed to generate a full utilization of labor and sustained enhancements in well-being in the developed world over the last three decades. Thus, an improved distribution of our socially necessary labor may be a superior way of improving the art of living than an expansion of those labors. This is not to deny that industrialization and macroeconomic policy management have yielded objective improvements in the general standard of living since Mill's admonition, but rather to suggest that beyond a threshold level of human needs, a better distribution of the social surplus may be a more expedient and sustainable way of improving welfare than the capitalistic clamor for more material throughput.

Mill (1929: 751) recognized that a stationary state of capital and population growth need not threaten social progress and could instead promote an improvement in the art of living. Mill's stationary state can be viewed as a post-scarcity utopia that promises a reduction in working time and a redistribution of social wealth to "cultivate freely the graces of life." It is a vision made possible by the perfection of the process of material transformation. Mill believed that the laws of production were largely governed by nature, while distribution was a social process. This frees individuals from the natural law imperatives of a competitive social intercourse and allows policymakers to address qualitative rather than quantitative social concerns. Thus Mill's (1929: 756) utopia is not one of stagnancy nor lethargy:

> It is scarcely necessary to remark that a stationary condition of capital and population implies no stationary state of human improvement. There would be as much scope as ever for all kinds of mental culture, and moral and social progress; as much room for improving the Art of Living, and much more likelihood of its being improved, when minds ceased to be engrossed by the art of getting on. Even the industrial arts might be as earnestly and as successfully cultivated, with this sole difference, that instead of serving no purpose but the increase of wealth, industrial improvements would produce their legitimate effect, that of abridging labour.

Clearly, Mill was one of the first political philosophers to propose a reformation of the industrial system along social and environmental lines that relied heavily on work time reduction for the masses. Mill's teachings are still rather apposite today. Certainly, some of the fruits of past technological advances have been widely distributed, but a better distribution of the dividends may have fostered a much more expedient improvement in the human condition. Furthermore, the prospect of some advanced industrial economies attaining a steady-state condition may shed light on recent economic trends. Rather than a reflection of continual macroeconomic failures, a secular decline in the ability of developed nations to generate ample jobs for a labor force swollen by social, technological, structural and demographic changes may be viewed as a barometer of an economy's progression towards a felicitous stationary state where there is simply less remunerative work to be conducted. If such is the case, maximizing the aggregate hours of work will become a fruitless exercise or one that entails an egregious encroachment on social norms and ecological systems in an effort to expand paid work.

The state of historical development also features prominently in the theories of Karl Marx. Given Marx's preferred methodology of critical historicism, it is not surprising that he criticized the assumption of scarcity as a mistaken generalization of economic relations within in a capitalist system to human nature at large. For Marx, both economic and human development were evolutionary processes. Industrialization was a necessary stage of development which made possible the expansion of human capacities in the non-oppressive context of material abundance. The material transformation of nature leads to a fuller development of human senses and it is this creative power that allows humans to realize themselves as sensuous beings. Marx writes that "the whole of history is a preparation, a development, for 'man' to become the object of sensuous consciousness." Historical development entailed an expansion of mankind's social definition of subsistence.

> With this development, his realm of physical necessity expands as a result of his wants; but, at the same time, the forces of production which satisfy these wants also increase. Freedom in this field can only consist in socialized man, the associated producers, rationally regulating their interchange with Nature, bringing it under their common control, instead of being ruled by it as by the blind forces of Nature; and achieving this with the least expenditure of energy and under conditions most favourable to, and worthy of, their human nature. But it nonetheless still remains a realm of necessity. Beyond it begins that development of human energy which is an end in itself, the true realm of freedom, which however, can blossom forth only with this realm of necessity as its basis. The shortening of the working-day is its basic prerequisite.
>
> (Marx 1975: 353)

Thus, Marx does not deny that individuals will have socially defined needs in an age of abundance, but questions whether or not those needs will be authentic. Inauthentic needs appear under capitalism when they are intentionally or artificially created for the purpose of realizing a profit; they are the needs of capital, not of autonomous individuals. Under socialism, the increase in material wants will continue, but the process of generating and realizing them will be a matter of both individual and collective action. A material abundance offers an escape from artificial necessity into freedom but not a complete suppression of culturally influenced needs. Marx envisioned a working day reduced to that needed for the material reproduction of society, but which also allowed for the expansion of free time, during which the authentic needs of the people can be discovered and realized.

The industrial stage of capitalism was a necessary condition in the pursuit of greater human liberation as the productive prowess of industrial capitalism could free workers from many of the tedious and excruciating forms of labor. G.A. Cohen (1978: 307) aptly summarizes Marx's view of the promise of abundance:

> The productive technology of advanced capitalism begets an unparalleled opportunity of lifting the curse of Adam and liberating men from toil, but the production relations of capitalist economic organization prevents the opportunity from being seized. *The economic form most able to relieve toil is least disposed to do so* [emphasis added]. In earlier periods of capitalist history the bias toward output conferred on the system a progressive historical role: capitalism was an indispensable engine for producing material wealth from a starting point of scarcity,

and there lay its 'historical justification'. But as scarcity recedes the same bias renders the system reactionary. It cannot realize the possibilities of liberation it creates. It excludes liberation by febrile product innovation, huge investment in sales and advertising, contrived obsolescence. It brings society to the threshold of abundance and locks the door. For the promise of abundance is not an endless flow of goods but a sufficiency produced with a minimum of unpleasant exertion.

Cohen (1978) identifies an intriguing modern paradox: why is it that the notion of scarcity was inculcated as a universal human condition during the most prosperous era of human history and in the very societies that could most afford to question the validity and usefulness of such a worldview? The paradox speaks to the stupendous success of neoclassical economics in cementing the ubiquity of self-interested behavior in the pursuit of utility maximization.

The protracted nature of the debate over the promise of abundance suggests that a central policy concern continues to be how government can be used to assist individuals and society during the transitional to a stationary state. Bleakley (1981: 2) warned that:

> If we are to cope with the problems of industrial transition it will be necessary to ensure that the burdens of re-adjustment are evenly spread: the gifts of the new technology must not be monopolized by those who are in a position to benefit by virtue their industrial power. Such was the tragedy of the industrial revolution. A repeat in today's circumstances would be a moral and social disaster: it would create a "two-nation" situation at the very moment in our history when we need communal unity as never before.

As Bleakley (1981) anticipates, the triumph of technology over material wants will eventually necessitate an alternative distribution of socially necessary labor and the social dividend. A crucial first step in the adjustment to an abundant society must then be a diminished social importance placed on paid work in terms of valuing and affirming the individual and regulating access to socioeconomic provisioning and participation. Indeed, an improved distribution of labor that increased socioeconomic participation might help to reveal that society is closer to solving the economic problem than is widely believed.

Scarcity and insatiability as axioms

If discussions of the possibilities of abundance strike the reader as ethereal or heretical, it is largely due to the success of neoclassical economics in cementing scarcity and insatiability as economic axioms. Neoclassical economic theory provided an alternative to a material surfeit of goods and a stationary economic state in which individuals turned their interests to non-economic pursuits. A primary assumption that girds the entire framework of mainstream economic thought is the notion that "more is better." Human nature is thought to possess an insatiable thirst for more commodities. As one popular economics textbook put it, "for practical purposes, human wants may be regarded as limitless. An occasional individual may have everything he needs, but man's capacity to generate new wants as fast as he satisfies old ones is well-known psychologically (Lipsey *et al.* 1972)." Adherence to the assumption of "more is better" subjects humanity to an insoluble dilemma—no matter how wealthy or productive our society becomes, we will always require greater levels of production and consumption.

Accepting the psychological axiom of unlimited wants fits hand in glove with the second methodological principle of orthodox economics—that of scarcity. Dating back to the classical period, most economists assumed that scarcity was part of the normal human condition. Adam Smith opined that some nations would be relegated by their size, laws, institutions, and inadequate resources to a condition of low wages and scanty profits. Thomas Malthus' population doctrine implied a struggle for the means of survival and the impossibility of eradicating poverty. Scarcity was consistent with the prevailing iron law of wages as it prodded men, indolent by nature, into the activity necessary for economic growth. Likewise, the economic thought of David Ricardo was based on the frustrations arising from the interaction between an expanding population and scarce natural resources.

However, the true permanence and ubiquity of contemporary notions of scarcity can be traced back to the intellectual contributions of the Marginalist school. Following Smith's groundwork, Marginalism viewed consumption rather than production as the starting point for economics. That meant that the analysis began with the individual rather than historically vested classes. This conveniently allowed the Marginalists to avoid making normative judgments about social conflicts and inequities. More important in relation to work time is the Marginalist definition of value in terms of subjective utility, which varied relative to the satisfaction obtained from scarce goods. Goods did not derive value from intrinsic qualities but from their scarcity relative to other goods. By shifting attention away from production and towards exchange, marginal utility theory represented a stark alternative to the traditional labor theory of value. The notion that labor was the ultimate source of value was ruled out as objects came to be valued by what they could secure in trade.

This variant measure of value allowed the Marginalist to escape the classical dilemma between natural and unnatural needs. There was no need for a moral or social limit to be placed on the quantity of goods desired. Cross (1993: 87) summarizes the import of the Marginalist thinking in terms of cementing the contemporary consumer culture:

> economic rationality was reduced to the maximization of choice between subjective preferences along an endless continuum of desire; in

turn, this eliminated the possibility of a stationary state economy where all 'true needs' would be satisfied and non-economic pursuits could take charge ... Marginalism's calculus of subjective preferences provided no moral or logical defence against endlessly expanding consumption.

The intrusion of the market into traditional or non-economic activities fell outside the province of the Marginalist economist. Marginal utility theory appeared to make economic theory more quantifiable and "scientific" and its related refinements have allowed the neoclassical view to achieve hegemony among Western practitioners of the economics discipline. The logic of endless growth and the rejection of a value distinction between legitimate and false needs accompanied the ascendancy of the Marginalist approach. Neoclassical economists argued that boundless consumption desires would ensure not only sufficient demand for output, but also adequate labor supply to produce the requisite goods and services.

The postulate of scarcity serves as a critical lynchpin of the marginal utility framework. Assuming that scarcity is a universal human condition provides neoclassical economics with a central focus and legitimacy as a "science" (Xenos 1989). Robbins' summary of the theory clearly reflects the "logic of scarcity,"

> We have been turned out of paradise. We have neither eternal life nor unlimited means of gratification. Everywhere we turn, if we choose one thing we must relinquish others which, in different circumstances, we would not wish to have relinquished. Scarcity of means to satisfy given ends is an almost ubiquitous condition of human behavior. Here, then, is the unity of the subject of Economic science, the forms assumed by human behavior in disposing of scarce means.

Decision-making was governed by an economizing calculation driven largely by a scarcity of means. A surfeit of individual needs may arise, but an endless variety of goods could ensure that the psychology of scarcity held full sway over society. Marginalism therefore required a great deal of faith in the emulative nature of consumption; a belief that the working class would succumb to relative desires rather than militate for more leisure time. The endless expansion of new desires, or insatiability, allowed the notion of scarcity to co-exist with the notion of diminishing marginal utility as needs in the aggregate became infinitely expandable. Marshall proffered the solution in his Principles of Economics (1890: 65):

> It is an almost universal law that each separate want is limited and that with every increase in the amount of a thing which a man has the eagerness of his desire to obtain more of it diminishes; until it yields place to the desire for some other thing, of which perhaps he had hardly thought, so long as his more urgent wants were still unsatisfied. There is an endless variety of wants, but there is a limit to each separate want.

The insatiability of consumer desires for new and different consumption experiences reinforces the notion of absolute and universal scarcity. If one can never achieve sufficiency, scarcity becomes a permanent affliction.

The relevant issue for Marginalists was the fact that a good has entered the economic realm by virtue of an individual desiring it. For Menger the very emergence of markets was linked to the universal condition of scarcity. Voluntary exchange was a means of maximizing satisfaction. Markets were crucial to the logic of scarcity for the Marginalists because they allow individuals to express their desires and create signals (prices) that measure that expression. The desirability or utility of an object was measured by the money price that would be paid for it.

Xenos (1989) points out the circular reasoning in this description of markets since the *existence* of markets is presupposed in the formulation of the economizing individual. Utility may appear to be commonly measured by prices only because individuals are already operating in market societies. Xenos (1989: 74) writes "neoclassical theory assumes that the individual responds to wants with an economizing rationality that leads him or her to propose exchange, but formulation of the theory suggests that it is because those wants are produced in a situation of property and exchange that the individual must economize in order to satisfy them." The chicken and egg debate over the origin of markets has important ramifications for the universality of scarcity. If Xenos' criticism is valid, then the postulate of universal scarcity is undermined. The logic of scarcity would only hold sway where private property and markets were the prevailing mode of expressing and satisfying needs. Indeed, markets tend to reinforce the experience of scarcity in modern society. Extensively developed money-payment systems increase the range of choices made available to individuals. Money serves as a common language in which a great variety of goods and services can be brought into a common dialogue. An expanding range of marketable products reinforces the psychology of insatiability as the individual faces a daunting array of consumption options.

The Marginalist thinkers effectively removed any responsibility from the buyer and the seller to anyone but themselves. A seller of goods has no responsibility to the environment, to conditions of production, or the means of the buyer; his sole responsibility is to earn the highest return possible on his wares. Schumacher (1974: 93) caustically summarizes the Marginalist view as a "metaphysical position of the crudest materialism, for which money costs and money incomes are the ultimate criteria and determinants of human action, and the living world has no significance beyond that of a quarry for exploitation." There is much that a market-based allocation ignores in the pursuit of good bargains and high profits, but those are generally viewed by Marginalists as market failures that stronger property rights and improved governance can overcome. Market failures due to externalities, non-exclusion, agency problems, and even market power are viewed as applications of the conditionally optimal individual choice model. Even macroeconomic stabilization is viewed as being an ephemeral problem to be resolved by rational maximization in the long run. The stabilization focus is to secure more resources that are presently available but underutilized. There is some room for the analysis of change in the orthodox model, as with growth theory and technological change, but the tendency is to fit these new givens (or assumptions) into the static maximization model of individual exchange.

A variety of dissenting thinkers—such as the German Historicists, Institutionalists, and Marxists featured in Chapter 2—have voiced opposition to the belief that economic motivations are paramount and ubiquitous in human affairs. Heterodox schools of thought generally concur that "economic man" is less prevalent when social inquiry is comparative, historical, and pluralistic in it focus. Castigating the overly deductive approach to economic analysis, or the Ricardian vice, these critics maintain that the institutions of commercial society, and the patterns of behavior they encourage, are specific to modern market societies. But with its ability to simplify and systematize market experience through a process of reasoning common to denizens of market societies, neoclassical theory prevailed beyond academia and public policy, permeating the depths of our social fabric. Temporary scarcity was made to appear as a general condition of insufficiency by the necessity of choosing between a vast array of alternatives. Scarcity no longer referred to an episodic shortage or insufficiency—as was the case in many non-market economies—but was transformed into a general condition of humanity that constantly frustrated the satisfaction of material desires. When coupled with the market mentality of industrial society, neoclassical theory was able to successfully transform the notion of scarcity from an occasional dearth of material needs to a self-imposed social condition that appeared to be ubiquitous and immutable.

Debates on abundance in the Industrial Age: the promotion of consumption

The experience of the 1920s and 1930s in the United States was a pivotal period in the construction of a social system built on consumption. The prospect of overproduction and "need saturation" that the Classical economists had contemplated arose again during the Roaring Twenties. This time economics played a pivotal role in promoting the importance of consumption and growth. As the Jazz Age came to a close, capitalists became increasingly solicitous about the willingness of middle-class Americans to expand their consumption. Many thought that America was approaching a material surfeit. As one industry spokesman of the time warned, "it is perfectly clear that the middle class American already buys more than he needs" (Grimes from Hunnicutt 1988: 41). Flooded markets, overproduction, underconsumption, increased productivity and saturated demand led to a fear of unemployment and contraction. Since many Americans had achieved a standard of living above their "need," an emerging view in the 1920s was that economic growth was doomed.

John Maynard Keynes anticipated a rapid progression toward Mill's stationary state and a diminished urgency of economic matters. Keynes (1972: 364) believed that, "the economic problem may be solved, or be at least within sight of solution, within a hundred years. This means that the economic problem is not-if we look into the future-the permanent problem of the human race." Thus, material scarcity was not a concern for Keynes but rather our ability to adjust to an abundant economy. Since our minds have been occupied with the problem of subsistence for thousands of years, Keynes wondered whether we would turn our thoughts to higher ideals once material sufficiency was achieved. Would we get on with the art of living or occupy our minds in less lofty pursuits such as invidiously distinguishing ourselves through acquisitive behavior? Adjustment to an age of abundance would require a moral renaissance in which "the love of money as a possession ... will be recognized for what it is, a somewhat disgusting morbidity, one of those semi-criminal, semi-pathological propensities which one hands over with a shudder to the specialists in mental disease (Keynes 1972: 369)." With material abundance, Keynes (1972: 365) writes, "we shall be able to rid ourselves of many of the pseudo-moral principles which have hag-ridden us for two hundred years, but with which we have exalted some of the most distasteful human qualities into the position of highest virtue." While there may still be some individuals deranged enough to pursue the accumulation of wealth in an age of abundance, society will no longer encourage and applaud them. Keynes (1972: 372) was hopeful that a material surfeit would cause emulative motives to wane, allowing us to "honour those who can teach us how to pluck the hour and the day virtuously and well." Certainly it would be difficult to turn off the acquisitive thinking in the short run. Perhaps, that is why Keynes preferred reduced work time as a long-run solution to unemployment, as it would allow for a gradual easing of the grip of acquisitive behavior.

In response to business fears of falling consumption, Hunnicutt (1988) argues that mainstream economists began to intensify their efforts to assure businessmen and some labor leaders that the motive to buy was not limited to a set of specific human needs and would readily expand in accordance with growing incomes. Neoclassical economists began speaking with a clarion voice when reciting their atomistic belief that human wants were insatiable. With its growing social acceptance, the formal economic paradigm of neoclassical economics would prove very useful in legitimizing and at times championing the high consumption movement. America thought that it had proven that the theory actually worked in the 1920s by manifesting an "almost insatiable appetite for goods and services, this abounding production of all things which almost any man wants (Hunnicutt 1988: 43)." By the mid-1920s, fatalistic attitudes were being replaced with a vigorous optimism that consumption could save economic growth and redeem employment. Americans would not work themselves out of jobs by producing more than they would consume. Edward Cowdrick (1927: 208), an industrial relations advisor to several of the largest American companies, referred to the movement as the "new economic gospel of consumption." Cowdrick recognized that the Industrial Revolution had brought about important macroeconomic changes. Writing in the 1920s, Cowdrick (1927: 209) opined that "the worker has come to be more important as a consumer than he is as a producer ... Production, which once reigned supreme in the industrial kingdom, has yielded the throne to distribution. Not to manufacture and mine and raise enough goods, but to find enough people who will buy them-this is the vital problem of business." Like many of his era, Cowdrick (1927: 210) advocated a high standard of living as an economic stabilization policy, writing that "this steadiness of buying power, through good and even through moderately bad times, should have important results in regularizing employment and making it easier to escape the most harmful manifestations of business cycles."

Businessmen became increasingly convinced that Americans could be persuaded to buy things produced by industry that they had never needed before. They were faithful that consumers would desire goods and services, not in response to some set of economic motives, but according to the "pursuit" of a constantly improving standard of living. Transforming the twentieth-century worker into a status-conscious consumer was quite revolutionary, as most people at the time still relied on home-made products. Advertisers took every opportunity to denigrate "home-made" products as old-fashioned or inferior in their efforts to promote "store-bought" and "mass-produced" items. Braverman (1974: 276) summarizes the success of advertising in cultivating a commercial spirit, "the source of status is no longer the ability to make things but simply the ability to purchase them." Advertising was a crucial component of the Fordist compromise that linked greater mass production with higher mass consumption—a productivist model centered on the hedonism of the pursuit of happiness through access to a greater number of goods.

Herbert Hoover's 1929 Committee on Recent Economic Changes, influenced by the National Bureau of Economic Research under the direction of Wesley Mitchell, promoted the high income/high consumption approach. The committee criticized pessimistic predictions about "saturation points" calling these predictions "abstract" and the likelihood of market saturation "remote." They pointed to economic theory and actual experience to counter the notion that the economy was reaching a steady state of abundance. From the theoretical standpoint, "economists have long declared that consumption, the satisfaction of wants, would expand with little evidence of satiation if we could so adjust our economic processes as to make dormant demands effective. ... With rising wages and relatively stable prices, we have become consumers of what we produce to an extent never before realized (Committee on Recent Economic Changes 1929)."

Although history eventually confirmed the resiliency of consumption, episodes of overproduction in the 1920s and the Great Depression continued to test the faith of business leaders in the adaptability of consumption.

Production in the 1920s was both plentiful and onerous. As the disutility of labor increased with the monotony of industrial work, the pull of consumption had to be that much stronger. After exalting work to the center of material, spiritual, and communal life, the competitive furor of business then proceeded to destroy many of the meaningful, rewarding, and self-fulfilling aspects of work. The later advent of Fordism and Taylorism, which endeavored to fragment and optimize the kinetics of work tasks, tended to alienate and demoralize the worker to the detriment of labor productivity. Reducing work to simple, monotonous tasks left the worker uninspired and resentful. The resulting disloyalty and labor turnover presented a colossal cost to the entrepreneur and threatened the work and spend culture.

John Commons suggested an extension of industrial goodwill as an alternative to scientific management as a solution to the emerging effort dilemma:

> At the moment when scientific management was achieving an evident success, another cost, less tangible but equally important, began to receive scientific investigation ... this hitherto unmeasured cost of labor received attention, and when, by a bold stroke of genius rather than science, the Ford Motor Company doubled its wages, but nevertheless increased its profits by the mere reduction in cost of labor turnover, it became evident to all that the intangible goodwill of labor may be as profitable as the scientific management of labor.

Ford's successful amelioration of chronic worker turnover in his plant by reducing the workweek and increasing the pay of his workers demonstrated that labor was a unique factor of production. Workers were reflective beings, concerned about equality in the workplace and the social impact of their labors. Unlike Eichner's (1985: 79) barrel of oil—which is indifferent to "whether it is used to heat a house of God or a house of prostitution"— workers are often concerned with the social impact of their labors. Unlike machines or bags of cement, employers had a moral obligation in their treatment of workers, and fairness was often reciprocated with greater work effort (Prasch 2004). Ford's experiment reminded other industrialists that workers were also consumers, whose collective prosperity was closely linked to their own.

When coupled with rising productivity that resulted from rapid technological development, the lessons of Fords' "five-dollar-day and five-day-week" presented the possibility of great social change—a democratization of leisure time and the social organization to support it. This first glimpse of a resolution of the "economic problem" of scarcity worried those content with the status quo while heartening those intent on social reform. This early munificence of the industrial system clearly delineated the battle lines between economic and social interests.

The capitalist class partially responded by promising a large and equitable sharing of the plenitude that would flow from a "technocracy" of production.

Technocracy held that workplace democracy and solidarity would afford a productivity bonanza that would result in a rested and well-paid worker efficiently producing for a mass market. When coupled with workplace harmony, an engineering-based approach to production was to yield a plenitude of goods and leisure to the working class. The productivity improvements that emerged in the wake of World War I offered a sanguine alternative to the nineteenth-century's bleak prognosis that the working classes were forever enslaved to long hours of work and the "iron law of wages".

Whereas organized labor in the United States responded forcefully to initial time and motion studies that threatened the skill and autonomy of the worker, unions became far more acquiescent to the concept of greater industrial output as a means of improving the lot of the worker. Responding to rebellious American shipyard workers, Frederick Taylor argued that his emphasis on technical efficiency would yield a "mental revolution" by ending class conflict in the workplace. According to Taylor (1947: 24), the scientific management of production would increase "the size of the surplus until the surplus became so large that it was unnecessary to quarrel over how it should be divided."

Many capitalists of the period offered either goodwill or gambits— depending on one's perspective—in the form of "social investments" in their workers. The hope was that a person would work harder as a partner, or family member, than as a servant. Company-sponsored Sunday schools, churches, housing, newsletters, recreation facilities, and employee representation plans were some of the devices designed to show that management cared for the worker. These benefits held the potential to foster a more productive and loyal worker, but, more importantly, they were believed to fend off unions. To suspicious observers, Taylor's "mental revolution" was a Faustian bargain from the beginning; designed to get labor to cede control over production in exchange for management's promise of higher wages and shorter hours. In any case, by shifting attention from the foreman to the engineer and from the micro level of the firm to the grander, macroeconomic notion of economic progress, Taylor was able to placate opposition from mainstream labor camps and set the groundwork for a compromise over the productivity dividend. Cross (1993: 29) argues that "Taylor's 'mental revolution' became the basic rationale for the eight-hour day that was won in Western Europe and in many American industries immediately after World War I."

Statements from labor leaders of the period confirm the compliant mentality. Cooke (1920) stressed that industrial engineers should join with leaders of a "new unionism" to raise productivity, increase wages, and reduce work time. The promise of the technocracy was formally endorsed by the American Federation of Labor (AFL) in 1925 in the following declaration:

> We hold that the best interests of wage earners as well as the whole social group are served [by] increasing production … and by high wage standards which assure sustained purchasing power to the workers …

Social inequality, industrial instability and injustice must increase unless the worker's real wage ... is advanced in proportion to man's increasing power of production.

This marked the emergence of a new approach, or what many would call a compromise, to the dialectic conflict between labor and management. Rather than a distributive struggle, increased output per worker could alone raise workers' pay. Labor's new compromise represented a radical departure from the older belief system that shortening working hours would create a scarcity premium that would in turn increase workers' share of national income. It is important to note that in terms of free time the technocracy of productivism has proven to be an empty promise. Beyond the achievement of the 8-hour day, progress toward more leisure time has largely stalled in the developed world. With few exceptions, higher wages and consumption in a mass-production economy have taken priority over shorter hours on the agendas of labor leaders, politicians, and managers.

Conservative mental remnants of the existing social order among labor leaders and the technocrats themselves arrested the development of a leisure society that could replace work as an organizing social structure (Cross 1993). The inability to conceive of a society that was not centered around the workplace continually tilted the bargaining balance toward higher income and greater consumption. Society lacked an effective counterweight against our highly visible consumptive lives and our relatively more private productive lives. Arguably Tugwell's (1927: 258) comments have even more relevancy today:

> Our social groups are consuming groups ... [W]e have almost completely divorced our producing lives from our consuming lives. At home and among friends we have no approval for our productive efforts, and so our neighbors, and, tragically, our very wives and children come to estimate us according to our incomes ... [F]or the old morality of service, of workmanship, and of pride in skill, there is substituted the morality of display.

The market mentality continues to tell us to build our character though hard work and by doing "productive" things in organizations. Yet as Zelinski (1997: 41) opines, "There is something seriously wrong with this: If we think we are what we do for a living, we have lost most of our character." The fragmented nature of production along with the obscurantism surrounding job functions and tasks needed to defend wage differentials based on the spurious marginal productivity theory of labor results in production being a largely private affair. Those in positions of power generally prefer to keep their "producing lives" private to frustrate external assessments of their true productivity. Narrowly defined, fragmented, hierarchical, and adversarial working conditions subject workers to a social inferiority complex with little relief outside emulative spending.

An additional impediment to a democratic and sustainable allocation of time and money was the resistance of business leaders. Even if technically driven, it is the rare capitalist that is enthusiastic about the implications of a leisure society. Although more palatable than a rebellious redistribution of income, any serious reshuffling of the spoils of production would undermine the disciplinary function of work. Many business leaders castigated the shallow consumerism and amorphous leisure time that might emanate from an abundant social system. In 1922, Andre Francois-Poncet (1922: 10) lamented that "the only benefactor of the eight-hour day was the cabaret."

From the perspective of the capitalist, mass productivity, with its promise of "high wages" and leisure time, threatened the work discipline and further economic growth. Most employers felt that the implications of worker prosperity were absenteeism, high turnover rates, and demands for shorter hours; in short, an erosion of the incentive to work. Similarly, cultural conservatives were solicitous that high wages and the spreading of a mass market would subvert social mores. A telling oration was given in 1926 by John Edgerton, president of the US National Association of Manufacturers:

> It is time for America to awake from its dream that an eternal holiday is a natural fruit of material prosperity ... I am for everything that will make work happier but against everything that will further subordinate its importance ... the emphasis should be put on work-more work and better work, instead of upon leisure.

Initially, Ford's capitalist peers were scornful of his five-dollar-day and five-day-week, arguing that it would lead to a life of frivolity among the working class. The argument that workers cannot be trusted to use leisure or wage gains in a meritorious fashion has been wielded so regularly against progressive improvements in working conditions over the centuries that it is now a rather threadbare shibboleth.

Despite the apparent success of the "social investments" in sharing productivity dividends to maintain consumption, some economists remained skeptical that the long-run dilemma had been solved. Their suspicions were stoked by the Great Depression—an era that challenged the resiliency of consumption as never before. The prolonged economic contraction of the 1930s revealed that consumer spending needed to be adequately cultivated and financed if it was to serve as the lifeblood of the economic system. The "economic threat" of abundance in the midst of poverty was portrayed most poignantly in Steinbeck's (1939: 476–77) *Grapes of Wrath*:

> The works of the roots of the vines, of the trees, must be destroyed to keep up the price, and the saddest, bitterest thing of all. Carloads of oranges dumped on the ground. The people came for miles to take the fruit, but this could not be. How would they buy oranges at twenty cents a dozen if they could drive out and pick them up? And men with hoses

squirt kerosene on the oranges, and they are angry at the crime, angry at the people who have come to take the fruit. A million people hungry, needing the fruit—and kerosene sprayed over the golden mountains. ... Burn coffee for fuel in ships. Burn corn to keep warm, it makes a hot fire. Dump potatoes in the rivers and place guards along the banks to keep the hungry people from fishing them out. Slaughter pigs and bury them, and let the putrescence drip down into the earth ... There is a crime here that goes beyond denunciation. There is a sorrow here that weeping cannot symbolize. There is a failure here that topples all our success.

The stalling of consumption-led growth during the Great Depression created fertile ground for the outgrowth of Keynesian thought. Importantly, however, the Keynesian revolution did not seek to supplant the role of consumption in economic growth but rather to stabilize it. Rather than work time reduction, Keynes advocated the "first aid" of government spending as it was the most expedient means of placing a floor on spending in the face of fickle investment and consumption expenditure. Government spending could stabilize aggregate expenditure that was ultimately responsible for employment, but as the Great Depression persisted it became clear that government had to be prepared to make prodigious expenditures to stabilize the market system.

Although it did not subvert the capitalistic structure of accumulation and distribution, the Keynesian rebellion did represent a partial threat to the market mentality as a socialization of investment, if extreme enough, could serve to subordinate the economy to social needs. Indeed, the subordination of the market, or what Polanyi called the "protective response," is visible in the few New Deal policies that continue to address critical market shortcomings in the United States. Yet, many interpretations of the "Keynesian revolution" conclude that it did more to save capitalism from itself than it did to resurrect the place of society in the economy. Zinn (1999: 393) observes that "the New Deal's organization of the economy was aimed mainly at stabilizing the economy, and secondly at giving enough help to the lower classes to keep them from turning a rebellion into a real revolution."[3] Indeed many of the New Deal protections designed to curb the callousness of the free market were temporary. Yet, a consensus emerged from the Keynesian policies that proved to be far more durable—the notion that economic growth could serve as a palliative for many social and economic afflictions.

Since World War II, the virtue of economic growth has been enmeshed in the political, economic, and cultural psyche of Western society. Keynes directed the eyes of liberals to the importance of production and the political successes that followed kept them focused there. Schor (1995: 70) writes:

the postwar regime was premised on steady increases in income and consumption in that the Keynesian alliance between business, labour and government was essentially an agreement to avoid conflict over shares by ensuring higher absolute levels for all ... Prosperity became key to the virtual elimination of political challenges to the system. Increasing consumption also solved the 'economic problem', that is, fear of stagnation. Productivity increases were channeled into growth of real wages and hence private consumption. Consumer credit enhanced consumer demand. The gap between what the economy was capable of producing and what people were willing to buy – the nightmare of prewar theorists – was kept to a minimum.

As Military Keynesianism racked up political victories, a generation of economists and politicians came to believe that government spending could be used to improve the material outcome of the economic game, with little concern for the destructive forces of economic growth. Debate over the efficiency of the form of government spending was tolerated; but its necessity was rarely questioned. As Minsky (1986: 30) writes, "the efficiency of Big Government can be questioned, but its efficacy in preventing the sky from falling cannot be doubted."

Growing the economic pie then became a central objective of economic analysis and policy while distributive matters waned in importance. In the 1950s, J.K. Galbraith (1958: 82) wrote that "few things are more evident in modern social history than the decline in interest in inequality as an economic issue." A strong argument could be made that a social indifference to inequality persists today, but clearly the scale of social inequities has begun to awaken a class consciousness. In retrospect, the growth consensus could be aptly described as a Faustian bargain, since the price paid for economic growth may have been larger than anticipated. Many of these costs are outlined in the next chapter, which examines some of the leading critiques of economic growth.

In addition to the premium placed on growth, the resiliency of the market mentality in the "age of Keynes" was also manifest in the pattern of assistance during the Great Depression and the rather rapid deterioration of public support for the New Deal programs. In the spirit of the New Deal and Marshall Plan, governments in advanced nations assumed a greater responsibility for creating adequate employment opportunities. This is not to say that they necessarily pursued full unemployment, but that creating "enough" jobs translated into considerable political success. The most expedient way for government to foster employment gains would have been through a rapid expansion of aggregate demand that served to increase consumption and production. Yet, even in the depths of the Depression the emphasis of government programs was on employment rather than cash assistance, as direct monetary aid was tainted with the same social suspicion that had tarnished public succor in centuries past. Trout (1973: 12) writes that "taxpayers often expressed the view that those on direct relief were getting nothing less than a soul-destroying handout, and for the duration of the depression, Americans vastly preferred work relief to cash relief. In city after city, investigations were staged to weed out welfare 'chiselers' and newspapers railed against 'boondogglers' and 'shirkers'."

As newspapers and other conservative forces accelerated their attack on welfare problems and graft related to cash assistance, many Americans began to question the work-oriented relief programs as well. By the late 1930s, negative evaluations of the Works Progress Administration exceeded positive responses in opinion polls (Trout 1973). The persistent ideology of individualism may have had its most pernicious effect on the day-to-day operations of the Depression relief programs. Local programs were often frustrated by stingy state legislatures. Consequently, work relief never came close to meeting the unemployment need, and local assistance agencies were chronically understaffed. Trout (1973: 39) estimated that "for every person on the federal payroll, at least four had been denied relief."

Not only was the New Deal relief modest relative to the need, but it was also fleeting. The soothing home fires of work relief programs had been reduced to smoldering ashes by 1941. With the demise of direct assistance and work relief programs, the relief revolution of the 1930s came to an end. Only one major piece of relief legislation survived—the 1935 Social Security Act—and that was not operational until it was validated by the Supreme Court as constitutional in 1937. Passage of the Social Security Act acknowledged some federal responsibility for relief of the poor, but the underlying philosophy of individualism and moral reform was little changed and remains intact today.

Scarcity in the labor-leisure choice model of work time determination

As scarcity and marginal utility theory came to dominate mainstream economic methodology, orthodox economists reduced human nature to a hedonistic existence. A shrewd calculator of pleasure and pain, economic man was seen to maximize his utility through the acquisition of more and more goods, and minimizes his pain by avoiding toil. Such hedonistic behavioral assumptions pervade every corner of neoclassical thought and are patently apparent in the mainstream explanation of the distribution of work hours. In the labor-leisure calculus the utility of the consumption made possible by greater earned income is balanced against the disutility of paid work to arrive at a work time preference. Veblen (1898: 78) describes the neoclassical approach to the labor market: "the economic beatitude lies in an unrestrained consumption of goods, without work; whereas the perfect economic affliction is unremunerated labor." The tradeoff between consumption and leisure relies on the belief that an individual's chief desire is to obtain the goods produced by labor while avoiding the effort by which the goods are produced. Furthermore, the neoclassical paradigm assumes the existence of robust competition in labor markets, to argue that working time allocations are a mere reflection of individual preferences for income and consumption versus leisure time.

Although the source of the disutility of work varies slightly within mainstream economic models, the assumption that workers possess an inveterate aversion to labor is ubiquitous to orthodox economic theory.[4] For instance, the atavistic resistance to work is given clarion expression in the contemporary work of New Institutionalist economists. Williamson (1985: 2) describes opportunism as a characteristic of "human nature as we know it." In this view, the traits and behaviors of man cannot be altered internally and must be constrained by institutional bounds.[5] Spencer (2003: 247) writes that, "against this backdrop, there has been no progress in uncovering the nature and transformation of work preferences. How and why workers acquire their motives for work remain important unanswered questions. The determinants of work motives, in short, continue to be consigned to a black box." The presumption of an innate disutility for labor has important ramifications for labor market reform. If work is irksome, granting opportunistic workers more control over their working conditions would lead to self-interested inefficiency, if not anarchy. In order to maximize efficiency, conventional wisdom holds that work organization must limit the opportunities that workers have to shirk. Workplace discipline must be maintained through rules, ceremonies, hierarchies, and segmentation within the firm and the maintenance of involuntary unemployment in the macroeconomy (Shapiro and Stiglitz 1984).

Employers, on the other hand, are disciplined by the competitive pressures of markets. In the neoclassical labor market, firms hire (demand) labor up to the point at which wages equal marginal products. Stiff competition in product markets ensures that all firms pay workers of homogeneous quality an equivalent wage. It follows immediately that the marginal product of like workers in all industries is equalized. The intersection of the labor supply and labor demand curve determines the real wage and the aggregate level of employment. The allocation of work hours is then a result of sovereign workers striking agreements with competitive firms based on worker preferences of income and leisure time. Firms, hiring workers in competitive factor markets, are subject to the prevailing wage and work time preferences of workers. Just as employers would be hard-pressed to find any workers when offering sub-standard wages, competitive factor markets would also restrain them from demanding excessively long work hours from employees. Furthermore, should employers fail to offer the desired work schedules, new firms will emerge and carve out a comparative advantage in the market based on a superior management of human resources. In the sovereign-worker model employers will offer a variety of work time regimes and employees will sort themselves into positions, industries, or occupations that reflect their preferred work time. If they cannot secure their preferred hours, workers will be offered a compensating wage differential. Thus, even if there is a dearth of short-hours jobs offered to employees, the competitive model characterizes workers as "choosing" long hours and compensating wage differentials. The orthodox assumption of perfect competition consequently results in work hours being primarily determined by labor supply phenomenon, representing the revealed preferences of workers rather than the might of employers.

The assumption of an aversion to labor has afforded the labor supply curve a special status in mainstream economic analysis. Although the bottom portion of the labor supply curve is upward sloping, most labor market theorists accept that the curve can bend backward as the income effects of higher wages dominate the substitution effects. As income rises, an additional hour of leisure has a higher opportunity cost, inducing workers into longer hours. This is the substitution effect. Normally, economists envision substitution effects dominating work time choices at lower wage rates. Under the income effect, increases in income induce workers to work less, or, in effect, consume more leisure. The substitution effects are reflected in the upward-sloping section of the labor supply curve, while the income effects are shown on the backward-bending portion. If history reveals workweeks to be recalcitrant, the sovereign-worker model indicates that wage levels have yet to reach the backward-bending region of the labor supply curve, where leisure time becomes more attractive.

Given their faith in competitive forces, neoclassical economists routinely appeal to protection of free will as an argument against work time regulation. A legislated reduction of hours, it is argued, would be an infringement upon the liberties of those who wished to work longer. This sovereign worker mentality also imbues the neoclassical interpretation of the historical record surrounding work hours. The Marginalists explain the late nineteenth-century movement for shorter hours as the propensity of workers to seek free time as real incomes rose. Reynolds (1974: 34) aptly summarizes the argument:

> Over the long run ... changes in hours reflect worker preferences. The main reason why weekly hours have fallen from about sixty at the turn of the century to around forty at present is that most workers find the increase in leisure preferable to the higher incomes they could earn on the old schedule. If and when most workers conclude that a four-day or a thirty-hour week yields a better balance between income and leisure, management and union policies will shift in that direction.

The history of the short hours movement and the potential for further reductions is thusly trivialized in mainstream economics as a simple consumer choice calculus between goods and leisure, rather than a larger societal movement to reform the social division of labor in a manner that would improve lives and livelihoods. Conversely, Hunnicutt (1988) argues that the struggle over work time represents more than a utility-maximizing choice for greater leisure. Free time "also represented freedom *for* something outside [work] – for an existence beyond the marketplace, 'outside' working, buying, and consuming and the control of owners, managers, and professionals (Hunnicutt 1988: 56)." Rather than a paragon of self-interested behavior, the militant worker demanding shorter hours and a new alternative culture represented the antithesis of "economic man."

Conclusion

From its adolescence in Mercantilism to the modern ascendancy of utility maximization, the motive of individualistic economic gain in the face of scarcity has played a central role in Western economic thought and, like religion, has profoundly influenced social policy. The obsession with insatiability is a direct result of an intellectual and social fixation on the "market form" of economic organization that largely eclipses alternative methodological approaches (Stanfield 1986). By examining the progression of economic thought on the market mentality and the mainstream exclusion of alternative perspectives (such as those featured in Chapter 2), this chapter has argued that the myopia of the market perspective is dependent upon a single economic perspective—the neoclassical paradigm. This neoclassical approach largely consists of promoting the maximization of insatiable human desires in the face of scarce resources. Neoclassical assumptions axiomatically treat wants as infinite while resources are limited. Moreover the moral substance of both the wants and the resources does not fall within the province of economic analysis for neoclassical economists, who eschew all normative subject matter. The contextual relevance of this view to employment policy is that under the market myth the division of labor comes to be governed by the pursuit of ever-expanding production in the service of unlimited wants. Rationally disposed to maximize utility, self-interested individuals recognize the advantages of exchange and their natural propensity to truck and barter generates a socially optimal division of labor. Yet, if either of the axioms of insatiable wants or scarcity break down, a market-driven distribution of labor becomes suspect and a reorganization of work time offers the potential for improving the life process.

2 Rethinking the Work Fetish and the Growth Consensus

"The stupendous industrial achievements of the market economy had been bought at the price of great harm to the substance of society."

Karl Polanyi (1944: 16)

"I have always been of the opinion that hard work is simply the refuge of people who have nothing whatever do."

Oscar Wilde (1997: 359)

Given its checkered origin, can we expect a persistence of the work fetish? Although it is difficult to predict the staying power of capitalist-infused notions, recent trends suggest that the idolatry of work is losing its magnetism. Indeed, diverse viewpoints antithetical to the supremacy of the market mentality have existed for nearly as long as capitalism itself. Although these heretical traditions have yet to alter the foundations of capitalist society, they have played an important role in protecting many aspects of society from the corrosive aspects of the free market. The history of capitalism is in large part a history of the continual curtailment of free market forces: the abolition of slavery; anti-trust legislation; prohibition of the sale and exploitation of women and children; Sunday as a rest day, the Poor Laws, the 10- and 8-hour working day; the maintenance of minimum wages; legal standards for quality, safety, and pollution; social, health and retirement insurance; and so on. Many of the labor market protections erected during the 1930s, grew out of the theoretical and applied works of radical economists, who have long been mindful of the limits of the market system. Indeed, heterodox analysis and interpretation of the capitalist system affords a useful understanding of the social implications of administering society on the basis of economic gain and provides inspiration for alternative social planning.

This chapter employs a heterodox perspective to investigate the emergence, efficacy, and implications of the market system with an eye toward informing an alternative distribution of social labor conducive to greater participation and well-being. It features some of the intellectual highlights in the debate surrounding the market mechanism and its impact on paid work. It offers a radical critique of the fundamental neoclassical assumptions of scarcity and insatiability that serve as the foundation of economic gain. The question of whether human nature or social organization compels modern man into acquisitive behavior is central to the issue of employment policy if that policy is concerned with maximizing human satisfaction. By extension, the critique of economic gain as a social lodestar calls into question the idolatry of paid work that is ubiquitous in the economic policy of market societies. Evidence from new psychological research on the failure of economic growth to improve life satisfaction (the abundance paradox) is offered to further challenge the wisdom of the growth consensus that fuels a preoccupation with paid work. Finally, the future of paid work in a post-industrial and post-service economy characterized by fewer employment opportunities is featured in this chapter as many observers contend that societies will be forced to drastically recast the relationship between remunerative work and social participation in the near future. In such an environment the erosion of the work fetish may be a foregone conclusion, which will test the sophistication and adeptness of social policy to adjust to technological change in a manner that ensures individuals the "tickets to participation (Tool 1998)."

The adolescent state of capitalism

In critically evaluating the rise of the market mentality, it is useful to remind ourselves that market economies have a relatively short history. Heilbroner (1993: 24) points out that in historical terms the ethos of economic gain is a recent development:

> It may strike us as odd that the idea of gain is a relatively modern one; we are schooled to believe that man is essentially an acquisitive creature and that left to himself he will behave as any self-respecting businessman would. The profit motive, we are constantly told, is as old as man himself. But it is not. The profit motive as we know it is only as old as "modern man." Even today the notion of gain for gain's sake is foreign to a large portion of the world's population, and it has been conspicuous by its absence over most of recorded history ... The idea of gain, the idea that each working person not only may, but should, constantly strive to better his or her material lot, is an idea that was quite foreign to the great lower and middle strata of Egyptian, Greek, Roman and medieval cultures, only scattered throughout Renaissance and Reformation times; and largely absent in the majority of Eastern civilizations. As a ubiquitous characteristic of society, it is as modern an invention as printing.

The historical record of labor markets provides ample evidence of the fleeting commitment to the principle of economic gain in pre-capitalist society. As chronicled in multiple anthropological studies, pre-capitalist societies, guaranteed an individual's survival by virtue of their membership in the group or society (Sahlins 1972; Applebaum 1984). With the introduction of a market-based social structure in seventeenth-century England, however, labor required the threat of hunger as seen, then and now, in the ascendant Ricardian theory and an assortment of social policies. The heavy-handed tactics needed to compel subjects to work in early capitalist and colonial societies calls into question the ubiquity of the economistic behavior of "economic man." In case after case, after destroying social structures in an effort to extract labor from local inhabitants, the expropriators were not able to rely on the allurement of high wages to bring forth productive effort; rather they had to rely on starvation and the use of corporeal punishment to extract physical effort from their subjects (Applebaum 1984; Zinn 1999). Polanyi (1944: 164) writes, "for the higher the wages the smaller the inducement to exertion on the part of the native, who unlike the white man was not compelled by his cultural standards to make as much money as he possibly could." The "economic motive" was also absent among early industrial workers who abhorred factory work. In the early stages of capitalism, virgin workers of indigenous make-up, unaccustomed to wage work, rankled by factory life, and unassimilated to the idea of an ever-rising standard of living, did not work harder when wages rose; they simply took more time off. As chronicled in Chapter 1, the prospect of penury and starvation along with a constant harangue about the amorality of unemployment was used to subordinate the poor to the factory system. Polanyi (1944: 165) offers sundry examples of coercion, "Legal compulsion and parish serfdom as in England, the rigors of an absolutist labor police as on the Continent, indentured labor as in the early Americas were the prerequisites of the 'willing worker'. But the final stage was reached with the application of 'nature's penalty', hunger."

Heilbroner (1993) also pinpoints a shared pessimism in the works of major economic theorists that raises doubts about the permanency of the capitalist system. He argues that Smith, Marx, Keynes, and Schumpeter all perceive capitalism as self-destructive. Heilbroner (1993: 103) asks, "why do none of our philosophers, not even Smith or Schumpeter, who are surely partisans of the order – foresee a long untroubled future for capitalism? Why can we not find any major figure in the history of economic thought who projects such a future?" Heilbroner (1993: 103) suggests that the answer lies in the difficulty of achieving macro- and micro-order in capitalistic society as well as the "nagging doubts regarding its political and moral validity." The inherent instability of capitalism presents a host of challenges: capricious investment flows, desultory social progress, inequitable income and wealth distributions, volatile credit extension, pressures towards monopoly or cartelization, the technological displacement of labor, inflationary tendencies of successful economies, and the depressive tendencies of laggard economies. Add to these challenges the moral misgivings related to surplus value flowing to those that "own" capital rather than those that "produce" or "use" it and it is easy to share the masters' apprehension regarding capitalism's long-run permanency.

A methodological alternative: radical political economy

Recognizing the inchoate and inherently volatile state of market-based societies should forestall ethnocentric interpretations of their development. Mindful of the influence of religious, social, and commercial institutions in the development of the market mentality, Polanyi (1977) warned economists against "formal ethnocentrism" that interpreted market capitalism as a spontaneous or natural outgrowth of embryonic market elements existing in pre-capitalist societies. Polanyi (1977: 125) writes:

> The temptation in our own age, to regard the market economy as the natural goal of some three thousand years of Western development is overwhelming ... Market trade itself, and eventually the modern market economy, were the results, not of a process of growth from small beginnings, but rather of the convergences of originally separate and independent developments that cannot be understood apart from an analysis of the institutional elements that went into their making.

Polanyi was able to avoid the temptation to ethnocentrism by pursuing a method of inquiry that was heavily dependent on economic anthropology and history. This evoluntary approach, which afforded Polanyi a unique insight into the role of the economy in society, is a defining characteristic of the Institutionalist method of social inquiry and provides a methodological foundation for the social effort bargain. Polanyi (1944: 46) observed that, "the outstanding discovery of recent historical and anthropological research is that man's economy, as a rule, is submerged in his social relationships." Accordingly, the social effort bargain recognizes that employment relations should be governed by a process that balances the social and economic functions of paid work as they evolve over time.

Polanyi was troubled by the influence of the market myth and the glorification of gain in the modern age that resulted in a perverse tendency for economic considerations to dominate social, cultural, and political life. Under industrial capitalism, Polanyi (1944: 57) writes, "instead of economy being embedded in social relations, social relations are embedded in the economic system." Polanyi argues that the disembedding of the economy from society is most apparent in the commoditization of land, labor, and money. He characterizes the transformation of these social institutions into commodities as "fictitious." The expropriation of the land is particularly emblematic of the economistic transformation. A symbolic step in the commoditization of land was the repeal of the British Corn Laws in 1946, which were established to protect agrarian traditions from destructive competition. Polanyi (1944) uses Ricardo's commoditization of marginally productive soil as a prime example of the economic role overshadowing other important social functions and uses. Polanyi (1944: 178) defends those social functions when he writes,

Land is tied up with the organizations of kinship, neighborhood, craft, and creed-with tribe and temple, village, gild, and church ... The economic function is but one of many functions of land. It invests man's life with stability; it is the site of his habitation; it is a condition of his physical safety; it is the landscape and the seasons. We might as well imagine his being born without hands and feet as carrying on his life without land. And yet to separate land from man and organize society in such a way as to satisfy the requirements of a real-estate market was a vital part of the utopian concept of a market economy.

The privatization of land gave control of its use to the legal, and often distant, owners whose financial claims usurped the interests of land users or inhabitants. Historical epochs of enclosure and foreclosure, such as those in seventeenth-century Europe or 1930s' America, respectively, illustrate the ability of financial owners to assert their property or "economic" rights over social customs and traditions.

Schumacher (1974) likewise views the functions of land as being "Meta-economic." That is, the proper use of land is not a technical or economic problem, but primarily a metaphysical dilemma. The issue of land use belongs to a higher decision-making process than economic rationalization. Ideally, enlightened property rights and land use would incorporate environmental, social, and moral considerations. Schumacher (1974: 88) writes:

There is no escape from this confusion as long as the land and the creatures upon it are looked upon as nothing but 'factors of production'. They are, of course, factors of production, that is to say, means-to-ends, but this is their secondary, not their primary, nature. Before everything else, they are ends-in-themselves; they are meta-economic, and it is therefore rationally justifiable to say, as a statement of fact, that they are in a certain sense sacred. Man has not made them, and it is irrational for him to treat things that he has not made and cannot make and cannot recreate once he has spoilt them, in the same manner and spirit as he is entitled to treat things of his own making.

If left unchecked, the market imperative toward extending commoditization would have altered human relations beyond recognition. Instead, protective mechanisms have been erected from time to time to insulate society from the most destructive aspects of the market mechanism. Governments have intervened with legislation regulating child and slave labor, working conditions, work time, wage minimums, bargaining equity, and income maintenance programs. Legislation restricting land use such as planning and zoning, resource conservation, pollution control, and environmental protection has also served as a buffer to unfettered market activity. Capital markets have operated under layers of regulation in an effort to curb moral hazards, the temptations of perfidious swindlers, systemic risks, and a hodgepodge of inequities. Given the disasterous results of the recent liberalization of financial markets, we can expect even greater social oversight of capital markets. Polanyi referred to the erection of these market restraints as the "protective response."

Polanyi's disembedded economy provides a useful framework for the investigation into how the methodological domination of the formal ethnocentric approach in economics has crystallized the market mentality and its concomitant fetish for remunerative work. For Polanyi, no misinterpretation of the past ever proved more prophetic of the future than the misplaced centrality given to the role of gain and profit made on exchange. He refers to the consensus among modern ethnographers concerning the lack of market-based institutions throughout history. In contrast to economists, Polanyi (1944: 47) states that anthropologists generally agree on, "the absence of the motive of gain; the absence of the principle of laboring for remuneration; the absence of the principle of least effort; and, especially, the absence of any separate and distinct institution based on economic motives." In his view, the free market system did not emerge as a spontaneous, historical force; rather it was installed as a matter of conscious design. Polanyi (1944: 57) explains:

> The nineteenth century—whether hailing the fact as the apex of civilization or deploring it as a cancerous growth—naively imagined that such a development was the natural outcome of the spreading of markets. It was not realized that the gearing of markets into a self-regulating system of tremendous power was not the result of any inherent tendency of markets towards excrescence, but rather the effect of *highly artificial stimulants* administered to the body social in order to meet a situation which was created by the no less artificial phenomenon of the machine (emphasis added).

For Polanyi, economic systems, market-based or otherwise, were not inevitable and natural evolutions. Social systems of accumulation and exchange were always and everywhere a product of society, molded by our thoughts and shaped by our actions.

Economistic behavior is glaringly absence among the manifold motivations to work in non-market societies. In such cultures, work is directed mainly to satisfy subsistence needs or religious and cultural traditions. Work relations are based on kinship, and exchange is based on reciprocity. Polanyi (1944: 49) notes that "in such a community the idea of profit is barred; higgling and haggling is decried; giving freely is acclaimed as a virtue; the supposed propensity to barter, truck and exchange does not appear." Work in non-market societies is embedded in the cultural fabric and linked to social institutions, exhibiting strong ties with family structures, religion, and taboos. Many work tasks such as hunting, fishing, clearing fields, thatching of roofs, and constructing shelters are preformed communally and in a festive manner. This cultural and communal governance of work has tended to promote gender equality. Applebaum (1984: 14) argues that, "in viewing non-market culture we have many examples of societies where women enjoy prestige and standing because all work is embedded in the culture and the communal aspect of work brings recognition to women's work as well as men's work." Pertinent to work time reform, anthropologists have observed that work in non-market societies is typically task-oriented rather than time-oriented. Time is not economically valued in non-market societies, and consequently work tasks are steadily pursued until they are completed. Workers do not conceive of themselves as "wasting" time but adjust their lives and livelihood to the course of natural events. Since there is little competition for rank or occupation, there is little differentiation between work and leisure. Indeed, the anthropological record suggests that economic incentives hold little sway in directing work activity in non-market societies.

This is not to say that individuals in non-market society do not pursue social esteem and recognition, but that they do not rely on financial or economic comparisons to differentiate themselves. Stanfield (1986: 47) contends that "the needs for social esteem and even invidious distinction may be insatiable but it is not inevitable that they be expressed through an endless treadmill of commodity consumption. Moreover, insatiability based on invidy is a neurosis, a sickness, more to be pitied and cured than celebrated and legitimated as a primary social force." The non-market society of Ponape, Micronesia, offers an example of bestowing esteem in a non-pecuniary manner. In this culture, farmers attempt to curry societal recognition by growing the biggest yam (Bascom 1948). Some of the prize yams weigh more than 200 pounds and must be carried on poles by a half dozen men. The Ponapean yam-growers are willing to work long, arduous hours, even for years, to produce something they will give away at feasts but will attest to their skill as farmers. They are motivated to work by a desire to be admired for their skills and generosity, not for their accumulated wealth. Under industrial capitalism people rarely share or exchange the product of their work directly; perhaps this is one of the reasons for the lessened solidarity among them and the enhanced desire for invidious financial distinctions relative to non-market cultures.

Although many heterodox schools of economic thought have criticized the organization of society around a market mentality, this analysis draws heavily on the works of Institutionalists (with later chapters highlighting the similarities to Marxian thought). Arguably, some of the most influential and widely cited critiques of the market system have been penned by Institutionalists, such as Thorstein Veblen, John Commons, Karl Polanyi, and John K. Galbraith.[1] The Institutionalist approach is particularly useful in the search for an alternative distribution and social function of paid work as its holistic methodology is less prone to the ethnocentric myopia that has led to the belief that acquisitive behavior is a congenital characteristic.

Rather than an exercise in the optimization of givens, Institutionalist economics is a study of the institutional adjustments necessary for the provisioning of society. The substance of individual wants and the resources available to satisfy those desires constitute a large part of the subject matter to be addressed and explained in the Institutionalist method. Since socio-economic outcomes are fundamentally influenced by power and habit, the Institutionalist method aspires to a holistic approach in order to address the many issues ignored by the neoclassical method such as market power, organizational structure, agency concerns, and other social, political, and ethical influences. Yet, the greatest difference between the Institutionalist and the conventional approaches is the evolutionary method employed by Insti-tutionalists. Unlike neoclassical economics which still operates under New-tonian constraints, Institutionalists used the Darwinian revolution to view the "social structure as something arrived at through a process of cumulative change and as something undergoing further change (Hamilton 1970: 35)." Indeed, Thorstein Veblen saw the evolutionary model as a means by which the whole fabric of economic thinking must be rewoven. Unlike scores of social scientists before and since, Veblen did not view the social universe as fixed and immutable. For Veblen, the impact of Darwinism was that eco-nomics needed to abandon preconceived notions that "the existing is normal" and that "the normal is right," and to devote itself to a theory of the evolution of institutions as they are.

The evolutionary methodology also places great store in Polanyi's anthro-pological approach to the study of economic problems and relations. Polanyi (1971: xviii) affirms the importance and usefulness of a holistic and evolu-tionary approach to inquiry that embraces technological advancement:

> Technological progress is cumulative and unbounded, but economic organization is not. There are only a few general ways in which the economy may be organized ... In the receding rule of the market in the modern world, shapes reminiscent of the economic organization of ear-lier times make their appearance. Of course we stand firmly committed to the progress and freedoms which are the promise of modern society. But purposeful use of the past may help us to meet our present over-concern with economic matters and to achieve a level of human inte-gration, that comprises the economy, without being absorbed by it.[2]

The "overconcern" of economic matters would become the central theme and legacy of Polanyi's research. For Polanyi, the vital challenge posed by capitalism was the ability of society to subordinate the economy and to keep it from exerting undue pressure on human relationships and the biosphere.

As Polanyi suggests, the evolutionary approach accentuates the impor-tance of technological development. In true Newtonian style, neoclassical economics has sought the principles that govern the mechanical changes of a natural economic system. It has taken technology and the continuity of tool development for granted and has sought the real explanation of the nature and causes of the wealth of the nations in the price system. Conversely,

Institutionalists claim that the price system has repeatedly disrupted the continuity of technological progress. Hamilton (1970: 126) explains, "the price system is a ceremonial system which is repeatedly menaced by the increasing productivity of modern technology. Profit, the end-all of the price system, is threatened by immense productivity of a non-scarcity technological system."

Polanyi warned that in the process of ethnographic or comparative social inquiry we should not consider manifestations of behavior under a particular structure of social institutions as inveterate human behaviors. Stanfield (1986: 59) summarizes Polanyi on this score, "if men appear here to be generous, there selfish, it is not their basic natures that are different but their social organization." Stanfield further suggests that the Institutionalist method championed by Polanyi is particularly suited to examining the role of paid work in modern society. Stanfield (1986: 15) writes:

> It is the essence of Polanyi's research programme, and, I think, the institutional dilemma of democratic industrial society, to find ways and means of getting a livelihood which are less disruptive of lives and less detrimental to the quality of life. It is this which vests the task of learning from the past with its practical import, indeed, urgency.

Given the intensification of labor market inequities, the growing dissatisfaction with a work and spend existence, and mounting ecological pressures, the conflict between lives and livelihoods has become particularly acute in the twenty-first century. Diminishing the importance of paid work in our lives while enhancing participation in family and community life may well be the most imperative social and environmental concern of wealthy countries in the modern age.

With its emphasis on a holistic, systemic, and evolutionary method of inquiry, Institutionalism is particularly well suited to the analysis of work time regulation. A holistic approach to the issue of work time regulation is imperative in order to achieve a true understanding of the relations between employers, workers, families, government, and other stakeholders in the formal employment process. Additionally, work time issues cannot be accurately considered without at least a modicum of evolutionary background to be used, if nothing else, for comparative purposes. For instance, knowledge of the historic struggle to reduce work time and the evolution of economic thought on the subject can afford a greater comprehension of labor market inequities and a broader insight into the most effective remedies. Furthermore, since the *regulation* of work time entails a continual assessment of societal objectives, it is consistent with instrumental value theory, which is a central feature of Institutionalist methodology. As is the case with income distributions (Peach 1987), instrumental value theory suggests that society must continually experiment with the distribution of social labor in order to balance competing social interests in a manner that advances the life process.

Thus the continual assessment of the socioeconomic outcomes of work time regulation and the adaptation of future regulation to evolving social needs is compatible with the instrumental value theory that guides Institutionalist economic thought.

Schultz (1978) recognized the variable nature of optimal work time when he tried to answer the question, "what is the optimal period of work time?" He recognized that the answer keeps changing; what is optimal in one society and in one historical epoch, may be considered excessive and unproductive at a later date or in a different society. Studies suggesting the efficiency of the 40-hour workweek were largely conducted when 48 to 60 hours per week were the norm. Schultz (1978: 340) writes that "the same studies conducted today would be in a totally different context. The 40-hour week is now expected – not 50 to 60 hours – and it seems likely that current research would show a workweek shorter than 40 hours to be the most effective."

Given the breadth of its methodology, the Institutionalist critique of mainstream economics represents far more than a nagging rant over minor shortcomings of an otherwise unassailable approach. In subverting two principal assumptions of the Neoclassical approach—insatiability and scarcity—the Institutionalist tradition represents a firmly lodged wedge in the cracks of the foundation of mainstream paradigm. Understanding the radical critique of insatiability and scarcity, enhances the cultivation of an alternative economic paradigm that is based on abundance and sufficiency and that, consequently, places less emphasis on economic growth and paid work.

Radical polemics of scarcity and the primacy of production

As outlined in Chapter 1, the orthodox concept of scarcity holds that men could never produce enough goods and services to guarantee everyone minimum security against want. This is largely ensured by an ever-expanding appetite for more possessions as society redefines the meaning of minimum living standards. A scarcity of goods and resources and a desire by men to obtain the most of what they could from limited sources have been enshrined as central tenets in mainstream economic thought. Thus, the very assumptions upon which mainstream economics is built necessitate the establishment and maintenance of a high consumption lifestyle. The insatiable nature of humanity serves as the foundation for the orthodox theory of consumer demand, which can be bifurcated into two broad propositions. The first is that the urgency of wants does not diminish as greater *varieties* of them are satisfied. Once man has satisfied his physical needs, psychologically based desires take over. The latter type of needs can never be satisfied, or at least cannot be objectively proven to be satisfied. The second proposition is that these wants originate from within the consumer. The putative primacy of consumer desires, limits the economist's task to maximizing the goods that satisfy consumer wants. Orthodox economics has therefore divorced itself from any judgment on the goods it seeks to proliferate. Any notion of necessary versus unnecessary has generally been excluded from the province of economics.

The issue of psychologically driven desires and the consequent inescapability of scarcity has been debated since antiquity. In his *Topics and Rhetoric*, Aristotle offered a taxonomy of human desires that has withstood the test of time. Aristotle bifurcated economic exchange into two categories: isolated exchanges and market exchanges. Isolated exchange is characterized by two parties exchanging goods in accordance with their own subjective preferences in the absence of market alternatives. Market exchange takes place when individual traders make decisions based on the influence of continuous, pervasive trading among large numbers of participants in an organized market. For Aristotle, isolated exchange arose from the existence of surpluses and differing subjective values among traders. Isolated trade existed, therefore, to satisfy humanity's "natural" desires. Market exchange, however, was quite different from the necessary exchange of households. Since market exchange was unbridled by the limited needs of the family and by diminishing marginal utility, it occurred merely for the purpose of accumulating wealth. Thus, although Aristotle condoned the use of exchange to satisfy (natural) individual and collective wants derived from material necessity, he condemned the use of exchange as a mere device for accumulating wealth. Since wealth accretion was without natural limit, its relentless pursuit ran the risk of impoverishing the many in order to profit a few.

Although the terminology has changed somewhat over the years, many economists have retained Aristotle's age-old classification of economic transactions. Marx employed terminology directly descendant from Aristotle when he delineated between "use-value" and "exchange-value." For Marx, a commodity's use-value reflected the innate or biological desires of consumers while exchange-values reflected the greed and oppression of the capitalistic system. Keynes' thinking was not far afield from that of Aristotle and Marx. Keynes (1972) found it useful to distinguish between relative and absolute needs. Absolute needs are those that, "we feel whatever the situation of our fellow human beings" (Keynes 1972: 364). Relative needs represent those desires that give us satisfaction by making ourselves feel superior to others, making them highly invidious or neurotic nature. Keynes (1972: 364–65) argues, "Now it is true that the needs of human beings may seem to be insatiable. But they fall into two classes – those needs which are absolute ... , and those which are relative in the sense that we feel them only if their satisfaction lifts us above, makes us feel superior to, our fellows. Needs of the second class, those which satisfy the desire for superiority, may indeed be insatiable." More recently, Daly and Cobb (1994: 138) have revived the ancient Greek term "chrematistics"—the accretion of money—to differentiate oikonomia, which they define as "the management of the household so as to increase the use value to all members of the household over the long run."

Institutionalists believe that consumption patterns in modern, market societies can only be fully understood when influences such as class distinctions, emulative behavior, and corporate influence are taken into account. Institutionalists have long recognized the power distinctions and ceremonial influences that pervade our economy and warrant inclusion in any economic analysis. The application of the evolutionary approach that Institutionalists inherited from the German Historicists is best able to recognize the institutional influences on human behavior and incorporate them into a system of economic inquiry. Indeed, much of the Institutionalist thinking on the notion of scarcity can be traced to the German Historicists and the American students that studied in Germany in the late 1800s.

One American student who traveled to Germany, Simon Patten, became one of the earliest social theorists to anticipate an age of abundance in America and incorporate it into his socioeconomic analysis and reform proposals (Fox 1967). Born in Illinois in 1852, Patten was concerned with the achievement of abundance and the limits that would have to be set on human desires as part of a societal adjustment to new economic conditions. Patten's views on the subject of abundance provide a helpful link between the German Historicists and the Institutionalist critique of scarcity that would later emerge in America. Patten's views also presage the Institutionalist role of technology in revamping the production process in a socially and environmentally friendly manner (featured in Chapter 5).

Given his 3 years of schooling at the hands of the German Historicists at Halle in Hamburg, Patten did not suffer from the ethnocentric myopia that Polanyi admonished against. From his German mentors—men like Gustav Schmoller, Adolf Wagner and, especially, Johannes Conrad—he learned to view the past as a gradual approach to the present, and acquired an active concern for those who suffered in the process of social change. Unlike the classicalists, who regarded men as rational maximizers of satisfaction and society as little more than the sum of hedonistic behavior, the Germans Historicists tended to view society as an organism that amounted to more than the sum of its parts. They viewed man's behavior as collective rather than individualistic and placed more store on traditions, empathy, and other moral influences as a motivation for action. For the Germans, human behavior and society could best be understood in the context of historical development. Their historical approach to social science taught them that economic and social life was in a constant state of interactive flux and that enlightened men could influence the direction of change in a benevolent manner. This approach sowed the seeds for the development of social policy in Germany that softened the callous aspects of the classical paradigm. Fox (1967: 23) argues that, "historical economists, committed to ethical relativism by their methodology, sought a middle course between extreme individualism and extreme organicism." With practitioners working as government consultants and administrators, the German Historical School was influential in the establishment of legislation that: recognized labor unions and their ability to strike, regulated working hours and labor conditions, and provided social insurance.

Perhaps the most influential lesson Patten learned from his German mentor, Johannes Conrad, was that the long-term trend was toward abundance rather than scarcity. The fertility of men and soil was as much a social as a natural phenomenon for Conrad. Birth control, agricultural, and industrial productivity gains, new sources of nutrition, growth of world trade, and the prospect of continual advancements in industrial technology created a hopeful outlook for the future. Conrad was convinced that when a particular resource or commodity neared exhaustion, men would be able to devise substitutes. (Chapter 5 outlines how a similar technological optimism allows the Institutionalists approach to avoid a Malthusian mentality and maintain human well-being while addressing the exigency of climate change.) Cognizant of America's rapidly expanding economy, Patten suggested that human intelligence properly applied to natural resource use and the social restraint of consumption could yield a material abundance. Thus, scarcity was not imposed by the natural world but emerged from social institutions. Patten (1885: 10) argued that scarcity resulted from consumers preferring "those forms of wealth of which nature is least productive."

Particularly during the transitional period to an age of plenty, there was a fear that men would simply increase consumption under the patterns established by the marginal-utility calculus—that as the costs of goods decreased, the amount of pleasure derived by consumers increased. Patten argued that unless society changed its habits, traditions, and prejudices, the age of abundance could produce communities of intemperate gluttons. An obvious way to condition an alternative pattern of consumption for Patten was through income redistribution. Low wages and poor working conditions prohibited the working class from seeking sophistication and variety in their consumption goods. Patten also advocated the use of tariffs to influence patterns of consumption rather than to protect infant industries or natural resources. Patten was optimistic that income redistribution, when coupled with growing abundance and modified consumption behavior, would afford the working class a condition of "restrained ease." Fox (1967: 57) summarizes Patten's view, "new methods of production and new standards of consumption, if brought to the 'partially civilized races,' would destroy the patterns of exploitation which kept the great mass of the world's population in economic and social bondage."

Since the choices made by consumers were often detrimental to societal contentment in an age of abundance, Patten's approach had to rely heavily on psychological analysis to elucidate what restraints would enable men to avoid the personal and social costs of a bountiful existence. The greater corporeal gratification resulting from material abundance would not satiate men's desire for the pleasures of spirit and the intellect. With proper guidance and encouragement, however, non-acquisitive pleasures—art, religion, patriotism, altruism, etc.—could gain greater importance as society matured in an abundant economy.

Patten was impressed by the new experimental psychology being developed in Germany and the United States in the late nineteenth century, including the work of John Dewey. Scholars of the time were building upon the psychology of Wilhelm Wundt to study the relationship between patterns of behavior and the organization of the mind. Fox (1967: 64) argues that:

> Psychological research confirmed Patten's suspicion that men would not seek new pleasures in consumption merely because they were made available. In addition, the new psychology might provide techniques for persuading and conditioning men in their adjustment to new environmental conditions ... Psychology could be used to educate men to prefer the pleasures of varied consumption and altruism – to develop habits suitable for the age of plenty.

Patten's critique of orthodoxy linked the notion of scarcity to a psychological view that was quickly becoming passé. Under an alternative psychology, mankind could be freed from the affliction of scarcity and the social structure of accumulation and exchange could be organized in a manner consistence with notions of sufficiency. Patten's work anticipated that the alternative psychological model eventually developed by Veblen, Dewey, and Ayres would provide a richer understanding of human behavior as it relates to consumer desires and the relevancy of scarcity.

The evolutionary approach of the German Historicists and the American Institutionalists revealed that mainstream economic thought was stuck in an eighteenth-century Behaviorist model of human psychology that envisaged man as self-interested and rational enough to avoid the harmful aspects of growth while reaping all that is benevolent. Behaviorism focused on the relation between people's environments and their behavior, not on what occurred within their heads. According to Behaviorism, unverifiable mental events were not the subject matter of psychology. This methodology is analogous to the neoclassical paradigm in economics which is disinterested in what consumers think or feel about the behavior they manifest. In this mindset, if consumer behavior is not utility-maximizing it will be altered.

The hedonistic view of human nature permeates the entire (neo)classical system. Smith (1776: 47) argued that (even in primitive) societies, "reasonable man would naturally take thought, weighing hedonistically the relative cost of procuring a beaver as against a deer, and would arrive at a reasonable answer based on the proportions of irksomeness and cunning in capturing each." Thus labor is irksome and goods, the product of pain and exertion, exchange for goods produced by equivalent units of agony. Humans have thusly been viewed by economists as passive responders to pleasure (Marginalists) and pain (Classicalists) buffeted about by the natural forces around them.

While mainstream economics retained a nineteenth-century psychology, Veblen's psychology was more "behaviorist" and "instinctual." For Institutionalists, the major objection to hedonism was not necessarily the use of the words "pleasure" and "pain", but in the conception of human beings as passive agents, mere receptors of pleasure and pain. The evolutionary approach to the study of institutions and behavior that grew out the Darwinian revolution led Institutionalists like Dewey and Veblen to break new ground on an Institutionalist psychology that paralleled the development of behavioral psychology. For Veblen and his disciples, human behavior is subject to a process of cumulative growth and adaptation. Habits are the product of past activity and are subject to modification and change. Indeed, later psychological theories, such as instinct, behaviorist, Freudian, and Gestalt, advanced man to an initiator of action.

For Institutionalists, specific human behavior is the product of the cultural milieu. In his "Instinct of Workmanship," Veblen (1898) argues that it is not instinct or nature that determines the social and cultural environment, but that social and cultural influences determine the type of behavior in which instinct (or impulse) manifests itself.[3] Hamilton (1970: 58) contends that, "this is what Veblen meant by his statement that instinctive behavior is subject to development and hence to modification by habit." Apropos the social effort bargain and work time reform, Hamilton (1970: 61) further writes that "in his analysis of economic behavior, Veblen holds that man is possessed of propensities such as the instinct of workmanship, the parental bent and exploit. In fact the first two have been frequently subordinated to the last in the development of human culture." Thus, paid work is a double-edged sword for Veblen; it provides for the development of constructive instincts, yet it also presents the pecuniary means for the destructive "contaminants" of emulation and predation.

Although most other professional disciplines have abandoned Behaviorist psychology, the economics profession has clung to its tenets. Meanwhile the field of psychology has offered many advances to the understanding of human behavior. Since the heyday of Behaviorism the psychology profession has seen the emergence of alternative schools of thought including, genetic epistemology, Gestalt theory, humanistic, cognitive, and biological psychology. Particularly germane to economics is the development of humanistic psychology. Humanistic psychologists insist that human nature consists of more than environmental influences, and that conscious processes, rather than unconscious reflexes, are what psychologists and social scientists should study. This approach, emphasizing human experience, choice creativity, self-realization, and positive growth, seems far better suited to a social science intent of improving human well-being than a hedonistic view of humanity.

Although Veblen may have established a unique psychological approach, he is perhaps best known for his strictures of hedonic man and orthodox consumption theory (Cordes 2005). Veblen (1899: 57) sarcastically summarized the concept of *homo economicus* when he wrote that, "the hedonistic conception of man is that of a lighting calculator of pleasures and pains, who oscillates like a homogeneous globule of desire of happiness under the impulse of stimuli that shift him about the area, but leave him intact." Rather than consumer wants originating "naturally" from within, Veblen (1899) viewed consumer behavior as "habits of thought" or "prevailing or dominant types of spiritual attitude and aptitudes." For Veblen (1899: 263), economic institutions (such as consumer demand) were not founded in immutable psychological or otherwise natural laws, but are "habitual methods of carrying on the life process of the community in contact with the material environment in which it lives."

Veblen maintained that the source of desires for ownership and accumulation of private property in market societies was emulation and invidious distinction rather than the innocuous search for subsistence and physical comfort. Since wealth confers honor, the desire for goods that display wealth may be limitless. In Veblen's estimation many denizens of market-based economies will attempt to evidence their affluence, be it real or feigned, through a display of conspicuous consumption. According to Veblen (1899), self-actualization or individuality has become the goal of consumption in the intense market environment, and such individuality is thought to be attained by assembling a unique collection of commodities. Some observers argue that the symbolism of consumption has accelerated since the 1960s (Sachs *et al.* 1998). According to Schulze (1993) in the "experience society" consumption is not a mere vehicle of instrumental utility. Consumption is loaded with significance in contemporary society; it constitutes a system of signs that convey information about the consumer and their peers. For many, what goods "say" counts as much as what they "do."

Since acceptance of the notion of insatiability in market societies was largely influenced by emulative or invidious behavior, Veblen opined that individuals might someday experience a surfeit of consumer desires if those wants were grounded in a different economic calculus. Reminiscent of Patten, Veblen (1899: 268) wrote that:

> If, as is sometimes assumed, the incentive to accumulation were the want of subsistence or of physical comfort, then the aggregate economic wants of a community might conceivably be satisfied at some point in the advance of industrial efficiency; but since the struggle is substantially a race for reputability on the basis of an invidious comparison, no approach to definitive attainment is possible.

The scarcity that mainstream economists treat as an immutable natural phenomenon was thus a social phenomenon for Veblen. Scarcity in Veblen's view was not a natural or economic constraint, but stemmed from abundant resources being allocated in a wasteful, unjust, and socially irrational manner. If wants are socially formulated, the tastes and preferences held by individuals have no more validity than the socialization process by which they are formed.

Later critics of orthodox consumption theory have advanced Veblen's view that scarcity is a socially created condition arising from a particular pattern of productive activity. According to Polanyi (1971) the centrality of the scarcity postulate was an artifact of a historically contingent convergence of the "formal" and "substantive" meanings of economics. The "formal" meaning refers to the "economizing" activity of the neoclassical model, which implies a set of rules regarding choice in a context of scarcity. Polanyi writes that the formal meaning "refers to a definite situation of choice, namely, that between the different uses of means induced by an insufficiency of those means." The "substantive" sense of the term "economic" refers to mankind's interaction with the natural and social environment and the manner in which this satisfies material want satisfaction. Polanyi (1971: 224) contends that the substantive approach is not dependent on a scarcity assumption, "the substantive meaning implies neither choice nor insufficiency of choice and, if choice there be, it need not be induced by the limiting effect of a 'scarcity' of the means; indeed, some of the most important physical and social conditions of livelihood such as the availability of air and water or a loving mother's devotion to her infant are not, as a rule, so limiting."

Polanyi (1971) argues that the ascendancy of the market system was part and parcel of a merger of the two meanings. Neoclassical economics "naively compounded" the "substantive" and the "scarcity" meanings of economics without a sufficient awareness of the dangers to clear thinking inherent in the merger ...

> The last two centuries produced in Western Europe and North America an organization of man's livelihood to which the rules of choice happened to be singularly applicable. This form of the economy consisted in a system of price-making markets. Since acts of exchange, as practiced under such a system, involve the participants in choice induced by insufficiency of means, the system could be reduced to a pattern that lent itself to the application of methods based on the formal meaning of "economic." As long as the economy was controlled by such a system, the formal and the substantivist meanings would in practice coincide ... their merging in one concept nevertheless prove a bane to a precise methodology in the social sciences. Economics naturally formed an exception, since under the market system its terms were bound to be fairly realistic. But the anthropologist, the sociologist or the historian, each in his study of the place occupied by the economy of human society, was faced with a great variety of institutions other than markets, in which man's livelihood was embedded. Its problems could not be attacked with the help of an analytical method devised for a special form of the economy, which was dependent upon the presence of specific market elements.

Thus the regulation of the economy through a market-based price system allowed the formal and substantive meanings of economics to coincide and reinforced the notion that scarcity was a universal and timeless condition. Moreover the ethnocentric analysis of the market economy blinded the economics profession to alternative ways of describing human behavior in broader (non-market) social settings.

Writing in the 1970s, William Leiss suggested that for the average individual living in a high-consumption economy a substantial amount of confusion exists between consumer needs and the sources of satisfying those wants. In *The Limits to Satisfaction*, Leiss (1976: 72) argues that most theories of needs are "incomplete because they attempt to analyze the components of human needs in isolation from actual social patterns of satisfaction." Consequently, a state of confusion arises between needs and commodities. Leiss maintains that people tend to misinterpret the relationship between their perceived needs and the possible sources of satisfying them. One reason that the modern consumer may experience difficulty matching their needs to the goods that will satisfy them is the expanding variety of products that are offered from year to year. The enormity of the opportunities offered as "want satisfaction" makes it difficult to base our decisions on knowledge of the quality of the commodities. Leiss (1976: 15) argues that the "knowledge that seems appropriate for judging the suitability of things in relation to the objectives of our needs is the knowledge that is applied to craft skills." Since craft knowledge provides an intimate understanding of the material and processes used in the production of a good, it affords a better way of determining what is suited to our needs. Consumer purchases founded upon even rudimentary levels of craft knowledge may provide a fuller, not to mention safer, existence than buying things because we are compelled by an invidious distinction.

As the division of labor becomes increasingly minute in market societies, our craft knowledge of goods is likely to become quite narrow. When an acute division of labor is coupled with long working hours, most individuals lose the opportunity to develop craft knowledge in a variety of fields or subjects. Consequently, the highly specialized worker is forced to rely on purchases of finished goods for the vast majority of their needs. The very same system that creates inordinately productive workers gradually renders those workers unsophisticated as consumers as their craft knowledge atrophies. If an extensive attachment to the labor process makes it difficult to attain the craft knowledge needed to make informed consumer decisions, consumers must then decipher and decide among the many commercial claims advanced by the self-interested promoters of goods and services. Given the prodigious number of goods available and the intricacy of their composition, consumer choice as a whole becomes a rather haphazard activity. Leiss (1976: 15) comments on the likelihood that such an arrangement will bring about an adequate level of want satisfaction, "Such 'choice' represents little more than subjecting one's body and mind to a grand experiment in the marketplace in order to determine whether any of the increasingly bizarre claims made on behalf of the products will prove to be valid. One-armed bandits in the dingiest of casinos offer better odds."

Advertising tends to compound the confusion that individuals possess over their needs and their satisfaction and perpetuates the high-consumption-long-hours lifestyle. It is estimated that the average American is exposed to approximately 21,000 television commercials per year (Mander 1991). Television, however, is only one medium of communication that has been commercialized by productive interests. When radio, print journalism, and other advertising mediums are mixed into the equation, it becomes much easier to grasp why consumers may be suffering from confusion over their wants and what will truly satisfy those wants. Just as there is little promotion of public goods relative to private goods (Galbraith 1958), the choice of less consumption and less work is greatly disadvantaged in face of a prolific promotion of private goods and services. Cohen (1978: 318) comments on the imbalance:

> No ads say: WHEN YOUR UNION NEGOTIATES, MAKE IT GO FOR SHORTER HOURS, NOT MORE PAY. ELECTRIC CARVING KNIFES ARE FINE, BUT NOTHING BEATS FREEDOM. There are no 'leisure ads' because firms have no interest in financing them, nor in paying for public reminders of the unpleasant side of labour which buys the goods.

The images employed in the construction of advertising messages often incorporate a set of ambiguities about consumer wants and objectives. Examples of this abound in the automotive industry. One of the most common forms of automobile advertisements features a sport utility vehicle in a remote and pristine natural environment—near mountain ranges, oceans, rural settings, and other relatively unoccupied locations. The implicit message in the advertisement suggests the vehicle's usefulness in accessing those settings that are inaccessible to others. If this were the primary reason for the purchase of a sport utility vehicle for millions of Americans, those settings would not remain remote and pristine for long. In reality, four-wheel drive and large engines are unnecessary, unused and expensive features for the vast majority of drivers. According to Ford Motor Company, 87 percent of Ford Explorer owners had never taken their vehicle off-road (Harpers Index 1998). Sport utility usage statistics suggest that drivers of such vehicles may be suffering from confusion over their needs for urban transportation—good gas mileage, maneuverability, and parking ease—and the status and independence that these vehicles promise through expensive advertising campaigns.

Advertisers have exploited the emulative process of material conformity to give consumer desires an upward creep. The market imperative is bigger and more, and rarely is this escalation mentality more evident than in the actions of consumers. The purchase of a new home serves as the impetus to replace the old furniture and, in some cases, the old wardrobe. Schor (1998: 145) offers the escalator as the operative metaphor, "when the acquisition of each item on a wish list adds another item, and more, to our 'must have' list, the pressure to upgrade our stock of stuff is relentlessly unidirectional, always ascending." The association between social conformity and consumer goods, instilled and perpetuated by advertisers, is part of what keeps the consumer escalator moving ever upward. Yet, if insatiability is an inveterate human condition why should advertising play such an important role? In short, the notion of primal insatiability is irreconcilable with the fact that hundreds of billions of dollars are spent each year on advertising and salesmanship in the effort to fabricate consumer demand.

In addition to, and perhaps corollary with, the pressure from advertising some critics have highlighted the pressures that workers and families face in "keeping up appearances" that smack of Veblen's invidious comparison. Even those aware of, and uneasy with, the emulative and invidious nature of certain expenditures are frequently cajoled to play the part in order to advance or ensure their own position within the system. The wrong suit, automobile, wristwatch or similar accoutrement could threaten or severely limit one's career in many professions. Likewise, sending a youngster to a birthday party with no gift or a homemade present may prompt emotionally-scarring ridicule. Lifestyles that resist the magnetic pull of the consumption are not forbidden, but generally scorned as "radical" or "eccentric." Galbraith (1973: 225) observes:

> It is possible to imagine a family which sets an income target as its goal; which has a husband and wife share in the provision of that minimum; which makes a considered and deliberate choice between leisure or idleness and consumption; which specifically rejects consumption which, by its aggregate complexity, commits the woman to a crypto-servant role; which encourages self-fulfilling as against useful education for the offspring; which emphasizes communal as opposed to individual enjoyments with the result that it resists industrial or other economic encroachment on its living space; which, in its public outlook, sets slight store by increased production of the goods of which it has a sufficient supply; and which is indifferent to arguments for expenditures on behalf of national prestige or military power from which it derives no identifiable benefit. This family is not formally condemned as wicked. It is not ostracized by the community. But such esteem as it enjoys is the result, primarily, of its eccentricity.

The observation is reminiscent of Polanyi's (1971) statement that, "if you question the money-happiness nexus people think you are not so much dangerous as mad." Indeed profound societal pressures to "fit in" create obstacles for consumers otherwise intent on making sustainable consumption choices.

Akin to Marx, many Institutionalists have argued that consumer competence is threatened by the growing tendency in high-consumption societies to identify human needs with commodities. Stanfield and Stanfield (1980: 444) state that, "the identification of needs with commodities is a learned orientation." Due to a fixation on commodities as a source of satisfaction, individuals become obsessively oriented towards earning and spending. When consumption and the work that affords it are reified, relations among people are made to appear as relations among commodities or things. The obfuscation of the social impacts of consumption further compounds consumer incompetence. A great deal of advertising does not relate relevant or accurate information to the consumer; it amounts to "selling the sizzle rather than the steak." Suggestive advertising "leads people to seek life satisfaction through commodities, to solve their frustrations and problems and establish social bonds with one another through commodities (Stanfield and Stanfield 1980: 446)." The pursuit of more and more goods typically fails to fulfill human needs due to an inability to relate personal and social needs to the commodities best able to fulfill them. The treadmill pattern of consumption—being passive, invidious, neurotic and self-justifying in nature—becomes inimical to the art of living as it results in a dearth of time available for other socially redeeming pursuits.

The lack of time required to realize the virtue of begotten possessions is a rather obvious, but rarely emphasized, shortcoming of the quest for commodities. Aristotle acknowledged the limits to acquisitiveness when he observed that the skill of the musician should not be attributed to the possession of a lyre, but to the time and effort the musician has invested in the mastery of the instrument. In *The Harried Leisure Class*, Linder (1970) likewise points out that consuming goods takes time and that an individual's time is limited. The full value of most goods is obtained when they are put to their fullest use. Having too many goods can interfere with the satisfaction derived from having adequate time in use. In a high-consumption society, goods will become increasingly cheap, and time more expensive. Time limitations will result in an increased intensity of goods consumption in the pursuit of enjoyment. If the clearest examples of pleasures are among those activities based on the use of things, consumption may be accelerated to increase the yield on time devoted to consumption. Greater levels of industrial efficiency result in more things being available for the same expenditure of real income. Consumption of goods must therefore rise to ensure that an equal benefit is achieved for each unit of time devoted to that pursuit.

By way of example, if the average person consumes $50 worth of goods in each hour devoted to a particular consumption activity, $50/hour would be the yield on that consumption time. However, if productivity doubles, the average person must now double the value of their consumption to $100/hour in order to maintain the same yield on consumption time as in production time. Attempting to maintain a constant yield on consumption in the face of rising productivity creates increasing pressure on an individual's time and a tendency for activities requiring the use of commercial objects to crowd out non-commercial activities. Linder (1970: 91) argues that the result of this time bind is that "more goods will not increase the pleasure derived, but actually reduce it." The time bind that results from overwork may result in many goods providing a rather ephemeral sense of satisfaction. A Gresham's Law principal arises in the realm of consumption as the satisfaction derived from ever-greater numbers of commodities tends to depreciate all types of satisfaction that are not dependent upon the consumption of things (Leiss 1976). In simpler terms, bad consumption, based on accumulation, drives out good consumption, based on craft knowledge or rewarding activities in the third sector.

Leiss (1976: 29) links the time bind and consumer confusion to the tenet of insatiability:

> the threat of scarcity is a permanent feature of our present society, no matter how vast the supply of available goods, because the escalation of material demands only plunges individuals more deeply into the ambiguous ensemble of satisfactions and dissatisfactions – and thus into greater confusion about the relationship of their needs to the many dimensions in the sources of possible satisfaction.

In a high-consumption lifestyle, the individual becomes more and more indifferent to their specific wants relative to the increasing amount of time and resources devoted to the total activity of consumption. Leiss (1976: 16) comments on the fickleness of desires, "the accelerating rate of product turnover provides a clue to the shallowness of wants in the prevailing market setting: things that appear so indispensable one day, only to be discarded in favour of others on the next, cannot be presumed to stir the wellsprings of desire very deeply." Indeed, the time bind that results from wringing more consumption from our growing productivity rates gives new meaning to the minimalist credo that "she who owns little, is little owned."

The primacy of production

Building on their criticisms of the primacy of consumer wants in contemporary market society, Institutionalists have also come to question the urgency of production in high-consumption economies. The orthodox emphasis on the sovereign consumer results in the view that primal human desires tend to direct production in a socially optimal fashion. This view maintains that as sovereign consumers make their desires felt in the free market, supply adjusts to demand, and production adjusts to consumption. In other words, supply follows the demands registered by self-directed consumers.

Observing the influence of large firms in market-based economies, Institutionalists have taken exception to the notion that firms are passively reacting to consumer desires that naturally or instinctively originate from within the consumer. John K. Galbraith has persuasively argued that just the opposite is likely true of most modern industrial democracies. That is, production calls the tune of consumption via the massive expenditures that firms devote to selling activities. The usefulness of commodities in the market system is subject to the fallacious test of "what can be sold" rather than "what is needed." Since large corporations wielding enormous advertising budgets can sell products of even the most suspect usefulness, Galbraith contends that producers have come to rule the planning system, and that consumers are subject to the choices that the productive system finds profitable to offer them. Galbraith (1958: 127) expounds, "So it is that if production creates the wants it seeks to satisfy, or if the wants emerge pari passu with the production, then the urgency of the wants can no longer be used to defend the urgency of the production ... Production only fills the void that it has itself created."[4] In relation to the labor market, Galbraith (1958: 239) then asks, "why should life be made intolerable to make things of small urgency?" Such questioning can easily be extended to the doubtful urgency of the long hours that prevail in many developed nations, especially when other wealthy countries have shown that an alternative distribution of labor is feasible, if not superior.

Galbraith's denigration of the capitalistic production and planning system is founded upon the notion put forth by Veblen and his disciples that in the modern market society the desire to get more and superior goods is a culturally driven phenomenon that takes on a life of its own. Galbraith expands on the theory of emulative and invidious behavior by illustrating the effects that powerful corporations have on consumers through advertising and political influence. Since powerful vested interests inevitably emerge within unregulated market systems, consumer desires become prostrate to what Galbraith (1973) calls a *technostructure* of influences. These external influences reduce the likelihood that individual desires are primal or urgent in the sense that the wants originate physically or instinctively from within the individual. The whole superstructure results in needs being culturally conditioned. Since the ruling class developed the *technostructure* that perpetuates the system, it is greatly biased towards economic output and economic growth (Galbraith 1973: 40). That is, the beliefs, laws, culture, religion, morality, and patriotism that have been culturally engrained support the ascendancy of the productive process, though not necessarily the maximization of output. Evidence of the technostructure's growth bias abounds in the market system: Protestant or Calvinistic work ethics; laws and social systems that promote work; schools that train students to be good workers rather than good citizens or independent thinkers; advertising that creates a fictitious demand for goods. In *Economics and the Public Purpose* Galbraith (1973: 323) highlights how Keynes overlooked the effects of such power in his famous forecast that economics would lose its relevance as society prospered,

> He did not see that, with economic development, power would pass from the consumer to the producer. And, not seeing this, he did not see the increasing divergence between producer or planning purpose and the purpose of the public. And he did not see that—since power to pursue the planning purpose is unequally distributed—development would be unequal. And therewith the distribution of income. Nor did he see that the pursuit of such purpose would threaten the environment and victimize the consumer. And he did not see that the power which allows producer purpose to diverge from public purpose would ensure that

inflation would not yield to a simple reversal of the policies that he urged for unemployment and depression. Nor did he foresee the problems of planning coordination, national and international, just mentioned.

Galbraith further claims that the culturally instilled growth fetish creates a false image of consumer choice that allows the ruling class to absolve themselves of the implications of the myth. Galbraith (1973: 6) maintains that an imagery of choice makes the pursuit of production exculpable, "economics and particularly the imagery of choice puts the business firm in the service of a higher deity. In consequence it is not responsible—or is only minimally responsible—for what it does ... If the goods that it produces or the services it renders are frivolous or lethal or do damage to air, water, landscape, or the tranquility of life, the firm is not to blame." The imagery of choice creates the semblance that production activities merely reflect individual choice—the firm is simply responding to the sovereign desires of the market. If people are abused by overwork, for instance, it is because they choose self-abuse. If productive behavior appears on occasion insane, it is because consumer desires may have taken leave of their sanity, but the producer is beyond reproach.

The cultivation of the imagery of choice induces the individual to abandon the goals they might otherwise pursue and accept those of another person or organization. Recently the cultivation has principally taken place through persuasion rather than force. However, as mentioned in Chapter 1, the threat of physical suffering was once a more prevalent means of inculcating the importance of production. Hunger or the disesteem of poverty if one does not work for wages and thereby accept the goals of the employer is an ancient form of compulsion that persists on a limited scale today. With increasing incomes, people have become less vulnerable to the threat of economic deprivation, making persuasion the chief instrument for the exercise of economic power.

The persuasion often takes the form of instruction designed to implant the imagery of choice. It persuades people that the goals of the productive system are really their own or at least sows the seeds for such persuasion. Economics has taken on this instructive role partly as a relic of its past (Galbraith 1973: 8). Since competitive agricultural firms produced the bulk of economic output during the genesis of the discipline, economics came to characterize firms as responding to changing costs of production and changing market prices. They were subordinate to the instruction of the market. However, as oligopolies and monopolies arose, economic theory remained captive to its origins. Galbraith (1973: 8) argues, "economics thus slipped imperceptibly into its role as the cloak over corporate power." As the power which the model protects has become much more palpable, disguising it has lost much of its intellectual decency as the obscurantism required an "infinitely interesting gadgetry of disguise" (Galbraith 1973: 324). Meanwhile, advertising and salesmanship have burgeoned where economics has withered, perpetuating the imagery of consumer choice.

Galbraith also challenges the notion of insatiability by questioning why the neoclassical application of diminishing returns does not apply to the entirety of goods. By claiming that the law of diminishing returns only applies to a single type of consumption, neoclassical theory avoided a normative discussion over the merits of different types of consumer behavior. For neoclassicalists, the powerful and largely immutable law of diminishing returns was not considered applicable to all goods on the whole and could not be relied upon to militate against the need for greater production. In his *Principles of Economics*, Alfred Marshall (1890: 78) asserts that, "there is an endless variety of wants, but there is a limit to each separate want." In the orthodox paradigm, while the marginal utility of an individual good undoubtedly declines with increasing stocks, the utility or satisfaction from a new or different good is not lower than the utility derived from the last unit of the initial good. Galbraith (1958: 122) summarizes the view with one of his signature similes, "so long as the consumer adds new products – seeks variety rather than quantity – he may, like a museum, accumulate without diminishing the urgency of his wants." Moreover, the rewards to those possessing the consumer "artifacts" are more or less proportionate to their supply. The production that satisfies these wants therefore assumes a position of exalted status. Galbraith (1958: 123) states, "The production that supplies these goods and services, since it renders undiminished utility, remains of undiminished importance."

Galbraith finds great folly in the fact that diminishing marginal utility is not capable of making intertemporal value judgments about consumption. He criticizes the orthodox denial that anything useful can be said of the comparative states of mind and satisfaction of the consumer at different periods of time. Galbraith (1958: 123) hints at the absurdity of the notion with the following parody:

> This position ignores the obvious fact that some things are acquired before others. Yesterday the man with a minimal but increasing real income was reaping the satisfaction which came from a decent diet and a roof that no longer leaked water on his face. Today, after a large increase in his income, he has extended his consumption to include color television and eccentric loafers. But to say that his satisfactions from these latter amenities and recreations are less than from the additional calories and the freedom from rain is wholly improper.

Since neoclassical theory cannot render a comment on the satisfaction derived from additional goods, and more precisely from different goods when acquired at later times, it likewise is incapable of arguing that future increases in a consumer's stock of goods does not diminish utility. Hence, neoclassical theory is vulnerable to the argument that the production of more goods diminishes the importance or urgency of the goods.

The inability of neoclassical theory to address value judgments has important implications for economic growth. Galbraith felt that economics should concern its self with the composition of economic growth and endeavor to make value judgments regarding the merits of expenditures on eccentric loafers vis-à-vis adequate housing. Many Institutionalist thinkers have shared this concern. Ayres similarly questioned whether the shoeing of a race horse should have the same social imperative as a plow horse. For Galbraith economic freedom was not represented by the ability to engage in superfluous consumption. True economic freedom could be achieved by granting access to basic human needs and the ability to make real choices regarding one's livelihood. Galbraith (1973: 226) writes, "The prime purpose of improving income, and *especially of improving the distribution of income*, should be to increase the number of people who are removed from the pressures of physical need or its equivalent and who are able, in consequence, to exercise choice as to their style of economic life [emphasis added]."

In summary, the Institutional view of technology and abundance, human psychology, and the structure of modern market economies challenges the validity of the neoclassical assumptions of scarcity and insatiability. If humans are governed by such principles it is due to social conditioning under the market form rather than ubiquitous human characteristics or natural laws. Invoking an alternative vision of abundance and sufficiency, diminishes the urgency of consumer desires and the inequitable social relations that attempt to satisfy those desires. In short, when we are able to make value judgments on the social merit of different types of consumption and production, the urgency of economic growth and paid work can be re-assessed in relation to other social and ecological goals.

Rethinking the growth consensus

It is important to acknowledge that the blind promotion of economic growth with no concept of bad or harmful growth is by no means "objective science." The growth consensus is itself a rhetorical construct with inherent value judgments (Fanfani 1934; Rowe 1999). Namely, the growth consensus represents the belief that more is better and that more of everything will generate more of what is good than what is harmful. Yet as basic human necessities become more readily available, the consumption needed to sustain the totem of growth is of questionable merit in terms of enhancing well-being. According to conventional wisdom, if people choose what they buy then the sum total of their purchases represents the greatest good for all. Yet, if choice is merely a mirage, then consumer theory could be improved by normative (value-based) reasoning and intervention.

Truth be told, a growing portion of consumption today is of a forced nature: private transportation in poorly planned cities, compulsory insurance, advertising and lobbying costs embedded in product prices, and collusive mark-ups. Even more consumption is foisted upon consumers by the corrosive aspects of economic growth. As commercial activity has expanded, substantial markets have emerged for products and services that merely abate the ill-effects of economic growth, including air and water purification, bottled water, sound insulation, and various forms of lifestyle coaching, including relaxation and nutrition assistance. Such markets suggest that greater economic throughput (not to be confused with progress) has not solved the economic problem itself but has created new problems requiring more consumption. Jonathan Rowe (1999) points out the paradox of the US economy in which some $21 billion a year is spent advertising food stuffs while the weight loss industry tops $32 billion annually in revenue.

Other types of consumption are largely addictive, forcing many to face the daily turmoil of consuming less of it. For moral, ethical and personal reasons, many people would prefer to eat, drink, smoke, gamble, and buy less (Rowe 1999). Yet, curtailing their tyrannical obsession stands in conflict with economic reasoning that declares growth as progress. Indeed, a great deal of growth and tax revenue is founded on addictive consumption that most people would ideally do without. Moreover, developing healthy and sustainable tastes and behaviors requires time and effort. Learning to appreciate art, wine, poetry, exercise, "slow" food, and so on often requires a substantial investment of time. When consumers have to conjure up such significant will power to resist some urges and cultivate others, the doctrine of the sovereign consumer is called into greater suspicion.

The growth consensus fails to comprehend that a great deal of material throughput is really an optical illusion of greater well-being. The idolatry of growth ignores crucial social and environment costs. Even worse, it actually counts such "bads" as growth and gain. Rowe (1999) observes:

> Pollute the lakes and oceans so that people have to join private swim clubs and the economy grows. Erode the social infrastructure of community so people have to buy services from the market instead of getting help from their neighbors, and it grows some more. The real economy – the one that sustains us – has diminished. All that has grown is the need to buy commoditized substitutes for things we used to have for free.

Likewise, Gorz (1980: 64) claims that people are living worse while consuming more as affluence dooms itself; "growth is causing more scarcity than it relieves."

The growth critique suggests that economists and policymakers need to differentiate between economic growth and economic development if they are intent on enhancing social well-being. Talberth *et al.* (2007) clarify that "growth refers to the quantitative increase in the physical scale of the economy, its throughput of matter and energy, and the stock of human built artifacts while development refers to largely qualitative improvements in the structure, design, and composition of physical stocks and flows that result from greater knowledge, both of technique and of purpose." A growing body of evidence suggest that the blind pursuit of economic growth does little to improve the standard of living in wealthy nations, and that we need to seek better ways of measuring and achieving greater life satisfaction.

Gaining prominence with the Club of Rome's foreboding warnings of the "Limits to Growth" in 1972, a growing chorus of social critics have been challenging the wisdom of unselective economic growth (Meadows *et al.* 1972). Growth opponents from motley backgrounds have largely focused on the social and environmental drawbacks of unmitigated economic growth. Recently economists have contributed to the debate by studying the impacts of economic growth on happiness and proposing alternative well-being indices to Gross Domestic Product (GDP). The critique of economic growth has emerged as a sub-discipline of economics with multiple indices reflecting a disconnect between traditional growth measures, such as GDP, and alternative measures of our well-being.

Introduced as a way of measuring wartime production capacity during World War II, the GDP is a relatively new economic index. Nevertheless, it has obtained prominence among economists, policymakers, financial professionals and the media. Jackson (2004) offers a telling commentary on the cultural ascendancy of growth accounting:

> Every society has a cultural myth by which it lives; ours is the myth of economic progress. So long as the national income continues to rise, we feel safe in assuming not just that we are doing well, but that we are living better than our parents or our grandparents did; that we are progressing—not just as individuals but as a society.

Most economists recognize that the GDP is ill-designed as a measure of our social well-being since it is simply a tally of goods and services bought in the economy. The chief innovator of the GDP measurement, Simon Kuznets (1934), acknowledged that "the welfare of a nation can scarcely be inferred from a measurement of national income." Since GDP ignores non-monetary activities and fails to distinguish between welfare-enhancing expenditures and those that are harmful to society and the environment, it yields a grossly inaccurate measure of socio-economic welfare. Talberth *et al.* (2007) write that in the calculation of GDP "needless expenditures triggered by crime, accidents, toxic waste contamination, preventable natural disasters, prisons, and corporate fraud count the same as socially productive investments in housing, education, healthcare, sanitation, or mass transportation." Perhaps the most eloquent questioning of the relevance of GDP was offered by Robert F. Kennedy (1968):

> Gross national product counts air pollution, and cigarette advertising, and ambulances to clear our highways of carnage. It counts special locks for our doors and the jails for people who break them. It counts the destruction of the redwoods and the loss of our natural wonder in chaotic squall. It counts Napalm, and it counts nuclear warheads, and armored

cars for the police to fight the riots in our city. It counts Whitman's rifles and Speck's Knifes and the television programs which glorify violence in order to sell toys to our children. Yet, the gross national product does not allow for the health of our children, the quality of their education, or the joy of their play; it does not include the beauty of our poetry of the strength of our marriages, the intelligence of our public debate or the integrity of our public officials. It measures neither our wit nor our courage neither our wisdom nor our learning, neither our compassion nor our devotion to our country it measures everything in short except that which makes life worth while. And it can tell us everything about America except why we are proud that we are Americans.

Forty years after Kennedy's admonition of a fixation on GDP, the growth consensus still reigns supreme, but a plethora of alternative measures have emerged.

One of the first alternative well-being measures was devised by Herman Daly and Clifford Cobb in the 1980s. Their Index of Sustainable Economic Welfare is still in use today and serves as the framework for many other indices, such as the Genuine Progress Indicator (GPI). The alternative measures are also referred to as "Green GDP" accounting systems as they seek to provide a more accurate barometer of welfare and the sustainability of economic activity. The calculation of alternative indices typically begins with the same personal consumption figures as GDP. They then deduct the social and environmental costs related to income inequality, crime, environmental degradation, and loss of free time, and then add in government expenditures on public infrastructure and the value of unpaid activities such as volunteering and housework. When these adjustments are made, the results reveal that GDP growth is a poor measure of social welfare in wealthy nations. In the United States, while GDP per capita tripled between 1950 and 2004, the GPI did not even double. Chart 2.1 illustrates GDP per capita growing by around 220 percent between 1950 and 2004, while the GPI increased by 73 percent.

Chart 2.1 also displays a measure of social health calculated by the Institute for Innovation in Social Policy since 1970. The Index of Social Health calculates an annual measure using the following 16 social indicators: infant mortality, child abuse, child poverty, teenage suicide, teenage drug abuse, high school dropout rates, unemployment, average weekly wages, health insurance coverage, senior poverty, out-of-pocket health costs for seniors, homicide rates, alcohol-related traffic fatalities, food stamp coverage, access to affordable housing, and income inequality. Although the index improved throughout much of the 1990s, it remains 12 points below its 1970 starting point.

Another important indicator of our social health that has deteriorated despite decades of economic growth is crime. Conservative reformers hoped that a large economic pie would sow the seeds for a less violent society.

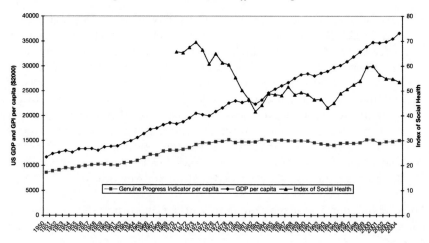

Chart 2.1 Alternative Well-being Measures
Data Sources: Talberth, Cobb and Slattery (2006) - www.rprogress.org; Institute for
Social Policy - http://iisp.vassar.edu/index.html

Instead, recorded crime increased by 300 percent in most countries between
1950 and 1980 (Layard 2005: 37). Although there have been substantial
reductions in crime of late in the United States, Australia, Canada and
Britain, the incidence of crime is still way above its level of 1950. Surely,
many factors influence national crime statistics, such as the emergence of
crack cocaine in the 1980s, but it is quite telling that this important measure
of our social well-being deteriorated so sharply during one the most robust
periods of economic growth on record in the capitalist world.

Alternative well-being measures are calculated across a variety of countries. Alarmingly, the trend in many countries is revealing a growing gap
between GDP and well-being. Applying the GPI to the case of Australia
reveals that the gap (measured in 2004 dollars) between the GDP and GPI
ballooned from $2,134 in 1950 to $15,916 in 2000. Per capita GDP in Australia nearly tripled during this period, rising at an average annual rate of
3.97 percent. Yet, Hamilton and Denniss (2000) calculate that per capita
GPI only increased 1.4 percent annually. The figures suggest that Australia
has experienced diminishing social returns to economic growth, reducing the
attractiveness of future growth.

New research on happiness: the paradox of abundance

In addition to devising alternative well-being measurements, a growing
legion of economists has been questioning the impact of economic growth
on our collective psychological well-being, or happiness. Revealing the seamy
side of growth, recent well-being research seriously questions whether the
preponderant emphasis placed on production over the last 50 years has

allowed individuals to "live wisely and agreeably well" (Keynes 1936). When the long-standing suspicions of heterodox economists of the primacy of consumption and production are coupled with recent psychological research on the effects of economic growth on happiness, the urgency of revisionist macroeconomic thinking is greatly heightened. Given the social, psychological and environmental fallout of the last 50 years of economic growth, it is unclear whether the "material abundance" achieved in wealthy nations is a reflection of social progress. Moreover, it is highly unlikely that greater throughput alone will contribute to the furtherance of the life process.

The discussion hitherto has made occasional reference to an abundance paradox. The term "abundance" has been intentionally chosen to differentiate from the notion of "progress." Although we have been conditioned to associate economic growth and material abundance with progress, recent environmental, social, and psychological research suggests that economic growth does not enhance well-being invariably. Although it may be slightly premature to claim that industrial society has reached a state of widespread abundance, recent trends suggest that there is little hyperbole in such a description. The advanced economies of the world now possess the resources and ability to provide the whole of their population with basic life necessities: food, shelter, healthcare, and education.

The pregnant question is what role economic growth should play in maintaining and expanding these achievements. Is it possible to further social progress with lower rates of economic growth? The role of technological advancement is central to the answer. Although it is true that citizens of wealthy countries have become healthier over the last century as manifest in longer life spans, lower rates of cancer, and less heart and lung disease, the technological advancements that rendered the improvements possible may have still been available at lower levels of economic growth.[5] Technological development is cumulative in nature and has been accelerating for some time now in both market and non-market societies. Indeed, it is possible that technological development could have been equally, or more, robust in the presence of slower, selective, or more equitable economic growth. Institutionalist economists have pointed out that mainstream economic thought falsely identifies the growth of the market economy as a precondition of industrial technological development, when it is likely the reverse (Ayres 1944). The consolidation of private enterprise within a market system was but one way of structuring the large-scale capital investments required by the technological discoveries of the Industrial Age. Throughout history other non-capitalistic social systems have organized large-scale investment projects: witness the mobilization to explore space in Russia and China. The connection between economic growth and general health is further complicated by the fact that market-based economic growth has introduced its own health risks: air and water pollution, food impurities, sleep deprivation, obesity, and mental disorders. In fact, a recent struggle for many governments has been finding ways to retard the excessive consumption of food and housing. Increasingly, the epidemics of obesity and urban sprawl have been recognized as creating large external costs to society in terms of the health, environmental and social problems they create.

The prospect of abundance is quite obvious in recent nutritional trends. In developed countries today a youngster is more likely to die of health complications related to obesity than to those related to hunger or protein deficiency. The pandemic of obesity has spread beyond the borders of affluent countries. According to the World Health Organization (2006) there were 1.6 billion people in the world that could be categorized as overweight in 2006. This figure is roughly double the 820 million people in the world that suffered from undernourishment in 2006, as tracked by the Food and Agriculture Organization (United Nations 2006). In a global context, there is clearly a sufficiency of food available, but its distribution and regulation leaves much to be desired.

Recent developments in housing are similarly suggestive of abundance. The typical new home in the United States is now over 2,250 square feet (208 m²), double the average area of a house just 50 years ago. The expansion of home size is even more staggering when one considers that the average size of families has fallen; the median household size in the United States has fallen from 4 to 2.6 in the last 25 years. Building trends are similar in Australia where the size of new houses now averages 2,484 square feet (230 m²). In Germany, housing space per person has expanded from 162 square feet (15 m²) in 1950 to 400 square feet (37 m²) in 1990. New homes are commonly equipped with central air conditioning and an array of under-utilized appliances and amenities, such as commercial grade stoves and refrigerators, extra dining rooms, and swimming pools. Clearly, construction trends in the advanced economies of the world indicate that adequate housing can be made available for the overwhelming majority of the population, but only if government regulation is implemented to ensure access and curb excesses that create expensive social and environmental externalities.[6]

Although far from universal, education is now more accessible than ever before. In the United States the average adult has completed 12.3 years of education, the highest in the world. One-quarter of American adults hold college degrees. Two-thirds of high school graduates enroll in a college, while less than 10 percent drop out of high school. While improvements are sorely needed in terms of degree completion and racial access to higher education, the United States is nearing the milestone of becoming the first society in which the majority of adults are college graduates. In addition to the expansion of formal education, new information technology has broadened the frontiers of knowledge. Information, of varying veracity, is now more readily available than ever before.

Given the societal will, many wealthy nations now possess the ability to feed, shelter, and educate unprecedented proportions of their population. Yet, the free-market does not possess a mechanism to foster a "shared" abundance. By their very nature, markets distribute goods or services by rationing them on the ability to pay. Private markets have proven to be problematic in the distribution of life's basic necessities. Thus, government action will be required to ensure that individuals have access to the mere necessities of life that our highly productive industrial process is capable of furnishing when it is not usurped by pecuniary interests (Veblen 1919).

If the basic necessities of life are readily abundant in the developed world, what role does greater economic growth play in improving well-being? Herein lays the paradox presented by a growing field of psychological research which concludes that growing affluence has produced little, if any, improvement in societal weal in wealthy nations. While economic growth indicators have tripled in the developed world in over the last 50 years, well-being indices have remained flat, mental illness has more than tripled, and unbridled individualistic behavior and thinking is unraveling our social fabric (Myers 1992; Putnam 2001; Layard 2005).[7]

A multidisciplinary cadre of researchers has been making a convincing case that happiness exists, can be objectively measured, has important personal and social consequences, and can be externally altered (Easterlin 1974; Clark and Oswald 1994; Diener 2000; Inglehart 1990; Kahneman 1999; Layard 2005). Blanchflower and Oswald (2008) have recently used physiological data on hypertension (blood pressure) to corroborate psychological well-being rankings, which critics claim are highly subjective. Their findings show that subjective measures of well-being (across multilingual and multicultural countries) track remarkably well with objective medical data. Blanchflower and Oswald (2008: 219) conclude, "happy countries seem to have fewer blood pressure problems."

The supposition that happiness can be measured and altered is a departure from the assumptions and policy implications of mainstream economics. Conventional wisdom in economics has held that individual wants were innately derived, or fixed, and that the pursuit of those wants in perfectly competitive markets would promote the greatest happiness for all. Government's role was to promote market flexibility and the pursuit of self-interested behavior. In concert, these forces would spontaneously yield the greatest possible happiness. With the ascendancy of the free market and the disembedding of the economy from society, gross national happiness became synonymous with gross national product.

In decades past, when many basic needs were unmet, economic indicators were a decent first approximation of how well a nation was performing. Yet, as wealthy nations have increasingly solved the economic problem of providing basic human needs to the whole of the population, growth indicators have proven to be largely ineffective at measuring our collective happiness. As suggested by Veblen, our desires do not arise from congenital sources alone and are prone to emulation and invidious comparisons, particularly in societies that celebrate individualism. Rather than deriving greater happiness from more income, research suggests that those living in developed nations would benefit more from increased security—at work, in the family and in the community—and stronger personal relationships. The policy implication is that politicians will have to assume a more nuanced approach to improving the human condition than simply increasing material throughput. Blanchflower and Oswald (2008: 3) anticipate that "This form of [happiness] research may even presage some move away from simple GDP targets of the sort that have been favored in post-war economic policy." Indeed, the accurate monitoring and effective promotion of well-being should be of utmost concern to Western governments as the pursuit of happiness ranks with life and liberty as an inalienable human right.

Easterlin (1974, 2001) was one of the first economists to suggest that economic growth does not enhance aggregate well-being. In 1974, Easterlin (118) concluded that "in the one time series studied, that for the United States since 1946, higher income was not systematically accompanied by greater happiness." His research further suggested that subjective measures of individual well-being are generally the same across poor and rich countries. Easterlin's path-breaking research on the topic lent credence to the notion that happiness is relative; that we should think of people as getting utility from a comparison of themselves with others close to them.

The lack of a national "happiness payoff" from economic growth has been corroborated by an extensive body of economic and psychological studies conducted over the last decade. In their review of the literature on income and happiness, Diener and Seligman (2004: 2) state that "it is clear that rising income has yielded little additional benefit to well-being in prosperous nations." Counter to microeconomic theory which teaches that greater income begets more consumer choice and greater happiness, the research suggests that once per capita income reaches a moderate level, greater income yields rapidly diminishing returns to aggregate measures of happiness. Inglehart *et al.* (2008: 265) write that "because the happiness levels of given societies do not seem to change over time, the idea that economic development brings rising happiness has been widely rejected. Although rich nations show higher levels of subjective well-being than do poor countries, these differences may reflect cultural differences in what happiness means." Nearly all studies have shown that national wealth only influences happiness up to a threshold level of income. This allows some researches to find a moderate positive correlation between income and well-being up to the threshold point. However, many of these studies rely on happiness and life satisfaction rankings from countries in economic and social chaos or transition. For example, most of the "unhappy," low-income countries contributing to a positive correlation between wealth and subjective well-being found by Inglehart *et al.* (2008) were either countries experiencing political chaos (Iraq and Zimbabwe) or economic transition from the Former Soviet Union. Indeed, when later data are used in lieu of survey results collected during and after the economic transition, the well-being rankings of many transitional economies are on par with other countries, and the positive correlation between

GDP per capita and subjective well-being is greatly reduced. Using the most recent data from the World Values Survey, Chart 2.2 suggests little correlation between happiness and national income in the 34 countries that have completed surveys in 2005, 2006, or 2007. When the correlates of national wealth, such as health, quality of government, and human rights, are controlled for, the effect of national income on well-being is insignificant. Helliwell (2003: 355) argues that the happiest people "are not those who live in the richest countries, but those who live where social and political institutions are effective, where mutual trust is high, and corruption is low."

Researchers at the New Economics Foundation estimate that only 10 percent of the variation in people's happiness is related to income and wealth, while our genes, upbringing, outlook, and our social interactions and activities account for roughly 90 percent of the variation in individual well-being (Shah and Marks 2004). Eckersley (2007: 148) summarizes the influence of *non*-economic variables on happiness:

> The evidence shows that a good marriage, the company of friends, rewarding work, sufficient money, a good diet, physical activity, sound sleep, engaging leisure and religious or spiritual belief and practice all enhance our well-being, and their absence diminishes it. Optimism, trust, self-respect and autonomy make us happier. Gratitude and kindness lift our spirits; indeed, giving support can be at least as beneficial as receiving it.

Thus adequate income is important insomuch as it provides the means to engage in these important social activities, but beyond a threshold of income having more money than time is of little value to well-being.

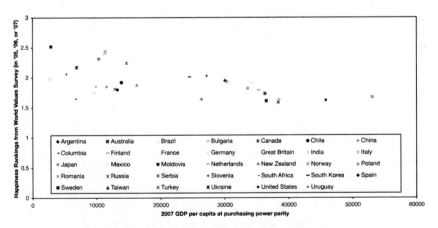

Chart 2.2 Happiness Rankings versus GDP per capita (2005–7)
Source: European Values Study Group and World Values Survey Association. EUROPEAN AND WORLD VALUES SURVEYS FOUR-WAVE INTEGRATED DATA FILE, 1981–2004, v.20060423, 2006, Inglehart *et al.* (2008), and The World Factbook, Central Intelligence Agency, 2008.

The putative correlation between income and happiness also breaks down at the regional or neighborhood level. Hagerty (2000) found that when personal income was statistically controlled, individuals living in higher-income areas of the United States recorded lower happiness scores than those living in lower-income neighborhoods. Similarly, Putnam (2001) suggested that higher statewide income was associated with lower well-being once individual income was statistically controlled. At various levels of aggregation, economic growth has exhausted its ability to yield greater well-being in prosperous regions. As Diener and Seligman (2004: 10) write, "income, a good surrogate historically when basic needs were unmet, is now a weak surrogate for well-being in wealthy nations."

Of utmost importance to the debate over the effects of economic growth is the impact of income *changes* on well-being. The international evidence suggests that growing national income has little impact on well-being in the developed world. Logically, the effects of income growth are larger in poor nations than in wealthy nations. But as basic human needs for food, shelter, clothing and healthcare are met, the return to well-being from greater income diminishes and eventually disappears. Many researchers have found that large increases in national income, often a doubling or tripling of real income, have yielded no improvement to a variety of national well-being measures (Easterlin 1995; Oswald 1997; Diener and Oishi 2000; Diener and Biswas-Diener 2002; Blanchflower and Oswald 2004). In the remarkable case of Japan, even a sixfold increase in per capita income from 1958 to 1991 failed to produce any increase in reported well-being (Diener and Oishi 2000). Since World War II, the Japanese economy experienced one of the most spectacular growth spurts in history, yet average life satisfaction hardly budged.

The case of Japan illustrates that there are cultural variations in the manner in which income is connected to well-being. People in many industrial nations, for instance, are socialized to work for pay and to feel as if they are contributing to society for doing so. They may also be encouraged to consume in a rigorous manner. Yet, a different culture might put more emphasis on non-market activities, nurturance or gift-giving. These cultural variations help explain why individuals living in poorer countries and communities sometimes report high well-being—because many of them are engaged in activities that are respected in their culture. The cultural influences are also consistent with findings that the unemployed in wealthy countries and regions are significantly less happy than other jobseekers, which is especially true if they are surrounded by a culture of high income and employment. Clark (2001) found that unemployment is associated more strongly with lower well-being in regions that have low unemployment than where it is high. Unemployed people on average are dissatisfied even if they had a relatively high income and a presumably larger accumulation of wealth to fall back on—perhaps because they are no longer performing a task that is respected by their culture. The elderly offer an interesting contrast. Retired people are not expected to work in most cultures, and consequently retirement does not typically harm their well-being the way unemployment otherwise would (Diener and Biswas-Diener 2001). Wilkinson (2007) suggests that such cultural heterogeneity undermines the reliability of happiness research and the redistributive policy prescriptions that tend to dominate the literature. But admitting that culture influences our happiness does not diminish the fact that national income does not. Indeed, if culture and other social influences disproportionately influence our happiness, the preponderant attention paid to economic growth has been misplaced.

The work fetish often suggests that non-employment is a social calamity on par with unemployment. The thinking is summarized in the aphorism that "the only thing worse than being exploited is *not* being exploited." This view holds that paid employment affords the worker structure for the day, social contact, and a source of respect, engagement, challenge and meaning. Yet new research on happiness suggests that those who choose not to partake in the labor force are not so lacking after all. Layard (2005) writes, "the data totally refute this [as a source of misery] ... Moves between work and being 'out of the labour force' involve much smaller changes in happiness than moves between work and unemployment ... And retirement is not bad for happiness either." The research therefore indicates that the social virtues that paid work provides in the existing social structure can be provided by other cultural or organizational means. Indeed the aged and the wealthy have established multiple social arrangements that provide social contact, respect, challenges, engagement and meaning in ways that may be more sustainable for the community and environment than remunerative employment.

At the micro level, studies of the association between *individual* income and well-being show mixed results. Following James Duesenberry's (1949) hypothesis that individuals care mostly about relative income, Blanchflower and Oswald (2004: 1375) find that "relative income has some explanatory power in a happiness equation even when absolute income is held constant." Yet, in US longitudinal studies, Diener *et al.* (1993) report the confounding findings that those with declining income reported an increase in their happiness, and the group whose income increased reported diminished well-being. In a study of job satisfaction, Clark and Oswald (1996) found that satisfaction with one's work depended on the pay relative to other similarly qualified workers, rather than on absolute pay. Most telling from a policy standpoint is the finding by Alesina *et al.* (2004) that greater income inequality is associated with lower well-being in Europe and the United States, even after controlling for income. The effect is statistically stronger in Europe than the United States. Defending the growth of redistributive policies in the United States and Europe over the last century, Alesina *et al.* (2004: 2010) point out that "even the net losers from distributive schemes (the wealthy) may favor them because they perceive poverty and inequality as social harms."

When it comes to windfall changes in personal *wealth*, the evidence is also mixed. An experimental study by Smith and Razzell (1975) found that gamblers who won large soccer betting pools in England were significantly more likely to report being happier than the comparison group. Conversely, Brickman *et al.* (1978) find that lottery winners are little happier, or even less happy, than they were before they won the big prize. More recently, Gardner and Oswald (2001, 2007) find that lottery winners and heirs receiving wind-fall inheritances reported higher well-being. Their 2007 study found that a small sample of Britons who experienced a moderate lottery windfall (between £1000 and £120,000 in 1998) reported less mental stress 2 years later as measured by the General Health Questionnaire.

It is important to note, however, that any positive effects related to finan-cial gains largely occur at the individual level and are often negated by the tendency for average incomes and desires to rise over time (Frijters *et al.* 2004). Kapteyn *et al.* (1976) estimate that up to 80 percent of the benefit of increasing individual income disappears due to rising aspirations and descriptions of "adequate" consumption as income rises. Van Praag and Fritjers (1999) have studied how people's actual income affects their desired income. Across nine countries the authors find that a dollar rise in actual income causes a rise of between 35 and 65 cents in desired income. Stutzer (2004) reports a rise in desired income of 40 cents with every additional dollar earned. The adaptation explanation of stagnating happiness argues that although greater income affords us luxuries and gadgets, we simply get used to them and eventually revert to our "set-point" of happiness. Myers (1992: 38) cogently summarizes the literature, "The second helping never tastes as good as the first. The second fifty thousand dollars of income means much less than the first. Thus the correlation between income and happiness is modest, and in both the United States and Canada has now dropped to near zero."

In an experiment with great relevance to work time reform, Solnick and Hemenway (1998) have shown that although people are not rivalrous with their leisure time they tend to make self-defeating comparisons to others when choosing their preferred income. The researchers asked Harvard stu-dents at the School of Public Health to choose between two earning situa-tions with constant price structures. Their choices were between: 1) receiving $50,000 per year while others average $25,000; or 2) receiving $100,000 per year while others average $250,000. The majority of students chose to make themselves materially worse off in order to improve their relative income (or social status). Conversely, only 20 percent were concerned with their relative position when it came to choosing between the following two vacation regimes: 1) receiving 2 weeks' vacation while others average 1 week; 2) receiving 4 weeks' vacation while others average 8 weeks. The policy impli-cation is that a non-rivalrous distribution of social productivity gains should take the form of more leisure time over income. The social and environ-mental costs arising from a mal-distribution of work hours feature in Chap-ter 4 underscore the importance for social scientists and policymakers to be mindful of the tendency for individuals to be rivalrous when it comes to relative income but not when it comes to relative leisure time.

The emphasis people place on relative income versus absolute income in shaping happiness is a crucial finding as work time regulation almost certainly entails a transfer of hours and income from the overworked to the underworked. Golden and Altman (2008: 21) observe that since the overworked are mainly high-income workers, "redistributing work hours from overemployed to underemployed individuals could yield a considerable net gain to social welfare. This would occur so long as hours gains provided to the underemployed outweigh the losses to all those currently employed at longer hours." Since the value of additional income is relatively low for many high-income, overworked individuals, it is likely that a redistribution of work time and income would result in a net welfare improvement. Layard (2005) contends that modern research has confirmed that extra dollars make less difference to happiness for a rich person than for a poor person. Logically then, if money is transferred from a richer person to a poorer person, the poor person gains more happiness than the rich person loses, feelings of injustice aside. Thus, the more equally a country's income is distributed the higher the average level of happiness, all else equal. If relative income is more important to well-being than absolute income, the compression of relative income that would result from work time regulation would enhance well-being at both the national and individual level.

The importance of relative income is extremely relevant to the issue of work time reform because, as Bosch and Lehndorff (2001) have shown, the reduction of average work hours in Europe has resulted in a more equitable distribution of paid work and earned income. If greater social equality improves well-being, a compression of the income distribution could be expected to improve well-being in the aggregate as the class of workers that are encouraged or compelled to forfeit some of their hours and income would not be experiencing a net loss. It is important to note that achieving greater socioeconomic participation through work time regulation can also enhance economic freedom which may be even more closely correlated with happiness than income equality (Ott 2005). Ovaska and Takashima (2006: 210) write that the results of happiness research "suggest that people unmistakably care about the degree to which the society where they live provides them opportunities and the freedom to undertake new projects, and make choices based on one's personal preferences." Work time reform that grants the over-worked more time and the under-worked more income to "undertake new projects" can therefore be a boon to happiness. Since greater income equality and economic freedom both contribute to societal well-being, increasing socio-economic participation through work time regulation may be more beneficial to our happiness than relying on traditional redistributive welfare programs alone.

As first blush the happiness research at the individual level appears to be inconsistent with the findings that aggregate happiness is not improved by economic growth. Yet, if the source of the individual happiness improvement stems from comparisons about relative income rather than the attendant increase in consumption, then the two findings can logically coexist. Clark *et al.* (2008) elucidate the issue:

> The broad consensus in the literature is that the paradox points to the importance of relative considerations in the utility function, where higher income brings both consumption and status benefits to an individual. Comparisons can either be to others or to oneself in the past. Utility functions of this type can explain the positive slope found in much of the empirical literature [for individuals]. However, since status is a zero-sum game, only the consumption benefit of income remains at the aggregate level. Since the consumption benefit approaches zero as income rises, happiness profiles over time in developed countries are flat.

Most importantly, individual income is largely irrelevant when forming national policy. It is impossible for national public policy to make everyone wealthier than everyone else. Yet, even if the government did attempt to produce more "winners," it is unclear that the net effect on well-being would be positive. The correlation between greater wealth and *lasting* happiness is still highly questionable for the individual.[9] At the level of society, the link between national income and well-being is highly spurious. As adaptive and emulative creatures, we tend to adapt our expectations about what will make us happy and continually compare ourselves to different groups of people. Yet, the race for status is a zero-sum game as one person's relative success comes at the expense of another person. If two people excel commensurately, there is no change in relative social status and the competition continues. Contemporary market societies that place a premium on individualism and social status therefore devote prodigious effort to changing what cannot be changed in total. Layard (2005) writes:

> The struggle for relative income is totally self-defeating at the level of the society as a whole. If my income rises relative to yours, your income falls relative to mine by exactly the same amount. The whole process produces no net social gain, but may involve a massive sacrifice of private life and time with family and friends. It should be discouraged.

Using individual income levels as a goalpost for success creates an endless source of angst. In the context of work time, the psychological importance attached to relative income, under current social norms, encourages many workers to opt for greater income and the consequent longer hours when given the choice between labor and leisure.

If the process of invidiously distinguishing one's self from their peers takes on a materialistic bent, it is likely to further diminish their personal happiness. Contemporary research on acquisitive behavior suggests that encouraging individuals to lead a highly materialistic lifestyle will not enhance well-being. Materialistic individuals have been characterized as having lower self-esteem, greater narcissism, a greater tendency for social comparison, less empathy, less intrinsic motivation and highly conflictual relationships (Kasser *et al.* 2004). Kasser and Ryan (2001) argue that people with intrinsic goals (i.e. they define their values by themselves) are typically happier than those with extrinsic goals (i.e. those motivated by some external reward such as financial success). Nickerson *et al.* (2003) also found that materialism predicts lower well-being later in life. Lyubomirsky *et al.* (2003) conclude that happiness is linked to what one gives rather than what they get. Materialism may result in lower well-being because materialistic individuals tend to downplay the importance of social relationships and seem to have a perpetual shortfall between their incomes and material aspirations (Solberg *et al.* 2004). Again the direction of causality is unclear; discontent might drive people to focus on extrinsic goals such as material wealth.

Nowhere is the need to buffer the callous aspects of economic growth more poignant than in the incidence of mental disorder and suicide. Diener and Seligman (2004: 16) write that "in stark contrast to the improvement in economic statistics over the past 50 years, there is strong evidence that the incidence of depression has increased enormously over the same time period." Allowing for population growth, ten times as many people in contemporary Western societies suffer from unipolar depression—unremitting bad feelings without a specific cause—than did 50 years ago. Oswald (1997) notes the continued presence of suicide in modern society and a weak positive correlation between income per capita and suicide rates. Using data from the US General Social Survey from 1972 to 1998, Blanchflower and Oswald (2004: 1366) conclude that, despite rapid economic growth, Americans have "become more miserable over the last quarter century."[10]

Although better diagnosis and lower stigmatism associated with depression can explain some of the higher incidence, it cannot account for a tenfold increase across a generation or two. Myers (1992: 43) writes, "no matter how we define depression, the finding persists: Today's younger adults have grown up with more affluence, more depression, and more marital and family misery." They are also more familiar with the consequences of depression—suicide, alcoholism, and substance abuse. A doubling of per pupil spending, smaller class and family sizes, declining household poverty, and increased parental education in America between 1960 and 1980 did little to reverse the social degradation of teenagers that was manifest in a doubling of the delinquency rate, a tripling of the suicide and homicide rates, and the quadrupling of unmarried births (Myers 1992). It would seem that household or governmental spending on adolescents is no replacement for parental supervision of teenagers. Indeed, antisocial behavior among adolescents may be the most immediate bellwether of the social costs associated with long hours and contingent work arrangements, but they are certainly not the only costs as these youngsters represent the future workforce.

Evidence of the staggering increase in depression among mature adults is provided by the Cross National Collaborative Group. In 1992, this study sampled nearly 40,000 adults from America, Puerto Rico, Germany, France, Italy, Lebanon, New Zealand, and Taiwan and revealed dramatic increases in risk for depression across the twentieth century, despite robust economic growth in the majority of countries. Furthermore, Klerman *et al*. (1985) found that 65 per cent of women born in 1950 had one depressive episode before the age of 30, whereas only 5 percent of women born before 1910 had such an episode. The growth of depression in Western society stands in stark contrast to the mental health of certain subgroups that have renounced a materialistic existence. In a study of the Old Order Amish living in Lancaster County, Pennsylvania, Egeland and Hostetter (1983) estimated that the Amish have about 1/5 to 1/10 the risk of unipolar depression than their neighboring Americans in modern communities. Despite repudiating the use of electricity, automobiles, and modern necessities, the Amish experience little mental despair and are equally satisfied with their lives as the Forbes magazine's "richest Americans" (Diener and Seligman, 2004). In the context of work time reform, it is noteworthy that the Amish devote very few, if any, hours to paid work in a hierarchical labor market.

The psychological literature clearly suggests that economic growth as a national public policy is rapidly exhausting its ability to generate greater well-being in the developed world. The lower levels of well-being reported by some poor individuals, and some poor countries, indicate that poverty can and does reduce well-being. Yet, once people attain threshold income levels, additional increases in wealth have a very small influence on well-being. There may be some improvement to individual well-being from a single financial windfall in the short run, but for a neighborhood, region or nation as a whole income growth beyond modest affluence provides very little bang for the buck. Thus, if economic growth continues to serve as the holy grail of economic policy, aggressive ancillary measures will have to be implemented if society is also intent on enhancing well-being.

In addition to the emphasis that individuals place on relative income, a number of other salient findings from the psychological research on well-being are of particular relevance to work time reform. The first is the influence of non-financial variables on human welfare. The findings suggest that marital status, social inclusion, education, religion, and labor force participation, independently of their influence on income, are more important than absolute income—dispelling the notion that income buys happiness. In a crude estimate, Blanchflower and Oswald (2004: 1373) calculate that to "compensate" an individual's happiness for being widowed or divorced it would roughly require an additional $100,000 income per year. Although such estimates should be treated cautiously, the relatively weak influence of economic variables on well-being has been corroborated by other studies. When college students—a typically materialistic age cohort—were asked, "what would make you happy-winning millions in the lottery, achieving fame/prestige in your career, enjoying physical pleasures (food, sex, drink), or falling (or staying) in love with your ideal mate?", Pettijohn and Pettijohn (1996) report that 78 percent chose love as their first choice. Such studies speak to the importance of non-economic matters in the average respondent's happiness index.

A second important finding is that well-being is "U-shaped" in age, meaning that happiness (U.S.) or life satisfaction (UK) usually reached its doldrums at midlife (Blanchflower and Oswald 2004; Clark 2008). In both Briton and the United States, well-being tends to hit a low around the age of 40 before rising again in later working life and rapidly in retirement. Few working parents would be surprised by this finding, as the mid-life low corresponds to the peak-earning and harried-parenting years of both American and British workers. When well-being reaches its nadir during peak earning years, it suggests that labor market trends in the United States and the UK—the feminization of the labor force, the growth of single parenthood, and the polarization of work hours—have not been managed in a favorable manner. Such findings suggest that there is significant scope for work time regulation to improve the well-being of harried, middle-age workers.

Another important finding relevant to work time regulation is that the strength of social relationships is one of the best predictors of well-being. After much investigation into the puzzling findings that higher income, education and health have not increased happiness since World War II, Lane (2000) espouses that people, not money, knowledge, or material possessions make us happy or sad. Lane (2000:147) emphasis the importance of social skills in fostering happiness, "Cooperativeness, leadership, and those skills that attract people of the opposite sex all contribute to a person's well-being. If one has poor skills of this kind, one loses that boon to happiness, companionship." Eckersley (2004) likewise concludes that well-being comes from being connected in a web of relationships and engaged in a variety of activities that give life meaning. In *A General Theory of Love*, Lewis *et al.* (2000) argue that the human desire for love and intimacy is a physical necessity that has evolved with humanity; that the brain evolved a chemical need for closeness as part of the stimuli that allow it to function properly. On the whole, married people are happier than singles, people from large families are happier than those from small families, and those that engage in multiple activities, where they interact with many other people, are happier than those who tend to stay at home (Lewis *et al.* 2000). Lane (2000) estimates that while 3 percent of Americans described themselves as "lonely" in 1957, the figure has grown to 13 percent today. Americans and Europeans are living longer and lonelier lives than ever before. When asked "What is necessary for your happiness?" or "What is it that makes your life meaningful?" most people cite satisfying relationships with family, friends, or romantic partners (Berscheid 1985). Studies of the sources of well-being reveal what many people in wealthy countries subconsciously know—that more money and more possessions do not increase individual happiness. The psychological research suggests that when unfettered capitalism is allowed to demand long hours, worker mobility, and alienating work, social relationships will suffer and create negative feedback effects on health, labor productivity, and civility. Indeed, shorter work hours may be a wiser way for society to share its social productivity gains.

The importance of the strength of social relationships is largely ignored by the vestigial fetish for work and economic growth that pervades thinking in the developed world today. For example, some social observers have suggested that much of the increased depression in the advanced countries relative to developing nations stems from a lack of distraction in the form of productive work. Easterbrook (2004: 165) suggests that depression is not as prevalent in the less developed world because "so many people there are focused on simply staying alive that they have no time or leisure in which to experience depressed frames of mind." He also claims that our pre-capitalist ancestors likewise lacked the time for developing a "depressed" state of mind. Indeed, Easterbrook (2004: 165) makes mental disorder sound like the tantrums of a spoiled child, "the United States and European Union generate enough wealth to spoil their citizens with depression; huge numbers of people in these places can, in terms of money or time, afford to feel badly."

Yet, such explanations ignore the alienating nature of modern capitalist society and the fact that contemporary workers have no more leisure time than our pre-industrial ancestors. Many historical accounts (Schor 1991; Reid 1996) have shown that prior to the Industrial Revolution workers enjoyed far more leave time for religious, family, and social ceremonies, including the occasional Saint Monday. Moreover, the masses of unemployed individuals in under-developed countries certainly have ample free time with which to become depressed. It is therefore more likely that the disproportionate mental anguish experienced in wealthy countries is related to paid work being both extensive (i.e. long weekly hours) and intensive (i.e. high levels of stress and job insecurity). The modern labor market is far more hierarchal, impersonal, and alienating now that production is governed by "exchange values" rather than "use values." Consumption is also becoming more impersonal. It is increasingly difficult to experience social relationships through consumption or material transformation in capitalist societies today. Thus growing levels of worker dissatisfaction are more likely the result of a fraying of social relationships than a mollycoddling of workers within industrial societies. The misplaced reverence for work as a means to occupy the mind ignores the principle determinants of well-being identified by modern psychological research: engaging social relationships and activities. As Institutionalists have pointed out, capitalism contains inherent contradictions in this regard. Progress requires perpetual implementation of new practices, technologies, and skills, while economic actors (firms, workers and families) are required to change their habitat, social and environmental linkages and patterns, and, most importantly in terms of well-being, their relationships with one another.

Recently the scales have been weighted in favor of the market mentality at the expense of society and ecology. The "economic rationalization" of the 1980s–2000s has been the pantheon of individualism. Deregulation of labor, trade, and domestic and international capital markets all represent the ascendancy of individual (private) interests. Market transactions have expanded at the expense of the reciprocity and redistribution that have been the source of familial and communal support and nurturance in the past (Polanyi 1944; Stanfield and Stanfield 1997). With worker mobility, labor market "flexibility" (i.e. job insecurity), international competitiveness, and individualism serving as hallmarks to modern capitalist society, it is little wonder that depression abounds. Past emphasis on family, faith, and community may have been confining, but it allowed individuals to view their personal setbacks as minor events within a larger context. Furthermore, a personal failure was less likely to be any one individual's fault alone. The cost of economic rationalization then seems to be the depression that arises from leaving people at the fate of pure individualism, without consolation or social context. Rampant individualism may cause us to think that our setbacks are of utmost importance and thus something to become depressed about. Individualism may also be depressing due to the meaninglessness of having few attachments to something bigger than ourselves.

It bears mention that many activities that enhance our well being—parenting, sex, love, friendship, social interaction—are also critical to the very propagation of our species. Curiously, however, many of these activities are not part of economics proper. We do not rely on the "market" or "voluntary exchange" to ration activities such as sex, love, parenthood, friendship, and democracy, and in many instances the marketplace is antithetical to them. Simply pursuing economic growth as an objective policy target is therefore unlikely to promote greater well-being. Layard (2005: 235) comments that, "Through science, absolute material scarcity has been conquered in the West, and we need to think hard about what would now constitute progress." Indeed, socioeconomic policy will have to be more subjective, nuanced and value-based if it is to improve life satisfaction in the future. Oswald (2006: 28) comments, "Economists' faith in the value of growth is diminishing. This is a good thing and will slowly make its way down into the minds of tomorrow's politicians." Psychological evidence arising from modern studies of the human impact of economic growth suggest that policymakers should aspire to reform economic activity around a concept of welfare that emphasizes material comfort, social involvement, and time for higher pursuits.

Large numbers of people in the developed world can now empathize with the plight of Midas and identify with Henry David Thoreau's (1854: 88) maxim that "a man is rich in proportion to the number of things he can afford to let alone." The psychological research suggests that a rapacious appetite for material goods has not translated into greater happiness. The research consensus that greater national income has done little to improve life satisfaction or happiness, suggests that the efficacy of growth-based public policy is quickly waning. Consequently, denizens of the developed world are re-evaluating the pinnacle of civilization as something more than material goods squirreled away in self-storage.[11] Myriad measures of well-being suggest that robust economic throughput over the last half-century has failed to improve many facets of lives. Whether the chosen index emphasizes psychological, environmental, social, or familial well-being, the conclusions are comparable; the developed world has been sold a bill of goods labeled the "growth consensus."

The future of paid work in "post-industrial" society

If the growing dissatisfaction with the fruits of economic growth does not militate for an alternative social division of labor, structural changes emerging in market societies will continually press the issue. Most developed economies have matured from agrarian societies to industrialized nations and then to a service-oriented economy. In their post-industrial condition, many countries have struggled to redefine the relationship between work, income and socioeconomic participation. Even more vexing, many observers anticipate a post-service economy that will further blur the delineations between work and social participation. This section addresses the growing imperative of labor market reform in light of the structural and technological changes taking place in the developed world.

The present stage of capitalism—whether one chooses the moniker of post-industrialism, post-Fordism, neo-colonialism, or globalism—has created a growing fissure in the relationship between income and work. The theoretical concept of marginal productivity—whereby economic resources are distributed on the basis of contributions to production—is increasingly irrelevant to workers as fewer human beings are needed in the provision of goods. For many economists, the notion of rewarding workers on the basis of their marginal productivity was always a myth, and a rapid technological contraction of employment possibilities may aid in revealing it as such. Technological developments (ranging from the bimolecular to the cybernetic) may soon render any lingering notions of "gainful employment" obsolete. Although it is true that alternative employment opportunities can be created as technology eliminates physical work, rapid dislocation of workers can dramatically alter the relationship between income and work and prompt a broader questioning of the social division of labor.

Many social observers contend that a new economic system is emerging which has the potential to eliminate paid work on a grand scale. This view holds that technological development will increasingly diminish the urgency and centrality of paid work in the economy and, consequently, the social psyche. Yet, political and social institutions have shown little ability to adapt to the changing structure of capitalism. The movement to a high-tech, post-industrial (or post-Fordist) economy represents a profound transformation that could feasibly reduce the incidence of work, dissolve the wage relationship, and reduce the fraction of the working population devoted to material production to around 2 percent of the labor force.

For decades now the lives of workers in the developed world have been emancipated from the exigencies of the agricultural or factory system. Employees may still face rigid and stressful work patterns, but such pressures are socially imposed; they are no longer an industrial necessity. Bertrand Russell (1935: 25) observed that "modern methods have given us the possibility of ease and security for all; we have chosen, instead, to have overwork for some and starvation for the others. Hitherto we have continued to be as energetic as we were before there were machines; in this we have been foolish, but there is no reason to go on being foolish for ever." Technological development has created the possibility for a greater flexibility of time use for the vast majority of workers. The prospect of further technological development into what Gross (1971) has called the "post-service" economy will require the wholesale reconfiguration of the labor market. Jones (1995: 1) describes both the metamorphisms and challenges in the labor market:

> Advance economies have now moved into a post-industrial era, in which services such as welfare, education, administration, and the transfer of information dominate employment. The displacement of agriculture by manufacturing as the dominate employer was the first of two major 'cross-overs' in economic history. The second was the displacement of manufacturing (industrial) employment by service (post-industrial) employment. The post-industrial era may be of short duration: the computerized revolution of the 1980s will contribute to a further major transition – to a 'post service' society in which routine and repetitive service employment will be significantly reduced, or eliminated. This change will raise unprecedented human problems: the whole relationship of people to time use, personal goals, economics, politics and culture must be re-examined.

Further clarification of the term "post-industrial" is useful. It was first used by Art Historian Ananda Coomaraswamy in 1913. The modern use of the expression refers to an economy where the majority of the labor force is no longer employed in agriculture, mining, manufacturing, construction and related storage and transportation. In its stead, employment in post-industrial societies has been found in the service sector: retailing, teaching, office work, transport, administration, entertainment, personal care, and the, now bloated, finance, real estate, and insurance industries. Jones (1995: 4) estimates that employment in the services reached 50 percent of the paid labor force by 1945 in Australia, 1947 in the United States, 1948 in the UK, 1955 in Canada, 1960 in Sweden, 1965 in New Zealand, 1966 in Belgium, 1972 in France and Germany, and 1972 in Japan. Today, well over two-thirds of employment takes place in the service sector in these countries.

A great deal of the employment growth in the service sector across developed nations can be classified as "in-person services." This classification includes occupations such as retail sales workers, waiters and waitresses, hotel workers, janitors, cashiers, hospital attendants and orderlies, nursing-home aides, taxi drivers, secretaries, hairdressers, auto mechanics, real estate agents, flight attendants, physical therapists, and security guards. Reich (1993: 177) points out that in the 1980s over 3 million *new* in-person service jobs were created in American bars, restaurants, and fast-food outlets alone, which was more than the *combined total* number of existing production jobs in the automobile, steelmaking and textile industries by the end of the decade. Yet, not all service sector jobs are people oriented. Contemporary work tasks are increasingly related to information with more people engaged in collecting, processing and storing data than are employed in agriculture and mining combined.

Given the momentum of the post-industrial economy, it is useful to anticipate what might follow. The optimistic view is that the productivist system will quickly adapt and generate positive employment effects. In this Panglossian perspective, firms operating in competitive markets will pass the lower production costs from technological change onto consumers in the form of lower product prices. The price savings will translate into greater output demand (for existing and new products), expanding employment in the aggregate.

While market "entrepreneurs," as Rifkin (2000) refers to them, maintain that technological development will increase production, profits, employment and consumption, the broader public has expressed hopes and desires for an alternative vision—one that replaces the perpetual expansion of work and consumption with a growth in leisure time. Some argue that market-based service employment will decline—perhaps even more rapidly than industrial employment—due to the introduction of miniaturized, sophisticated, low-cost technology. The labor market in such a society would be characterized by a reduction in the number of people working in large-scale service employment with routine and repetitive tasks that can be replaced by computerized operations that are cheaper, faster, and more accurate. By directing the free time generated by the automation of service-oriented tasks toward the liberation of the working class from the work and spend cycle, the next major economic transformation could be managed far more equitably than the process of de-industrialization.

The capitalistic tradition of distributing economic resources on the basis of contributions to production is being challenged by new computer-based technologies. Imminent advances in robotics threaten to make the military, manufacturing, and service worker as redundant as the farm hand. The technological unemployment caused by recent automation has been highly visible in manufacturing and mining. The employment effects of automation at US Steel are emblematic of trends in the manufacturing sector in general. In 1980, US Steel employed 120,000 workers, but by 1990 it was manufacturing the same amount of steel with 20,000 employees (Rifkin 2000). The mining industry has also experienced severe technological unemployment. In 1925, it required around 588,800 miners to extract 520 million tons of bituminous coal and lignite. By 1982, 774 million tons of coal was processed by less than half (208,000) as many workers (Rifkin 2000). Automation of the service sector is the next frontier. Wallace (1989: 366) comments that "with such capabilities as voice communication, a general purpose programming language, learning from experience, three dimensional vision with color sensitivity, multiple hand to hand coordination, walking and self-navigating skills, and self-diagnostic and correction skills, the goal is to approach, as closely as possible, the human capabilities to process environmental data and to solve problems, while avoiding the problems [like absenteeism and shirking] presented by human agents." Experts estimate that each robot replaces four jobs in the economy, and that it will pay for itself in just over a year through near-continuous use (Rifkin 2000). Indeed, once robots master the ability to stock selves, hoards of service sector employees— including one million Wal-Mart workers—will be rendered redundant.

Some corollary developments of post-industrial societies are worthy of mention when anticipating the effect of technological change on the labor market. First, technological development and information-based employment has arguably accelerated the rise of the global economy. With instant worldwide communication, vastly reduced transportation costs, and footloose financial capital, multinational corporations have challenged the political capacity and will of nations to regulate the impact of international trade on their economies. Second, the occupational base of the post-industrial society, requiring less physical exertion, has increased labor participation rates, primarily driven by a feminization of the work force and retention of aged workers. It has also introduced the possibility for a more flexible (part-time and/or contingent) attachment to the work force. Lastly, there has been a growing divide between the "information-rich" and the "information-poor." All of these developments have the potential to intensify the labor market inequities and class conflict brought about by the post-industrial system.

The social impact of large-scale technological unemployment is likely to be more problematic in a post-industrial world than it has in the past as it is unclear what new sector could provide large-scale employment opportunities.[12] Social and environmental objections to more economic growth will diminish the potential for traditional employment growth to absorb the losses. Jones (1995: 6) contends that, "there will be increasing anxiety about the rate of depletion of the world's resources, and [consequently] the adoption of a 'stable state' economy in which materials are recycled and miniaturised technology is used to save energy." Given the growing awareness of social and environmental externalities, the two competing visions of technology are coming into greater conflict with one another. Rifkin (2000: 74) points out that the resolution of this conflict has important ramifications for society, "the vision of the entrepreneur keeps us locked in to a world of market relations and commercial considerations. The second vision, one championed by many of America's best-known utopian thinkers, brings us into a new era in which the commercial forces of the marketplace are tempered by the communitarian forces of an enlightened society."

Although technological development may represent a Silverado for the "efficiency cult," a failure to harness it in the best interest of society presents the possibility of severe social disruptions. Gorz (1999) argues that while capital has orchestrated its "exodus" from the Fordist system quite adroitly, society has failed to transform itself to allow labor a similarly munificent evacuation. In addition to minimizing its reliance on labor, capital has increased its mobility in order to access a larger army of workers and lower costs. The capitalists' need to perpetuate the work ethic has resulted in a labor market segmentation that shifts the traditional antagonisms between management and labor to animosity between the "elite" workers in the primary sector and those in the peripheral sector. The insiders are chosen for their passion for, devotion to, and identification with work. Capitalists have already begun to create the macro-social conditions needed to maintain the work fetish and mask the liberating potential of technological change by concentrating the shrinking amount of necessary work in the hands of a few, who will gratify themselves with the pride of being distinguished from the "losers." Economically and technically, a sharing of the work by a larger number of workers is feasible, but such a development would threaten the preservation of "traditional" attitudes regarding paid work.

It is important to recognize, however, that the establishment of an elite sector of chosen workers comes at the expense of social welfare. Since they simultaneously produce wealth and unemployment, elite workers impact both the fortunes and miseries of society. Gorz (1999: 45) writes of the externalities wrought by workaholics in the primary sector:

> The greater their productivity and eagerness for work, the greater also will be unemployment, poverty, inequality, social marginalization and the rate of profit. The more they identify with work and with their company's successes, the more they contribute to producing and repro-ducing the conditions of their own subjection, to intensifying the com-petition between firms, and hence to making the battle for productivity the more lethal, the threat to everyone's employment – including their own – the more menacing, and the domination of capital over workers and society the more irresistible.

The social costs of such labor market segmentation are most apparent in the modern management trend toward outsourcing. When the firm retains a small, elite group to orchestrate outsourcing of erstwhile work tasks, the negative social externalities resulting from the squeeze on labor become quite obvious. Recently, such troublesome outsourcing has been institutionalized by the much heralded "Ohno" production techniques closely associated with Toyota and other Japanese producers. Since approximately 85 percent of the labor force involved in the production of the final product is now employed by subcontractors offering varying wages and working conditions, cost effi-ciencies arising from the Ohno approach may merely represent a sophisticated segmentation of the labor market. Lebaube (1991: 18) summarizes the Japanese system:

> Whilst the company refocuses on its core activity and tends to upgrade the jobs of its personnel, it shifts the most painful constraints, which often take the form of Taylorized working conditions, on to a network of subcontractors. The "fragmented" enterprise hypocritically closes its eyes to the social consequences of this division, and to the implications of the specifications it imposes on its suppliers.

The growing army of contingent workers must be added to the ranks of the peripheral sector to fully appreciate the social impacts of the post-industrial production system. These freelance, self-employed, or marginally attached workers are not covered by many labor laws, have little social insurance protection, and assume most of the economic risk in their piece-meal employment arrangements. Contingent workers often perform the same work as the permanent staff, but are deprived of the equivalent status, benefit entitlements, and pay levels. Expansion of the ranks of the contingent sector could well lead to the abolition of wage labor and a return to the cutthroat labor market conditions that prevailed in the early stages of industrialization. By throwing more workers into competition with one another as self-employed contractors, capitalists could avoid many of the restrictions erected by the labor movement over the last two centuries. The social status of workers would no longer be protected by labor law, and companies would be at liberty to treat contractors quite inequitably in the absence of competitive markets. Evidence from the ranks of contemporary self-employed workers serves as a harbinger of the social inequities that may follow. Sergio Bologna (1996) reports that "[self-employed workers] can achieve a decent level of income only by working a great many hours, and they are more liable than employed workers to fall below the poverty line." He cites a European Commission survey finding that more than half of self-employed men, and one-third of women, work 48 hours or more per week throughout the European community (Bologna 1996). In France, the figures are as high as 70 percent and 50 percent, respectively.

The new economy is restoring the worst forms of domination, subjugation and exploitation by forcing workers to compete with each other in a quest to obtain the very work that it is abolishing. Yet, it is not the dissolution of traditional employment that we should object to, but the charade of perpetuating the same social structure as an immutable wellspring of human rights and dignity. It is important to note that embracing the dissolution of traditional paid work is distinct from the ongoing physical human action that provides essential philosophical and anthropological purpose. As Gorz (1999: 3) claims, "we have to exit from 'work' and the 'work-based society' in order to recover a taste for, and the possibility of, 'true' work." Yet, as long as the abolition of work also restricts access to social participation, a flourishing of unpaid work in the third sector is unlikely to fill the void created by post-industrial development. In order to maintain its privileged position in the class struggle, the establishment denies that traditional work is being eliminated. Gorz (1999: 58) writes:

> We are a society of phantom work, spectrally surviving the extinction of that work by virtue of obsessive, reactive invocations of those who can imagine no other future than the return of the past. Such people do everyone the worst service imaginable by persuading us that there is no possible future, sociality, life, or self-fulfillment outside employment; between inclusion through employment and exclusion; between 'identity-giving socialization through work' and collapse into the despair of non-being.

Capitalism has systematically entangled the need for adequate, stable income with the need to interact, strive, and be appreciated and accepted by others. Yet, the anxieties of the working class suggest that permanent paid work as a means to social and personal identity and fulfillment is threatened by the marginalization of increasingly large segments of the labor force. In post-industrial societies, the remedy may not lie in creating more work hours, but in ameliorating the distribution of socially necessary labor and socially produced wealth. If it can overcome the invocations of the work fetish, the growing welter among disenfranchised workers may crystallize an alternative method of producing and distributing the means of social continuity. Unlike the Industrial Revolution, which was oriented towards increased material output, the information revolution has the potential to yield greater leisure time for the masses in developed countries. A democratic expansion of leisure is more likely to prompt genuine human progress than an expansion of throughput because greater leisure time provides the potential for satisfying a variety of needs (i.e. social, intellectual, familial, and spiritual), as opposed to the satisfaction of mere physiological and invidious desires.

Some futurists even argue that the traditional work ethic may be counterproductive to societal needs in the age of technology (Jones 1995; Gorz 1999; Rifkin 2000). They foresee the need for a fundamental change in the notion of time use and the relationship between employers and employees in post-industrial society. New types of employment will have to complement new patterns of time use that will be devised to be time absorbing—activities such as craftwork, gardening, research, sport, leisure, hobbies and do-it-yourself projects. Gorz (1999: 98) opines, "to change society, we have to change 'work' – and vice versa. To change it by divesting it of all its reifying constraints (hours, hierarchy, productivity), which reflect its subordination to capital and which, so far, have determined the essence of what is currently known as 'work'." An obsession with efficiency and speed could taint the enjoyment otherwise yielded from non-work activities. Voluntary activities in the third sector should not be perceived as lamely supplementing the market economy, or as a quid pro quo for social support (as suggested by some basic income proponents), but as a critical component of improving socio-economic participation.

Given the appropriate social arrangements, a diminished or discontinuous attachment to the labor force would not create insecurity for workers. In reality the less extensive and intensive the connection to work, the greater the employment security in aggregate. Since the growth in the contingent workforce is essentially a reduction in total work hours, discontinuous employment means that work will be spread out over a greater number of people. Constructing a social system that embraced a sporadic attachment to paid work would recognize that the right to work and the right not to work are of equal social importance.[13] As featured in Chapter 5, many European countries, such as the Netherlands and Denmark, have incorporated the right to discontinuous work regimes into their social and labor market policy with positive macroeconomic outcomes (Gorz 1999; Hayden 1999).

Rifkin (2000) argues that the expansion of the "third sector" is the preferred way to supplant the psychological and social benefits that workers currently derive from paid work. The third sector is distinct from the private market and the government sector and is analogous to household or communal production. Rifkin (2000: 220) writes, "this is the arena where men and women can explore new roles and responsibilities and find new meaning in their lives now that the commodity value of their time is vanishing." The third sector includes the panoply of activities carried out by hundreds of volunteer organizations serving millions of people across the globe today. In the United States, the value of the volunteer activities has been estimated at $131 billion in 2004, or $447 per capita (Talberth *et al.* 2007).

In the UK, the "New Labour" government that took office in 1997 embraced the growth of this alternative sector, culminating in the recent (2006) establishment of an Office of the Third Sector. Since 1997, New Labour has been encouraging volunteerism through a variety of policies, including infrastructure improvement grants. Despite the long hours worked by one-fifth of the British workforce, there is evidence of growing activity in the third sector. The number of charities operating in the UK has increased from 98,000 in 1991 to 169,000 in 2004 (Haugh and Kitson 2007). These social enterprises are not motivated by a desire to maximize profits but to provide a number of activities in the public interest—such as reversing the social ills related to economic exclusion and environmental degradation. In 2003, the non-profit sector in the UK employed a permanent paid workforce of 608,000, which amounts to 2 percent of the total workforce (Wilding *et al.* 2006).[14] But the unpaid voluntary labor provided to the sector dwarfs permanent employment; 13.2 million people volunteered once a month in 2003, the equivalent of 1.1 million full-time employees (Home Office 2004). Although the policies and initiatives of Britain's New Labour have been moderately successful in encouraging more activity in the third sector, the long hours worked by large numbers of British workers clearly constrains the growth and achievements of this sector.

The importance of a thriving third sector is supported by recent research showing that reliance on financial or economic motives alone does not always lead to optimal results. Titmuss (1970) found that when people donated blood for the sake of human welfare, it was safer (as in Britain) than when people were paid for it (as in the United States). In a study by Deci and Ryan (1985) two groups of students were given puzzles to complete; one group was paid for each correct solution while the other group was unpaid. At the conclusion to the allotted time, both groups were allowed to keep working. The researchers observed that the unpaid group did much more extra work than the paid group. In this case, the intrinsic value of the work led to the unpaid team doing twice as much additional work than the paid group. Perhaps the external motivation of monetary rewards reduced the internal rewards for the paid group. More evidence comes from Switzerland, where two communities were being considered for radioactive waste storage sites. One group of local inhabitants was asked, "Would you be willing to have the repository here?" Frey and Oberholzer-Gee (1997) report that 50 percent responded "yes." A second group was asked, "If you were offered a certain amount of compensation [unspecified], would you be willing to have the repository here?" When it became a financial proposition the "yes" rate fell to 25 percent. People were less willing to act in the social or national interest when financial motives were involved. A final example that is rather apposite to the issue of work time comes from an Israeli childcare center. When parents were becoming chronically late to pick up their children, the center implemented modest fines for being late. Gneezy and Rustichini (2000) observed the economically irrational result that even more people were late and more often. Now that they were paying for it, they felt that being late was more acceptable. These experiments suggest that converting an activity from the third sector to the private market may have unintended consequences. Indeed, financial and economic incentives are not always the most powerful or appropriate motivators of human activity. Volunteer, communal or familial arrangements may be the most effective mechanism when goals are not purely profit-based.

In the postindustrial economy, there is the real potential for escalating tension between the information rich, who possess claims to income, and the information-poor, who will be increasingly unskilled, bored, frustrated, and impoverished. If public policy fails to address adequately the "technological divide," economic power will become even more inequitable than it is now, economic resources will be the subject of continual struggle, and protracted unemployment will traumatize society and retard its progress. If left unbridled, aggressive competition and individualism will become highly divisive in contemporary capitalist societies. If technological advance leads to widespread destitution and disenfranchisement and the concentration of wealth in the hands of the few, not only will capitalism be threatened but democracy as well. Alternatively, enlightened policy could foster a post-service society that affords a golden age of leisure and personal development based on the cooperative use of technology and resources. Economic stability and progress depend on the socioeconomic participation of the vast majority of citizens.

In order for democracy to thrive, leaders in capitalistic countries will need to implement policies that foster a more equitable and inclusive economy. In our postindustrial condition of growing abundance, it has become less important to hatch new ways of creating more jobs for the sake of jobs alone. Growth of the third sector offers a much needed antidote to the materialism and rapacious consumption that grips contemporary society. Engagement in the third sector can serve as a source of the dignity and respect that humans seek as social beings. Once workers are liberated from paid work and secure an alternative means of social integration, society may reflect upon its erstwhile obsession with paid employment in terms similar to the way in which the slave system in the Americas was defended. Testaments to the physiological, psychological, and social well-being of the subjects of the wage system will be revealed as spurious as claims about the putative weal of African slaves in the Southern United States and the Caribbean prior to emancipation (Carlyle, 1849).

Conclusion

The radical critiques and approaches featured in this chapter shed a penumbra of doubt on the urgency of the productive process in high-consumption, industrialized economies. Questioning the exigency of the productive system casts suspicion on the urgency of paid work and particularly long work hours. Arguably there are few recurring exigencies within the capitalistic system that would justify the economic, social and environmental costs associated with the current polarization of work hours. Long work hours may be tolerable in a state of war or similar national emergency, but in normal times there appears to be little urgency to the consumer desires that the productive process both satisfies and inflames. In short, if the primacy or urgency of the production process is suspect, then a maniacal attachment to the workforce may be of questionable social worth.

Evidence of the seamy side of economic growth in the developed world is emerging from research on the inability of national income growth to enhance collective happiness. Indeed, the data available from a variety of measures of national well-being should prompt serious sociological introspection. A pregnant question that emerges is whether a curtailment of much of the invidious consumption that has taken place over the last half-century would have improved society weal? If the resources devoted to "relative" consumption, including advertising, were instead channeled into work time reduction and activities in the third sector, might societies have achieved improved levels of well-being? The remaining chapters investigate why an organized effort to regulate work hours represents the best single-policy mechanism to improve societal well-being in a post-industrial, climate-constrained world of growing abundance.

3 Work Time Regulation as a Macroeconomic Policy Tool

Growth-oriented capitalism is dead.

Andre Gorz (1980: 11)

If economic value means anything at all, its meaning is that of a gradual and continuous realization of a more effective organization of the life process.

Clarence Ayres (1944: 228)

Having outlined the broad divisions in economic theory in general, this chapter turns to an analysis of economic thought relating to the salient macroeconomic issues of unemployment and inflation. Since World War II, market economies have struggled to achieve the elusive macroeconomic goal of full employment and price stability. Indeed, many economists have abandoned the quest by accepting the existence of an immutable trade-off between employment and inflation. Yet, since that trade-off is increasingly being challenged on theoretical, empirical, social, and environmental grounds, the door is now open to alternative approaches to macroeconomic management. Being cognizant of how various schools of economic thought approach the topic of unemployment aids in the assessment of modern full-employment policy and proposals. This chapter therefore begins by comparing and contrasting the various viewpoints surrounding the causes and possible cures of unemployment, including some of the political implications related to the elimination of unemployment. Since an underlying goal of a fully employed economy is greater social inclusion, the chapter also explores the Institutionalist meaning of greater socioeconomic participation. Presuming that the elimination of involuntary unemployment emerges as a political objective, the analysis then turns to a comparative assessment of competing full-employment programs and their ability to redress the socioeconomic and ecological anxieties emerging in wealthy nations. Since abandonment of the work fetish opens the door for enhanced socioeconomic participation to serve as a new objective for full employment policy, the narrative suggests ways in which work time regulation could serve as an effective macroeconomic policy lever in a post-industrial, climate-constrained society.

Views and viewpoints regarding unemployment

The manner in which we approach the unemployment problem is an important looking glass into the nature of things to come. Competing employment policies contain varying degrees of homage to the market mentality, which not only influences the future success of the policy but the vision of the society we confer on our progeny. The recognition of a pressing socioeconomic problem, and our collective response to it, is a reflection of our values, our view of humanity and our vision for the future. The society our grandchildren inherit hinges on the social policy choices we make today. It remains an open question whether future generations will be able to obtain greater well-being by better balancing their lives and their livelihood or if they will continue to "live to work" under the yoke of the work fetish. It is useful then to examine how competing schools of thought have chosen to approach the role of paid work in social provisioning. The goals and expectations of alternative employment programs prove to be extremely revealing in anticipating specific policy outcomes and the consequences to society. Thus, this section is devoted to the governing principles of alternative approaches to the issue of unemployment.

For most of the twentieth century, a clear delineation existed between orthodox economics and heterodox views over the characterization of unemployment. Neoclassicalists, as well as many NeoKeynesians, believed that persistent unemployment was largely voluntary. Their theories held that obstinate wage demands and other wage rigidities kept labor markets from clearing at full employment. Conversely, heterodox observers of capitalist economies have insisted that long-term unemployment is involuntary, stemming from political and economic forces that maintain an insufficiency of jobs.

Recently, however, the distinctions have blurred. Mainstream economics has gradually come to acknowledge the existence of structural unemployment, embracing it as a necessarily evil that should be accepted on the grounds of efficiency and stability (Shapiro and Stiglitz 1984; DeVroey 1998). Given the putative tradeoffs associated with unemployment, the mainstream policy objective becomes the maintenance of optimal unemployment rather than its outright elimination. The occasional mainstream economist, such as Edmund Phelps (1996), recognizes the prodigious social costs of unemployment as worthy of government intervention. By way of example, Phelps (1996) and Layard (1996) advocate wage subsidies as a means of generating positive externalities associated with lower unemployment while not disrupting the firm's labor cost structure. Without delving into the efficacy of wage subsidies at this juncture, it should be noted that the very advocacy of such programs by mainstream economists is a patent acknowledgement that the labor market cannot achieve full employment on its own accord and that government intervention is necessary.

A uniting cause for many heterodox economists has been a condemnation of involuntary unemployment and the promulgation of policy prescriptions designed to reduce it. The issue of unemployment is central to the radical critique of capitalism's inability to devote its vast productive powers to first satisfy ubiquitous human needs and then promote unparalleled levels of human freedom. However, subtle differences do exist among the broad heterodox approaches that have important implications for public policy. A comparative assessment of Post-Keynesian, Institutionalist, and Marxist views on the issue of unemployment is useful therefore in formulating a full-employment strategy that is capable of achieving broadly held macro-economic objectives in a socially and environmentally sustainable manner.

The post-Keynesian approach to unemployment

Mindful of Keynes's (1936) exposition of the structural inability of capitalism to provide adequate employment levels, post-Keynesian economists often argue for greater government spending as a means of stabilizing and maximizing employment. Indeed, post-Keynesians can be broadly characterized as under-consumptionists—believing that unemployment arises from a failure to utilize all of the potential social surplus (that is, to eliminate dormant savings). Post-Keynesian policy often relies on demand-side management to redress the bulk of unemployment. Yet, the short-term nature of such action has led many Marxists to question whether such policy ever eliminates the social surplus that is the underlying cause of the unemployment. As featured below, Marxists and Institutionalists suggest that although demand management has had sporadic success in addressing the symptom of unemployment it has failed to correct the cause of recurrent crises. In an economy characterized by highly efficient, capital-saving technology controlled by oligopolistic firms, a stimulation of aggregate demand may simply accelerate the capitalist tendency toward crises of overproduction. Indeed, Keynes (1932: 525) himself warned that the Great Depression was "not a crisis of poverty, but a crisis of abundance."

Accepting that structural issues play a complicating role, some post-Keynesians have recently advocated that the government directly employ all those individuals willing and able to work on a temporary basis as part of a job guarantee program that manages a buffer stock of unemployed workers (Mitchell 1998; Wray 1998). Yet, such a program is essentially an aggregate demand stimulus that uses the existing level of desired labor force participation as its fiscal target. Other things equal, aggregate demand will be larger with a buffer stock program at every phase of the economic cycle as it addresses unemployment by placing a floor under spending. Other post-Keynesians subscribe to a basic income approach, which provides individuals with an unconditional or participatory income stream (Widerquist *et al.* 2005). Income guarantees impact unemployment by removing some job seekers from the labor force while stimulating consumption to increase the labor demand for those still seeking work. In essence, both job and income guarantees rely on a stimulation of aggregate demand to achieve employment gains. They could be thought of as having "level effects" rather than altering the structure of the capitalistic system. Although they may marginally improve the work and living conditions of the under-privileged, they do little to improve the bargaining position of the working class, as employers will still be in a situation to segment the working class into over-worked and underutilized cohorts. Since both policies attempt to grow their way out of unemployment they offer little hope in reversing the environmental damage caused by large and growing levels of economic throughput.

The Marxian approach to unemployment

Marxian economists believe that the persistence of involuntary unemployment results from a class struggle. According to Marx, there is always and everywhere an excess supply of labor, which depresses wages and ensures that surplus value (and concomitant profit) is positive. The disparate social and political power of the capitalist class grants them the wherewithal needed to maintain a reserve army of surplus workers. The ranks of the reserve army are swollen by technological unemployment, labor market segmentation, and footloose capital that fuels geographical imperialism. A conversancy in Marx's approach to work time as well as his critique of capitalism helps clarify the urgency of work time reform. Given that Marx viewed the length of the workday as the chief tool of capitalist exploitation, work time regulation then becomes the preferred method for addressing the misuse of labor that is at the heart of the struggle between capitalists and workers. The Marxian analysis helps explain why employers have historically resisted past work time reductions even while the evidence suggested that short hours would not hinder production. Marx was one of the earliest economists to argue that the efficiency of labor improved with shorter work durations. In addition to greater worker productivity, Marx held that capitalists possessed a variety of techniques to maintain output levels in the wake of work time reductions. He believed that capitalism had a tendency to raise the average level of work intensity and that this greater intensity, in conflict with human limitations, would make periodic reductions in work time necessary.

A prominent theme in the Marxian approach is that the exploitation of labor is accomplished through an underutilization of labor. By controlling the means of production, the capitalist maintains a "surplus army of unemployed workers" that tilts the employment relation in favor of the employer. Moreover, even those individuals that remain employed will become increasing alienated in a commodified, capitalistic system. Marx used the term "alienation" to describe the situation in which individuals fail to grasp the nature of the social order in which they live because of their subordination to its demands. The situation in which no one produces what they consume or consumes what they produce would become a source of frustration and disenfranchisement for the working class in the Marxian critique. Alienation distorts our vision of the losses that result from our surrender to the commodity system and reduces our vigilance against an artificially imposed social order. We begin to use a new vocabulary of efficiency, rationality, and value in our evaluation of social provisioning.

The human experience of work is a central and defining element of Marxian thought. The post-industrial transformation of material by labor envisioned by Marx and his followers would restore to mankind the powers of self-expression and fulfillment that flow from social production but have been stolen from most workers by the hierarchical nature of the capitalistic labor market. Work would be imbued with an almost philosophical virtue as "to know the world, is to transform the world."

After solving the economic problem through a stint with capitalism, work could begin to assume a more social function for Marx. He offers a vision of a humanistic productive process in a postindustrial world:

> In my production, I would have had the direct satisfaction of the awareness of having satisfied a human need through my work ... I would have had the satisfaction of having acted as an intermediary between you and the human species ... Our products would be so many mirrors from which our being would shine out to us.
>
> Fetsher (1971: 37)

The operative term in Marx's statement in relation to work time is the *awareness* of satisfaction. Under the current division of labor, workers are rarely knowledgeable about the end-users of the products they produce. Perhaps more troubling, consumers know little about the products they consume or the conditions under which they are produced. This commodity fetishism is greatly reduced however when households are freed to engage in more activity in the third sector—home production, volunteerism, and community development. In producing and sharing vegetables, bread, ale, quilts, and other goods or services, they not only realize personal growth but achieve greater social integration. The Marxian approach therefore informs work time discussions by allowing us to differentiate between paid work and autonomous activity. A reduction of paid work hours becomes a means of engaging in the purposeful activities that give life meaning. Gorz (1994: 61) writes that work time reduction then takes on a social function as well as a pragmatic, macroeconomic function:

> Reducing working hours will not have a liberating effect, and will not change society, if it merely serves to redistribute work and reduce unemployment. The reduction of working hours is not merely a means of managing the system, it is also an end in itself in so far as it reduces the systemic constraints and alienations which participation in the social process imposes on individuals and in so far as, on the other hand, it expands the space for self-determined activities, both individual and collective.

It is useful to contemplate how a revamped social system might generate an alternative to a labor "market". Marx (1977: 178) writes "what distinguishes the worst of the architects from the best of the bees is this, that the architect raises his structure in imagination before he erects it in reality." In the Marxian ideal, work should become a means by which individuals may express and recognize their existence as social creatures. There would be a waning of the current incentives to work—poverty, avarice, and the coercion of society or religion—and workers will be drawn to work as if to a festival, carnival, arts project, humanitarian effort, or sporting event. Assured of the necessities of life, the protean worker would have more freedom to choose the type of work they enjoy most. Work hours would be short, and monotonous jobs could be changed frequently. Gibson (1990: 110) defines a free society as "one in which there is no social coercion compelling the individual to work." Other socialists would tolerate a moderate social compulsion to work in order to complete the servile and disagreeable tasks that would be shared by everyone in rotation. Yet, the drudgery of such tasks is expected to be greatly reduced by technological development and superior social planning. Socially directed work will become less feverish, less tyrannical, and more harmonious and rewarding. Tilgher (1977: 114) describes Marx's future society as one in which "the free worker will labor with the enthusiasm of the artist creating a thing of beauty, will be as eager as a fine athlete to beat all previous records, and in which production, nourished by these joyful life-forces, will race eagerly forward along the endless roads of illimitable progress."

Clearly, the continuing optimism of socialism rests with Marx's conviction that mankind's inescapable labor can become the means of its self-expression, rather than its self-imprisonment (Heilbroner 1980). It is not denied that such a transformation would be a Herculean undertaking, requiring significant authority over economic activity and outcomes. The prodigious apparatus of market society would have to adapt to a different set of objectives. If the work experience of socialism is to differ from that of capitalism, the structure and organization of both the productive process and society will have to be redesigned. In abolishing the work-based society, Gorz (1999: 78) writes:

> Social time and space will have to be organized to indicate the general expectation that everybody will engage in a range of different activities and modes of membership of the society. To indicate that the norm is for everyone to belong—or at least be able to belong—to a self-providing co-operative, a service exchange network, a scientific research and experiment group, an orchestra or a choir, a drama, dance or painting workshop, a sports club, a yoga or judo group, etc.; and that the aim within the sports or arts 'societies' is not to select, eliminate or rank individuals, but to *encourage each member to refresh and surpass him/ herself ever anew in competitive cooperation with the others, this pursuit of excellence by each being a goal common to all* [sic].

A first step in such a social reconstruction should be the regulation of work time as it goes to the heart of the dialectic conflict between capitalists and the working class. Marx's (1977: 412) view of work time determination remains apposite today, "The history of the regulation of the working day in certain branches of production, and the struggle still going on in others over this regulation, prove conclusively that the isolated worker, the worker as a 'free' seller of his labour-power, succumbs without resistance once capitalist production has reached a certain stage of maturity." Marx (1977: 334) made clear in his chapter on the working day in Capital, that work time is the principle instrument of exploitation wielded by the capitalist, "the establishment of a norm for the working day, presents itself as a struggle between collective capital, i.e. the class of capitalists, and collective labour, i.e. the working class." Thus, for Marx, the process of work time reduction was the result of a perpetual class struggle, driven by emerging social institutions and technological development.

It is extremely telling that Marx used time rather than output as a way of illustrating the source of surplus value. Marx called the time required to produce the daily means of subsistence "necessary labor time." He then defined "surplus labor time" as the additional time that workers were required to toil beyond "necessary labor time." The rate of exploitation, or surplus value, was then given by the ratio of surplus to necessary labor time. Regulating this avenue of exploitation represented an ongoing transformation of society toward a higher plane of social development. Marx (1977: 496) believed that work time reduction was an essential step in achieving a true realm of freedom; "the shortening of the working-day is its basic prerequisite."

The modern relevance of Marx's work is perhaps best seen in the many contemporary analyses of unemployment that focus on the class incentives revolving around the maintenance of a reserve army of unemployed workers.[1] Marxists suggest that capitalists will act against their own self-interest in order to protect their class interests. In kindred spirits with Marx, Michael Kalecki believed that the opposition to sustained full employment was driven by political motives related to class rather than economic principles. Kalecki (1943: 351) writes that:

> Obstinate ignorance is usually a manifestation of underlying political motives ... among 'economic experts' closely aligned with banking and industry ... With permanent full employment the sack would cease to play its role as a disciplinary measure. The social position of the boss would be undermined, and the self-assurance and class-consciousness of the working class would grow.

Kalecki points out that maintaining the power inequity is so important that the business class often forfeits profits in order to perpetuate the bargaining advantage it has over workers. Kalecki (1943: 351) contends that "discipline in the factories and political stability are more appreciated than profits by business leaders." History has shown that even the more-progressive capitalists have deferred to an irrational class interest when faced with hours regulation by the state. Commons (1921: 817) sites a Massachusetts debate over work time restrictions:

> In the Massachusetts hearings even the paper manufacturers who have already adopted the eight-hour day in competition with others on the twelve-hour day nevertheless, with one exception, opposed state legislation requiring their competitors to adopt it. Their objection is incomprehensible from the standpoint of self-interest. It can only be explained from a standpoint of class interest. They oppose a law which would benefit themselves individually because they stand by other employers who would not be benefited by it.

As long as the business class wields its disparate political clout, counteracting an economic slump by means of stimulating private investment will not result in lasting full employment and the largesse offered to employers to maintain employment will have to become increasingly generous.[2] Kalecki (1943) argues that after successive recessions the interest rate would have to fall to negative and the income tax would have to be replaced with an income subsidy to encourage employers to stabilize their payrolls. According to Kalecki (1943: 353), traditional aggregate demand stimulus becomes problematic when "the entrepreneur remains the medium through which the intervention is conducted." Wage subsidies to employers and income and job guarantees that leave the employer's ability to Balkanize the labor market intact will not tighten labor markets sufficiently. By definition, labor underutilization will persist until workers can achieve their desired work hours. The underutilization of labor, as well as the concurrent problem of overwork, will only be improved by reducing labor market segmentation. Since work time regulation directly influences the division of labor and the worker's interaction with the employer, it is the most expedient and effective means of curtailing labor market segmentation and granting workers the wherewithal to attain their desired work time regimes.

Gilman (1965: 233) likewise admonished that "as long as private enterprise predominates in an economy, so long will the drive toward private accumulation of capital remain the controlling factor of the rates of investment and employment." Gilman's (1965) solution to the conditions of growing unemployment and economic crises is the absorption of the "uninvestible" social surplus by means of increased social spending and a shortened work week without reduction in pay. Gilman suggests that the most essential reform of the New Deal era was one that was not aimed at increasing mass consumption—the move from the 50-hour work week to 40 hours. Gilman (1965: 100) writes:

The commonsense rationale for this action was the "share-the-work" slogan, but fundamentally the effect was to reduce the excess surplus-value which a fifty-hour work week was then capable of producing. The alternative was to keep twelve to fifteen million workers from producing surplus-value. Cyclical unemployment had always been a means of halting the accumulation of uninvestible social surplus, but at the unemployment rate precipitated in the 1930's, this traditional means had become *politically* [sic] intolerable. A reduction of work hours had become imperative if capitalism was to be saved from the Midas curse of its potentially overwhelming riches.

The average American workweek has been rather recalcitrant since the New Deal reforms, although there has been a greater polarization from the average. Instead of the productivity gains of the last five decades flowing into greater leisure, capitalists used their substantial political clout and advertising persuasion in an effort to eliminate the "uninvestible social surplus" through greater consumption and the regular maintenance of moderate unemployment.

Political motives against full employment have remained intact under the growth consensus. Consequently, prodigious government spending and subsidies have been needed to stimulate a level of investment that approaches full employment. Marxian economists generally subscribe to a "social conflict theory" that questions the effectiveness of aggregate demand policy due to its dependence on the state of the relative bargaining power of the two opposing classes (Rowthorn 1977; Goldthorpe 1978). Through the autonomy they exercise over investment decisions, capitalists wield tremendous influence over politicians, employment levels and their own incomes. Short of a large-scale socialization of investment, employment policy intent on reversing the capitalist's bargaining advantage requires direct regulation of working conditions. Full employment programs that fail to improve the workers' bargaining position beyond a tightening of the economic system essentially retain the entrepreneur's role as the medium of government intervention. In order to achieve lasting employment gains, labor market policy must reduce the class conflict between workers and employers. Aggregate demand policies might be targeted on the least privileged workers, but the temporary (in the case of buffer stock employment) and the growth-dependent nature (in the case of both income and job guarantees) of the programs yield little improvement in the power imbalance between workers and capitalists. This is particularly true when make-work programs are designed to have minimal impact on inflation as they must maintain a certain level of labor market segmentation in order to curtail the wage demands that arise from the additional government spending. The regulation of work hours, however, offers the prospect of significantly reducing labor market segmentation as it goes to the source of the conflict between the capitalist and the worker.

The Institutionalist approach to unemployment

The Institutionalist approach to unemployment is in many ways a hybrid of the Marxian and post-Keynesian views. Institutionalists generally accept the post-Keynesian premise that macroeconomic stimulus can ameliorate some of the suffering related to unemployment, but they also contend that fiscal responses alone are incapable of addressing the inherent power structures and institutions within capitalism that often result in the social mismanagement of resources. Generally, Institutionalists have been more concerned with increasing economic participation and improving the life process than maximizing paid work per se. Stanfield (1999: 240) writes, "by extending participation, a democratic culture draws from a larger pool of society's skill and insight, first, in the tinkering from which scientific and technical advances flow, and, second in grappling with the problems of institutional adjustment."

For Clarence Ayres and the Institutionalists, the failure of conventional wisdom to grasp the pervasive and powerful force of technological development has led to a misplaced emphasis on the market's ability to ensure widespread socioeconomic participation. According to Ayres (1935), the material arts were the foundation of Western civilization, not the market. Capital accumulation was engendered by the continuous development of technical efficiency—an expansion of matter-of-fact knowledge through a continuous process of material culture. The market was a deliberate collection of regulating institutions: "property, the price system, rent rolls, and loans at interest—these institutions are important so far as they define the reservoirs of accumulation and the channels of permissive use; but they no more account for the existence of the excess they regulate than a dam accounts for rainfall (189–90)." In the Veblen–Ayres tradition, technology—which grew of its own inherent nature—became the dynamic force in social evolution. Mainstream economic thought falsely identified the growth of the market economy as a precondition of industrial technological development, when it was likely the reverse (Ayres 1944). The consolidation of private enterprise within a market system was but one way of structuring the large-scale capital investments required by the technological discoveries of the Industrial Age. While Marx viewed the social pressure toward work time reduction as an impetus for the employer to increase automation, Institutionalists envisioned the development of the machine process as a continuous phenomenon that provided for the continual re-assessment of the social division of labor.

Recognizing technological development as the true source of progress allowed Ayres (1961) to espouse a democratic welfare state as the preferred political-economic system because it drew most broadly upon the skills and attributes of the entire population. To make such a claim, Ayres had to abandon long-standing notions of a conflict between economic security and incentive toward purposeful action. Furtherance of the life process did not depend on the consumption sacrifices and risk-taking of the wealthy. On the contrary, the wealth and income inequality perpetuated by the "veneration of savings" was inimical to economic progress. Ayres held that under-consumption was the principal source of instability and the main obstacle to full employment. Insufficient consumption stems from an inequitable dis-tribution of income, and therefore the solution is to be found in the redis-tribution of income from those that save too much to those that would consume more. The extent of the income redistribution should be governed by macroeconomic objectives; redistribution should increase consumption until all output at full employment is absorbed. The amount that should be seized from the rich is exactly equal to the amount of savings in excess of investment. Ayres (1938: 84) writes that the "pressure of excess funds at the top is directly proportional to the consumptive vacuum at the bottom." According to Ayres (1944), redistribution could eliminate recessions and create a new age of economic progress. Once redistribution has taken place, the multiplier "does all the rest (Ayres 1944: 274)."

Although Ayres (1946) acknowledged that the government was capable of printing money to bolster personal spending or public works to stabilize the economy, he argued that such an approach did not address the excess of saving untaken by the wealthy and could therefore be inflationary. Financing government spending with progressive income taxes could absorb the redundant savings, but in the case of public works programs the economy would progressively become socialized. This led Ayres (1944: 277) to his favored redistribution program—a guaranteed annual income financed by a progressive income tax designed to "recapture and reactivate sequestered funds." Sequestration occurred through "spurious investment and outright hoarding" (Ayres 1944: 109). Spurious investment took place when a finan-cial investment resulted in no increase in real investment. Explaining why greater savings does not lead to greater investment, Ayres (1944: 109) writes:

> Faulty distribution of income permits (and even obliges) some funds to be accumulated for which no real investment in actual capital goods can be made. This impediment is due to the deficiency of consumer pur-chasing power, a deficiency which is caused by the excess flow of funds into large incomes and is precisely commensurate to it.

According to Ayres, economic growth was not contingent on the savings of the wealthy, but rather excessive money savings were inimical to growth. Economic growth in credit-based economies is self-financing. Credit is cre-ated based on the assets that the credit brings into existence, so the financing of investment is largely a matter of paper transactions (Ayres 1946: 1961).

In 1952, Ayres outlined his plan for a guarantee annual income, making him the earliest modern proponent of such a policy (Walker 1979). In order for it to serve as a non-inflationary policy of redistribution, a critical compo-nent of Ayres's plan was that it be financed by progressive income taxes. But since hoarding and spurious investment are difficult to detect, the amount to be taken directly from the wealthy would be impossible to pinpoint. Tax flows from the rich would vary, and taxation would have to err on the side of caution in order to avoid an economic contraction. Ayres relied on economic growth to offset the variable nature of excess savings and to ensure that full employment was attained without overtaxing the rich. Although progressive taxes could contain some of the inflationary effects of government spending, a guaranteed annual income was clearly reliant on greater consumption and production to eliminate unemployment. While advocating a guaranteed income, Ayres (1943: 480) wrote, "The citizens of industrial society must consume more abundantly ... because if they do not industrial society will collapse." However, regulating work hours may be a superior redistribution tool than a guaranteed income, as the side effects of greater economic growth are far more obvious today. Since work time regulation clearly influences access to income and consumption it can serve as an effective way of reactivating the sequestered funds of the overworked in order to achieve full employment. But since work time regulation may also be used to reduce the surplus output that needs to be absorbed at full employment, it is more consistent with modern conceptions of economic progress that place less emphasis on material throughput. Ayres (1961: 235) likely would approve of the idea of using work time regulation as a redistributive tool as he viewed an American economy of abundance and was willing to "be done with the bugaboo of scarcity."

The goal of greater socioeconomic participation

Economists of the radical tradition (Institutionalists, Marxist, Feminists, etc.) have long recognized the "non-market" virtues that individuals offer the economic system. These heterodox approaches place more store on increasing social inclusion than maximizing output or total work hours. The humanistic goal of improved socioeconomic participation proves useful in devising full employment policies that are not contingent on greater throughput and are therefore more compatible with "green" approaches to social provisioning. Such an alternative approach forces one to acknowledge that unemployment is a definitional concept which is inextricably tied to our social definition of what is an acceptable attachment to the labor force and what jobs are appropriate for paid work. From time to time societies have erected limits to the types of activities and products that could be provisioned for pay. Many of the most intimate and meretricious activities, such as love and sex, have long been excluded from social definitions of paid work. Social mores have also led to the regulation of an individual's attachment to the labor force. The prohibition of childhood labor, regulation of wages and hours, and the granting of retirement status all manifest an evolving social concept of acceptable labor force participation. The principle thesis explored here is that society should continue to regulate paid work in order to strike a better balance between socioeconomic participation and self-interested wealth maximization.

For Institutionalist economists, any serious economic theory must consist of two elements. First, there must be an acknowledgement of an evolutionary adjustment process. Second, the theory should lead to a furtherance of the life process—"doing more things or doing them better." In the context of full employment policy, reliance on threadbare Keynesian spending programs fails to acknowledge the evolution toward an abundant post-industrial economy in which the need for physical work is less urgent. In an abundant society, more production is capable of doing more harm than good when measured by life satisfaction and ecological sustainability. This relates to the second principle in that blind devotion to more material throughput may lead to society doing more but with little betterment to mankind.

A close reading of Institutionalist writings on the subject of "participation" suggests that a prudent employment policy would incorporate more than a stimulation of aggregate demand intent on increasing employment and industrial output. Absent prudent labor market regulations; stimulating the economy may only result in current workers toiling longer and harder, reducing their socioeconomic participation without increasing the participation of the involuntarily unemployed and underemployed. In his analysis of the Institutionalist approach to distribution and economic progress, Peach (1987: 1500) writes that individuals are "poor because the institutional (or distributional) arrangements of society have not adjusted to the productive potential of the economic system." Since Veblen's recognition of the "incredible productivity" of modern industrial society, Institutionalists have embraced a view of an abundant society, where, due to the accumulation of technological knowledge, extremes of inequality are not necessary. In this view, degrading and disenfranchising poverty is not a result of society's inability to produce goods and services in sufficient quantities or of a scarcity of resources, but rather due to institutional inhibitions that perpetuate a system of income distribution in accordance with status.

The Institutionalist approach to the distribution of general economic resources is highly relevant to the issue of work time reform because a better distribution of work hours is more likely to provide relief to marginalized workers than a consumption-driven expansion of economic throughput that would largely result in longer hours for relatively well-off fulltime workers. Greater socioeconomic participation is likely to foster human development and social advancement. Stanfield (1999: 240) advances the alternative vision of greater social inclusion, "once clearly understood, the next step is to convert the welfare state into the Creative State that celebrates and mandates universal and diverse participation toward the greatest possible achievement and progress." Consistent with the Institutionalist approach, Bertrand Russell (1935: 25) recognized the centrality of work time reduction in promoting human flourishing, "In a world where no one is compelled to work more than four hours a day, every person possessed of scientific curiosity will be able to indulge it ... and since they will not depend upon these pursuits for their livelihood, their originality will be unhampered."

The Institutionalist goal of enhanced socioeconomic participation is better suited to post-industrial economies as it emphasizes a process of technological development and institutional change designed to further the life process, without relying on greater material throughput. Greater participation not only captures the contributions of the previously unemployed, but also those previously discouraged from a callous labor market. More individuals may choose to participate in the paid workforce if humane and bilaterally flexible hours are offered to workers. By expanding the aggregate supply of labor, work time reduction could bring forth more human capital to be mixed with greater physical capital for longer operating periods to achieve greater efficiency and material sufficiency. As individual working times are shortened, firms will be pressured to decouple working time from operating hours. Operating hours can then be extended to improve the cost efficiency of the capital stock. In addition to greater industrial efficiency, the demonstration effect of having more people participating in society can lead to a greater human flourishing and furtherance of the life process. The view is philosophically consonant with John Ruskin's (1860: 105) worldview as expressed in his description of wealth:

> There is no wealth but life. Life including all its powers of love, of joy, and of admiration. That country is richest with nourishes the greatest number of noble and happy human beings; that man is richest who, having perfected the functions of his own life to the utmost, has also the widest helpful influence, both personal, and by means of his possessions, over the lives of others.

All too often, the contributions of Institutionalists on economic participation have been misinterpreted into a paean for greater paid work. In an attempt to "fit" the Institutionalist interpretation of enhanced participation into contemporary, market-based ideology, many scholars have yielded to the temptation of achieving greater economic "participation" through an expansion of remunerative employment (Tool 1998). By extension, it is often suggested by economists that the chief cause of poverty and other social problems is unemployment. However, the sociological literature suggests that marital divorce is the single largest "cause" of poverty (Heath and Kiker 1992; Arditti 1997). Furthermore, an examination of the US labor force relative to the population suggests that unemployment is not the salient cause of poverty as there are substantial numbers of individuals that are not in the labor force who do not live in poverty while far too many employed individuals are impoverished. This suggests that poverty is caused by a lack of access to income, but not necessarily "earned" income. Indeed, the low incidence of poverty among the aged—due to the success of Social Security—suggests that remunerative work is not the only way to increase the economic participation of population subgroups. Figure 3.1 clearly shows that tens of millions of American homemakers, students, artists, retirees, and

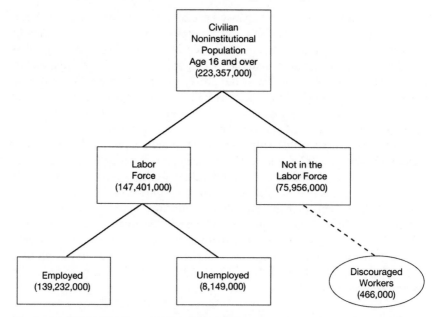

Figure 3.1 US Labor Force Proportions (2003)
Source: Bureau of Labor Statistics, Employment and Earnings (January 2005).

unpaid volunteers would beg to differ with the prevailing sentiment that paid work is a necessary condition to achieve a sense of personal identity, character, and social status. Prasch (2002) cites a great diversity of activities conducted outside the paid labor market to refute ideological arguments in favor of wage subsidies that are based on employment being essential to the social status and self-esteem of workers. Jenkins and Sherman (1979: 141) dismiss the importance of work in fostering human character and social status:

> We do not believe that [paid] work per se is necessary to human survival or self-esteem. The fact that it appears to be so is a function of two centuries of propaganda and an educational system which maintained the 'idea' of work as its main objective, but which singularly failed to teach about leisure and how to use it … This need for [paid] work is, we would argue, an ingrained and inculcated attitude of mind.

Paradoxically, the paean to the virtues of paid work is quickly abandoned at the first suggestion of severing social benefits from the obligation to work. Skeptical of the intrinsic merits of work, socioeconomic policies routinely guard against weakening the incentive to work. Gorz (1999: 98) offers a sarcastic commentary, "work isn't actually so attractive, gratifying, satisfying or integrating that you don't need to give people 'incentives' by setting benefit rates for the unemployed at a level below subsistence income."

Although it is true that in many of the less-forgiving capitalistic societies, individuals and families are largely responsible for their own fate and that failure to obtain paid work has a dire impact on the unemployed, it is not true that this must be, and always will be, the case. Societies are always capable of devising alternative ways of distributing the dividends of the social product. Indeed, for public policy to be truly progressive and sustainable it will have to address the structural changes occurring in post-industrial societies by recasting the emphasis placed on paid work.

Current market societies manifest a disconnect between the usefulness of individuals as consumers, voters, nurturers, volunteers, and citizens and the value we place on them as workers. Remunerative work—be it the tangible bias of production or the questionable "service" of persuasive advertising—is engrained in our social psyche as an activity worthy of reward. Unpaid work is treated as far less valuable. The disparate treatment is patent in many public policies and programs in the industrialized world. Governments have increasingly made employment a condition of material and physical well-being, ostensibly signaling that individuals are valued more for their productive qualities than their many other social attributes.[3] Despite technological advance and labor specialization that have rendered possible an improved distribution of a larger social dividend, paid work has become a prerequisite to economic participation in many growth-obsessed societies. However, the link between paid work and economic participation is under serious threat in post-industrial economies as globalization and technological unemployment have inflamed labor market inequities and threatened to deepen the chasm between the haves and the have-nots. Eventually society will have to address the growing numbers of excluded and disenfranchised workers by increasing their participation in a socially and environmentally sustainable fashion.

As post-industrial production techniques reduce the relative amount of labor demanded by employers, how will individuals continue to participate in the economy? How will they obtain the means to be effective members of a socioeconomic system that requires fewer workers? As the urgency and primacy of paid work evaporates, the distribution of the means of social participation will need to be commensurate with the volume of wealth socially produced rather than the quantity of work performed. A greater societal recognition of the usefulness of individuals as consumers, parents, volunteers, companions, household producers, or merely engaged citizens is essential in eroding the link between employment and socioeconomic participation. A rethinking of the division of socially necessary labor should be the basis of a comprehensive employment policy that is intent on increasing socioeconomic participation rather than simply creating jobs for employment sake alone.

Consistent with the role of material transformation fostering self-expression in Marxian thought, the goal of reduced work time is not a condemnation of purposeful effort for Institutionalists. Indeed, Veblen pursued a similar objective to Marx—a deliquescence of the capitalist labor market hierarchy, which would remove much of the irksomeness of labor and allow mankind's instinct of workmanship to flourish. Veblen and his followers also envisioned a world of abundance flowing from the technological march of the machine process. The waning urgency of material needs meant that society would need to increasingly focus on the institutional barriers to a rich and reward-ing life. The implication of our instinct for workmanship is that a freedom from the obligation of paid work does not entail a diminution of purposeful activity.

In the context of regulating work time in post-industrial economies, the Institutionalist concern of properly situating the economy in the larger social structure is quite useful. In particular, Polanyi's promotion of an economic methodology that subordinates economic forces to the fundamental objec-tives of individual freedom and development serves as a valuable lodestar when considering alternative social provisioning schemes. As Stanfield (1986: 25) writes, "Polanyi's conviction was that the good economy is one that provisions the lives of individuals, provides for their fullest development, and does so without disrupting or distorting those lives or their development." The broad thesis of this book is that the clash between "lives" and "liveli-hood" has become considerably inflamed in the developed world and that work time regulation governed by an instrumental value theory should be implemented as a preferred method of ameliorating that conflict.

The emphasis on the *regulation* of work time in balancing the social effort bargain was suggested by another Institutionalist economist renowned for his work in labor economics—John Commons. Commons suggested that the regulation of hours might be used to stabilize output and employment.[4] Commons (1969: 71) writes:

> Elasticity has to be provided somewhere to meet the fluctuations [in labor demand]. The elasticity may be provided by laying off a part of the force in hard times and taking them back in good times, or by reducing hours all around in hard times and increasing them in goods times. The one method is the method of unemployment for some, the other the method of distributing unemployment and regularizing employment for all.

Although sparsely explored by Commons and his students, this chapter endeavors to show that prudent work time regulation could be used as a macroeconomic policy tool to achieve much more than a softening of unemployment.[5] In addition to tightening labor markets to achieve full employment, regulating average working times in concert with productivity increases could bring about greater price stability and more stable and sus-tainable levels of economic activity. Thus, work time regulation should be viewed as macroeconomic policy rather than simply labor market regulation. Hours regulation should become a central policy tool to influence the social effort bargain over employment, price stability and sustainable economic output.

The fiscal feasibility of a fully employed economy

In contemplating full-employment programs, it is important to recognize that governments are not fiscally constrained in an under-utilized economy. Although the government is capable of fully funding a shift to full employment, its primary role should be to influence the social effort bargain to achieve social objectives while maintaining as much distributive neutrality as possible. In the case of a work time reduction, government fiscal policy should be used to balance productivity gains, wage concessions from workers, and profit concessions from employers to achieve some distributive neutrality among the various social partners. Government spending has played a significant role in work time reduction experiments to date. Policymakers have used fiscal spending to offset payroll expansion costs that were not defrayed initially by productivity gains or wage concessions to achieve some distributive neutrality in the wake of work time reform. For instance, in an effort to appease French employers and environmentalists alike, France's 35-hour law used taxes on polluting sectors—chemicals, metals, and energy—to finance reduced payroll taxes on the hiring of low-income workers. Moreover, short time compensation programs (outlined in Chapter 5) have utilized unemployment compensation benefits to encourage the take-up of shorter hours in lieu of layoffs.

Although collective negotiation over the distributive effects of work time reductions and taxation burdens is important, it should not be governed by traditional notions of fiscal austerity. Under a "Chartalist" or "State money" approach to fiscal management, the sovereign issuer of a currency faces few restraints on its ability to spend money, particularly at less than full employment. Keynes (1923: 67) reminds us that, "the creation of legal tender has been and is a government's ultimate reserve; and no state or government is likely to decree its own bankruptcy or its own downfall so long as this instrument still lies at hand unused." Typically only federal governments possess the power to collect taxes and define that which legally discharges money contracts and tax liabilities. Unlike state and municipal governments or members of a common currency (such as the Euro), the sovereign issuer of a currency is less beholden to credit markets. The widespread use of non-convertible, fiat money in modern credit-based economies means that a monopoly issuer of currency that possesses a sovereign right to tax is at great liberty to regulate its fiscal spending to achieve macroeconomic objectives (Wray 1998). It is critically important, therefore, that work time reform be funded at the proper level of government. Since US state governments and Euro-member countries do not issue their own currency, they must align their expenditures within a certain ratio of their tax revenues in order to appease credit markets. But, as the fiscal management of the United States government has proven time and again, the normal or routine fiscal position for a federal (or currency-issuing) government can be one of deficit. Although currency-*using* governments can and do run deficits for extended periods of time, their persistence and magnitude are extremely restrained relative to those that can be achieved by currency-*issuing* governments.

The "Chartalist" or "state money" approach to government spending finds its genesis in Abba Lerner's doctrine of "functional finance." Lerner extended the work of Knapp and others to argue that there is no need for policy-makers to cower to the nostrums of "sound finance" in the implementation of full-employment policies and programs. Lerner (1943: 471) refers to this "breach with tradition" when he writes:

> Spending by the government must be regarded not as something to be done when it can be afforded ... but as a regular and painless way of maintaining prosperity, to be undertaken when the society is poor on account of unemployment ... Taxes must be regarded not as a means to which the government has to resort in order to get money ... but as merely a device for reducing the income and therefore also the expenditures of members of society. The quantity of money must be regarded not as something to be regulated strictly according to the sacred rules of some gold standard ... but as something that is of no account in itself ... completely subservient to the rules for maintaining the right amount of spending and investment. An increase in government debt must be regarded not as a measure of last resort ... but as a matter of very little consequence ... completely subjected to the rules for maintaining prosperity and preventing inflation.

Under "functional finance" fiscal policy is not hamstrung by traditional financial doctrines about what is sound and unsound. The government may run fiscal surpluses or deficits for long periods of time. Lerner writes (1943: 470) "in neither case should the government feel that there is anything especially good or bad about this result; it should merely concentrate on keeping the total rate of spending neither too small nor too great, in this way preventing both unemployment and inflation." Adopting function finance would not entail a large expansion of national debt since "full employment can be maintained by printing the money needed for it (Lerner 1943: 471)." Taxation then assumes importance as an automatic stabilizer rather than a source of revenue generation and would be used interdependently with monetary policy to influence the rate of spending. Lerner (1943: 470) suggests that:

> Taxation therefore should only be imposed when it is desirable that the taxpayers shall have less money to spend, for example, when they would otherwise spend enough to bring about inflation ... No matter what unimaginable heights the national debt might reach ... No matter how much interest has to be paid on the debt, taxation must not be applied unless it is necessary to keep spending down to prevent inflation ... The interest can be paid by borrowing still more.

Although such statements may sound heretical to financial markets, judicious government spending that increases socioeconomic participation, investment, employment and private wealth will result in greater tax revenue to offset the debt-financed spending. There is no reason to fear crowding-out caused by the private sector (households and firms) refusing to lend to the government. From a macroeconomic prospective, the private sector is faced with the choice to hoard or spend their money. If they hoard, the government is still able to print money to meet its payment obligations. The only effect is that the private sector is now holding non-interest government liabilities (cash) instead of interest-bearing government bonds and the government saves the interest payments. If the private sector spends its cash, then the government does not need to and its "financing needs"—printing money or borrowing—are diminished. If consumer and investment spending are robust enough, then taxing can commence to reduce inflation and principal payments can be made to reduce the level of public debt. Moreover, it is likely that full employment would actually "crowd in" higher levels of investment, minimizing the need for government spending. There could also be portfolio effects that have an expansionary effect on private spending. That is, the greater is the private wealth held in government bonds, the less incentive to add to wealth by saving out of current income and the more available for current consumption by the private sector. Again, the higher private spending then makes the achievement of full employment possible with lower government spending. Lerner (1943: 472) acknowledges that, "there is an automatic tendency for the budget to be balanced in long run ... even if there is no place for the *principle* of balancing the budget." The debt-financed infrastructure expenditures made in the United States in the early 1990s that contributed to the largely unintentional fiscal surpluses of the Clinton Administration in the late 1990s offers a recent example of the fiscal relationships that Lerner envisioned.

Regulating government fiscal operations with the "functional" objective of achieving full employment need not create price pressures. Indeed, Lerner (1943: 469) is mindful of demand pull inflation when he advises governments "to keep the rate of spending in the country on goods and services neither greater nor less than that rate which at the current prices would buy all the goods that it is possible to produce ... by all who want to work." Notice that the target level of spending for Lerner is a "socially defined" full employment of resources. Lerner warns that the "instinctive revulsion" against printing money is the tendency to identify it with inflation. Yet, the printing of money is distinct from the spending of it, and as more money is hoarded, more can be printed without triggering inflation. In summation, the "functional finance" or "state money" view suggests that the monopoly issuer of a currency possesses the fiscal prowess to achieve socioeconomic objectives such as full employment with little need to appease financial markets or conservative doctrines of fiscal discipline. Currency-issuing governments are not debt-constrained in their ability to spend to achieve full employment, but they must be mindful of not igniting excessive demand-pull inflation by spending too far beyond the full-employment threshold.

Like Abba Lerner and the contemporary Chartalist movement, Institutionalists express little concern for the fiscal costs related to achieving full employment. Most Institutionalists subscribe to Foster's (1981: 966) maxim that "whatever is technically feasible is financially possible." Institutionalists rarely allow parsimonious concerns over capital scarcity to stand in the way of genuine human progress. Ayres (1952) employed the phrase the "myth of capital" to admonish against confusing the role of physical capital (technology and knowledge) with the accumulation of money. The myth was built on the notion that "the whole progress of opulence seemed to derive from the fecundity of money (Ayres 1952: 110)." For both Ayres and Veblen, the productive potential of the economy resulted from society's accumulated knowledge of how to produce: that is, a continuous development of the technological arts and crafts. While mainstream economics attributes physical capital to the accumulation of savings and foregone consumption, Ayres (1944: 49) counters that "no one secretes steel rails by going without lunch." In his pillory of savings-based growth policies and the encouragement of personal savings, Ayres (1944: 52) further explains that, "funds are accumulated not because some people are more abstemious than others, or more far-sightedly prone to idealize the sweet by-and-by, but because some people are richer than others, and for no other reason." In other words, despite the best efforts of the rich, they cannot consume in sufficient quantities to avoid saving. Savings are the result of inequality, not differing time preferences for consumption or the outcome of prudent fiscal policy.

According to Ayres, the reliance of savings on income inequality contributed to economic instability rather than growth. Near the end of the Great Depression, Ayres argued that "the present extreme discrepancy in the distribution of income" was the chief cause of the economic instability. In contrast to Keynes, Ayres' solution to economic instability was not greater aggregate demand, but greater income equality, which would allow for higher levels of consumption but in a less volatile fashion. For Institutionalists economic progress results from society's accumulated technical knowledge of how to produce, not from the savings of inequitably distributed incomes. Indeed DeGregori's (1973: 261) summary of the Institutionalist approach is apposite: "development is a process of doing, not abstaining."

Many advocates of work time reduction devote substantial energies devising tax revenue schemes to help "pay" for the more egalitarian sharing of wealth and work (Gorz 1999; Hayden 1999; Rifkin 2000). They propose higher taxes on activities that lead to financial instability, environmental damage or social disintegration. Yet, "functional finance" and the Institutionalists' recognition that whatever is technically and politically feasible is also financially possible, frees work time reform from the need to engage in "budget scoring" (Foster 1981). A "Tobin tax" or an "eco-social VAT" may be useful in encouraging socially benevolent behavior, but they are not necessary to fund comprehensive work time reform in an under-employed economy. Any currency-issuing government possesses the financial prowess to exert a profound influence on the distribution of wealth and work within a society, and need not be held hostage by the prejudicial conventions of financial markets. If government spending is used prudently—to achieve greater socioeconomic participation—it will not lead to excessive levels of government debt, inflation, or crowding out.

A comparative assessment of full-employment programs

Given their view that the bulk of unemployment is involuntary and that governments are not debt-constrained by a scarcity of capital, heterodox economists have espoused a variety of full-employment programs. This section compares and contrasts two of the most popular proposals—job and income guarantees—with a program of work time regulation in order to assess the potential for hours regulation to serve as a macroeconomic policy tool. Although work time regulation is by no means a panacea for every macroeconomic shortcoming, its superiority over any other single policy in achieving the macroeconomic objectives of greater socioeconomic participation, stable and sustainable economic output and price stability is rendered evident by a comparative analysis of competing programs.

Job guarantees versus work time regulation

Recently, job guarantees have re-emerged among post-keynesian economists as a way of achieving a more direct labor market intervention than fiscal stimulus alone (Wray 1998). Also known as the buffer stock employment model, the program posits that government manages a buffer stock of unemployed workers by providing jobs to all those willing and able to work for a living wage. The chief virtue of a job guarantee is its ability to quickly create jobs. A government policy of directly employing the jobless could certainly be viewed as expedient. It is also likely to be the most appropriate fiscal spending target for developing countries suited to Abba Lerner's "Functional Finance," as it can ensure adequate spending levels during slack times and reduced spending during robust economic activity. Accordingly, a buffer stock employment program represents a vast improvement over the current application of the "non-accelerating inflation rate of unemployment" (or NAIRU) in assisting developing countries to target the proper level of government spending needed to achieve low unemployment with minimal risk of demand-pull inflation. For the industrialized democracies of the world, however, a buffer stock model has many important disadvantages relative to a regulation of work hours. In light of the drawbacks delineated in this section, an alternative labor market policy that uses the government's fiscal prowess and regulatory powers to influence the social effort bargain surrounding

working time may be a more effective, sustainable and certainly more equitable, way of increasing socioeconomic participation.

One of the most troubling aspects of job guarantees is the promotion of
greater work and consumption. By furthering the "work fetish" and the "gospel
of consumption," a job guarantee strengthens and expands the capitalist's
sphere of influence in everyday life (Cowdrick 1927). With its emphasis on
more remunerative employment, as governed by exchange value, the buffer
stock employment model addresses the social ill of unemployment by introducing what many would consider another social pathology—growth of the
consumer culture. Perpetuating the market mentality by expanding aggregate
work hours further strengthens the capitalists' position in the dialectic
struggle between capital and labor and represents a contraction of the
worker's "space for development" (Marx 1991: 493).

Like nearly all macroeconomic policy since the Industrial Revolution, the
buffer stock model is guided by the pursuit of economic growth and paid
work. The buffer stock is designed to absorb employment from the private
sector and employ the workers at similar tasks so that they can be rehired by
private firms at a later stage. By virtue of the fact that the buffer stock model
temporarily employs workers until they can be rehired by the private sector,
the program will have to offer jobs that are of private value, but not necessarily public worth. The activities undertaken by buffer stock workers will
have to be governed by exchange value rather than use value. This precludes
public good functions (such as environmental clean-up), leaving activities
that were previously provided by households or the community via the third
sector as prime candidates for "privatization." As such, the operation of a
buffer stock expands output and the reach of the market, bringing with it the
potential for relative public decay, environmental damage, growth of a consumer culture and inflationary pressures. Joan Robinson, one of the earliest
"post-Keynesians," was herself solicitous of suffering a work fetish. Robinson
(1969: xi) pondered the zealous pursuit of employment growth:

> If we are to be guaranteed full employment in any case, the question to be
> discussed is what the employment should be for. Do we want more
> investment or more consumption? If more investment, should it be in
> the infra-structure of industry – the supply of power, transport and
> communications-should it be in private profit-seeking business or should
> it be in the improvement of social services-education, health, housing- and
> general amenities? If more consumption, should it be to reduce poverty
> or to give everyone a proportionate share? These deep divisive questions
> are smoothed over by the making of employment an end in itself.

In terms of Keynes's three ingredients for full employment, a buffer stock
model (as distinct from permanent public sector employment) owes its success
at achieving full employment largely to the "first aid" of greater consumption.
In a post-industrial setting, however, any policy dependent on more

consumption is likely to inflame the social and ecological costs of indiscriminate economic growth outlined in Chapter 4.

A buffer stock scheme essentially redefines unemployment by expanding the functions of paid work. Since the buffer stock is not limited to the permanent employment of workers in the provision of public goods, it will have to expand the social definition of acceptable market work. It is not denied that greater throughput, at some magnitude, could eventually reduce unemployment to inconsequential levels. Yet, in a post-industrial economy of declining job opportunities, the redefinition of work and consequent expansion of output will have to be both prodigious and perpetual. Stubbornly high levels of labor under-utilization in some industrialized countries suggest that the level of economic expansion will need to be in excess of 10 to 15 percent of real GDP growth per year in order to ameliorate existing labor surpluses and to continually absorb the technologically unemployed.

Job guarantee proponents recognize this as a potential drawback to greater throughput. Cowling *et al.* (2003: 12) write, "while higher levels of output are required to increase employment, the composition of output is a pivotal policy issue." To soften the social and ecological impact of this greater throughput, job guarantee advocates claim that make-work jobs could be environmentally sustainable, add value to the community, and promote upward mobility for current and future workers. Yet, if the private sector jobs they are temporarily replacing do not already possess such virtues, it is difficult to see how they will be imbued with these characteristics when they are performed in the public sector without re-defining the boundaries of work activities. Since the intention of the buffer stock is to temporarily employ workers and keep them trained for later private sector expansion, finding new tasks for them represents a permanent expansion of the functions of paid work. It is likely, however, that such job tasks will have to be permanently provided by the public sector as the private sector has little motivation to provide such socially beneficial functions.[6] Nels Anderson acknowledged the tendency for public employment to become permanent in his 1938 book *The Right to Work*. Anderson (1938: 65) links chronic unemployment to technological advance, "Technological advances in factory and office are constantly disemploying large numbers of workers, and despite assurances from American business that new industries will spring up, creating new occupations and new jobs, the truth is that such few new industries as there are do not want the unemployed from the relief rolls." If they are intent on maintaining full employment through job guarantees, governments will need to be prepared to permanently retain the bulk of unemployed workers on public work projects.

A permanent expansion of public sector employment could certainly be used to reverse the Galbraithian social imbalance of private opulence in the face of public squalor, but if it goes beyond the provision of public goods and the amelioration of market failure it will itself be contributing to the growth of the private sector and the need for more public expenditure. If the provision of public goods is a persistent and growing need—the refitting of "clean technology," for instance—then an appropriate response would be a permanent expansion of public sector hiring, not a buffer stock of temporary workers, who may disappear again when private sector hiring resumes. Thus, any full-employment program that entails an expansion of economic output works at cross purposes as it simultaneously causes social and ecological externalities that diminish well-being.

By contrast, work time regulation has the potential to reverse the Galbraithian social imbalance by reducing the scale of the private sector while expanding activities in the third sector. A redistribution of work time would afford the over-employed the time needed to partake more fully in the third sector, while the greater income received by the under-employed could help to increase their social involvement as well. Since work time reduction is a form of productivity dividend that does not necessitate more consumption and production in the private sphere, it would not exacerbate the social imbalance between public and private sector activities.

The difficulty surrounding the temporary nature of the buffer stock, has led some advocates to propose a bifurcated program with a "stable core buffer stock component and a flexible buffer stock" (Mitchell and Wray 2005: 240). As addressed below, wages of buffer-stock workers cannot be very attractive since low wages in the buffer stock serve to restrain the wage demands of primary sector workers. That is, primary sector workers will not demand higher wages if there is still some risk of having to accept a relatively lower buffer-stock wage. Effectively, a buffer stock model commits the government to achieving price stability by perpetuating the insider–outsider labor market segmentation that currently frustrates improved labor market outcomes. Assuming all buffer stock workers earn comparable wages, the stable core then becomes a permanent expansion of public sector employment at reduced wages. The risk of establishing and sustaining low-skilled, low-wage jobs has led Sawyer (2003: 888) to refer to the buffer stock plan as "underemployment or unemployment by another name." Permanent public sector employment at low wages might be preferable to chronic unemployment, but is clearly inferior to a redistribution of work time that results in an expansion of private sector payrolls at prevailing wages.

Full-employment programs that fabricate jobs also present ideological hurdles related to the growth of market activity. For better or worse, the growth of the "free market" has resulted in many household or third-sector activities being commodified. There is a very real risk that make-work programs will accelerate this trend as they search for activities that can be preformed initially by public sector workers and then be fully privatized when the economy expands. Indeed, many of the potential occupational activities that buffer stock proponents envision (companionship, safety and environmental supervision, daycare provision, etc.) are functions that are frequently provided through non-market mechanisms. Payment for such activities could easily corrupt the very meaning of non-market functions, pulling many caring and nurturing tasks into the orb of the market. Make-work programs run the risk of devolving into a program in which we are paid to "take in each others laundry" and the children and parents too! A full-employment model that succumbs to such "work fetishism" effectively redefines household production, volunteerism, and nurturing care as a market activity in order to fabricate jobs for the unemployed. It consequently puts its proponents in the uncomfortable position of facilitating the commodification of social activity or the "creep" of the free market into erstwhile non-market activities. Activities in the third sector should not be regarded as a source of paid work tasks to be colonized by the capitalist market economy or as a quid pro quo for basic income and social assistance.

In addition to the commercialization of social activities, make-work programs run the risk of creating ecological and social burdens that swamp the benefits generated by the employment gains. In the 1990s, a backlash emerged in Japan against "make-work" infrastructure projects such as dams, airports, and bridges that were characterized as state-sponsored degradation of the environment and local communities (Economist 1999). Given the social and ecological ramifications of public development projects, the expansion of infrastructure should be governed by necessity and sustainability, rather than a zeal for job creation. Anders Hayden (1999: 38) writes:

> An ecological approach demands that we refuse to create jobs artificially at the expense of nature and society, and that we begin the phase-out of unnecessary and destructive forms of production, from land mines to lawn chemicals ... Rather than furiously scrambling to make new work that is often meaningless and of low or no social utility, we should seek to share equitably the work that needs to done, the leisure dividend from the work we choose to no longer do, and the wealth generated.

As detailed in Chapter 4, ecological imperatives dictate that alternatives to make-work programs must be examined as a way to balance the convoluted social and ecological aspects of a fully employed economy. Thus, in a climate-constrained, post-industrial world—with its diminished need for workers—even a job guarantee program would be forced to implement a long-term trend toward work time reduction.

Aggregate demand will always be larger with a job guarantee as more people will be receiving wages for activities that were previously provided by the community, the household, or no one. Moreover, the capitalist has a strong motivation to ensure that future productivity increases are directed toward greater aggregate demand. Capitalists prefer that any productivity benefits that are shared with workers take the form of higher wages rather than reductions in work hours (Philp 2001). This is because higher wages entail greater consumption to absorb the increased output that has threatened the capitalist's planned scarcity or, in Veblenian terms, "capitalistic sabotage." The use of buffer stock wages rather than a redistribution of labor and leisure amounts to the government distributing the social product in the capitalists' favored form. The wage dividend perpetuates the inequities of the market system by inflaming the commodity fetish. Furthermore, it is naïve to think that the capitalists will maintain the status quo as the government expands output that competes with private sector sales. Since buffer stock work functions are governed by exchange value, a job guarantee would compete with the private sector in both input (labor and capital) markets and output markets. Insomuch as the increased output of buffer stock workers threatens the profitability that stems from both surplus labor and capitalistic sabotage, employers will truculently oppose the program and seek to maintain the labor market segmentation that is the source of their surplus labor extraction.

Although aggregate demand will always be larger with a job guarantee than without it, the question remains whether it will be large enough? If government spending is tied to unemployment and more unemployment is not forthcoming during an economic slowdown (due to a shift to part-time work, for instance), a job guarantee may not be able to stimulate spending sufficiently to bring the economy out of its doldrums. The recent economic slowdowns in Japan and the United States offer fruitful examples. Throughout the anemic economic growth of the 1990s the unemployment rate in Japan never rose above 5.5 percent. The situation has been similar in the United States where during recent recessions and the global financial crisis of 2008–09 unemployment has yet to rise above the levels recorded in the 1981– 83 recession. Given that the unemployed in these cases were such a small segment of the population, it is doubtful that providing them with a government paycheck could ensure that deficit spending was large enough to equate desired net savings with actual net savings and keep the economy out of recession. If a sufficient number of individuals do not feel the compulsion to work for a government paycheck during an economic contraction, the economic stimulus will have to take some other form. It is worth noting that roughly 35 percent of the working age population does not offer its labor for paid employment in most industrial countries. Moreover, if the "graying" of the baby-boomers results in the labor market shortages that are expected, using unemployment as a target for fiscal spending would be ill-advised as an underperforming economy could still have relatively tight labor markets.

In contrast to a job guarantee, work time regulation could reduce the overall sphere of influence of the marketplace, improving the bargaining position of the working class vis-à-vis the capitalist class. Linking future productivity increases to leisure payments instead of pecuniary payments, for example, could reduce the thirst for more mass-produced goods. If well-paid, part-time work (say 20 hours per week) became the norm there would be less scope for the capitalist to engage in exploitative tactics with any one worker. Under the right conditions, namely an equitable distribution of material necessities, the urgency of consumption in the private market could be diminished. This is not to deny that there would be some pressure toward speed-up or an intensification of work during the initial work time reductions, but such pressures would be forced to ease as labor markets tightened and the capitalist blunderbuss of unemployment and labor market segmentation was splintered.

The redistributive effects of work time regulation could offer greater stability to the economic system at lower levels of aggregate expenditure, including government spending. If economic contractions are caused by a poor distribution of income and consumption, as suggested by Ayres, work time regulation could effectively redress the distributional problems. Levitan and Belous (1977: 26) also extol the stabilizing virtues of work time regulation on the economic multiplier:

> When a recession hits, something has to give. If prices, wages, and workweeks show little adjustment, all weight is placed on production levels and the number of workers employed. The results have been huge gyrations in output and employment. The argument is that if more variables – such as work time – are allowed to absorb some of the shock, the oscillations of the pendulum will be smaller and equilibrium – including full employment and vigorous output will be restored at a far quicker pace.

Work sharing could be used to attenuate the roller-coaster effect of economic activity by stabilizing employment and consumption and, by extension, investment and output. Currently, hours adjustment serves this absorption function to a limited degree in the United States. Charts 3.1 and 3.2 suggest that variability of hours in the private sector already absorbs some of the impact of reduced labor demand during economic slowdowns. Chart 3.2 is particularly illustrative in this regard as it manifests a pronounce spike in the number of employees working part-time hours for economic reasons prior to and during official economic recessions in the United States. A policy of work time regulation would take the pragmatic step of improving this adjustment process by making work-sharing more practicable for employers and more equitable for workers. A systematic, predictable, transparent, and equitable hours adjustment process could substantially improve economic stability by stabilizing incomes with relatively low levels of government spending.

Another ideological objection to a buffer stock arrangement relates to the government assuming the social costs of unemployment caused by layoffs. If private firms are able to rely on the buffer stock as a temporary "storage shelf" for their workers in their search for short-run profits, the program would amount to a financial subsidy for firms with a fickle commitment to its workers. Temporary public sector employment (or a buffer stock of workers) promotes an undesirable shifting of the social costs of unemployment and underemployment from private firms to the government. By absorbing the expendable workers from the private sector, the government will be subsidizing the social costs of unemployment for employers. Stabile

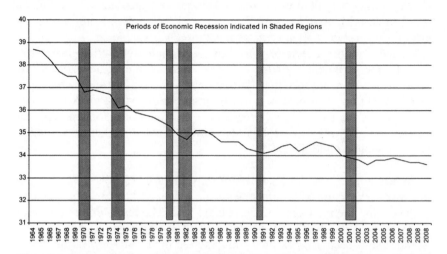

Chart 3.1 Average Weekly Hours of US Production Workers (Total Private- Includes Full-time and Part-time workers)
Data Sources: Bureau of Labor Statistics and National Bureau of Economic Research

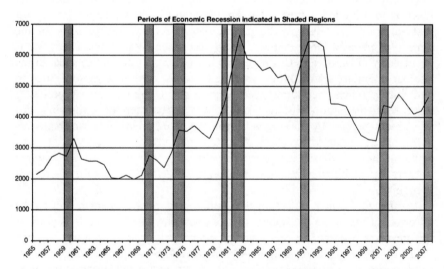

Chart 3.2 US Workers on Part-time Hours for Economic Reasons (thousands)
Data sources: Bureau of Labor Statistics, Current Population Survey and National Bureau of Economic Research

(1996: 151) summarizes the social costs of unemployment originally outlined by JM Clark (1923):

> Regarding workers, this means that they must feed, clothe and house themselves and their families, whether they are working or not. These costs will not go away, if workers cannot pay them, so someone else must, whether it be friends and relatives, eleemosynary institutions, or government. If these other agencies helped the social costs of labor, businesses were being subsidized by them.

Like so many capitalist policies and practices before it, a job guarantee therefore creates an untoward socialization of the losses and privatization of the profits. By relieving employers of the obligation to maintain long-term commitments to workers, the operation of a buffer stock of workers represents a subsidy to those employers least committed to their employees. In essence, the buffer stock employment program temporarily hires private sector workers during a slowdown and attempts to keep them "employable" until corporate profitability (or the expectation of profits) is robust enough to hire them back again. By fostering a short-term time horizon in hiring, a buffer stock runs the very real risk of encouraging ephemeral work arrangements and shifting the costs to society at large. Although this is largely the case under current social structures, there is still some stigma attached to a myopic pattern of hiring and firing. Pension funds, consumers and workers themselves often react unfavorably when a firm engages in layoffs for short-term financial gain. Under a job guarantee that makes such short-term layoffs more palatable to society, it is reasonable to expect that firms will more readily resort to layoffs to boost short-run profitability. Rather than encouraging firms to pass the costs of unemployment onto society in general, prudent public policy should encourage firms to internalize the social costs of unemployment. As outlined in Chapter 5, work-sharing programs have been used to encourage firms to assume a longer time horizon in their employment commitments by making it less expensive to expand and contract work hours in accordance with the economic cycle.

As with wage subsidies, subsidizing the social costs of unemployment could actually result in lower money wages being paid to workers. The experience of the Speenhamland income scheme of 1795 illustrates the intricacy of keeping an intended income floor from becoming an income ceiling. The poor design of the Speenhamland and other assistance programs of the Poor Laws epoch often allowed employers to lower wages so far that the workers experienced a lower level of absolute income even after receiving public succor. Indeed part of Marx's preference for work time reduction was the view that the poor laws between 1795 and 1834 played a central role in the immiseration of the rural working class by allowing English farmers and landlords to pay below-subsistence wages, while the parish relief system mitigated the social costs of the sub-par wages. Although there are some bona fide reasons why firms would not take advantage of income and employment subsidies to lower wages (e.g. efficiency wages), it remains a theoretical possibility that job and income guarantees could have perverse effects on worker well-being (Block and Somers 2005).

Another important shortcoming of a job guarantee is that it does not adequately address the polarization of work hours that is endemic to capitalism. Marx (1968: 477) warned that overwork and unemployment will be twin problems under capitalism, "Capitalist production provides for unexpected contingencies by overworking one section of the labouring population and keeping the other as a ready reserve army consisting of partially or entirely pauperised people." Although the fall-back position of the overworked individuals who might quit their jobs is more generous with a job guarantee, significant labor market segmentation will still place pressure on workers to maintain long hours. Elevating the position of secondary sector workers will not substantially improve their bargaining power relative to primary sector workers. Nor will it improve the prospects of the over-worked in their effort to secure humane working hours. A job guarantee would likely have "level effects" on the conditions of work, but the structure of the labor market will be little changed as employers would intensify their efforts to maintain labor segmentation and extract surplus labor value from their existing workforce. Direct regulation of hours is the most effective means of protecting workers from the labor market segmentation that is often maintained through work time polarization. Barring a direct regulation of work hours, the pressures that Marx outlined nearly two centuries ago, will continue to militate toward longer hours for primary sector workers.

It is also unclear if the underemployment of those currently working short hours or below their career qualifications will be adequately addressed by a job guarantee. Proponents of make-work programs contend that the part-time workers could take on a second job or full-time work within the buffer stock program. However, employing workers at a second and third part-time job or fabricating full-time jobs, very quickly runs into logistical, bureaucratic and efficiency hurdles. It is therefore unclear how a second part-time job with the government is a better utilization of the underemployed than expanding their hours on existing private payrolls as well as creating more hours for them in the primary sector through a tighter regulation of work time.

Payroll expansion could encourage firms to pay more workers primary-sector wages to perform tasks that are more complex and sophisticated than the public works programs typically envision. Work time trends in many industrial democracies increasingly display relatively long work hours for high-paid primary-sector employees and a reduced role for low-wage secondary-sector workers (Bluestone and Rose 1997; Jacobs and Gerson 1998). A work-time-regulation policy could therefore address the current mal-distributions of hours in a manner that improves both social and economic efficiency. Socially, because it could afford the overworked more time to spend with family or community; economically, because reduced work time has been shown to make the overworked more productive.

An additional advantage of work time regulation is that it does not throw buffer stock workers into competition with public sector employees or other low-paid private sector workers. Indeed, work sharing is a much more solidaristic means of shouldering the burden of an aggregate reduction of work hours. Since work time reduction endeavors to expand private payrolls, it is more immune to the criticism that the output of buffer stock workers would "crowd-out" private sector output (Sawyer 2003). Moreover, as work time regulation can be designed to encourage participation across a diversity of industries and firms, the plan possesses more industrial, demographic, and geographic neutrality than a job guarantee that targets pockets of unemployment. Since payroll expansion is not targeted towards a particular sector or segment of the labor force, it encourages greater employment across all occupations and wage levels. In addition to being income and industry neutral, payroll expansion also has the ability to increase economic participation across geographic boundaries. Whereas job guarantees chiefly aid those geographic areas with high unemployment (mostly urban regions), a payroll expansion scheme would not be limited to areas that manifest high levels of unemployment and could ameliorate both underemployment and overemployment cross all regions. This is increasingly important in the wake of growing technological unemployment that has created a more heterogeneous group of unemployed and underemployed individuals. Work time reduction has the potential to stretch into every pocket of a country, increasing employment and social participation across a variety of regions, industries and income levels. As a result of this widespread potential for payroll expansion, work time reduction should be able to garner broad-based political support.

Taken together, the assorted drawbacks of job guarantees have led critics to characterize the program as a palliative that fails to alter the dialectics of capitalism by altering the class relations that are at the heart of labor market frustrations. Employment alone does not provide secure incomes over the long term. Creating jobs, training people for jobs, retraining people for different jobs and stimulating a greater consumption of commodities to do so, all misses the mark. Since the threat of obsolescence confronts every worker in the post-industrial labor market, direct work time regulation coupled with stronger individual claims to the nation's social surplus (or capital stock) provides a superior assurance of economic security. In their advocacy of broader access to capital, Kelso and Hetter (1968: 145) observe that, "it is the institutions of society, not parental genes, that bestow the blessings of ownership of productive capital." Granting individuals more access to productive capital and more leisure time is an effective and sustainable way of enhancing socioeconomic participation.

Leading job guarantee proponents have also expressed some concern over the role of work in capitalist society but their policy proposals often stand in contradiction to those concerns. Mitchell and Wray (2004: 10) write:

The future of paid work is certainly an important debate. The traditional moral views about the virtues of work-which are exploited by the capitalist class-need to be recast. What is the best way to make the transition into a system of work and income generation that expunges the yoke of the work ethic and the stigmatization of non-work?" While a broader concept of work is the first phase in decoupling work and income, we do not advocate imposing this new culture of non-work on to society as it currently exists. Social attitudes take time to evolve and are best reinforced by changes in the educational system.

In this sense, advocates of job guarantees and work time reduction proponents share a criticism of income guarantees. Both agree that immediately abandoning a societal role for paid work, with no concurrent reform of educational and cultural support systems, will lead to growing disenfranchisement of the unemployed and underemployed. Where the two part company is how society will achieve the needed labor market reform in transition to a workerless society, or at least one in which work is less urgent. By reinforcing the work fetish, it is difficult to see what mechanism a job guarantee would use to reduce the urgency of work and begin eroding the nexus between work and income. Incongruously, a job guarantee program endeavors to reduce the role of remunerative work by expanding it. Yet, it is difficult to conceive how a diminution of paid work will be more effectively accomplished by expanding it rather than regulating it. If the intent is to re-embed the economy within a dominant social structure, then we should be reducing paid work and its control over our personal lives and space. If we are to recast social mores surrounding the role of remunerative work, regulating the labor market with policy mechanisms that are already in place can be an effective first step.

Work time regulation has a built-in mechanism that allows society to gradually lift the yoke of market work while simultaneously filling the space that is liberated with redeeming activities through educational and cultural reform. Gorz (1994: 96) envisions work time reduction as the principal policy lever,

> That is why, in my opinion, we have to come at the problem 'from below', by reducing the number of working hours. And this has to be conceived not as a single measure but as a long-term, general policy, concerning both government and trade unions, and embodying an alternative view of civilization ... A new contract for society has to be established so that social relations can be transformed. A universal allowance created by a law and paid out by an administrative agency would not have the same scope.

Regulation of the labor market is a more expedient way to diminish the significance of remunerative work than expanding employment through make-work programs and hoping that educational enlightenment will eventually alter future attitudes toward work. Work time reduction immediately launches society on a trajectory towards a new culture in which the work/income nexus will be continually reassessed.

Many Marxists would prefer a reduction in wage-labor time to make-work programs that escalate the commodity fetish and labor market segmentation. Burkett (1998) makes the case that since the production of a "surplus product" is a social process the most democratic allocation of the surplus would be a reduction in wage-labor time. Alternative policies to redistribute the benefits secured by labor market insiders to the outsiders, such as the wage and income subsidies proposed by Rothschild (1991) and Phelps (1997), ignore the use value of the third, unpaid, sector of the economy. Burkett (1998) considers work-sharing to be the most egalitarian and socially efficient method to redistribute the social surplus in an environment of segmented labor markets. Burkett (1998: 71) explains that "while individual workers still contribute to wealth production, they do so only collectively, as part of a social process which is more than a mere sum of individual parts— a process utilizing the natural resources and historically accumulated knowledge of society as a whole." When production is viewed as a social process, the notion of marginal labor productivity is revealed as a fallacy. Rather than reflecting predetermined differences in the productive abilities of individual workers, wage inequalities represent the uneven development of capital accumulation, disproportionate bargaining power between capital and labor, and an arbitrary and discriminatory distribution of the socially produced surplus product. Thus, proposals that address the insider–outsider distribution of the surplus product need to be mindful that they are not built upon the same reasoning as marginal productivity theory. Burkett (1998: 73) points out that a major fault of Phelps' (1996) proposal to subsidize the wages of low-wage workers is that "its proposed maintenance of wage inequalities among workers is motivated by the same principle as neoclassical marginal productivity theory." From a Marxian perspective, the social effort bargain that is manifest in the allocation of the surplus product needs to be governed by the recognition that production is a social process and that individual and class claims to highly disproportionate allocations are suspect.

An additional Marxian criticism of wage and employment subsidies is that they ignore the value of socially useful activities conducted in the third sector. An important Marxian observation is that the conflict between social production and private appropriation results in the undervaluation of many goods and services that satisfy important human needs, and that focusing on redistributions from insiders to outsiders limits the policy response to subsidizing outsider employment to yield the equivalent of wage income. Burkett (1998: 72) contends that, "there is no logical reason why outsider compensation should not be extended to domestic labor and the various forms of community work, which while not eliciting positive wages from capitalist markets, nonetheless yield (or could under changed circumstances) important social benefits." Recognizing social use values in the allocation of the surplus product could foster policy responses that transform the status of "outsiders" to socialistic insiders, that is, to increase their socioeconomic participation.

The extension of Rothschild's insider–outsider redistribution scheme to include leisure time would represent a social recognition that society's total surplus time—all time in excess of the work time required for the reproduction of society at its current living standard—is the original source of its social wealth (Marx 1977). Under capitalism the lion's share of this potential free time is appropriated by capital in the form of surplus value, which is essentially the monetary form of surplus wage-labor time (Marx 1991: 530). Increasing the social valuation of non-market labor time would promote a democratic sharing of surplus time in a manner that is far more sustainable than traditional policy proposals that are largely based on the expansion of market-labor time. Burkett (1998: 73) extols the virtues of elevating the use-value of leisure time in the social effort bargain:

> Aside from the benefits of increased time with children and other household members, and the well-being connected with having more of a break from [paid] work, reductions in worktime required for material security help open up opportunities for cooperative networking throughout civil society including participation in political and self-governmental activities. Indeed, when people deemphasize work-oriented and commercial-privatist forms of social status and contacts in favor of increased leisure and less expensive leisure-time activities, this can be seen as a popular and progressive struggle for increased autonomy and freedom of human development-regardless of its social dysfunctionality *for capitalism* [sic].

Work time regulation that recognizes the social nature of the production process and the use value of non-paid labor time represents a superior approach to conducting the social effort bargain over the surplus product. If we view the social product as a "fund for social change" as suggested by Stanfield (1992), work time regulation becomes an obvious choice as an equitable, sustainable, and practicable mechanism to improve socioeconomic participation. Work time regulation can foster an enlightened social compromise that makes inroads into the present structure of capitalism. Certainly, a policy of reduced work time that placed more emphasis on non-market activity, household production, civic engagement, and the like would be more acceptable to those seeking more fundamental and permanent labor market reforms than are offered by traditional growth-based employment policies.

The effort to expand remunerative work confuses Veblen's instinct for workmanship (or Marx's ideal of defining ourselves through our daily labors) with "paid" work. It is not denied that greater social integration can result from make-work programs targeted to unemployed individuals. The objection is that the expansion of paid work (through greater aggregate work hours) is used as the primary vehicle for social interaction. In a post-industrial environment of declining private employment opportunities, social participation should not be vetted by the government's determination of which activities are worthy of remunerative reward through public employment schemes. Although the outcome of the government's "task prioritization" may be favorable when compared with the private sector solution, it is not preferable to the alternative of regulating the entire labor market to achieve the greatest socioeconomic participation for the greatest number of people.

With its predilection for more work and indifference to household production, the job guarantee operates under the same mentality as the workhouses of yesteryear. Although the conditions may be more humane under public sector employment, the paternalistic spirit of the nineteenth-century workhouse would persist. Make-work programs that place preponderant value on remunerative work over the plethora of social activities available to individuals in the post-industrial era represent an antiquated policy response. Surely we can aspire to a more progressive social policy that provides opportunities for underutilized workers without enslaving all workers to a work and spend existence.

Price stability

The trifecta of macroeconomic policy since the Industrial Revolution has been the achievement of consistent economic growth, full employment and price stability. Since these goals relate to competing class interests, macroeconomic outcomes in industrial democracies largely reflect the bargaining power of the vested interests. Few issues illustrate the class struggle inherent in the social negotiation over macroeconomic goals more lucidly than the curtailment of inflation. The mere hint of inflation has long been the bugaboo of progressive social policy. Overly ambitious economic growth or a full utilization of labor has been thwarted repeatedly by the political economy of inflation. It is sometimes argued that the bond-holding class wields disproportionate power and influence in the macroeconomic balancing act (Canterbery 2002). Orr and Frank (2003) suggest that the bond market's fear of inflation and kindred spirits with the central bank affords the wealthy substantial influence over the US Congress. Since politicians realize that the Federal Reserve will take preemptive anti-inflation action—at great costs to the whole of the economy—they are loathe to pass progressive legislation that does not curry favor with the bond market. Greider (2003: 53) likewise writes, "finance capital shapes and polices the 'social contract' in American far more effectively than the government, which has largely retreated from the role." Having a hand on the blunt cudgel of monetary policy, the bondholding class is thusly able to assert a preponderant influence on socioeconomic policy in the United States.

A chief objection to fighting inflation with blunt monetary tools is the disparate impact anti-inflationary policies have on low-wage, minority workers. In his treatise on the US Federal Reserve Bank, Greider (1987) pointed out that central banks are rarely equal opportunity "dis-employers" when they apply the brakes to monetary policy. Wray and Forstater (2004: 262) similarly write that, "perhaps a reasonable case could be made that inflation can be and should be fought by raising unemployment rates if all workers shared equally in the pain." Since anti-inflationary policy in capitalist societies tends to be highly discriminatory, employment policies should be mindful of the need to fairly distribute the sacrifices caused by anti-inflationary monetary regimes. This section attempts to illustrate how work time regulation could "spread the pain" of an anti-inflationary policy bias more equitably than a buffer stock of workers that perpetuates labor market segmentation. It also illustrates how work time regulation could serve as an incomes policy by distributing future productivity gains in the form of work time reduction rather than wage increases to achieve greater price stability than a job guarantee that simply creates a price floor with no upper bound to wages. Perhaps most importantly, the approach outlined in this chapter (and empirically corroborated in Chapter 5) illustrates how work time reduction can increase labor productivity to reduce inflationary pressures in a full-employment economy.

Buffer stocks as a wage buoy

Although a job guarantee represents a vast improvement over the current paradigm of a non-accelerating-inflation-rate-of-unemployment (NAIRU), its ability to achieve upward price stability is limited. A job guarantee would have little influence on the wage and price spiral in robust economic times and tight labor markets. Job guarantee programs are often described as a buffer stock system to stabilize the price of a critical economic input which will then have salutary effects on inflation (Wray 1998b). Although the notion of achieving full employment may be consistent with a post-Keynesian income policy intent on stabilizing prices, using buffer stocks to fight inflation seems to presume the neoclassical market mentality of inflation being caused by "market forces" such as labor scarcity or monetary excess.

While inflation is mainly a monetary phenomenon for neoclassicalists, post-Keynesians traditionally view inflation as a result of the conflict over the distribution of real output or the struggle over income shares (Holt and Pressman 2001). Inflation is a reflection of the bargaining power of those groups with vested interests in the economy, not a simple market failure in the commanding heights of the economy that can be managed by buffer stocks. Concerned that inflation results from wage growth in excess of productivity growth, post-Keynesian inflation policy has sought to resolve the struggle over income shares in an organized and equitable fashion (Moore 1978). The favored policy has been an incomes policy that tames inflation by making money-wage increases commensurate with productivity increases (Weintraub 1961). The traditional post-Keynesian view of inflation is consistent with the social conflict theory arising from the Marxian tradition. Proponents of the social conflict theory hold that inflation arises from the conflict between capitalists and workers over the total income generated by the economy and that the effectiveness of aggregate demand policy is dependent on the state of the relative bargaining power of these two classes (Rowthorn 1977; Goldthorpe 1978).

The view of inflation inherent in buffer stock employment programs represents a departure from traditional post-Keynesian inflation policy. The buffer stock model assumes that the government will be able to manage stockpiles of inputs (labor or energy) in sufficient quantities to stabilize prices throughout the entire economy (Wray 2001). However, since buffer stock programs merely attenuate prices swings, managing a stockpile of workers will not eliminate wage pressures, especially during a shortage. It may be possible for the government to place a floor on wages by standing ready to employ those willing and able to work. But in periods of robust labor demand, a buffer stock will not be able to relieve price pressures stemming from wage demands of emboldened workers. Since the buffer stock cannot create more workers in response to tight labor markets, it could do little to ease the wage and price spiral that tends to arise from tight labor markets. The buffer stock model therefore has to rely on the threat of primary sector workers losing their jobs and having to accept a less desirable buffer stock job as a means of containing the inflationary pay demands of private sector workers. This draconian method of achieving price stability conflicts with the ideology of traditional post-Keynesian inflation policy. King (2001b: 5) argues that such a policy positions buffer stock advocates "on the right of the Post Keynesian debate on inflation control, while advocates of a formal incomes policy might be said to occupy the left." Since a buffer stock serves as a price buoy rather than an anchor, the government would still need to resort to traditional post-Keynesian incomes policies to address demand pull inflation.

If inflation is caused by the conflict over national income, placing a floor under the price of a key commodity will not eliminate that conflict. In fact a job guarantee program that stimulates aggregate demand by requiring individuals to engage in more exchange-value activities will intensify the dispute over national income as the bargaining power of all workers will be increased. Empowered by a tighter labor market, all workers will theoretically be able to militate for higher wages, although the insiders will still enjoy a significant bargaining advantage. The resulting inflationary wage and price spiral is resolved in the buffer stock model by having temporary, buffer-stock workers serve as "a better inflation-fighting force than the jobless" presumably because employers can hire them rather than concede to wage demands of primary sector workers (Mitchell and Wray 2005: 238). But a buffer stock of workers is more likely to affect the "level" of wages rather than the structure of the labor force as it does not directly regulate existing working arrangements. The inflationary demands of primary sector workers will be particularly pressing during robust economics times and fiscal policy will have to revert to an anti-inflationary bias.

The difficulty arising from tight labor markets has been acknowledged by buffer stock advocates. Ulmer's (1972: 157) proposal for a public employment program relied on "temporary use of direct price and wage controls," but provided no explanation as to how they would be removed. More recently, Mosler states that, "if a shrinking ELR (employer of last resort) pool is not answered with demand reducing measures, other prices will rise relative to the ELR [buffer stock] wage and old fashioned inflation can follow (Mitchell 1998: 551)." As outlined below, work time regulation offers a superior method of addressing "old fashion inflation" by altering the negotiation over the social product in a manner reminiscent of an incomes policy.

During robust economic times, buffer stocks offer little prospect of abating wage pressures in the primary sector. Since buffer stocks target a minimum price of labor, an earnings floor if you will, and do not create a wage ceiling they will have little impact on primary sector wage demands. Capitalists will be able to maintain a significant degree of labor market segmentation, allowing them to avoid hiring from outside the primary sector. As such they will avoid payroll expansion and attempt to squeeze more from existing workers in the form of longer hours and greater work intensification. One only has to look at the history of commodity prices (such as oil) to realize that buffer stocks do not place a ceiling on prices. Buffer stocks may mitigate priceswings, but they tend to prop prices up rather than restrain them, particularly when the commodity is in short supply. Buffer stocks, therefore, do not serve as a price anchor but rather a price buoy. That is, they represent an earnings floor rather than an earnings ceiling. Public and private sector employees alike will still face pressure to work long hours under a job guarantee—either to maintain insatiable consumption desires or to retain jobs that offer long hours on a take-it-or-leave-it basis. Such behavior would certainly become inflationary as Mitchell and Wray (2005) concede when they write, "if the government decides not to deflate demand, the ELR pool still allows the economy to operate with higher aggregate demand and lower inflation pressures [than under a NAIRU], although inflation can still result." It may be true that with a buffer stock of workers, employment can be higher before an inflation barrier is reached, but such an arrangement is still more inflationary than a work time regulation scheme that directly influences that barrier.

The job guarantee confuses incomes inflation with spot price inflation and offers buffer stock solution rather than the incomes-based policy that post-Keynesians have traditionally advocated in abating wage-price inflation. If inflation is caused by the conflict over national income, stabilizing the price of a key commodity will not eliminate that conflict and will in fact intensify the dispute as the bargaining power and income of workers is increased. Indeed, post-Keynesian proposals for incomes policy grew out of the observation that macroeconomic booms led to inflation and that the successes of anti-inflationary policy were ephemeral. Long-term price stability then required an incomes policy. On the whole, post-Keynesian inflation policy has been concerned with preventing increases in gross profit margins and limiting changes in money wages to the changes in labor productivity. Few, if any, policies have focused on productivity growth itself. Although most post-Keynesians would agree that greater price stability could result from labor productivity growth, their macroeconomic policies—such as job and income guarantees and tax-based income policies—do not feature enhanced labor productivity as a central objective. By contrast, productivity improvements among the underworked and overworked alike are central to the anti-inflationary effects of work time regulation.

Work time regulation as an incomes policy

Since it is possible for price pressures to emanate from the labor market as workers and employers struggle over national income shares, one aspect of a comprehensive inflation policy should be to link average compensation growth to productivity growth. A work time regulation regime that targeted productivity increases could achieve price stability with minimal additional administrative burden. Since overtime thresholds and maximum weekly work hour limits already exist in many countries, governments would simply need to strengthen their regulatory tools and then start using them in a regulatory fashion. Nations might decide, for instance, to devote half of the average annual productivity growth rate to work time reduction and reduce the maximum and overtime thresholds accordingly. In addition to relieving demand-pull inflation in the labor market, work time regulation could also mitigate price pressures among the other factors competing for national income. The ability of raw material producers to command a larger share of national income—as was the case with oil producers in the 1970s—is reduced in an economy with a larger third sector that is not as dependent on economic throughput for its livelihood.

Contrary to the operation of a buffer stock that creates a floor for the price of labor, work time regulation could be viewed as an incomes program that targets a wage growth ceiling. By encouraging or mandating that a portion of productivity dividends be distributed in the form of reduced work time rather than pay hikes, work time regulation could operate much like an incomes policy that links increased worker compensation with productivity gains. If demand-pull inflation was particularly acute, work time regulation could be used to make it expensive, or even illegal, for firms to grant productivity dividends in the form of wages rather than leisure time until inflation was curtailed. If cost-push inflation was a concern, workers could be asked to temporarily forfeit both wage and leisure gains and enter into an agreement with employers to devote all productivity improvements to price reductions. This sort of social effort bargain would require firms to make credible commitments to workers that the productivity gains would not be funneled into greater profits. Indeed, a chief virtue of tax-based (TIP) or quota-based (MAP) incomes policies is their ability to penalize price-setting firms that raise prices above productivity achievements. It may be possible to design a work-time incomes policy with similar attributes to protect both workers and consumers in the social effort bargain.

If the secular trend towards reduced work time somehow caused a temporary increase in per unit labor costs, work time regulation could entail a slower reduction, or even an expansion, of individual work hours. Although a long-run expansion of work time should be avoided due to the pernicious effects on labor productivity, there may be temporary adjustment costs that militate for a short-term protraction of hours. If there is a credible threat of cost-push inflation or some other national exigency, it is feasible that policymakers could ease work time restrictions in the short run to achieve vital national interests. For example, in the course of retiring the baby-boom generation of workers, work time reduction might not be pursued as aggressively as it otherwise would on account of demographic pressures placed on labor markets. Thus, it is important to recognize that work time *regulation* does not always entail work time *reduction*; but since improved labor productivity is central to achieving the desired macroeconomic objectives, the secular trend would be towards reduced work hours. After an initial, and largely voluntary, redistribution of work hours that brought the economy close to full employment, a further tightening of the labor market could be achieved in a non-inflationary manner by devoting a portion of annual productivity growth to shorter hours. If the outcome of the social effort bargain resulted in an average productivity contribution to work time reduction of around 2 percent per year, a 40-hour week could be reduced to 32 hours in the course of a decade through productivity gains alone ($0.02 \times 40 = 0.8$ hours $\times 10 = 8$ fewer hours).

The inflationary effects related to fiscal spending are less pressing under work time regulation because the government will not have to offer the full-wage equivalent of a public sector job in order to encourage payroll expansion. Although Lerner's Functional Finance frees policymakers from the confines of traditional fiscal nostrums, work time reduction provides greater leverage to public spending than job or income guarantees. In terms of fiscal efficiency, payroll expansion through work time reduction is a superior full-employment strategy as it can be operated at much lower cost for the same employment impact. In other words, the same level of spending dispensed under a job or income guarantee could be leveraged into a far greater impact on employment through a work time regulation scheme. For instance, Wray (1998) estimates that a job guarantee for the United States would cost somewhere in the neighborhood of $50 billion a year, creating less than $50 billion worth of public payroll expansion after subtracting administrative expenses. Alternatively, a work time reduction plan that offered private firms payroll expansion incentives totaling $50 billion could generate earned income growth many multiples higher since private firms would be paying a major portion of the compensation package offered to new hires. Wage subsidy plans offer a similar "fiscal efficiency" but they fail to harness the societal, environmental and productivity benefits that result from presently employed workers reducing their work hours and thereby increasing their socioeconomic participation.

Expecting firms to contribute to the cost of payroll expansion is not impracticable as they will be reaping the benefits of government subsidies (or payroll tax incentives), greater labor and social productivity, marginally enhanced aggregate demand (due to initial income redistributions), and the lower societal costs associated with greater economic participation (e.g. lower unemployment compensation). Rather than the government bearing the full cost of directly employing a worker, work time reduction operates on the margin. The government will only need to offer financial incentives equivalent to a fraction of the total hiring costs of an additional worker to encourage firms to expand their payrolls and reallocate work hours. By leveraging payroll expansion, more goods and services are likely to be produced per unit of government spending, reducing the inflationary impact of work time regulation relative to traditional full-employment programs. Thus, rather than the government serving as an "employer of last resort," it would be far more prudent for the government to assume the role of "payroll expander of last resort."

Price stability through increased productivity

In addition to reducing inflationary spending, work time reduction has been shown to have positive feedback effects on labor productivity.[7] Work hour reductions tend to have salutary effects on productivity at the firm level because they encourage a re-organization of operating hours that often results in greater utilization of non-labor inputs. Bosch and Lehndorff (2001) contend that the productivity gains from the re-organization of work were critical to achieving "distributional neutrality" and subsequent job growth in many work time reductions across Europe in the 1980s. Historically, experiments with work time reduction have revealed a favorable impact on labor productivity through what might be conceptualized as an "efficiency week (LaJeunesse 1998)." The benefits of an efficiency week mirror those of efficiency wages as outlined in Table 3.1. Yet, an efficiency week offers important productivity advantages over an efficiency wage at both the firm and societal level.

Whereas an efficiency wage reduces the costs to the firm associated with monitoring worker behavior, an efficiency week reduces the need to monitor both worker behavior and the quality of their output. Although it is true that a well-paid worker is less likely to intentionally shirk than an under-paid worker, they are just as likely to make mistakes as they become fatigued. By contrast, if the "efficient compensation premium" takes the form of short hours, the well-rested and alert worker is both less likely to shirk or make production mistakes. (The relationship between long work hours and the greater incidence of accidents, injuries, and illness is examined in Chapter 4.) Thus, the efficiency week offers the firm all of the productivity advantages of

Table 3.1 The virtues of efficiency weeks vis-á-vis efficiency wages

Efficiency wages	Efficiency weeks
• More money to invest in nutrition, education, transportation, training	• More time to make these human capital investments
• Higher costs of shirking compels workers to behave – the cheat-threat argument	• Loss of compassionate work hours likewise represents a cost to shirking and reduces "petty-pilfering of work time"
• Higher morale and lower turnover reduces recruitment and retention expenses	• Well-rested, less-harried workers also have high morale and low turnover
• Lower cost of monitoring worker behavior (not necessarily output)	• Lower monitoring costs for both behavior and quality – well-rested, alert workers make fewer mistakes
	• Societal benefits of increased leisure

the efficiency wage with the additional benefit of reducing the costs of fatigue. A second advantage of efficiency weeks relates to the improved social productivity that will flow back into the production function of the firm. Through a variety of avenues, an efficiency week that improves socio-economic participation will enhance the social productivity of the entire economic system. Indeed, many of the most egalitarian societies in Europe also possess some of the highest hourly productivity levels in the developed world. Boules and Cette (2005: 76) conclude that:

> The United States is no longer setting the 'technical efficiency frontier' now defined by these European countries. In other words, some of the other industrialised countries have already closed the productivity gap. By 'opting' for shorter working hours and/or lower employment rates, the European countries with high hourly productivity would also seem to be promoting more of a leisure society than the United States.

In the aggregate, even as more and more firms offer efficiency weeks there are still gains to be made, which is not the case with widespread payment of efficiency wages. Although the productivity benefit that accrues to the individual firm may diminish as work hours are redistributed and reduced by more firms, there is still a benefit to society, a portion of which accrues back to the individual firm. The societal benefits of a social effort bargain that increases socioeconomic participation are not available under an efficiency wage that simply inflames a work and spend existence.

Greater social productivity can also result from the improved income equality achieved by a compression of the work time distribution. Countries with relatively short working hours, such as Germany, France, Sweden, and the Netherlands, have considerably more egalitarian income distributions. This is another avenue to greater social productivity as it has been shown that greater equality correlates with greater growth and employment (Galbraith *et al.* 1999). Since productivity is widely acknowledged to be procyclical, a more equitable sharing of work time has the potential to stabilize economic growth and improve social productivity. With greater employment stability and job security, consumer confidence and aggregate demand will be less erratic. It should be noted that compressing the distribution of work time is not an attempt to achieve absolute equality, but rather a way to restrain those inequities built on anti-social work hours.

Even if the net aggregate effect of a redistribution of work hours was slightly less work, income, and consumption, it could yield an otherwise more productive economy than could be achieved under a less egalitarian division of labor at higher throughput. It is important to differentiate here between the stabilization of economic growth and its curtailment or maximization. For social and environmental reasons, it is important that work time reduction is not co-opted by the productivist vision and combined with traditional Keynesian spending to generate more consumption and irresponsible growth. It is also important that economic output is not contracted beyond a level needed to maintain technological advance in order to ameliorate pressing social and ecological needs. How society uses its greater productivity to influence the scale and composition of economic growth is an important societal question that should be debated and resolved through a social effort bargain that considers the interests of a diversity of stakeholders.

In the context of price stability, it is important to emphasize that the productivity benefits of work time regulation accrue at both the firm level and the macroeconomic level. By tightening the entire system, the whole economy operates more efficiently, reducing the need for anti-inflationary policy measures. Indeed, this is true of any policy that moves the economy closer to full employment because it promotes efficiency of the private sector, reduces shared social costs related to social exclusion (crime, poor health, etc.) and increases the education and skills of the formerly unemployed workers. But work time reduction offers productivity dividends over and above those achieved by a mere tightening of the system. Shorter hours not only make individual workers more productive, but the extra time they have with their family and in their community yields social productivity benefits in addition to those derived from full employment in general. The social productivity gains associated with an improved distribution of societal labor therefore represent an advantage over traditional full-employment programs in terms of fighting inflation.

There is a growing body of empirical evidence suggesting that an immediate work time reduction would tighten the slack in the workday and place little pressure on prices under existing workplace arrangements. When "beeped" during work hours, Csikszentmihalyi (1990) found that the average worker admitted that they were not working 25 percent of the time. This provides modern evidence that workers use the reservoir of untapped work time to engage in what Marx called a petty pilfering of work time. The finding is consistent with Liebenstien's (1980) "X-efficiency" and Weber's (1922) "engrained habituation" explanations of why firms may not optimize the use of production inputs such as labor. Provided that workers are protected from an intensification of their work tasks, eliminating idle time in the workplace could be a boon to productivity at both the firm and societal level. Further evidence of the productivity benefits related to past work time reduction experiments is presented in Chapter 5.

An important macroeconomic ramification of work time regulation is the liberating effect it would have on monetary policy. Using labor market policy to achieve price stability allows monetary policy to assume low and stable interest rates. This would foster greater price and economic stability as the central bank would not have to restrain the entire economy to fight price inflation arising from specific sectors. Moreover, a low interest rate regime would discourage booms and busts in particular financial assets. As financial speculation has historically led to the privatization of profits (during the boom) and the socialization of the losses (during the bust), a more predictable interest rate policy would result in a more egalitarian spreading of the costs related to the instability of capitalism. Low and stable interest rates will also moderate swings in the foreign exchange value of the currency and stabilize output related to foreign trade. Furthermore, since hours regulation would be debated and implemented as part of the conventional political process, it would reflect a more democratic consensus than the monetary policy decisions currently made by autonomous central bankers.

The impact of work time reduction on consumption and monetary policy provides an important contrast to a job guarantee that increases the risk of imported price inflation. Palley (2001) has pointed out, that the fiscal stimulus provided by a job guarantee is likely to add to the demand for imports, especially since the earnings of buffer stock workers will induce greater domestic income. This presents the possibility of expanding trade deficits and exchange rate depreciation. In a small open economy, exchange rate depreciation creates the risk of imported price inflation that could trigger a domestic wage-price inflation.

Conversely, using work time regulation as an incomes policy chokes off this open-economy inflationary channel by curtailing the growth of aggregate income and throughput. Distributing productivity gains in the form of time rather than income places a constraint on the growth of imports and trade deficits, thereby stabilizing the exchange value of the currency. Moreover, capital flight due to the inflationary effect of tight labor markets is less likely when full employment is achieved by tying work time reduction to productivity gains to achieve price stability. As such it frees monetary policy from external financing constraints and affords a lower interest rate regime, which will reduce the cost of finance for firms engaged in a re-organization of work and place further downward pressure on prices.

Ideally a work time incomes policy would be managed so that the inflationary pressure of greater bargaining power resulting from full employment would more than offset the deflationary pressure of greater labor productivity resulting in modest levels of inflation. If the deflationary effects stemming from the greater productivity of shorter hours were to dominate the inflationary effects of improving workers' bargaining power, policymakers would still be at liberty to engage in expansionary fiscal policy, especially since the fiscal cost of work time regulation is expected to be far less than job or income guarantees. The advantages of modest inflation relative to zero price growth or deflation are well established (Keynes 1972; Minarik 1980; Levine and Renelt 1992). Acting as a tax on wealth, inflation constrains the spending of the wealthy and thereby abates future inflation. In addition to the "leveling" effect that moderate inflation has on income distributions, inflation may encourage investment and economic growth as profit expectations rise with price gains. As Keynes (1972) pointed out, firms are speculators on the prices of the products they produce, and inflation creates a forgiving environment for firms, especially those that are highly indebted. Indeed, the economic woes that have plagued the Japanese economy for more than a decade serve as a powerful reminder that zero price growth exacts an expensive toll. Therefore, policymakers should regulate work hours with an eye toward achieving modest and predictable rates of inflation. Once a superior macroeconomic balance of low unemployment, low inflation and sustainable output growth has been achieved, it would be relatively straightforward to link productivity gains to work time reduction to maintain egalitarian macroeconomic outcomes.

To summarize, a regulation of work time provides multiple inflation release valves. First, a redistribution and reduction of work hours can increase productivity at the firm level through the "efficiency week" effect. Second, productivity dividends also accrue at the societal level due to a tightening of the economic system, greater social inclusion and the liberation of monetary policy. Third, less fiscal spending is required to encourage firms to hire unemployed and underemployed workers vis-à-vis a job or income guarantee. Finally, an incomes policy designed to distribute productivity dividends in the form of time rather than money reduces future inflationary pressures. As such, work time regulation represents a novel way of achieving price stability while maintaining full employment and sustainable economic activity.

Income guarantees versus work time regulation

If the customs and mores surrounding remunerative work were to become more malleable, a viable proposal to ensure future economic participation could be found in the various proposals classified as income guarantees.[8] Although a network of sociologists, economists and activists has recently revived the prospect of guaranteed annual incomes, and a few countries (Brazil and South Africa) have endorsed the idea as a mechanism to fight extreme poverty, the policy offers little promise in tackling important macroeconomic objectives in the developed world and could only be considered environmentally sustainable if large numbers of individuals choose to use their basic income payment to buy down their hours of work, thereby reducing their consumption. Given the sophistication of labor market segmentation that has fueled the polarization of work hours, it is unlikely that many recipients of a basic income would be in a situation to reduce their work hours. Since it does not directly regulate the ability of labor market insiders to distinguish themselves from outsiders (through long hours, for example), an income guarantee offers very limited potential to ameliorate unemployment rates, work time polarization, socioeconomic inequities, and ecological damage. When coupled with the problems of instantly allowing some income recipients to shirk all socially necessarily labor, the inability of an income guarantee to achieve these important socioeconomic objectives greatly diminishes its economic feasibility and political palatability.

In addition to the equity objections raised by conservatives of giving people money with very few strings attached, there is a well-founded concern that a guaranteed annual income would inflame acquisitive behaviors with damaging inflationary and ecological consequences. Rather than arresting the pernicious aspects of the work and spend cycle, a guaranteed income would likely encourage invidious consumption habits in the same manner as traditional aggregate demand stimulus policies. The encouragement of greater growth is likely to exacerbate inequities in a two-tiered labor market consisting of a core of full-time, high-waged, educated workers on the one hand, and a marginalized group of contingent, less-skilled and poorly paid workers on the other.

In essence, income guarantees possess the same drawbacks as traditional Keynesian policies that rely on "pump-priming" in that they run the risk of overheating the economy. Income guarantees are likely to be even more inflationary than targeted government-spending programs as they do not trigger capacity-expanding production. An income guarantee that universally distributes purchasing power with no requirement of a productive contribution by recipients is a clear recipe for inflation. Income guarantees effectively amount to an expansion of aggregate demand with no commitment to increase aggregate supply. The political acceptability of universal income guarantees will be severely hampered by their inflationary tendency. As the threat of inflation so often sounds the death knell for progressive social policy, it is likely that the bond-holding and capitalist classes would quickly mobilize to defeat a basic income program in most nations of the developed world today.[9]

As with job guarantees, recent variations of income guarantee proposals have been shaped by the work fetish. When income and job guarantees were first being debated in the 1960s, Feagin (1975) conducted surveys of Americans' views on aid to the poor. His findings show that only 38 percent of Americans supported an income guarantee program over the existing welfare and relief payments. The survey respondents were more supportive of a job guarantee plan; 72 percent agreed "that the federal government [should] guarantee a job to every American who wants to work even if it means creating a lot of public jobs like during the depression (Feagin 1975: 134)." Thus for many Americans, the notion that the right to income could be separated from the need to work was repugnant. There is little evidence that these attitudes toward the poor have changed today.

Some proponents of income guarantees admit that a "participation income," which is a payment conditioned on recipients performing some socially useful task, is the only variant of the program that would be politically feasible in the United States and Europe.[10] In advocating a guaranteed annual income, Tobin (1968: 113) wrote, "the widespread, if largely groundless, fear of freeloading can be met by making part, if not all, of the assistance to families conditional on the willingness of employable members to present themselves for work or training, and by providing assistance in a way that rewards self-reliance." Be it Nixon's "Family Assistance Plan" or Friedman's (1962) "negative income tax," paid work has been a crucial "selling point" in the advocacy of guaranteed incomes. This "participation income" might be viewed as a gradualist approach to a universal income guarantee. Indeed, in post-industrial economies the list of exemptions from the labor market will have to gradually be extended to more and more individuals. This would put the government in charge of selecting which occupations or groups of workers were worthy of a social exclusion from work. Which activities will be deserving of a work exemption and which will be required for a "participation" income? Will we reward political action, poetry, push-pin poetry, community service, or religious-based activities? As trends in technological unemployment in the post-industrial economy cause the list of potential paid-work activities to shrink, the list of labor market exemptions will grow. Rather than the government picking winning and losing activities, prudent public policy should empower all individuals to reduce their attachment to paid labor. The best way to do so is to make work time reduction a possibility for all workers.

Income guarantees also fail to introduce greater economic stability as most proposals fail to address demand deficiencies or inflationary pressures. Although an income guarantee or negative income tax could be tied to the level of private spending to have a counter-balancing effect on economic activity, most advocates do not champion the program as such, focusing instead on the libertarian aspect of lifestyle choice and the efficiency advantage over traditional welfare programs (Friedman 1962; Tobin 1968; Van Parijs 1995). Even if a basic income was administered as a stabilization policy—being generous in recessions and parsimonious in expansions—it would still have difficulties fighting the price pressures arising from the wage and price spiral as it only influences the labor market indirectly.

Another important critique of work-based-minimum-income plans is that socioeconomic participation would be limited to the minimum that money could buy. Gottschalk (1973: 235) objected to such plans as perpetuating "the assumption that 'nonworking' persons should be consigned to live on a defined minimum income." It may be difficult to foster greater socio-economic participation for both the underemployed and the overemployed by guaranteeing incomes if, in doing so, society becomes even more materialistic. A low minimum for those who cannot find decent or suitable work undermines their sense of self-worth and self-respect. The stigmatism of a work-based minimum income would separate the recipients from the rest of the community which would then be even more entrenched in an individualistic market existence as a result of the economic stimulus provided by the income guarantee. Since it is not growth neutral, a guaranteed income would perpetuate labor market segmentation, contributing to the maintenance of a core of full-time, high-paid, skilled workers and a periphery of marginalized, low-paid, unskilled workers. Gorz (1992) refers to this as the "basic income apartheid" because, although living conditions of the most disadvantaged workers would improve marginally, lasting progress toward a more egalitarian society of shared work will be arrested. Gorz argues that we should attempt to take back the public space currently dominated by paid work in order to make room for political and social activities designed for the common good. He contends, however, that work will not be ousted from that space by granting a guaranteed income that allows individuals to remain outside the economic sphere. Gorz (1994: 95) admonishes against the implementation of a universal financial allowance on its own:

> An allowance program of this kind, in exempting people from performing any paid work, fails to create a public space for non-economic activities. Economic activity today occupies the public space to an exaggerated extent ... It will not, however, be ousted from that space by paying allowance to those who stay outside the economic sphere, and thereby remain outside what is today the most important dimension of the public sphere. On the contrary, an allowance that exempts people from any work within the economic sphere will deepen the split within society. Economic activity will become the province of production-mad, profit-hungry individuals.

Aznar (1988) likewise points out that income guarantees would intensify the social conflict between an elite group of labor market insiders and the outsiders that have been excluded from the job market. So long as the work fetish maintains its magnetism on the social psyche, labor market reform will initially require expanded access to both income and paid work. Hayden (1999: 173) writes "given a society in which employment continues to play such a central role in granting status, identity, and opportunities for self-realization, a gradual reduction of hours for all, with some form or income guarantee, is preferable to the relatively enlightened marginalization of a guaranteed annual income without the sharing of work." Thus, a "second check" or "part-time salary" could serve as an ancillary policy to work time reduction but a guaranteed annual income guarantee alone will not achieve sufficient labor market reform to ameliorate the underutilization of labor (Aznar 1993).

If autonomous activities are to replace paid work in the public space, then the centrality of work has to be reduced through organized public action, governed by a desideratum of greater socioeconomic participation rather than economic rationality. Barring an organized plan to regain the public sphere, such as a regulation of work hours, the anarchy of production will remain in force and social inequities will persist. Since they stoke the work and spend fires, income guarantees encourage acquisitive individuals to monopolize the public space while the non-working income recipients will be marginalized into social oblivion. If robots eventually replace workers in large numbers, there may be a need to implement a social dividend program akin to a guaranteed annual income as a way of distributing the social surplus. But movement toward the goal of zero work hours needs to be shared and gradual in order to arrest the work and spend mentality and to ensure the adequate development of the human faculties needed to occupy greater autonomous time in a redeeming manner. If non-market activities are to replace paid work, then the culture of work has to be reduced by an organized process that gradually shares social productivity gains as well as the remaining social labors in an equitable fashion. A gradual redistribution of socially necessary labor creates public space for non-market activities, initiating the societal transformation toward a post-industrial existence that places less importance on paid work.

Work time reduction is the only welfare reform program that promotes the full dignity and citizenship of all members of society because it recognizes that the social tasks that need to be performed can be made as pleasant and fulfilling as possible by distributing them in a manner that decreases their duration and intensity. Unlike job guarantees or participatory income programs, work time reduction discourages the "outsourcing" of important, and often intimate, social functions such as the nurturance, entertainment, and education of our youth. Employment programs that suffer from a work fetish run the risk of forcing such third sector activity into the sphere of paid work by encouraging greater labor market specialization and segmentation.

Gottschalk (1973) proposes a community-based welfare system as an alternative to income guarantees. In such a system, recipients would become shareholders in a community-controlled organization that dispenses welfare aid in return for beneficial tasks to the community, including child rearing and caring for the aged. Yet, a plan of this sort is highly dependent on a redistribution of work hours. The time to complete these community tasks is precisely what work time regulation would afford overworked employees, while their paid work hours could be taken up by those who are underemployed. The erstwhile underemployed would then have the financial resources to participate more fully in the community and still have the time to join their neighbors in more non-market activities and production.

Another obstacle to income guarantees is the potential that the payment could be squandered on nonessentials rather than being devoted to more judicious expenditures such as healthcare, childcare, education, adequate nutrition and supplemental retirement savings. Conversely, payroll expansion typically encourages individuals toward such socially redeeming expenditures. Therefore, until social provisioning is enhanced in many countries and the societal predilection towards paid work is eased, enhanced socioeconomic participation can best be promoted by policies that encourage a redistribution of society's necessary labors without creating inordinately more work hours in aggregate.

Providing a "no-strings-attached" income could easily lead to inflation with little or no improvement in unemployment. If the greater aggregate demand stimulus was taken far enough, income guarantees could reduce unemployment but the cost would be unsustainable economic growth. The sizeable expansion of throughput needed to address labor underutilization in the developed world and the attendant social and environmental ills associated with such rapid economic growth represent the most objectionable consequence of a full-employment income guarantee.[11] Given the social and environmental costs of economic growth, full employment policies should be governed by the goal of increasing socioeconomic participation with a minimal expansion of the free-market system and resource utilization. Full employment policies that do not consider the urgency of environmental protection and relieving the pressure on the earth's natural resources are unsustainable in the long run and therefore inferior to work time regulation. This is not to say that there is no social role for income guarantees; only that they cannot be considered a sustainable full-employment policy. It might be wise for a society to grant limited income guarantees or negative income taxes to societal subgroups in an effort to improve the efficiency of income support or to address chronic income inequalities, but universal implementation as a method to address unemployment will only invite the aforementioned economic, social, and environmental problems. In a sense, work time regulation represents a median ground between job and income guarantees as it seeks a balance between a more equitable distribution of remunerative work under current institutional arrangements and the free will to pursue more non-market activities both now and in the future.

Conclusion

Economists generally defer to one of two main explanations for unemployment: 1) the rigidity of wages (or artificially high real wages); or 2) class conflict. This chapter has shown that work time reduction reduces both of these sources of unemployment through its favorable impact on productivity and by linking those productivity gains to an expansion of life outside the realm of capitalist relations, thereby diminishing a primary source of class conflict. Whatever its source, unemployment is always a distributional issue. It amounts to a choice of visiting the burden of an economic downturn on a small portion of disadvantaged workers or spreading the pain more equally.

If it makes sense for the government to subsidize the employment of some workers through a wage subsidy or job guarantee during an economic contraction, why not subsidize all workers through a work-sharing plan? Unemployment insurance-supported work sharing plans (examined in Chapter 5) have done just that in the 1970s and 1980s by reducing the hours of all workers and affording them a portion of the full-time equivalent unemployment insurance benefit. Through such programs, the State temporarily absorbed some of the costs of unemployment while individuals were kept on private sector payrolls in a far more equitable and solidaristic fashion than inflicting unemployment on an unlucky minority of workers (Best 1988). Since it attenuates income and consumption contractions, widespread work-sharing has the potential to stabilize economic activity without relying on substantially greater economic stimulus and material throughput.

As it goes to the heart of the inflation issue—labor productivity and income distribution—work time regulation offers the potential of achieving greater economic participation and price stability in a sustainable manner. An expansion of employment and economic participation through work time reduction will have countervailing pressures on prices that can be harnessed to achieve modest and stable inflation. The productivity-enhancing benefits that are increasingly being realized through reduced work time experiments will place downward pressure on prices. On the other hand, the tightening of the labor market that would result from a work time reduction could strengthen the bargaining power of all workers, placing upward pressure on wages and potentially on final prices. In order to balance these countervailing price pressures, a policy that links productivity growth to greater leisure time for all workers should be implemented to serve as an incomes policy designed to avoid an inflationary struggle over national income. Designed in this fashion, work time regulation offers the very real possibility of achieving price stability and low levels of unemployment without relying on make-work solutions that result in more material throughput. Work time regulation is less inflationary than both income and job guarantees, as it improves labor productivity at a fraction of the fiscal spending and can be designed to attenuate excessive consumption in the future by granting productivity dividends to workers in the form of reduced work hours rather than larger absolute incomes. Moreover, the expansion of private sector payrolls through work time regulation would arguably be less inflationary than make-work employment in the public sector. Sawyer (2003) argues that "mainstream" private sector jobs would provide greater output than those offered as part of a job guarantee. Certainly, the greater output resulting from the expansion of private sector payrolls would be less inflationary than the fiscal spending associated with job and income guarantees that have a limited effect on the aggregate supply of goods and services. This not to say that net output would have to expand indefinitely, as productivity gains could be continually directed toward work time reduction as part of a long-run incomes policy.

Since they fail to address the central and exploitive issue of the determination of working hours, income and job guarantees do little to alter the dialectic relations of capitalism. The lodestar of an employment policy should not be an obsession with keeping everyone busy, but rather an effort to increase socioeconomic participation by increasing the work hours of some while reducing them for others. In a post-industrial world characterized by automated and global production processes, employment policies should place a new emphasis on bolstering economic participation that is not solely defined by remunerative work. In the "weightless" economy of the information age, an employment policy that creates jobs for the sake of employment alone, will increasingly lead to a misallocation of societal resources as the time and effort employed in those tasks may be better spent in non-market activities. Economists and policymakers should therefore begin to envision progressive employment policies that are not subject to current ideological proclivities toward paid work. As more regions of the world come to struggle with the paradox of abundance, the merits of traditional Keynesian employment policies that rely on ever-increasing levels of aggregate spending will be quickly negated by the social and ecological damage caused by a growth-oriented work and spend ethos. Thus, full-employment policies that rely on traditional aggregate demand stimulus and more material throughput represent a twentieth-century solution to the problems of the twenty-first century. A modern full-employment policy should seek to improve the economic participation of both the underemployed and the over-worked through a redistribution and reduction of work hours that not only stabilizes economic activity, but also benefits families, communities, and the enviroment.

4 The Ecological and Social Sustainability of Work Time Regulation

Neoclassical economics, as even its most prideful communicants would agree, did nothing to prepare people for the explosion of concern over the environment – something that might have been expected of a good and competent science. So economists would be wise to be restrained in recommending remedies that grow out of these ideas.

JK Galbraith (1973: 288)

… the general march of industrial democracy is not towards inadequate hours of work, but towards sufficient hours of leisure. Working people demand time to look about them, time to see their homes by daylight, to see their children, time to think and read and cultivate their gardens – time, in short, to live.

Winston Churchill, President of the Board of Trade, UK (1908: 111)

The role of work time regulation in sustainable development

When discussing the sustainability of economic activity, it is important to distinguish between growth of material throughput—a physical phenomenon—and the expansion of wealth and income—a social phenomenon. While increased material throughput is now a controversial national objective, economic growth as measured by income flows can still be a feasible social goal. Herman Daly (1996: 192) contends that "sustainable growth is impossible." Yet, the arguments against growth often confuse the measurement of the financial value of economic transactions with the level of material transformation. When general economic growth is distinguished from development or progress, it is possible to envision a social system of production and distribution that is physically sustainable and still able to generate higher levels of income and wealth. But the focus should not be on growth alone; we will have to become more accepting of moderate growth rates as we begin to target the things that matter in the furtherance of the life process. With improved environmental stewardship, economic growth as measured by GDP may slow or even contract in the short run, but that need not diminish human welfare. Since much of the prolific rise in output over the last two centuries has been related to mining the earth on one side and filling it with waste on the other, curtailment of these activities may reduce material throughput. Widespread implementation of renewable energy may alone contract the monetary value of output as we will cease paying for the mining and burning of fossil fuels. On the other hand, if significant value is added by green technologies, the monetary value of output need not fall. In place of extractive industries, for example, society could choose to develop an "eco-industry" that competed for government contracts to reduce and recycle industrial and household waste and to innovate and implement green technologies. Such activity could maintain rather constant levels of GDP while greatly enhancing human welfare. Indeed, many of the "greenest" European countries, such as Holland, Denmark, Sweden and Norway, have seen their economies grow more slowly than average while quality of life measures have improved. When we measure the things that are most important—such as the integrity of the environment, free time to build relationships, democratic participation, volunteerism, lower crime and inequality, job and health security, and overall well-being—maximizing the output of material goods is revealed as a rather pedestrian pursuit.

The question of the environmental sustainability of unfettered economic growth is twofold: the continuing availability of natural resources and the capacity of the ecosystem to absorb a growing level of material transformation. The evolutionary approach of Institutionalist economics again proves useful in conceptualizing a social structure of production that is in closer harmony with the natural world. For Institutionalists, technological change is central to the economy and the institutional adjustments that govern it. With technological change, productive capital is not a stock of natural resources fixed by natural law. Resources do not "exist" for Institutionalists, but rather they "become." Institutions—be they markets, governments or otherwise—define resources and capital by promoting certain production processes over others. The environmental implication of this approach is that technological advance can ensure the availability of productive inputs and relieve disposal pressure on the ecosystem.

The Institutionalist method offers a rather optimistic view of technological development, suggesting that productive practices tend to follow abundant resources, which at one time included fossil fuels. Particularly if the institutional conditions are favorable, technological adaptation will militate toward abundant resources. Today, for example, bio-fuels are in greater abundance than ever before due to the meteoric rise of agricultural productivity, and, accordingly, technology has adapted in the form of alternative fuels and engines for automobiles and composting operations for energy production. As is usually the case, the technology has been available long before social institutions have been willing to adapt to its use. Recognizing the adaptability of technology is important to the ecological debate because as Sachs *et al.* (1998: 29) argue "ecological sustainability is at present endangered more by the damage human activities cause to eco-systems than by shortage of raw materials." This suggests that it is not necessarily the scale of activity that has been problematic, but rather the methods and processes used in the transformation of nature—especially the burning of fossil fuels.

As the Institutionalist approach emphasizes economic "development" or "progress" over traditional economic "growth," it represents a departure from the "growth model of environmental stewardship" without sacrificing the furtherance of the life process. The last 50 years of industrial economic growth have clearly manifest the conflict between unselective growth and ecological degradation, diminishing faith that the environment would eventually benefit from long-run growth. During the halcyon days of economic expansion, many held the belief that growth would eventually provide the means to repair the environment and protect it from further damage. Walter Heller, former Chairman of the US President's Council of Economic Advisor's (1961–64), espoused the view thusly:

> We need expansion to fulfill our nation's aspirations. In a fully employed, high-growth economy you have a better chance to free public and private resources to fight the battle of land, air, water, and noise pollution than in a low-growth economy. I cannot conceive of a successful economy without growth.
>
> (Schumacher 1974: 98)

Economic growth has also been defended as necessary to tackle poverty. The "rising tide lifts all boats" aphorism holds steadfastly to the notion that conventional economic growth will eventually trickle down into poor countries. But the growth solution offers a false choice by pitting the health of the environment against the well-being of the poor in developing nations. In a global context, the growth consensus has become a veil for aggrandizing the wealth of the fortunate fifth of the world's population, while the poor are abandoned to deal with the environmental consequences. Not only are the benefits of economic growth more inequitable today, but the ecological consequences caused by the rapacious consumption habits of the developed world are more apparent and severe than ever before. The Sustainable Development Issues Network (2008) calculates that under current distribution patterns the rich have to get very much richer for the poor to get slightly less poor. It now takes around $166 worth of global growth to generate a single dollar of poverty reduction for people in absolute poverty, compared with just $45 in the 1980s. In a climate-constrained world, serious poverty reduction—at home and abroad—can only come to fruition by deploying a new development model that is oriented toward redistribution rather than unequal economic growth. In the search for a more sustainable social system we would do well to remember J.S. Mill's (1929: 496) time-honored delineation between economic growth and progress, "A state of constant capital … is not equivalent to a stoppage in human inventiveness. There would be great latitude for all kinds of intellectual culture, for moral and social progress, and just as many possibilities of improving the conduct of life; and it is more probable that this would occur."

The Institutionalist approach represents an alternative to the price mechanism that is often espoused as a way of rectifying most environmental problems. Although internalizing the ecological costs of trade would go some distance in ameliorating environmental damage, Institutionalists generally agree that relative prices fail to reflect important normative values. When social issues revolve around matters of moral value, a holistic analysis becomes imperative. The price mechanism alone cannot tell us why the Alaska Wildlife Preserve should not be encroached upon; why the wetlands should not be developed into agricultural or commercial land; or why cherished open spaces should not be sold to the highest bidder. Sachs *et al.* (1998: 95) describe an approach that most Institutionalists would endorse:

> Anyone who does not want poisons in mothers' milk must ban production of toxics; if the preservation of a specific landscape is desired, the preconditions must be established. That starts with a value judgment. Only then can it be asked how an objective viewed as being right can best be achieved. And only after that will it also be relevant to determine what contribution the possibilities open to a market economy can make towards attaining what seems an ecologically meaningful objective.

This approach—which retains some scope for the market mechanism—is highly congruent with the Institutionalist practice of "letting a thousand flowers bloom." Institutionalists would not forsake the market mechanism entirely, but would recognize its limited ability to govern man's interaction with the environment.

Given capitalism's track record of ecological degradation and the eminent threats related to global warming, prudence seems to dictate that "selective" growth represents the most pragmatic approach to our current ecological woes. Targeting manageable or sustainable growth holds the prospect of both reducing our net claims on the environment and the damage associated with future levels of extraction and disposal. Rapidly contracting output or maintaining business as usual practices offers little escape from the ecological dilemma as both would entail an exclusion of large portions of the populace from the solution. A policy of enhanced socioeconomic participation under selective growth is likely to provide more "ecological breakthroughs" than the status quo or a knee-jerk contraction of economic activity as more minds and manpower will be recruited to the process of sustainable development. As argued above, conceiving of a successful economy that is less dependent on market-based growth would almost certainly require an expansion of the third sector. Combining environmental stewardship with humanity's innate parental bent, it should be possible to direct human activity in the third sector toward the objective of improving life satisfaction in a sustainable manner.

The concern for environmental sustainability in a society of greater socio-economic participation is not motivated by the Malthusian specter that seems to guide so many apocryphal critiques of the industrial system. Schumacher (1974), for instance, warns that prodigious production is based on the profligate use of irreplaceable natural capital. This fixed and Newtonian view of capital—allowing little scope for technological change to alter the definition of "capital inputs"—is characteristic of many of the modern polemics of contemporary production methods. For instance, Princen (2005: 16) also views efficiency and sufficiency as irreconcilable:

> Sufficiency principles such as restraint, respite, precaution, polluter pays, zero, and reverse onus have the virtue of partially resurrecting well-established notions like moderation and thrift, ideas that have never completely disappeared. They also have the virtue of being highly congruent with global ecological constraint, a congruence not shared by efficiency.

Likewise, Lester Brown (1999: 29) has long argued that, "Such conflation of the notions of efficiency and satiability promote a false choice for environmentalists."

Yet, we should not be rash in tarnishing efficiency with the brush of insatiability. Notions of efficiency and sufficiency need not be mutually exclusive. Indeed, we can embrace the ideals and consequences of material sufficiency, while still striving for greater efficiency in our resource use. A chief virtue of the Institutionalist approach is that it offers a reconciliation of the conflict between sufficiency and efficiency. As outlined above, Institutionalist thought does not assume scarcity and non-satiation. It is therefore accepting of the notion of sufficiency—that it is possible to define when individuals and societies have obtained enough. Given the centrality of technological change, however, there is always the potential for achieving enough with less. Just because the pursuit of efficiency has been hijacked by and for the purposes of economic growth in the past, it does not mean that we will be forever committed to growth as the "end all, be all" of economic activity. An Institutionalist view of technological advance recognizes the severability of efficiency and insatiability and consequently eschews the long-run pessimism expressed by Malthusian warnings of resource depletion.

Institutionalists would agree however that short-term limits to the destructive aspects of industrial production are imperative so that the "point-of-no-return" in terms of environmental damage is not broached. In the early 1990s, Paul Ekins (1993: 92) estimated that sustainability entailed a 50 percent reduction in environmental impact. He cites three broad factors impacting the environment: population, consumption, and technology. Since population is expected to reach 10 billion by 2050 and economic growth of 3 percent per year amounts to a fourfold increase in consumption in the next 50 years, technological improvements would have to reduce the impact of consumption by 93 percent over the next five decades in order to achieve sustainability. Given the Herculean nature of such a task and the inequities of consumption between northern and southern countries, erecting some short-term limits to growth in Northern countries seems practicable. By Ekins' calculations, zero growth for rich countries could allow consumption to quadruple in the developing countries while technology is left to tackle 78 percent of the environmental impact. Lamenting the fact that roughly 20 percent of the Earth's population is responsible for 80 percent of the resource use, Sachs *et al.* (1998) calculate that by the year 2050 carbon dioxide emissions must be reduced by 50–60 percent in Germany and 85–88 percent in Canada and America if ecological space is to be made available for even meager growth in living standards in developing countries. Although the various sustainability estimates are imprecise, they illustrate the need for a multifaceted and pragmatic approach to sustainable economic management.

A pragmatic approach to sustainability requires that if any economic growth is to occur in the short run it will have to be highly "selective." Indeed, some selective growth might be preferable to no growth as it has the capability of "crowding-in" environmental improvements throughout the rest of the economy through increased socioeconomic participation. The benefits gleaned in rich countries could then be shared with the rest of the world. By reducing the north's consumption footprint, policies such as work time reduction not only create ecological space for poor countries, but they also create the possibility that the Fordist industrial model will not be reproduced throughout the rest of the world. The technological discoveries spawned by greater socioeconomic participation in developed countries will hopefully be exported abroad to help less-developed nations avoid, or leapfrog, many of the "dirty" practices utilized by the industrial pioneers. At a minimum, we should ensure that the production and use of some of the world's worst pollutants and contaminates would remain under international bans, as would the most pernicious labor and business practices.

Environmental pragmatism recognizes that behavior modification takes time and that relying on market mechanisms—such as enlightened capital markets to penalize carbon producers—might take too long from an ecological point of view. Government intervention is needed therefore to avoid ecological catastrophes by interrupting the positive feedback loops of self-reinforcing mechanisms. Meadows (1997: 80) provides some useful examples of feedback loops that could be ecologically troublesome, "The more babies that are born, the more people grow up to have babies ... The more soil erodes, the less vegetation it can support, the fewer roots and leaves to soften rain and runoff, the more soil erodes." In this sense, work time regulation could serve as a thermostat that retards positive feedback effects before they become too large for long-run technological advances to resolve or reverse. Confronting an increasingly fragile ecosystem with accelerating feedback loops, government intervention should seek to limit material throughput in the short run as a means of curtailing environmental damage during the adoption of improved technology. Such temporary restraint can be achieved while embracing a long-run belief in the ability of technological change and institutional adjustment to bring about more sustainable production processes.

Smarter growth should also entail an expansion of traditional environmental regulation in order to eliminate the immediate ecological threats of the "production for profit" system. Noting the inability and inefficacy of market (i.e. Coasean) solutions to internalize the cost of environmental damage, Galbraith (1973) suggests that a reduction and regulation of economic growth is a preferred means of controlling the market's assault on the biosphere. Yet, he acknowledges that reducing economic growth could achieve, at best, a lagged and gradual amelioration of the environment. Since growth reduction tends to freeze relative living standards, this form of environmental protection only becomes an appropriate remedy as the distribution of income becomes more equal. Galbraith (1973: 289) emphasizes distribution when he writes, "The prime purpose of improving income, and especially of improving the distribution of income, should be to increase the number of people who are removed from the pressures of physical need or its equivalent and who are able, in consequence, to exercise choice as to their style of economic life." Thus, in an affluent economy, income distribution can take on greater importance than income growth, which then places less pressure on the environment. This is extremely relevant to work time regulation as the first goal of reform should be to redistribute work hours from the overworked to the underemployed.

Given the limitations posed by current income inequities, Galbraith's view suggests that growth reduction should be coupled with legislated parameters within which growth can occur. Regulation of the amount of waste, heat, noise, social strain, familial stress, community degradation or other negative externality realized during production, makes the State, not the market, the arbiter and protector of the public interest. After reducing income inequality through work time regulation, environmental policy could then consider further curtailment of economic growth. In the short run, however, selective economic growth coupled with strict environmental regulations could encourage more sustainable lifestyles in wealthy nations.

As a society, we may choose to do more things, or we may choose to simply do them better. By combining the principles of efficiency and sufficiency wealthy countries can endeavor to optimize inputs, without necessarily maximizing outputs. For extended periods of time, we may *choose* a smaller economy in order to curtail the destructive aspects of the free market approach. But if society is able to adapt to technological change in a manner that alters the composition and callousness of economic growth, ecological restraints need not entail a significant contraction of economic activity over the long run. Work time regulation can therefore serve as an effective mechanism in restraining the interim ecological damage caused by society's measured adoption of technological advancement. It should be noted that societal deliberation in adapting new technologies is often beneficial. Indeed, choosing the proper path of technological development is complex and has convoluted social consequences. Haste has often made waste when antic-ompetitive behavior or government funding has favored an inferior techno-logical option which led to a path dependency that magnified the costs to society. At the other extreme, the potential harm of a desultory adaptation of technology is that the capitalist system will race onward, catapulting society dangerously close to the "point-of-no-ecological-return." Work time regulation can then serve as a useful brake on consumption-driven produc-tion during this deliberative stage and allow for the fullest long-run techno-logical development possible by increasing the participation of the greatest number of societal members. Sachs (1993: 16) speaks to the importance of such a growth thermostat when he writes, "an increase in resource efficiency alone leads to nothing, unless it goes hand-in-hand with an intelligent restraint on growth." Brundtland (1987: 8) describes a sustainable growth mentality that also embraces short-term restraints:

> The concept of sustainable development does imply limits – not absolute limits but limitations imposed by the present state of technology and social organizations on environmental resources and by the ability of the biosphere to absorb the effects of human activities. But technology and social organization can be both managed and improved to make way for a new era of economic growth.

Achieving ecologically neutral production practices through the use of effi-ciency measures, environmental taxes, and other reforms, is futile if the reduction in pollution levels is negated by large increases in production. Automotive technology offers a case in point. Although modern vehicles are inordinately more efficient than the cars of yesteryear, meteoric growth in the number of cars and miles driven has offset any ecological gains. Work time reform can therefore help ensure that efficiency gains are not cannibalized by irresponsible growth. Regulating hours can play an essential role in directing productivity gains towards activities with a smaller ecological footprint. Hayden (1999: 52) argues that "channeling productivity gains towards more time rather than more production clearly does not in itself lead to *absolute reductions* in the demands that Northern societies make on the environment; but it could be extremely effective in *limiting* or even *halting* increases in consumption and further environmental degradation so that action on other fronts can lead to environmental improvements [sic]." As it can constrain overall economic activity, the continual adjustment of work hours can respond to the environmental exigencies caused by the composition of eco-nomic output prevailing at any point in time. Work time regulation can serve an essential role in a process of sustainable development that endeavors to "keep the volume of human extraction/emission in balance with the regen-erative capacities of nature" (Sachs 1993: 17). The current state of the environment suggests that output *growth* should be curtailed until its com-position can be transformed into a less destructive form—at which point society might choose to expand work hours and accelerate economic growth in a sustainable manner.

Ecological reform will need to go beyond the mere imposition of new constraints and limitations to economic rationality that appear in the "market-based" solutions to environmental damage. The ideal ecological approach should involve a paradigm shift that alters the tendency of capitalism to extend the sphere of economic rationality and increase the value of expanding stocks of capital. Gorz (1994: 95) argues that the "less but better" slogan "aims to reduce the sphere in which economic rationality and commodity exchanges apply, and to subordinate it to non-quantifiable societal and cultural ends and to free development of individuals." Embarking on an ecological paradigm shift through work time reform need not impinge on our individual or social welfare. As suggested in Chapter 2, we could live and work better and more "lightly" upon the Earth by earning and consuming less, provided that we consume differently. Importantly, a non-material vision of progress that enhanced social participation would afford more individuals the opportunity to contribute to technological improvements and to ply them in a sustainable manner.

The ecological urgency of work time reform

The ecological urgency of re-thinking the scale and composition of economic growth has been underscored by an assortment of climate change studies over the last decade. The Intergovernmental Panel on Climate Change (IPCC), commissioned by the United Nations, concludes that "warming of the climate system is unequivocal, as is now evident from observations of increases in global average air and ocean temperatures, widespread melting of snow and ice and rising global average sea level (2007: 2)." In relation to economic growth, the IPCC (2007: 5) identifies a strong link between global greenhouse gases (GHG) and industrial activity, "Global GHG emissions due to human activities have grown since pre-industrial times, with an increase of 70% between 1970 and 2004 ... Most of the observed increase in global average temperatures since the mid-twentieth century is very likely due to the observed increase in anthropogenic GHG concentrations (2007: 5)." The meteoric increase in GHG emissions, such as carbon dioxide, does not impugn all forms of economic growth. It does however challenge the composition of economic output, which currently relies on fossil fuels to transform vast quantities of resources into consumption goods. The IPCC (2007: 6) warns that "global increases in CO_2 concentrations are due primarily to fossil fuel use, with land-use change providing another significant but smaller contribution." Even with growing recognition of the problem of global warming and the implementation of some mitigation policies, global GHG emission will continue to grow at a dangerous pace over the next few decades. The IPCC Special Report on Emissions Scenarios (2007: 7) projects "an increase of global GHG emissions by 25 to 90% (CO_2-eq) between 2000 and 2030, with fossil fuels maintaining their dominant position in the global energy mix to 2030 and beyond." Thus, curbing the growth of consumption and output in the short run, while altering the composition of economic output in the long run, is essential to avoiding the cataclysmic and potentially irreversible climatic changes related to global warming. Invoking the same sense of urgency, the Stern Report (Stern 2007: iii) warns against a blasé approach to global warming, "the scientific evidence points to increasing risks of serious, irreversible impacts from climate change associated with business-as-usual paths for emissions." Ackerman and Stanton (2008: vi) use an updated version of the Stern model to calculate the impact on the US economy and find that "the true costs of global warming – including economic losses, noneconomic damages, and increased risks of catastrophe – will reach 3.6 percent of US GDP by 2100 if business-as-usual emissions are allowed to continue." The implications of climate change point to the inevitability of a curtailment of current levels of material consumption in wealthy countries; whether it is done proactively of our own volition or forced upon us by natural disasters is the only remaining matter of choice. With estimates of the economic costs of status quo emissions ranging from a 5 to 10 percent annual reduction in global GDP, it makes little sense to pursue unsustainable short-term economic growth if it will only prompt large reductions in well-being and untold human suffering in the wake of cataclysmic climate changes. Stern (2007) estimates that business as usual climate change will reduce welfare by an amount equivalent to a reduction in global consumption per person of around 20 percent per year. This is roughly equivalent to a 1-day reduction in the average workweek. The calculus is clear; we can reduce working time (and its attendant market consumption) today with some prospect of improving the environment or have the lifestyle changes forced upon us by ecological collapse in the near future.

The consequences of global warming will not be isolated to the industrial countries that have produced the bulk of the GHGs. Instead, those countries that have contributed the least to atmospheric changes are expected to suffer the brunt of global warming as livelihoods in non-industrialized countries are closely linked to subtle climatic changes. Ackerman and Stanton (2008: vii) write, "the sad irony is that while richer countries like the United States are responsible for much greater per person greenhouse gas emissions, many of the poorest countries around the world will experience damages that are much larger as a percentage of their national output." It therefore becomes a moral imperative for industrial countries to restrain their rapacious consumption habits until the composition of economic growth can be transformed into more sustainable practices. Work time reform that channels productivity dividends into more autonomous time for workers rather than more consumption should be viewed as an effective way of halting the assault on the environment and reducing the risks of climatic change in third-world countries.

Lipietz (1995) argues that Keynesian-style economic management is now passé in light of global ecological challenges and that work time reduction should be at the core of an "ecological macroeconomics." Lipietz (1995: 47) writes:

> It is therefore the height of cynicism to claim that 'only growth will reduce unemployment'. In fact, the only way to stop unemployment growing is to reduce the individual's working time ... Creating a society which gauges progress by the growth of free time more than by the accumulation of wealth is an imperative stemming from responsibility – the crisis of waste matter and climate change through greenhouse effect is merely the consequence of a model of the indefinite growth of mass consumption.

Indeed, the superiority of work time regulation relative to traditional full-employment policies that owe their efficacy to an expansion of economic output is the restraint of the ecological damage caused by unfettered economic growth. The economic stimulus associated with job and income guarantees, for instance, would commit us to significantly higher levels of consumption and material throughput with little improvement in labor market inequities. Even if some of the functions performed by job guarantee workers were socially and environmentally friendly, there is no guarantee that their greater consumption would be. When a full-employment economic stimulus is added to current consumption levels, the carrying capacity of the environment becomes a serious concern. Granted short hours may provide greater leisure time which can also be spent on activities of questionable social value, but at least such "time consumption" is beyond the immediate sphere of influence of the capitalist and tends to be less harmful to the environment than the consumption of mass-produced goods and services. Indeed, many of the homespun activities conducted in the third sector tend to be service-oriented and more sustainable (not requiring packaging, promotion, and transportation) than activities conducted on the hedonic treadmill of a work and spend existence. Furthermore, the "cleaner" activities of the third sector may become more attractive once the full ecological cost of market activity is internalized into the price of private sector goods and services through government regulation.

Although "expending" leisure time is intrinsically less damaging to the environment than market-driven expenditures, government policy and ecological taxes should still attempt to direct both commercial and leisure activities into "sustainable" practices. This is especially true in the short run as a redistributive work-sharing program may stimulate effective demand and economic activity *in the aggregate* during the initial stages, before stabilizing at more sustainable levels. Many of the macroeconomic benefits of work time regulation, such as improved productivity, result from more egalitarian patterns of employment and consumption, which in turn lead to a tightening of the economy system. A redistribution of work time may result in greater aggregate demand since the underemployed, who will be able to expand their work hours and earnings, are likely to have a higher marginal propensity to consume. Depending on the level of income inequality prevailing in a particular economy, a redistribution of work time may initially increase material throughput. But as productivity dividends are devoted to work time reduction, economic growth could be reduced to slower and more sustainable rates. Hayden (1999: 95) anticipates this in his advocacy of ecological tax reform, "to the extent that sharing work as a job-creation strategy provides a short-term boost to economic growth, measures to promote eco-efficiency become increasingly important as a means of limiting, and possibly negating, the ecological consequences of that growth." It is important to note, however, that any increase in absolute output would be a one-time event related to an improved distribution of social labor. Moreover, work time regulation operated as an incomes policy would restrain the level of economic growth far below those levels that would prevail under traditional full-employment programs.

Social sustainability

Writing in 1883, Paul Lafargue was nonplused as to why workers were willing to risk so much by working long hours:

> Cannot the labourers understand that by over-working themselves they exhaust their own strength and that of their progeny, that they are used up and long before their time come to be incapable of any work at all, that absorbed and brutalized by this single vice they are no longer men but pieces of men, that they kill within themselves all beautiful faculties, to leave nothing alive and flourishing except the furious madness for work.
>
> (Lafargue 1883: 59)

In retrospect one may be tempted to answer that the workers of the industrial revolution had little choice but to submit to the harsh working conditions in order to obtain a means of subsistence. A corollary question then becomes why would their employers ask them to damage their health and long-run productivity? Unfortunately, the question is still relevant to the contemporary labor market as the empirical evidence suggests that extensive attachment to the workforce still creates substantial physical and social costs.

Long hours as an addiction

Since a polarization of work hours is prevalent in many wealthy countries, this section further explores the personal and social costs associated with long work hours. In some cases it is unclear whether the costs of over-work are of a personal or social nature. The impact of long hours on personal health is foremost a personal sacrifice but also exacts a toll on families, communities and healthcare systems. Since the provision of healthcare is collectively financed (through a socially or privately coordinated pooling of risk), long hours that result in more health problems represent a social burden. Indeed, any activity that results in poor health generally creates a drag on social productivity and efficiency. With the imposition of sin taxes on activities such as smoking and alcohol consumption, many developed countries have acknowledged the social nature of unhealthy lifestyles. It is therefore appropriate to explore workaholism as a social ill with a cost structure similar to other addictions. Exploring the costs of excessive work hours helps elucidate the true costs of overwork and suggests one reason why happiness has stagnated since 1975 in long-hours countries, while it has risen in some of the short-hours countries of continental Europe.

Conceiving of the desire to work long hours as an addiction helps to illustrate the potential social costs of the pathology. McNamara (2004) writes of a compulsive work syndrome that can degenerate into a vicious cycle:

> Workaholism is an addiction. It's the illusion, and associated destructive behaviors caused from that illusion, that a person can effectively address challenges in life and work exclusively by working harder at work. The addiction seems to follow this cycle. Discomforts in life and work cause the person to seek relief from those discomforts. The primary form of relief that the person has access to, and believes in the most, is to feel good by accomplishing something as part of their job at work. So the workaholic attends to getting something done at work. However, as the workaholic attends increasingly to getting things done at work, their personal life begins to suffer from lack of attention.

The social costs of long work hours relate to both the direct effects on the individual worker as well as the spillover effects onto workers and family members close to the "workaholic." If long hours decrease the well-being and lifespan of workers, society may have to shoulder a large portion of the costs inflicted on the workaholics' family members.

Unlike well-known addictions to cigarettes, liquor, food and gambling, the time-honored idolatry of work suggests that workaholism is not only a socially accepted, but a socially conditioned addiction. Evidence of its prevalence, therefore, should not come as a surprise. Although addictions are difficult to define and measure, growing evidence of workaholism has been coming to light as social scientists increasingly wrestle with the polarization of work hours. The Canadian General Social Survey of 2005 asked people whether they considered themselves to be workaholics. Nearly one-third (31 percent) responded yes (Keown 2007). The survey also found that workaholics are significantly more likely than other people to report poor health. Hamermesh and Slemrod (2008) also conclude that workaholism is prevalent and has large spillover affects on the utility of both co-workers and family members. Since many workaholics have the ability to determine their own hours and influence the hours of their co-workers and spouses, they create negative spillovers by compelling others to work longer hours and realize lower utility levels than they would in the absence of an addict (Hamermesh and Slemrod 2008). Robinson *et al.* (2001) found that workaholics experience more marital strife than typical workers, as indicated by their fewer positive feelings about marriage, greater rates of marital estrangement, and higher divorce rates. Clearly, the adverse impacts of overwork are not limited to spouses, "children are affected by parental work addiction in ways that are mentally unhealthy and can cause problems well into young adulthood (Robinson 1998: 65)."[1]

The individual costs of excessive hours

A growing body of empirical research is suggesting that excessive work hours adversely impact the health, well-being and longevity of workers. Overtime and extended work hours have been linked to a variety of health problems, including hypertension (i.e. high blood pressure), cardiovascular disorders, mental health problems, reproductive disorders, musculoskeletal abnormalities, chronic infections, immunologic deficiencies, diabetes, and general health complaints (van der Hulst 2003; Sparks *et al.* 1997; Dembe *et al.* 2005). In a meta-analysis of 21 medical studies using both self-reported and non-self-reported health measures and a qualitative analysis of 12 additional studies, Sparks *et al.* (1997) find a positive relationship between hours of work and ill-health, including physiological and psychological health symptoms. In a meta-analysis of studies conducted between 1996 and 2001, van der Hulst (2003: 183) similarly concludes, "these studies show that there is good reason to be concerned about the possible detrimental effects of long work hours on health, in particular cardiovascular disease, diabetes, illnesses leading to disability retirement, subjectively reported physical health and subjective fatigue."

Some of the most alarming evidence of the cardiovascular problems caused by long work hours comes from Japan where Uehata (1991) reports 203 cases of "karoshi"—fatal cardiovascular attacks linked to the stress of long hours. Two-thirds of the causalities had been regularly working more than 60 hours per week with more than 50 hours overtime per month before the heart attack. In addition to death from overwork, "karojisatsu" (work-related suicide) has been receiving attention as a growing social problem in Japan. In an analysis of 22 work-related suicides, long working hours were noted in psychiatrists' "psychological autopsies" (conducted for the plaintive) in 19 of the cases (Amagasa *et al.* 2005). In nine cases, individuals had been working between 10 and 16 hours per day for at least 25 days and, in some cases, up to 11 months. Certainly, more factors than long work hours contribute to workers becoming suicidal, but the fact that extended hours are a common denominator in so many cases suggests that excessive hours are compounding workplace stress.

Since middle-age cardiovascular attacks are common and the heart attack fatalities in Japan are not large in epidemiological terms, other studies need to be referenced before drawing conclusions about the direct impact of long work hours on hypertension and coronary heart disease. A variety of large-scale studies have corroborated the link between cardiovascular disorder and long work hours. Sokejima and Kagamimori (1998) found that the risk to Japanese men of a heart attack increased with a prolongation of work hours. Russek and Zohman (1958) found that 71 of 100 coronary patients in a US hospital under the age of 40 had worked more than 60 hours per week over a sustained period, more than four times the number in a matched control group. Similarly, nearly 50 percent of 50 patients admitted to an Oklahoma hospital with a heart attack regularly worked more than 60 hours per week, compared with 25 percent of a matched control group (Thiel *et al*. 1973). Analyzing a United States Census file of 22,176 Californians collected over a 3-year period, Buell and Breslow (1960) found that working more than 48 hours per week doubled the chance of dying from coronary heart disease. In a logistic regression of more recent data from the 2001 California Health Interview Survey, Yang *et al*. (2006) reveal a positive association between hours worked per week and likelihood of having self-reported hypertension. Compared with a reference group that worked between 11 and 39 hours per week, individuals working exactly 40 hours per week were 14 percent more likely to report hypertension, those working 41 to 50 hours per week were 17 percent more likely, and those working more than 51 hours per week were 29 percent more likely to report hypertension after controlling for a variety of alternative influences (Yang *et al*. 2006). Spurgeon (2003: 48) summarizes the research on work hours and cardiovascular health, "regularly working more than 60 hours per week and perhaps more than 50 hours per week appears to increase the risk of cardiovascular disease."

Long hours have also been linked to musculoskeletal problems and other workplace injuries, particularly in jobs that place heavy and repetitive physical demands on workers. A variety of studies have revealed an association between long working hours and an increased risk of occupational injuries among workers in specific occupations and industries, including construction workers, nurses, anesthetists, veterinarians, healthcare professionals, miners, bus drivers, long distance truck drivers, fire-fighters, and nuclear power plant workers (Dembe *et al*. 2005). For example, in a study of female grocery clerks in the United States, Morgenstern *et al*. (1991) found that the average number of hours worked per week and years employed in that occupation was significantly related to the prevalence of hand/wrist injuries characteristic of carpel tunnel syndrome. At the industry level, Trinkoff *et al*. (2007) studied a group of randomly selected registered nurses from Illinois and North Carolina, and found that hours worked per day, weekends worked per month, working other than day shifts, and working 13 or more hours per day at least once a week were *each* significantly associated with needlestick injuries. The researchers conclude that "despite advances in protecting workers from needlestick injuries, extended work schedules and their concomitant physical demands are still contributing to the occurrence of injuries and illnesses to nurses (Trinkoff *et al.* 2007: 163)." Long hours can also have less visible effects on psychological health, which adversely impact labor productivity. In an American automotive plant, increased overtime was significantly associated with impaired performance on various cognitive tests and associated with more feelings of depression, fatigue and confusion (Proctor *et al.* 1996).

There is growing evidence that the health impacts of long hours within specific occupations and industries also holds in the aggregate. This suggest that there are more occupations in which long hours are pernicious to health than not. Analyzing the responses of 10,793 Americans participating in the National Longitudinal Survey of Youth between 1987 and 2000, Dembe *et al.* (2005) estimate the risk of long working days, long workweeks, long commute times, and overtime schedules causing a (reported) work-related injury or illness. After controlling for age, gender, occupation, industry and region, the authors finds that working in jobs with overtime schedules was associated with a 61 percent higher injury hazard rate compared with jobs with no overtime (Dembe *et al.* 2005). Furthermore, working at least 12 hours per day was associated with a 37 percent increased hazard rate and working at least 60 hours per week was associated with a 23 percent increased hazard rate (Dembe *et al.* 2005). Dembe *et al.* (2005: 588) conclude that "job schedules with long working hours are not more risky merely because they are concentrated in inherently hazardous industries or occupations, or because people working long hours spend more total time 'at risk' for a work injury." Thus, the research on the health and safety implications of long work hours indicate that workers who work longer hours place themselves at greater odds of suffering an injury than the risks associated with simply being exposed to workplace injuries for a longer period of time. In other words, if the work hours were performed by a different, refreshed worker, the risk of workplace injury and illness would decline. A diminution of workplace injuries and illnesses, it should be noted, represents a significant cost saving to employers and a consequent boost to productivity and profitability.

The direct effects of long work hours on health tend to be compounded by the indirect effects on lifestyle habits, or what medical researchers refer to as "maladaptive behaviors." Long hours have been linked to a variety of unhealthy behaviors such as smoking, alcohol abuse, lack of exercise, insomnia, poor eating habits, and fewer medical examinations (Sparks *et al.* 1997). These lifestyle habits indirectly affect the health of overworked employees. Analyzing Canada's 1996–1997 National Population Health Survey, Shields (1999) found that switching from standard to long hours between 1994–1995 and 1996–1997 increased the odds of cigarette consumption for both men and women, unhealthy weight gain for men, and alcohol consumption for women. In a survey of coping behavior among Australian charter bus drivers, Raggatt (1991) identified long hours as the most significant predictor of stimulant use and sleep disorders. Long work hours were also linked to the irregularity of daily life, meals and sleeping patterns for Japanese middle managers (Maruyama and Morimoto 1996). The cumulative effect of unhealthy lifestyle habits is a greater incidence of cardiovascular disease and other debilitating illnesses.

Long hours that result in sleep deprivation represent both a serious health concern to the individual worker as well as a safety risk to the general public. The US National Transportation and Safety Board has vehemently publicized the fact that fatigue is the most frequent, direct cause of truck accidents in which the driver is killed. In 1991, researchers asked 602 truck drivers, "When do you feel you should stop driving?" Shockingly, 82 percent of the drivers responded that they usually stopped driving when they had a startle resulting from a head drop, or when they saw something in the road that wasn't there—a hypnagogic hallucination (Dement and Vaughan 1999). Government regulations have likely improved the situation today, but short of these regulations it is unlikely that conditions for truck drivers would have improved.[2]

Yet, should we only be concerned with the impacts of fatigue on transportation workers? Even if lives are not riding on our decisions at work, our own livelihoods and longevity certainly are. Indeed, the alertness, proficiency, and safety of the entire workforce affect our national competitiveness, health, and standard of living. Van der Hulst (2003: 184) points out that "the association between long work hours and short sleep hours suggests that a lack of recovery may be the most important pathway that links extended work hours and health." Dement and Vaughan (1999) present a convincing case for the restorative virtues of diurnal sleep patterns. The authors assert that adequate daily sleep improves our mood, mental and physical performance, immunity to disease (including cancer), vitality and longevity. Since sleep improves our resistance to diseases as diverse as the common cold to cancer, access to adequate daily sleep should become a matter of national priority. Dement and Vaughan (1999: 267) write that:

> TNF [a potent cancer killer] naturally increases tenfold while we sleep and then drops again when we awake. Staying up all night doesn't appear to affect their levels during the sleepless night, but the next day the number of natural killer cells available to fight off invaders can be severely reduced. Investigators in San Diego and elsewhere have found that people who simply stayed up until just 3:00 am before falling to sleep had a 30 percent reduction in the number of natural killer cells the next day and depressed activity in the natural killer cells still present. In addition the production of interleukin-2 was diminished. This suppression of immune function could result in greater susceptibility to viruses such as common colds. Since these immune cells also protect the body against tumors, it is possible that chronic sleep deprivation increases cancer risk.

The economic costs of sleep deprivation are staggering. Chronic sleep debt degrades nearly very aspect of human performance, including vigilance (ability to receive information), alertness (ability to act on the information), and attention span. Australian sleep researchers have clinically equated the effects of sleep loss to alcohol intoxication. The researchers found that after 24 hours awake the sleep-deprived group had the same test scores as drinking volunteers with blood-alcohol levels of 0.1 percent, which is more than legally drunk in most locales (Dement and Vaughan 1999: 231). Such research begs an interesting question; if long hours are tantamount to intoxication, should society limit the use of overtime hours in the interest of public safety and social productivity? The overuse of workers to the determent of adequate sleep levels has profound impacts on worker health and performance.

Dement and Vaughan (1999: 324) comment on the myth of sedulous individuals owing any success they may achieve to "burning the midnight oil":

> Rather than making them more productive, forgoing sleep for the sake of work makes people much less efficient and prone to making mistakes that can require even more work to fix ... Every individual needs a specific amount of sleep, and this amount cannot be altered. It is analogous to our body temperature set point. No matter how much our temperature goes up or down during the day, it must average 98.6 degrees F when we are healthy. Getting less sleep over many nights only builds up the amount of sleep debt we are carrying. For a time we can fool ourselves into thinking we are adapting to a shorter sleeping time, but eventually the sleep debt catches up with us.

The amount of sleep required varies between individuals and can change with age. But the authors' central point is that attempts to alter our individual sleep requirements in search of better performance will be fraught with frustration. Based on his 30 years of research on sleep and dreaming, Dement estimates that the typical American carries a sleep debt of between 25 and 30 hours (Dement and Vaughan 1999). Although some sleep debt is useful in acquiring and maintaining nightly sleep, sleep researchers have consistently shown that we accumulate large sleep debts to our personal and social detriment. Intuitively, sleep-deprived U.S. workers will find it difficult to achieve the hourly productivity levels of presumably better-rested European workers

Given the advent of the information age and the "new weightless economy," worker motivation is increasingly important in improving labor productivity. New psychological research shows that intrinsic pleasure may be an equally powerful motivator in the creative work process as external rewards. Openness to pleasure is an important element of the creative process, but our ability to experience pleasure is disabled by a heavy sleep debt. Dement and Vaughan (1999: 318) write that "sleep is a potent tonic for the creative process because it helps put us in a receptive state of mind where we feel motivated, are open to new ideas, are able to grasp complex and subtle relationships, and are capable of reaping pleasure from the creative process." Moreover, research into lucid dreaming—the ability to recognize a dream during REM sleep and partially influence the direction of the dream—offers promising possibilities for unlocking the creative mind during sleeping hours. In the new economy that places a premium on the use of knowledge and information, fostering creative work time through improved sleep and other leisure activities should assume more importance than simply burning the midnight oil in a misguided effort to succeed.

Many workers view professional success and sleep as a trade-off. A recent survey indicates that more than 80 percent of Americans believe that you cannot be successful at work and get enough sleep (Dement and Vaughan 1999). Since sleep research underscores the importance of *diurnal* rest, public policy should be designed to discourage the accumulation of sleep debt. Consequently, "flexible" work time regimes that require long weekly hours as a trade-off for shorter work years, or even careers, impose significant health and social costs on workers, families and communities. The importance of *daily* sleep establishes the workday and the workweek as preferred work time regulatory periods. Given the importance of daily sleep and the fact that sleep needs generally decline with age, our public policy should challenge the wisdom of racing to retirement. Rather than celebrating individual pursuit of maniacally long work hours, public policy should foster an improved lifetime distribution of work, sleep, and the other important lifestyle habits that improve our health and productivity.

Social costs of excessive hours: gender and family issues

One of the most important social issues related to work time reform is gender equality in the distribution of market and household labor. On average, women continue to perform a disproportionate amount of unpaid household labor, while working fewer paid hours than men. According to the 2007 American Time Use Survey, female workers with children under age 6 devote an average of 7.07 hours per day to household activities, shopping and nurturance, while men devote 4.16 hours on average (BLS 2007). As women have assumed more paid work hours over the last four decades, a gender-neutral society would require men to engage in more household production. The realization that employers can no longer offer "jobs with wives," which rely on the "unpaid market labor" of spouses, creates the need for an urgent redistribution of social labor along gender lines (Philipps 2008). Probert (1995: 49) articulates the urgency for change,

> The traditional pattern of full-time employment from the age of 18 to 65, with a 40 hour week and four week annual leave, was only ever offered to men, and only possible because armies of women were available to do all the socially necessary work. However, women are more

and more likely to be in the paid work force. Fewer and fewer will be available to staff the voluntary social services, run the school canteen, take care of older relatives. And it's not just the social implications, but the environmental ones that need to be considered. Those women carrying the double burden have little time for sorting their garbage into glass, plastic, paper and compost components for recycling.

Rather than continuing the double standard of asking women to be more like men while conducting paid work but not while performing unpaid work, a redistribution of remunerative work could free labor resources to be used more equitably in the third sector. Making work time regimes more androgynous needs to become a central focus of work time reform. It should begin with the recognition of the masculine structures and practices that dominate the contemporary labor market in most countries. After gaining a consciousness of gender inequities, genuine reform should endeavor to redistribute both paid work and unpaid household production. Significant progress could be made by making shorter hours available across a wider range of industries and occupations, which would increase their attractiveness to both male and female workers. As more men then opt for shorter paid hours, they will be freed to make a greater contribution in the third sector. McInnes (2005: 292) writes that:

> A genuinely family-friendly work-life balance will only be achieved by 'taking parenting out of competition', through greater state regulation of the negotiation of working hours, and much more extensive parental leave and childcare provision. The aim should be to regulate the labour market in such a way as to place parents and non-parents on an equal footing, overcoming, as far as possible, the penalties imposed by the cumbersomeness of children. This task will become even greater as the legacy of the male breadwinner system fades.

Liberation of and from work and the consequent growth of the third sector would go a long way in recognizing the supreme form of work performed by mothers. Negt (1989: 32) offers a fitting description of the profound social contribution made by nurturers, "Work in the household ... , where identity and the capacity to live and love are produced, in order that subjects capable of work may take their place in the system of social labor – i.e. *the true process of the production of life* – is placed at society's disposal *free of charge*, mainly by women [sic]."

The dual role performed by women may be diminishing the satisfaction that they derive from both paid work activities and their unpaid activities in the third sector. Research by Stevenson and Wolfers (2007: 2) concludes that "measures of subjective well-being indicate that women's happiness has declined both absolutely and relative to male happiness ... Our findings raise provocative questions about the contribution of the women's movement to women's welfare and about the legitimacy of using subjective well-being to assess broad social changes." Such findings are corroborated by a diminished enthusiasm for paid work expressed by many working mothers. In the last decade, American mothers have been seriously rethinking the merit of full-time work hours under the current social structure. After a long struggle to gain greater equality in the labor force, working mothers are reassessing the attractiveness of competing in the rat race. A 2007 survey by the Pew Research Center indicates that mothers have lost their zeal for full-time work over the last decade. Among working mothers (with children 17 and under), only 21 percent viewed full-time work as ideal in 2007—down from 32 percent in 1997. Among stay-at-home mothers, only 16 percent were interested in finding full-time work—down from 24 percent in 1997 (Pew 2007). A significant portion of the reduction came from the group of mothers with children younger than 4 years old. Whereas 31 percent of mothers with young children preferred full-time work in 1997, only 16 percent held such preferences in 2007. Although their eagerness to work full time is greatly diminished, working mothers are not interested in retracting from the labor force entirely. A full 60 percent still prefer a part-time employment arrangement.[3] These preferences suggest a significant disconnect between employee work time preferences and actual experience. While the Pew (2007) survey shows that 60 percent of working mothers say they'd prefer to work part time, the US Bureau of Statistics reports that only 24 percent of all working mothers are on part-time hours.[4]

Perhaps the work time desires of American working mothers are derived from their first-hand knowledge of the damage done to young people by the lack of time spent with their parents. Indeed, mothers would be the first to perceive such problems. This mother's intuition has been confirmed recently by new research identifying the social costs of parental time famine. UNICEF's *Child Poverty in Perspective: an Overview of Child Well-being in Rich Countries* (2007) suggests that economic growth achieved in countries with long work hours and higher levels of economic inequality has not translated into improved social outcomes for children. Likewise the Relationship Forum's *An Unexpected Tragedy: Evidence for the Connection between Working Hours and Family Breakdown in Australia* (2007) manifests the large social costs associated with a work fetish that is maintained at the expense of family time. Similarly, the Study of Early Child Care and Youth Development (2007) financed by the US National Institute of Child Health and Human Development—tracking more than 1,300 children in various child care arrangements—found that keeping a preschooler in a large day-care center for 1 year or more increased the likelihood that the child would become disruptive in class. The study used teacher ratings of each child to assess behaviors such as interrupting class, teasing and bullying, and found that the effect persisted through the sixth grade. Such findings suggest that if long hours result in a dearth of parenting time the social costs will be apparent in deviant youth and teen behavior. Yet the social costs of long hours are much more severe and persistent when one considers that today's under-supervised children are tomorrow's workforce. Essentially, labor market regulation that subordinates the economy to social needs should be viewed as crucial industrial policy since it affects a nation's future productivity and international competitiveness.

Work time regulation that aspires to a secular decline in working hours is consistent with the five work time policy objectives outlined by Fagan (2004) to promote gender equality in employment and work-life balance. Fagan (2004: 137) delineates the following goals:

> The first objective is to reduce working time barriers to labour market participation and thus contribute to raising women's employment rate. The second objective is to address any particular working time obstacles to women's entry to management and other male-dominated activities, thus contributing to the reduction of gender segregation, and particularly vertical segregation. Both of these objectives are about increasing women's labour market integration, and the third has a more ambitious vision: to develop working time arrangements that improve the quality of reconciliation of employment and family responsibilities and work-life balance more broadly. The fourth objective underpins the preceding three, and is concerned with developing equal treatment between full-time and part-time workers, including opportunities to make transitions between full-time and part-time hours at different life stages. The final objective focuses upon adapting men's working time patterns and increasing their time involvement in parenting and other care activities, hence contributing to reforming the gender division of labour in households.

Therefore, a gender-neutral work time reform should include the collective reduction of full-time hours as it makes full-time employment more compatible with nurturing commitments and other time-intensive domestic activities. Again, it is important that work time regulation targets a weekly reference period rather than an annual focus in order to ensure that critical, daily needs of families are not usurped for weeks and months at a time by the "exigencies" of the production cycle.

By limiting the ability of full-time workers to compete for promotion on the basis of long hours, work time regulation can begin to elevate the status of women in full-time employment. Work time reform that encourages full-time male workers to assume more part-time work across more industries and occupations could enhance the gender integration of both market and household work. Such a redistribution of time helps to establish the "psychological space" needed to break down the existing barriers to gender integration of both the market and household sphere. The work fetish has provided men with a ready excuse for not pulling their weight at home. If they were discouraged or proscribed from long hours, it is likely they would feel greater compulsion and capability to increase their contribution to household production. As the Dutch experience featured in Chapter 5 suggests, a redistribution of work hours is capable of freeing up longer work hours for women who desire them while simultaneously giving men more time for activities in the third sector.[5] Although work time reform does not represent a panacea for gender inequality, it is a necessary precondition for a greater societal integration along gender lines. As such, a work time policy that aspires to greater socioeconomic participation is consistent with the central ideals and objectives of feminist economics. Since work time regulation can bring about more time with family and a more equitable distribution of market and household production it is a rare example of a public policy that can appeal to conservatives and feminists alike.

Work time preferences: Is the work fetish losing its grip?

The labor-leisure choice model featured in Chapter 1 suggests that the long work hours of many workers (and the recalcitrance of average workweeks) are largely a reflection of workers continually choosing to reap the benefits of labor productivity growth in the form greater income and consumption rather than leisure time. Although modern consumption habits suggest that this is partially true, an alternative explanation of the rigidity of the workweek is that workers are not free to choose their work hours due to the "lumpy" proportions in which work time is offered. Blaug (1985: 313) writes that labor is demanded by employers "in lumpy amounts on a take-it-or-leave-it basis; the laborer may have to work far in excess of the point at which the marginal utility of income equals the marginal disutility of effort." Copeland (1931) likewise observed that the factory system utilized standardized hours that are influenced by firm, trade union, and government policy. Consequently, the factors influencing the disutility of work, such as duration, intensity, and the general conditions and quality of work are largely beyond the control of the individual worker.

Empirical research on work time choice finds scant evidence of the income preference explanation. When asked to assess their ability to adjust working hours (up or down), only 15 percent of workers reported the possibility of doing so (Kahn and Lang 1987). Maume and Bellas (2001: 1148) find no evidence of Hochschild's (1997) supposition that workers seek refuge from family life at work, concluding that "personal choice is unrelated to work schedules." In a comparative analysis of work time preferences across a variety of countries, Stier and Lewin-Epstein (2003) find that large numbers of individuals are dissatisfied with their workloads and that the preference for work time reduction is greatest among those workers who are full time, highly educated, older and from higher-income families. Seemingly, these highly skilled, high-wage workers would be the best equipped to make their work time preferences a reality. If elite workers are not in a position to secure their preferred work time regimes, then the mass of workers in the secondary sector are likely to have even less prerogative in setting work hours. At the macro-level, Stier and Lewin-Epstein (2003: 322) find that "in countries with high levels of economic development (as measured by GNP per capita) and low economic inequality, employees (both male and female) prefer to reduce the time spent in paid work."

When employers offer inflexible work time regimes, workers may have to resort to frequent job changes in order to achieve a semblance of their preferred hours. Böheim and Taylor (2004) find that work time constraints were a significant determinant of British workers changing employers or leaving the labor market entirely. In the extreme, workers sacrifice their desired hours in the short term for the hopes of an early retirement. Clearly, a growing body of evidence refutes the preference theory of work time determination and suggests that working time has been imposed on the majority of workers, particularly in America where the lack of choice contributes to many employees feeling overworked (Schor 1991; Jacobs and Gerson 2000; Maume and Bellas 2001).

Although there are signs of deliquesce, contemporary social attitudes still regard paid work as necessary for human dignity. The value of work goes beyond the pay check, and significantly influences the individual's own sense of place, identity, self-respect and self-worth. Over 80 percent of Americans say that work gives them a sense of self-worth as a person and provides some sense of meaning for their lives (Wuthnow 1996). The feminization of the workforce and the achievement of unprecedented labor force participation rates across the developed world suggest that these psychological effects hold fast across gender lines. Given the role of paid work in shaping personal identity and self-worth, it is little wonder then that the vast majority of workers indicate that they would continue to work even if they had sufficient means to retreat from the workplace (Blyton and Noon 2002).

When squared with the banality and tedium that most workers experience in their jobs, the commitment to work shown by modern workers represents one of the most important social paradoxes of our time. According to a review by Gini and Sullivan (1989: 69), "in well over one hundred studies in the last twenty-five years, workers have regularly depicted their jobs as physically exhausting, boring, psychologically diminishing, or personally humiliating and unimportant." Despite such drudgery, people still seek work as a source of personal identity and self-worth. Gini and Sullivan (1989: 17) conclude, "what we think this data means is that for most men and for an increasing number of women there is no alternative to work, no other activity that absorbs time, uses energy, taps creativity, demands attention, provides regular social interaction, and is a source of status, identity, self-respect, and financial remuneration." It is indeed a troubling social commentary and a monumental failure on behalf of policymakers that capitalistic society has provided so few sources of personal identity and character growth outside the realm of paid work.

The lack of a social means of identity and character development may help to explain why women have fought so hard to achieve equality in a male-dominated economy and labor market when the end result was the drudgery of a double shift—one at work and one at home. The realization that paid work offers less intrinsic meaning and reward (beyond that of a paycheck and job title) than previously derived from the household or third sector is likely linked to the declining desire for full-time work among mothers as well as the increase in mental health disorders in the developed world. Indeed, the postponement or abandonment of the socially important and generally rewarding function of rearing and nurturing children in order to compete in the labor force may deprive parents of significant "psychic" and "social" rewards. Instead of work being an all-or-nothing choice for parents, countries like the United States should devise ways to afford harried workers more time to share their human capital at home and in the third sector in order to ensure social continuity.

Although most individuals are still keen to participate in the formal labor market, there is a clear desire for a *less extensive* attachment to the labor force. The discontent with current work structures is most patent among members of Generation X. With their preference for free time and work-life balance over lasting employment relationships, Generation X both anticipates and pre-empts the insecurity of work in the post-industrial age. Far more so than their Baby Boom parents, members of Generation X value and embrace short and varied careers, flexible work hours that allow them to pursue authentic pleasures, and permanent part-time work. As Generation X matures, its value system seems to be spreading in wealthy countries throughout the entire working population. For example, a 1991 Gallup poll indicated that only 10 percent of the working population in Germany valued their work as the most important aspect of the lives. In the United States, the figure was 18 percent, down substantially from 38 percent in 1955. For Western Europeans aged 16 to 34, "work" or "career" rank behind five other priorities—time with friends, having enough free time, being in good physical shape, spending time with one's family, and having an active social life.[6] In a sample of upper-middle-class, full-time workers in the United States, Schor (1995) finds that 73 percent of employees report that they would have a better quality of life if they worked less, spent less and had more time for themselves.

A growing number of surveys and studies suggest that significant proportions of full-time workers—especially parents and the overworked—would opt for shorter hours if offered even a partial trade-off of current real income maintenance. Although there is still great alacrity for participation in the paid workforce under decent working conditions, a clear preference is emerging for a less demanding attachment to the labor force. One way to evaluate whether workers are freely choosing longer hours—out of loyalty to their employer or an obsession with income and consumption—or if they face constrained choice in their labor-leisure decision is to investigate their working-time preferences as identified in surveys. If actual working time accords with worker preferences, there would not be large proportions of workers seeking longer or shorter work hours.

As with any collection of survey data, the manner in which the question is framed can influence the outcomes and conclusions of the research. Many work time surveys fail to clarify the impact that an hours reform would have on future income. Most surveys have assumed that incomes will fall commensurately with the hours reduction, implying significant lifestyle changes for workers on shorter hours. For example, multiple studies have analyzed data from the 1989 International Social Survey Programme (ISSP) to conclude that a greater percentage of workers desire more hours and more pay than desire fewer hours with less pay across a variety of OECD countries (Bell and Freeman 1995; Souza-Poza and Henneberger 2000). The verbatim wording of the ISSP question is: "Think of the number of hours you work and the money you earn in your main job, including regular overtime. If you only had one of these three choices, which of the following would you prefer? (i) Work longer hours and earn more money; (ii) Work the same number of hours and earn the same money; (iii) Work fewer hours and earn less money." Yet, relying on this sort of questioning to assess the desirability of short hours is flawed because it only presents the choice of fewer hours at a lower income level, ignoring any productivity offset. Indeed, when one considers the responses to an alternative ISSP survey question which makes no mention of a trade-off between work hours and income, a clear preference is revealed by workers (and job seekers) for fewer work hours (see Chart 4.1). Stier and Lewin-Epstein (2003) analyze responses to the 1997 ISSP survey question that asks "would you like to spend more time in a paid job," and conclude that "as a general pattern, we find that in the majority of countries, the proportion of those who would prefer to decrease their market time is higher than the proportion of those who want to increase it."

In deciphering the results of work time surveys it is important to recognize that survey questions inferring a one-for-one trade-off between income and reduced work hours represent a false choice for workers as they completely ignore future productivity gains. There is no historical or theoretical explanation for why shorter hours must come at the cost of a commensurate income reduction, especially in the long run. Thus, surveys that enquire whether or not workers will opt for more free time at lower pay are of little relevance to work time reform. Work time reduction that is linked to future productivity growth need not entail a significant reduction in income. A more realistic and useful survey question would ask workers how they would prefer to realize their future productivity dividends.

When forward-looking questions are asked of workers, they are much more desirous of shorter hours in lieu of pay rises. Hart and Associates (2003) found that while only 15 percent of survey respondents would work fewer hours for less pay today, the number increased to 42 percent that would definitely or probably do it in the future. Yet, even this result is misleading because, with productivity gains and a redistributive economic stimulus on their side, workers should not have to reduce their future incomes and standard of living at all. It is also important for survey questions to

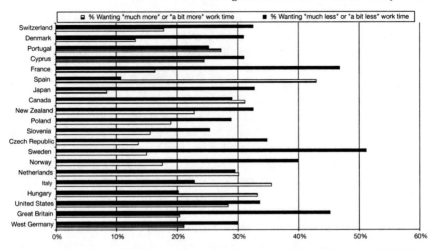

Chart 4.1 Percent of ISSP Respondents Wanting Less and More Time in a Paid Job
(compiled from the 1997 ISSP work orientations II survey)

stipulate that the intensity of the work will remain the same with shorter hours so that workers do not interpret the shorter hours option as implying "fewer hours, less pay, and *harder* work." Thus, an accurate reflection of worker preferences for future work hours should ask workers if they prefer to receive future productivity dividends—"in the form of more income at constant hours and workload?", or "constant income with fewer hours and a proportionate reduction in workload?"

Although few surveys ask workers how they would prefer to realize their productivity dividend, Statistics Canada's 1985 Survey on Work Reduction came close to assessing worker willingness to use future productivity increases to secure shorter hours. The survey asks respondents if they would trade some of their pay *increase* in the next 2 years for more time off. The other questions asked by the survey may have clouded the results, but even during the recessionary times of the 1980s, Benimadhu (1987) reports that 30.7 percent of respondents were willing to trade fewer hours for either less pay or by forfeiting their pay raise. Since the evidence from past work time reductions indicates that income levels have either been maintained or fallen only marginally (see Chapter 5), those surveys that assess workers' desires for work time reductions with no income reduction or those with a partial income loss are the most relevant to work time reform.

Another complication related to the analysis of work time preferences is the possibility of hysteresis, or "path-dependency." If workers, for whatever reason, are compelled to work long hours, consumption preferences may shift from household production to market production. The shift from time-intensive to money-intensive goods may orient workers to consumption patterns that become difficult to alter in the future. If rampant consumerism causes a loss of craft knowledge and a diminished social acceptance of homemade goods, consumers are more likely to become permanently reliant on mass-produced goods. Since highly indebted workers have grown accustomed to a work-and-spend existence, surveys that refer to current trade-offs between income and leisure time may not distinguish between workers "getting what they want" or "wanting what they get" (Schor 1995: 74).

However, the process may also work in reverse. Until they actually experience it, many individuals may not be able to contemplate a lifestyle that is less dependent on market production and more dependent on activity in the third sector. The experience is reflected in the oft-heard statement made by retirees that "I don't know how I ever had time to work?" Once individuals realize greater autonomy from the market, they may embrace a further curtailment of market-based activities. Such was the case with Canadian telephony workers in the wake of a work time reduction experiment in 1994. When Bell Canada initially asked its technicians whether they would voluntarily accept an 8 percent cut in their workweek with a proportionate reduction in pay, only 10 percent responded favorably. After receiving a no-layoff guarantee, 70 percent of workers voted in favor of the 36-hour workweek. Four months after the policy had been implemented for *all* workers only 15.4 percent of the workforce wanted to return to full time. The workers came to value their 3-day weekends more than the loss of pay, which averaged only $30 a week after accounting for lower income taxes. A Canadian Advisory Group on Working Time and the Distribution of Work (1994) came to a similar conclusion regarding Chrysler workers forced to reduce their regular and overtime hours at a minivan plant in Windsor, Ontario, "the loss of overtime is less resented as time passes and as people begin to live their lives in a new way." In their case studies of 36 firms McCarthy *et al.* (1981) find similar evidence of employees and employers coming to embrace a permanent reduction in hours after experimenting with shorter hours on a temporary basis. It appears then that once workers realize that they can combine greater free time with alternative consumption patterns to improve their standard of living, they often have little desire to return to long hours. Importantly, surveys show a greater alacrity for work time reduction when workers are given some assurance that their income sacrifices will be used in an egalitarian fashion rather than solely boosting firm profitability. Cette and Gubian (1998) find that while a minority of French workers expressed a willingness to reduce work time and compensation in general, a majority would do so if jobs in their workplace were protected or created.

Working time preferences in the United States

When work time reduction entails a commensurate income reduction, surveys show a willingness among American workers to accept such a trade-off ranging from 8 to 52 percent of the workforce (Golden and Gebreselassie

2007). Jacobs and Gerson (2000) calculate that that nearly half of American workers prefer shorter hours, 90 percent of whom desire at least 5 fewer hours per week. Conversely, only 17 percent of American workers would prefer to work longer hours (Jacobs and Gerson 2000).[7] When asked in a Work in America (2003) survey, "If you had more high quality ... part-time options available to you right now, how likely do you think you would be to use them and reduce your schedule?" more than one-third of workers (33 percent union and 36 percent non-union) responded that they would be likely or somewhat likely to use them (Friedman and Casner-Lotto 2003). Similarly, the National Study of Families and Households found that 36 percent of husbands in dual-career couples "would prefer to work less than [their] present work schedule" (Clarkberg and Moen 2001). Particular sub-groups, such as parents of pre-teen children, have shown a greater desire to forgo income for work time reduction. In its 2006 survey of full-time work-ing mothers with children at home, CareerBuilder.com found that 52 percent of working mothers were willing to take a pay cut to spend more time with their children. Thus, even when large income tradeoffs are at stake, sig-nificant portions of the US workforce are willing to forfeit a day's work and the associated wages for more free time, suggesting that access to nominal income is not as important to workers as actual work hours might suggest.

Although US surveys do not typically ask workers how they would like to receive future productivity dividends, some surveys allow for the possibility of productivity gains by simply asking workers if they prefer more or fewer hours. Furthermore, a growing number of American surveys have been asking how much income workers are willing to forfeit for fewer work hours. Based on past work time experiments, those surveys that posit a 20 percent work time reduction (roughly 1 day per week) with less than a 10 percent reduction in pay posit the most realistic scenario. Schor (1995) asked workers, "[would you] take the option of a four day week, for a 10 percent pay cut? 20 percent pay cut?" She reports that 51 percent of survey respondents were willing to forfeit at least 10 percent of their pay. Hahnel (1998) likewise reports that 50 percent of full-time workers would accept a 10 percent income loss in exchange for a 4-day workweek.

Recent surveys of general priorities suggest that parents are not the only group suffering from a dearth of time. In a survey of middle-class respon-dents, the Pew Research Center found that having enough free time was the overarching socioeconomic concern among Americans. Some two-thirds (68%) of middle class respondents say that "having enough free time to do the things you want" is a very important priority in their lives. Having suffi-cient leisure time was a priority to more people than any other priority offered in the survey including: having children, being successful in a career, being married, living a religious life, doing volunteer work/donating to charity, or being wealthy (see Chart 4.2). Consistent with previous work time research, those demographic groups that placed a high priority on free time were the ones least likely to have it—such as the employed, the middle-aged, and mothers of young children. Clearly, a growing number and variety of surveys suggest that American workers are not content with their current work hours. They recognize other social activities as being more important than being wealthy, especially when wealth accretion entails long hours. The evidence also reveals that many workers are willing to reduce their hours and even forfeit some income if it helped them achieve shorter hours and less time on the "hedonic treadmill."

Work time preferences in Australia and the UK

The growing incidence of long work hours is not unique to the United States (see Chart 4.3). A handful of industrialized countries, are in league with the United States by having more than 15 percent of the workforce reporting hours of 50 or more per week, including Australia (20 percent), the UK (15.5 percent), New Zealand (21.3 percent), and Japan (28.1 percent). Furthermore the data presented in Chart 4.3 manifest a worrisome trend toward more people working long hours between 1987 and 2000 in all but four of 18 developed countries.

The growth of long hours has been particularly acute in Australia where the percentage of full-time, male employees working 50 or more hours per week increased from 23 percent in 1982 to 35 percent in 2002 (ABS 2003). The pressure toward extended work hours in Australia has been felt by female workers as well. In 2003, average full-time hours for both male and female workers were well above the standard workweek of 38 hours, with

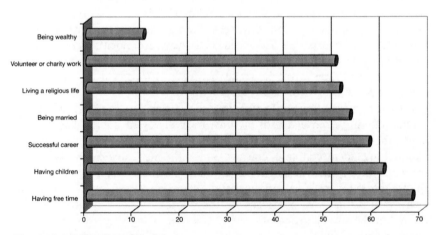

Chart 4.2 Middle Class Priorities
Percent of (self-identified) middle class respondents saying this is "very important"
Source: "Inside the Middle Class: Bad Times Hit the Good Life" Pew Research Center, April 9, 2008

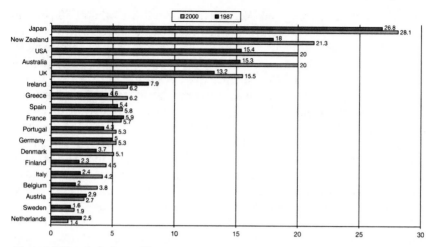

Chart 4.3 Trends in Long Hours
Percent of non-agricultural employees working 50 or more hours per week (49+ for USA and Japan)
Credit: Reproduced from data compiled by Lee (2004), Figure 2.5 Trends in Excessive hours (p. 47)

men averaging 47 hours per week and women 43 hours. Much of the growth in hours over the last two decades has taken the form of unpaid overtime. Campbell (2002) estimated that unpaid overtime was more commonplace than paid overtime in Australia. Given employers' avoidance of overtime penalties, it could be argued persuasively that many Australian workers have been working more hours for the same pay and are now deserving of fewer hours at no income loss. In fact, 6 percent of respondents to a government survey in 2000 insisted that their desire for less work at constant pay be recorded in that manner (van Wanrooy 2007). If that 6 percent is added to the 7 percent of workers willing to work fewer hours for less pay, the proportion of "over-employed" workers in Australia becomes more substantial.

When the preferences of the self-employed are combined with the preferences of paid employees (the ABS excludes "owner managers" from large surveys) the extent of over-employment is more even striking. Approximately 42 percent of the self-employed desire fewer hours, while only 8 percent prefer more hours (ABS 2002). Combining the preferences of all workers (including the self-employed), the Negotiating the Lifecourse survey in 2003 reveals that, when no income loss is stipulated, 39 percent of all Australian workers would prefer to work fewer hours, while 9 percent would prefer more hours. Van Wanrooy (2007) finds that Australian workers are more likely to identify themselves as being over-employed if they are older, work longer hours, perform the higher share of paid work in the household, and have children under 15 years of age. It seems equally difficult for households as a whole to achieve their preferred hours distribution. In their analysis of coupled individuals, Tseng and Wooden (2005) find that "almost 50 per cent of dual-earner couples work a combined number of hours each week that exceeds their combined preferred hours. Further, for many of these couples the gap between preferred and actual hours is substantial – almost 20 per cent reported a net gap of 20 hours per week or greater."

One of the best assessments of how workers prefer to receive future productivity dividend comes from the Australia Institute's analysis of annual leave. Denniss (2003) finds that over half (52 percent) of Australian workers would prefer to receive an additional 2 weeks' paid leave in lieu of the equivalent 4 percent pay increase. This was despite the fact that 57 percent of Australian workers did not take their entitled four weeks' leave in 2002. Although some workers chose to save their leave, 42 percent cited work-related difficulties or wanting to work and make more money as the reason for their minimal leave usage (Denniss 2003). When such large numbers of workers are not able to access their "legally protected" annual leave, it suggests that work times are being unilaterally determined or strongly influenced by Australian employers.

In 2006, 77 percent of Australian respondents agreed with the statement: "A government's prime objective should be achieving the greatest happiness of the people, not the greatest wealth." When asked "What is the most important thing for your happiness?" almost 60 percent of surveyed Australians cited partner/spouse and family. A further 8 percent identified community and friends. Ostensibly, a large proportion of the Australian population believes that a primary responsibility of government is to support and protect their happiness, grounded in relationships with their family, friends and the broader community. At the same time, only one-quarter of those surveyed thought that life is getting better. Obviously the preponderant emphasis placed on paid work in Australia is not translating into greater societal weal.

Preferences for work time reduction are quite patent in the UK as well. The 2002 British Social Attitudes Survey (BSAS) revealed that roughly 40 percent of working adults would prefer to reduce their hours while only 3 percent were interested in increasing their hours, even when they "would be paid the same amount per hour."[8] Survey evidence from the UK indicates that a substantial portion of male workers are willing to forfeit income for fewer hours. Stewart and Swaffield (1997) find that 36 percent of working age men (21–64 years old) desire to work fewer hours at the prevailing *hourly* wage rate, entailing a reduction in net income. Predictably, the proportion rises to 50 percent for those working in excess of 51 hours per week. Consistent with other developed countries, those working the longest hours in the UK are the least satisfied with their work time regime.

Stewart and Swaffield (1997) suggest that the minimum hours that firms expect their employees to work in the UK is positively correlated with the unemployment rate. Bluestone and Rose (1997) echoed this premise in the United States, where American workers are compelled to work long hours out of growing job insecurity. Seemingly, the long hours of British workers also results from a "make hay while the sun shines" attitude rather than sovereign workers exercising their free choice in a competitive labor market. British attitudes suggest some gender solidarity in resisting the greater job insecurity through work time reform. The desire for a redistribution of hours in the UK is in large part driven by changing social views of gender-based participation in the workforce and household production. The BSAS survey revealed a majority consensus that both partners should contribute to household income and that there should be greater participation by men in unpaid household work and childcare (MacInnes 2005).

Financial pressures to meet housing costs and to maintain purchasing power are rather acute in the United States, UK, and Australia. In the United States, falling real incomes and greater job insecurity make work time reductions seem like an impossible choice for many workers (Bluestone and Rose 1997). Yet, if current incomes were maintained and workers had bona fide discretion over their future productivity dividend, work time reduction may become a viable option for more workers. Indeed, Europe serves as an edifying case study for those who think that workers in the United States, UK and Australia cannot "afford" work time reduction, as many workers in short-hours countries of central Europe display a willingness to give up even more wage gains to secure shorter hours.

Work time preferences in Europe

Even in many European countries, where average annual work hours are significantly lower than in much of the developed world, surveys suggest that roughly half the labor force would like to reduce their work hours further. The Employment Options Survey (2000) of some 30,000 working-age respondents from 16 European countries revealed that two-thirds of employees wanted to change their work hours in 1998. Half of European workers (51 percent) preferred fewer hours when choosing between lower current hours or *future* pay rises. Only 12 percent of workers desired longer hours. Moreover, the desired magnitude of change was substantial. On average, employed men preferred a 37-hour week while women sought a 30-hour week; an average reduction of 6 and 3.5 hours, respectively.[9] European survey data suggest that the percentage of the workforce that desires shorter hours has increased since the mid-1980s, even in countries that had already achieved significant work time reductions (Lehndorff 2000). In Germany, where working hours were relatively low, 28 percent of full-time workers were willing to reduce work hours further even when it entailed a commensurate earnings loss (Holst and Schupp 2002).[10]

Full-time workers in Europe possess a latent desire to reduce work hours and assume a part-time attachment to the workforce; 23 percent of women and 19 percent of men currently working full time prefer to work part time. Additionally, 38 percent of all job seekers in Europe prefer a part-time arrangement, making the achievement of full employment through work time redistribution a feasible objective (Employment Options Survey 2000). In a meta-analysis of work time preferences and actual working hours in developed countries, Fagan (2004) concludes that, "the amount of adjustment that most people want to make is substantial ... Overall, there is a general tendency to prefer to exit the extremes of very short or very long hours of work and move into the middle ground of substantial part-time/ short full-time hours in the 20–39 hour range."

Other studies also reveal some convergence of preferences toward a shorter full-time workweek, but still find large proportions of workers that are content with their part-time arrangements. Across the 22 countries surveyed as part of the ISSP, large proportions of part-time workers were happy with their hours. Stier and Lewin-Epstein (2003: 317) write, "those who work long hours (the overworked) indeed prefer to shorten their time in the labor market. Part-time workers, however, do not prefer an increase their market time (as the bifurcation theory would predict) [*sic*]." Since part-time workers and the unemployed prefer a "shortened" workweek, a redistribution of work hours could have a large impact on employment. Thus, even in countries where it would seemingly be difficult for workers to reduce their hours, given their relative short work times, surveys reveal a desire for less paid work. Such findings support the notion that the social effort bargain could distribute future productivity gains in the form of work time reduction in a manner that accords with worker preferences, social welfare, and environmental protection.

Conclusion

The evidence surrounding work time preferences suggests that across a wide variety of socioeconomic conditions, contemporary workers are prepared to move down the path to shorter hours, especially if given adequate incentives and protections. In the estimation of many workers the use-value of time spent not working is more valuable than the exchange-value of the time spent doing paid work, but they have few means of realizing their preferences. The majority may be willing to choose fewer hours, but they are not free to choose. The gulf between actual work hours and desired work time suggests that optimal work time distributions will not be achieved through a laissez faire approach. When nearly two-thirds of workers express ideal work time regimes that differ from their actual arrangements, the labor-leisure choice model is devoid of explanatory power.

In the 1920s, Henry Ford convincingly demonstrated that the technology and managerial know-how existed to achieve substantial work time reductions with no reduction in output. Ford was not deluded by neoclassical theory into thinking that shorter work times came to fruition as a result of the workers' desire for greater leisure. Absent labor market regulation—Ford realized that the employer's prerogative was the dominant influence in determining work time regimes. Ford (1926: 11) writes, "the hours of labor are regulated by the organization of work and by nothing else. It is the rise of the great corporation with its ability to use power, to use accurately designed machinery, and generally to lessen the wastes in time, material, and human energy that made it possible to bring in the 8-hour day." Ford's view was affirmed by Samuelson (1971: 7) when he observed that "in contrast with freedom in the spending of the money we earn, the modern industrial regime denies us a similar freedom in choosing the work routine by which we earn those dollars." If workers lack the bargaining power to access their share of productivity dividends—the real compensation of the typical American worker has been stagnant over the last two decades—then they cannot be expected to have much influence over the form (i.e. wages or free time) of any productivity dividends they may receive. Government intervention in the social effort bargain is therefore justified to promote a division of labor that minimizes social and ecological costs while improving socioeconomic participation.

Even if work time regulation entails a short-term increase in aggregate consumption and production (due to a redistributive stimulus), its path-dependency effects make it a viable option for achieving living patterns that are compatible with long-term social and environmental sustainability. As Hayden (1999: 74) writes, "even productivist trade-offs in the short term can serve as a useful way of gaining acceptance for the idea of WTR [work time reduction] and illustrating the benefits of a new conception of the good life focused more on quality of life then quantity of consumption." Contemporary evidence suggests that the lion's share of workers would embrace fundamental reform of the division of social necessary labor. Gorz (1999: 64) contends that the hurdle to such a reformation is not cultural, but political:

> It does not lie in the difficulty of gaining acceptance for a lifestyle in which employment has a much smaller place within *everyone's* [sic] life. It does not lie in everyone's identification with his/her job. It does not lie in 'everyone's urgent desire' to occupy a full-time job on a permanent basis. It does not lie in social attitudes not having caught up with the potential for a more relaxed, more multi-active life. It lies, rather, in *the political world not having caught up to the change in attitudes* [sic].

A major obstacle to work time reform resides in the fact that access to full socioeconomic participation is closely attached to full-time employment status. The growing disaffection for more income and longer hours suggests that work is not valued chiefly for its financial and intrinsic rewards, but for the rights and entitlements that are accessed through employment with few alternative avenues of access available. Powerful vested interests frustrate the reformation of the labor market by perpetuating a work fetish, which conflicts with recent technological and cultural changes that require us to go beyond problematic attempts to extend wage relations to activities not yet infiltrated by the market. Although widespread social or ecological calamities could prompt a collective counter-response to the political status quo, astute governments do not have to wait for catastrophic events before responding. Recognizing the technical, environmental and cultural need for change, governments can serve as a guiding influence intent on improving socioeconomic participation in a civil, sustainable, and liberating manner. By defining new rights, new freedoms, and new social norms, an effective countervailing power to the work fetish can foster labor market reform that does not result in social disenfranchisement and ecological devastation. Regulatory direction is needed to create the space in our lives for "true" work— the creative, poetic activity that is the source of all wealth and self-fulfillment (Gorz 1989). When workers lack genuine discretion over their work hours, they tend to adjust the one factor that they do control under incomplete labor contracts—effort levels. When workers are pressured to spend long hours away from their homes, families and communities their subsequent withdrawal of efficiency represents a cost to both the firm and the broader society. Viewing employment negotiations as a social effort bargain makes it clear that the state has a vested interest in promoting equitable and sustainable outcomes through the regulation of work time.

5   The Employment Effects of Work Time Reduction

If the ordinary wage-earner worked four hours a day, there would be enough for everybody, and no unemployment – assuming a certain very moderate amount of sensible organization.

Bertrand Russell (1935:18)

So long as there is one man who seeks employment and cannot find it, the hours of work are too long.

Samuel Gompers (1887) (from Schnapper 1972: 250)

To serve as an effective macroeconomic policy tool, work time regulation must have some potential to redistribute work in a manner that ameliorates under-employment and its related labor market inequities. When conceptualized as a macroeconomic policy tool along the lines of an incomes policy, the objective of hours regulation should be a long-run reduction in the average workweek. If the societal goal is to harness technological development to increase socioeconomic participation in a socially and ecologically sustainable manner, work time regulation will need to achieve a secular drift toward shorter hours. Although most economists are not opposed to shorter hours in principle, many question the ability of the policy to have employment effects on the scale needed to address the underutilization of labor prevalent in advanced economies today and the growing joblessness anticipated in the future.

This chapter therefore investigates the potential for work time redistribution and reduction to achieve positive employment effects when implemented on the appropriate scale and in an effective manner. It bears repeating, however, that improving unemployment does not necessarily entail a creation of net new hours of work. The chapter begins by examining the lump-of-labor fallacy that is often marshaled against proposals to reduce work hours. It then features some of the difficulties related to the various methodologies of measuring the employment effect of shorter hours. The bulk of the chapter is devoted to an investigation of the success of various types of work time reduction experiments. Since the potential for job creation is tightly linked to the productivity effects of an hours reduction, the chapter concludes by investigating the productivity impact of past work time experiments. The objective of the chapter is to show that positive employment effects are possible, and to elucidate the conditions under which work time regulation will have the greatest employment impact.

Regulating a "lump of labor"

A common rebuttal wielded by mainstream economists to suggestions of work sharing for the common good is that the amount of work to be done (or labor demand) is not constant and that attempts to redistribute work will be confounded by substantial fluctuations in total labor demand. They contend that policies targeting the supply of labor are conceived under a lump-of-labor fallacy that ignores the dynamic nature of economic growth and employment. The alleged dynamism of labor demand results in a defeatist view of labor market regulation. Any attempts to regulate access to paid work will alter the scale of output and employment and obviate the intended policy objectives.

This debate over the impact of shorter hours dates back to the classical period of political economy. Nyland (1989) argues that as the agitation for a 10-hour day in the UK swelled to rebellious proportions, political economists were forced to abandon their argument that work time restrictions were an infringement of free will. Clearly, the British factory worker of the 1830s possessed little bargaining power with which to exercise their free will. Economists then turned to the analysis of production costs to argue that work time limits would be harmful to capitalists and workers alike through the deleterious impacts that higher labor costs would have on trade. Thus, the lump of labor fallacy owes much of its origin to the British Factory Acts and Nassau Senior's specious analysis of the affect of shorter hours on per unit labor costs. The Factory Acts dealt primarily with the restriction of hours of child and female workers, but a series of Ten Hours Bills between 1847 and 1878 which prohibited the employment of children under the age of ten and restricted the hours of "young persons" and women eventually allowed male workers to reduce their hours to 60 or less (Blaug 1958). In what has become known infamously as "Senior's last hour," Nassau Senior's (1837) opposition to the Factory Acts failed to separate individual work times from production times (or establishment hours). Senior (1837: 215) argued that the "whole net profit is derived from the last hour [in a cotton mill that worked] 12 hours for 5 days in the week, and nine on Saturday." According to Senior, a legislated work time reduction to 10 hours per day would destroy firm profits and have dire effects on investment and output. Senior cites a Manchester Businessman Mr. Ashworth, "When a labourer lays down his spade, he renders useless, for that period, a capital worth eighteen pence." Although the example of the spade was intended to underscore the cost of an entire factory remaining idle, Senior and others failed to ask why someone else could not pick up the spade or man the expensive machinery in the factory. According to Blaug (1958: 217) the notion that reduced work time would lead to a proportionate fall in output "became an essential feature of the classical analysis of factory legislation."[1] The fear that the regulation of individual working hours would clash with operating hours to raise per unit costs of production has influenced mainstream economic thought on the topic ever since, underlying modern claims of a lump-of-labor fallacy argument.

However, some economists of the classical era, such as Marx, Mill, Rae, Thornton, and Owen, began to challenge the Panglossian conclusion that nothing could be done to alter the distribution of wages and work time due to the wages-fund doctrine and Senior's "last hour." They were increasingly able to draw on firm level data that supported the notion of an efficiency week. From Owen to Leverholme in Britain, to Kellogg and Ford in the United States, industrialists began experimenting with work time reductions to achieve greater labor productivity. Marx illustrated the historical inaccuracy of assumptions made about the rigidity of wages, output, and labor productivity. Responding to arguments made by Senior and Weston against higher wages and shorter hours, Marx (1970: 14) wrote:

> If our friend Weston's fixed idea of a fixed amount of wages, a fixed amount of production, a fixed degree of productive power of labor, a fixed and permanent will of the capitalists, and all his other fixedness and finality were correct, Professor Senior's woeful forebodings would have been right and Robert Owen, who already in 1816 proclaimed a general limitation of the working day the first preparatory step to the emancipation of the working class ... would have been wrong.

Marx's optimism regarding Owens' experiment with short hours and better pay has been validated by history. The long and successful history of minimum wage legislation and work time reductions—from the battle over the 10-hour day to contemporary demands for part-time work—have revealed the concern over falling investment and output to be more shibboleth than substance.

Mainstream economists have revived the putative link between individual working times and output to oppose working class desires for shorter work time on multiple occasions since the battle over the 10-hour day. A new wrinkle to the argument was added during the struggle for the 8-hour day that relied on competition yielding an optimal work day. If shorter hours were really more efficient, competition would ensure that employers adopted such schedules. According to this assumption, competition invariably ensured that employers would utilize the most efficient work regimes and any forced reduction in the national standard represented a threat to production costs and the nation's ability to trade competitively in the global marketplace. In this view, the regulation of working conditions posed the risk of a contraction of output and employment. As John Rae (1894) pointed out, the central issue surronding work hours was industrial efficiency and not the vague notions of the income-leisure trade-off later envisioned by the Marginalists.

Mainstream economists continue to employ the lump-of-labor fallacy argument at both a microeconomic and macroeconomic level. The microeconomic argument relies on work sharing making the factor of labor more expensive so that employers shift away from labor in their production mix.[2] The theoretical paradigm finds its origins in the wages-fund doctrine that assumes that relative income shares (wages, profits, and rent) are immutable. If, however, income shares are arbitrary rather than given, there is scope for a fruitful regulation of labor supply.

At the macroeconomic level, the lump-of-labor fallacy argument against shorter hours is confronted with another fallacy—that of composition. In economics what is true at the level of the individual or the firm is rarely true for society as a whole. As with many neoclassical economic theories, drawing conclusions about the macroeconomic effects of work time reductions from microeconomic reasoning is subject to the perils of methodological individualism. For instance, if work time reduction somehow causes higher per unit labor costs, firms may initially shift away from labor in their production mix. Yet, if higher hourly wage rates result in greater consumer spending in the aggregate, then firms will have an incentive to expand aggregate output and employment. This disconnect between micro and macro phenomena should be quite familiar to neoclassical economists who routinely conclude that technological advance that supplants labor with capital at the firm level tends to "create more jobs than it destroys" in the aggregate.

The macroeconomic aspect of the lump-of-labor fallacy argument holds that proposals to regulate the supply of labor erroneously assume a fixed level of total output. It is argued that the "lump-of-labor fallacy" leads work-sharing advocates to assume a fixed level of output that can be parsed out in a variety of ways with little or no impact on subsequent output levels (Katz 1998). It is more accurate therefore to refer to the argument as the "lump-of-*labor/output*" fallacy. Many mainstream economists admit to short-run employment gains but only at the cost of higher inflation (Layard *et al.* 1991). Katz (1998: 37) employs the inflationary death knell for work sharing when he writes "a reduction in the unemployment rate is likely to increase the bargaining power of incumbent workers and lead to wage increases that reduce the employment gains." In the mainstream view, the market or government response to higher inflation will reduce the level of output, reducing labor demand in the aggregate. As with expansionary fiscal policy under the "natural rate of unemployment" theory, labor supply regulation is futile as the market automatically adjusts back to an equilibrium level of participation.

Clearly, a critical assumption of both the microeconomic and macroeconomic explanations of the lump-of-labor/output fallacy is that work time regulation will increase the per-unit costs of labor. Higher labor costs cause a substitution of capital for labor in the firm's production mix and a macroeconomic adjustment that leads to a higher price level and no long-term improvement in employment levels. History has shown, however, that greater per-unit labor costs are not a forgone conclusion because productivity improvements have more than offset the costs of past work time reductions at both the firm and aggregate level. Thus, history has corroborated Chapman's (1909: 356) observation that "I have found no instance in which an abbreviation of hours has resulted in a proportionate curtailment of output." As explained in Chapter 3, full employment achieved through work time reduction would not trigger a deflationary contraction of output or inflation since it would distribute productivity dividends in the form of time rather than money. When workers—emboldened by lower unemployment—pursue "time raises" rather than "pay raises," the inflationary fears of macro-economists are rendered baseless. Implementing an "incomes policy" by linking work hours to productivity gains could dispel any lingering notions of a Phillips curve trade-off between inflation and unemployment. Breaking the theoretical link between inflation and unemployment liberates policy from the restrictive confines of the natural rate of unemployment hypothesis—a far more damaging fallacy than the "lump-of-labor/output" presumption.

Many economists admit that with long adjustment periods work time reduction can reduce unemployment and improve labor productivity to alleviate price pressures. But most still maintain that work sharing is not a suitable employment policy in the short run due to rigid work structures or higher wage costs. Bosch and Lehndorff (2001: 210) point out the inconsistency in such an argument, "what is considered self-evident in the long term is regarded as unfeasible in the short term. Such a position can hardly be considered satisfactory unless it is assumed that we have reached the 'end of history' as far as working time is concerned." Thus the lump-of-labor/output fallacy is only binding when production conditions make relative income shares immutable and when work sharing makes labor usage more expensive. Yet, even if an overly aggressive work time reduction rendered labor so scarce that per unit labor cost did escalate, firms would face an incentive to substitute capital for labor in a manner that increases efficiency. The productivity dividends that resulted from shocking firms into more efficient production techniques could then be shared with all of the social partners to production—perhaps in the form of even shorter hours. Each substitution of capital for labor brings us one step closer to our ultimate goals of reducing paid work hours to inconsequential levels. So there should be no fear of productivity-enhancing substitutions of capital for labor.

Walker (2004) has shown that the benefits of work time reduction do not depend on an absolute rigidity of output and that short-hours advocates have never relied on the presumption of a strictly fixed level of output and labor demand. Indeed, even a moderate rigidity of output can give potency to public policy intervention. If labor productivity declines with the length of the workday, there is scope for work time reductions to generate productivity improvements and (net) positive employment effects. Since work time reduction can serve as an independent source of productivity improvement, particularly when working time is decoupled from operating hours, lower per unit costs can neutralize any perverse output effects and vitiate the "lump-of-labor/output fallacy" argument that is used to thwart shorter hours.

Another criticism of the "lump-of-labor/output fallacy" argument against short hours is the inconsistent application of the theory. It is seldom argued that the fallacy would operate in the direction of long hours if labor markets were deregulated. What would happen, for instance, if overtime restrictions and other working time limits were removed under the advice of economic rationalists? Would there be an increase in output and employment, making more goods and services available to the average consumer, even though workers would have less money and time to purchase and enjoy them? Would there be a glut of goods and an economic slump due to under-consumption? Would capitalists watch idly while profits evaporate as firms find it difficult to maintain the artificial scarcity that bolsters prices of final goods? More likely, the removal of work time restrictions would result in a further polarization of work hours to the benefit of primary sector workers and firms' profit margins. Veblen's analysis of capitalist sabotage suggests that output restrictions would remain in place to the detriment of society. Veblen (1919: 67,69) laments the social costs of constrained output and labor market segmentation that result from the capitalists deliberate retardation of efficiency:

> the loss suffered by the rest of the community is necessarily larger than the total gains which these maneuvers bring to business concerns; inasmuch as the friction, obstruction, and retardation of the moving equilibrium of production involved in this businesslike sabotage necessarily entails a disproportionate curtailment of output … It should be added, as is plain to men, that these ordinary and normal processes of private initiative never do provide employment for all the men available.

Marxian interpretations of the production process similarly maintain that production would be curtailed as capitalists seek to maintain the labor market inequities that are the basis of their profits by only expanding the hours of select workers. In short, there is no reason to be optimistic that a deregulation of working time would lead to an expansion of output and employment. Indeed, it is more likely that greater capitalistic sabotage and segmentation of the labor market will result in less output and employment. Under both work time contraction and expansion, output is not as dynamic as the lump-of-labor/output fallacy would have us believe, giving hours regulation some potency as a public policy tool.

The de facto dynamism of output and employment is also challenged by the arbitrary application of the lump-of-labor/output fallacy. Although the notion of there being a fixed amount of work or output applies to many public policy matters, the lump-of-labor/output fallacy has been rather selectively deployed to torpedo progressive policy proposals that impact the supply of labor such as early retirement and work time reductions. Curiously, the concept is not used by mainstream economists to explain why the natural rate of unemployment boundary is soft, making tight monetary policy premature. If output is dynamic, why do monetary authorities continue to subscribe to "natural unemployment rate" and "output" (Taylor) rules in their management of the monetary system? Indeed, it would be near impossible to predict the "Taylor gap" between potential output and actual output if output levels were so dynamically responsive to things like changes in the composition of labor supply. The same dynamic nature of output and employment that foils efforts to regulate labor supply, should also apply to efforts to regulate output via monetary policy. If output is dynamically flexible, low levels of unemployment should not pose a threat as output can be expanded (by adding more capital to a more productive workforce) to alleviate any lasting inflationary pressures. The selective application of the "lump-of-labor/output" concept can only be explained as a political, or class, issue. It is highly disingenuous for central bankers and economists to hold that output is recalcitrant when it serves the interests of the bondholding class in fighting inflation, but not when progressive work time regulation is proposed to ameliorate the living standards of the working class.

Immigration offers another example of output rigidities enhancing the effectiveness of public policy. Proposals to restrict immigration assume a lump of labor/output argument when they hold that there is only a limited amount of work to be shared between domestic and migrant workers. If output were dynamically flexible, there would be no need to protect domestic workers from the competition of migrant workers as output and employment would expand to create sufficient jobs. Yet, the fact that every developed nation has established restrictions on the mobility of labor suggests that there is some rigidity to output and employment. Moreover, where immigration has taken place, there is convincing evidence of detrimental impacts on native workers that compete directly with migrant workers (Frey 1994; Borjas *et al.* 1997; Shulman and Smith 2005). If the concept of a lump of labor/output is a fallacy, why do politicians around the world forsake the advice of free-trade economists by keeping migration restrictions in place? Xenophobia may explain some of the clamor for immigration controls, but the harm done to low-wage workers by immigration attracts substantial political attention. The ubiquity of immigration barriers in the developed world suggests that output and employment is not as dynamic as orthodox economists would have us believe and that policy intervention can be used to improve labor market outcomes.

Finally, and most importantly, since one of the goals of work time regulation is to enhance the stability of output and aggregate employment, the lump-of-labor/output fallacy argument loses its relevancy as a critique of short hours. In fact, no fallacy arises when work time *regulation* policy is designed to stabilize the amount of output and employment. Layard *et al.*

(1991: 502) write that "there can be no doubt that, *so long as output is unaffected* (sic), this [work-sharing] argument is decisive. But the question is, Would output be unaffected?" Yet, when hours regulation is utilized as a macroeconomic policy tool, the proper question becomes "*could* output be unaffected?" A constant or a relatively fixed number of total work hours should not be considered a misguided assumption of work time regulation, but rather a policy objective. Given the social and ecological implications of greater economic growth, our societal goal should be to achieve a more sustainable level of economic throughput and to adjust the distribution of individual work time in a manner that enhances societal welfare. As a non-inflationary means of achieving full employment, work time regulation can serve to stabilize the scale and scope of output and employment. Prudent work time regulation would only allow work time expansions when vital social and economic interests were threatened. Likewise, if greater output was needed to pay for the initial work time redistributions or reductions required to achieve full employment, the policy could pursue "selective" growth that is socially and ecologically sustainable.

Minimum output thresholds could be maintained through government spending on payroll expansion that is linked to work time reduction. That is, firms would only receive assistance with their fixed costs of labor when workers benefited as well. Although it is debatable whether or not the lump-of-labor/output fallacy has limited the effectiveness of work sharing in the past, the social and ecological costs associated with more economic growth suggest that action should be taken to achieve a rather stable "lump" of total employment. Just because labor demand may have been allowed to expand and contract to a varying degree in the past, it does not mean that society must be beholden to such fluctuation in the future. Students of the labor market from Chapman (1909) to Walker (2004) have observed that total labor demand is rather lumpy; and contemporary social and environmental problems suggest that it should be made even "lumpier."

The employment effects of work time reduction experiments

Since the employment effects of work time regulation hinge closely on the structure and design of the policy, this section is devoted to investigating the success of past work time regulation schemes in preserving or expanding employment. In order to be environmentally and socially sustainable, a work sharing program should endeavor to increase aggregate employment (jobs) rather then aggregate hours. It is possible to identify three necessary conditions for a strong job creation effect from work time reduction (Whitley and Wilson 1986). First and foremost, the productivity offset needs to be collectively managed. Although some productivity offset is unavoidable and welcome in order to balance the competing needs of stakeholders in the social effort bargain, pernicious sources of productivity improvements such as speed-up and inflexibility of work hours should be avoided. The social effort bargain must then determine how much of the social productivity dividend will be devoted to job creation and how much will flow to existing workers and capitalists. Second, the use of overtime in lieu of hours redistribution or payroll expansions should be discouraged in order to maximize job creation. Lastly, a work-sharing program might be designed to reduce the short-term costs associated with payroll expansion and retention at reduced hours until long-run productivity improvements have been realized.

Before exploring past work time experiments, the notion of positive employment and its measurement must be clarified. For the exploratory task at hand, a positive employment effect is not limited to a decline in the unemployed population alone. Since most work time policies at the firm and industry level were not intent on expanding payrolls but rather protecting them, the preservation of employment can be viewed as a positive employment effect. If modest, or "defensive," work-sharing policies have been successful at preserving jobs, it is likely that a more ambitious policy, designed to have maximum employment effect, could substantially reduce unemployment. Yet, policy should not be singularly focused on creating net new jobs but also on ameliorating the Balkanization of the labor market apparent in many developed countries today. Indeed, the intent and purpose of limiting long hours and redistributing our social labors is to reduce both unemployment and the labor market segmentation that contributes to labor market inequities. Providing longer hours at the short end of the distribution through a redistribution of hours may be a superior way of addressing labor underutilization than redirecting part-time workers into new full-time jobs or additional part-time jobs for which they are not suited (as make-work programs tend to do). Moreover, a redistribution of work is certainly a more sustainable solution to labor underutilization than increasing government spending to the point of satisfying all desires for more work hours.

Some observers claim that the final assessment of employment programs can only be accurately conducted by using an hours-based measure of labor utilization that is calculated by asking the employed and unemployed alike how many more hours they wish to work. Although such a measure would provide a more accurate reflection of the tightness of the labor market, it cannot serve as the ultimate touchstone of a full employment policy because it makes the achievement of full employment nearly impossible. So long as employed workers are desirous of more hours, unemployment will persist under an hours-measure of full employment. Even if the government provided a 35-hour-a-week job to all those willing and able to work, for instance, a preference by workers to work more hours (say 55 per week) would create persistent unemployment. Government would then be committed to boost spending and production to accommodate the collective definition of unemployment rather than influencing the social definition of unemployment through hours regulation. Given the social and ecological constraints facing developed countries, it would be extremely imprudent for governments to maintain the level of macroeconomic stimulus needed to satisfy the work hour demands of all workers.

In a seminal article exploring the macroeconomics of work time reduction, Bosch and Lehndorff (2001) show that working time reductions do not necessarily lead to more overtime, increased unit costs, and reduced growth, but rather result in positive employment effects. The authors outline four ways that the employment effects of work time reductions have been measured: regression analysis, surveys and case studies of firms, macroeconomic simulations, and statistical decompositions. Exploring results yielded from each measurement methodology is useful in assessing the general employment impact of work time reduction.

Regressions analysis

Metric analysis attempts to estimate the employment elasticities related to work time reduction from statistical time series data. Regressions are problematic as the impact of work time reduction is difficult to isolate from other macroeconomic and aggregate labor force dynamics. The problems are analogous to those faced in minimum wage studies. Yet, unlike minimum wage research that has benefited from various cross-border experiments, there are relative few work time experiments to be analyzed. As a consequence of the difficulties involved, the results of econometric regressions have been quite variable. Studies have yielded mostly positive employment effects but some results have been flat or slightly negative. Bosch and Lehndorff (2001: 221) summarize the regressions results in various Western European countries as showing an increase in employment of 2 to 3.5 percent for a working time reduction of 5 percent.

Case studies and surveys of firms

Although research at the level of the firm often only represents a snapshot of the employment effects, it can provide important information about the way in which firms react to work time reductions over the economic cycle. For example, some firms may choose to use overtime in the short run rather than hire more workers. However, over a longer period they may be forced to hire more employees as initial levels of work intensification cannot be sustained. If payroll expansion is lagged to the end of the next economic cycle, case studies may capture some employment effects that were missed by short-sighted regression analysis. Knowledge of firm-level responses can be useful in refining the reform and regulation process. Anecdotal evidence can also inform macroeconomic simulations because it illuminates how the parameters of overtime use, shift systems, and operating hours respond to work time reductions. Bosch and Lehndorff (2001: 223) conclude that "none of the surveys known to us has concluded that the collective working-time reduction in question has had no employment effect, or even a negative one."

Macroeconomic simulations

Simulations of macroeconomic events attempt to clarify the interaction of economic variables and their influence on employment. Alternative scenarios can be developed ex-ante and the impact of various assumptions can be estimated. Importantly, such ex-ante assumptions (i.e. productivity effects and operating hours) should be based on the evidence gleaned by the case studies and surveys of relevant firms or industries. Most studies of the employment effect have used a 1/3 to 2/3 productivity offset. For instance, the French government's macroeconomic simulations of the 35-hour law prior to its implementation assumed a one-third productivity offset and no change in operating hours. This productivity offset proved to be far too low and resulted in the government overestimating the potential job creation. Ex-post simulations tend to be more reliable and have shown overwhelmingly positive employment effects. Gorres (1984: 56) conducted a meta-analysis of the simulations carried out in Europe prior to the 1980s and revealed "a relative employment effect of over 40 percent ... as an average of all variations and studies." Macroeconomic simulations have to be viewed with caution as their predictive prowess depends on the decisions made by the modeler, who may not be any more qualified to exercise better judgment regarding the model's parameters than anyone else.

Decompositions

Under the final measurement approach, total hours worked in the economy are separated into the various types of employment (overtime, full-time, part-time, etc.) in an effort to isolate job creation. The second challenge is to calculate which hours changes are attributable to productivity versus work time reduction. This method has been used by both employer organizations and trade unions. Bosch and Lehndorff (2001: 227) conclude that "although the results obtained differ enormously, employment effects achieved were positive."

The paucity of large-scale work time reductions, the difficulty in measuring the employment effects, and the variability of the methodological approaches make precise measurement of the employment effects elusive. Yet, virtually all studies of work time reductions, using variegated methodologies, show positive employment effects. The disparate findings of employment studies conducted to date suggest that the ancillary conditions of work time reform are critically important to job creation. Bosch and Lehndorff (2001: 227) write, "the most important thing is to agree on the kind of *conditions* that have to be *created* if the employment policy pursued is to be as successful as possible in creating jobs [sic]." The employment impact of work time reduction cannot be predetermined as the design of the policy is pivotal to the job creation effects. The decisive factor in generating jobs is not necessarily the magnitude of the work time cuts but how they are put into practice. Recent experience suggests a role for the state in addressing the compensation of low-wage workers, the high fixed cost of payroll expansion, training of low-skilled workers, and bi-lateral work time flexibility that avoids work intensification. In anticipating the employment effects of work time reduction a useful admonition is offered by Bosch and Lehndorff (2001: 210, 240):

> it cannot be argued that the reduction of working time is not in itself an instrument of employment policy simply because researchers have concluded that a particular form [and scale] of working-time reduction in one country has not lead to higher employment ... a potentially effective instrument of employment policy can be put to good or bad use.

Work time reduction and flexibility schemes have been implemented at the firm, industry, and national level, in an effort to preserve or expand employment while boosting productivity. In an effort to identify the conditions most conducive to employment gains, this section focuses primarily on large-scale work time reduction experiments. That is, statutory or collectively bargained work time reductions and government-supported work-sharing programs. These large-scale forms of work time reduction are the most relevant to macroeconomic policy and also the most controversial. However, some space is devoted to work time reduction at the firm level as policymakers need to be mindful of what happens inside the "black box" of firm production to better understand how hours regulation impacts payroll expansion, operating hours, productivity, and the like.

Although the bulk of the modern evidence comes from Europe, there has been some experimentation with work sharing in North America over the last century. As the "scientific management" of production in the 1920s reversed the tendency of the rate of profit to decline, many firms and government organizations began to experiment with work time reduction (Nyland 1989). Although never fully embracing Tayloristic time-motion studies, labor unions realized that scientific management could be used to abandon rule-of-thumb production methods in favor of more efficient methods. Utilizing the data yielded from a government-funded study of the 8-hour day in one of his Detroit automobile plants, Henry Ford implemented the 5-day, 40-hour week in 1926 as a cost-cutting initiative. The success of Ford's new work time regime in reducing costly employee turnover led to the widespread implementation of the 40-hour week in the automotive sector as well as a few other heavily unionized industries such as construction and textiles.

Soon thereafter, the Great Depression made work sharing a reality across many industries. The depression brought about an aggregate reduction of work hours in the United States of approximately 20 percent. President Hoover supported spreading the work as an alternative to layoffs, but provided little more than moral suasion through his Commission for Work Sharing. Nevertheless, employers responded with a somewhat egalitarian reduction in hours; in March of 1932, 56.1 percent of all workers and 63 percent of those in manufacturing were employed part time. Large employers like Sears, GM, Kelloggs, Akron Tire and Standard Oil all scaled down their workweeks. In an effort to avoid the future expansion of work hours in the face of high levels of unemployment, the 1933 Senate passed a 30-hour bill authored by Hugo Black, which would have made the 30-hour week compulsory in all industries. The bill was sponsored in the House of Representatives by William Connery. Although Roosevelt originally supported the Black-Connery bill and would later regret not signing it, he withdrew his support for the legislation citing concern for a provision that forbid the importation of goods produced by workers who worked longer than 30 hours per week. Nevertheless, the popularity of the 30-hour legislation forced the newly elected President Franklin D. Roosevelt to emphasize work time reduction in his National Industrial Recovery Act and, to a lesser degree, in subsequent labor legislation. Hunnicutt (1988) argues that an implicit deal was struck in the NIRA with labor leaders who were lured by the provisions of Section 7a that guaranteed union organization and collective bargaining. When specific industry codes were finalized by the NIRA, shorter hours were deemphasized. Whaples (2001: 4) writes "despite a plan by NRA Administrator Hugh Johnson to make blanket provisions for a thirty-five hour workweek in all industry codes, by late August 1933, the momentum toward the thirty-hour week had dissipated." Roughly half of the employees covered by NRA codes were placed on 40-hour weeks and nearly 40 percent had longer workweeks. In the end, the Fair Labor Standards Act extended the 40-hour week to most firms engaged directly or indirectly in interstate commerce, but had few incentives for work sharing below this level. Work sharing would not receive serious political discussion again until the economic slowdown of the 1970s and 1980s. Many American states followed the German and Canadian governments in utilizing proportional unemployment compensation benefits to promote the spread of work in lieu of layoffs that were mounted during the difficult economic years of the 1970s and 1980s. Since state and national governments have played a critical role in financing past work-sharing programs through flexible unemployment compensation arrangements, briefly investigating the structure and outcomes of the larger work-sharing plans is useful in envisioning the proper role of government in future labor market regulation.

Unemployment insurance-supported work-sharing schemes

One mechanism that governments have used to avoid mass layoffs and unemployment is partial payment of unemployment insurance benefits to employees that have reduced their average work hours in lieu of layoffs or dismissals. Such policies are also referred to as short time compensation (STC) programs. European governments were the first to experiment with STC programs. Since it is more difficult to terminate an employment relationship in Europe, most European countries have adapted their social safety nets to accommodate part-time or reduced hours in order to make layoffs and discharges less necessary (Van Audenrode 1994). Rather than employment status being an all-or-nothing prospect, STC allows workers to access unemployment compensation on a proportional basis. A general example would be an employee who experienced a 25 percent reduction in their hours and pay receiving a weekly unemployment benefit that partially offsets the loss in income—the replacement rates range from 60 to 80 percent of the income loss. Although most STC programs have been temporary in nature and design, they offer useful insights into the efficacy of a permanent work time regulation program.

STC is often viewed as being more efficient than layoffs, since it eliminates the costs of employee separations.[3] Aside from some of the most senior workers, who typically receive seniority premiums, most employees also view work sharing as being more equitable than layoffs since the burden of economic uncertainty is shared more equally across the workforce. Beyond the benefits that accrue to firms and their employees, there are also important social benefits derived from STC programs. Although the financial costs to the unemployment compensation scheme are relatively similar whether benefits are granted to a small number of beneficiaries or a larger group receiving partial benefits, the social costs of spreading the unemployment are substantial lower. Sharing the burden of an economic contraction through STC reduces the usage of public support programs such as welfare payments, food stamps, and rent assistance. Moreover, the "full-time unemployment" that results from traditional layoffs has been linked with a greater incidence of alcoholism, drug abuse, child and spousal abuse, and other anti-social behavior. Intuitively these problems would be less prevalent under a system of work sharing that promoted "part-time unemployment." In the American context, Nemirow (1984: 37) points out that distributing reduced employment among many workers on shorter weekly hours will "also help public policy deal in a more rational way with the problem of health insurance for the unemployed." There are also important equity implications for the labor market. Work sharing can insulate the employment of minorities, who are often the last hired during economic expansion, but the first fired during contractions.

Work sharing can also yield important macroeconomic benefits. STC can bring about greater macroeconomic stability than layoffs because work sharing disperses the burdens of an economic slump more equitably by maintaining a portion of fringe benefits and pay for more workers, thereby stabilizing consumption levels and attenuating the severity of the downturn.[4] A small loss suffered by many workers will result in less pain and panic selling of real estate and other assets than unemployment that is concentrated on fewer individuals. Equally important to the stabilizing effects on consumption are the macroeconomic benefits related to the hysteresis effects of unemployment. The expensive and recalcitrant costs of the path-dependency effects of unemployment are well known (Blanchard and Summers 1987). Intuitively, spreading the unemployment would eliminate many of the hysteresis effects related to both the skill and behavior of workers as well as those related to the attitudes of employers and governments regarding "equilibrium" rates of unemployment. Indeed, STC could serve as a mechanism for maintaining and developing important human capital investments during an economic contraction or transition. A large portion of workers placed on 4-day weeks could use their day off to attend classes or similar retraining activities. Such investments would reduce the path-dependent drag on employment when economic output recovered. Commenting on the broader socioeconomic benefits of work-sharing, Best (1988: 4) has argued, somewhat prophetically, that STC programs are worthy of study because, in a harried world, "the idea of using hours rather than dollars to address social and economic problems may become an important issue in the future." Indeed, using unemployment insurance benefits to finance work sharing identifies time as an important social resource.

The German origins of STC

Recognizing the ability of STC to achieve the goals of income maintenance and greater job security, European governments have generally been the most experimental in using social benefits to compensate for shorter work time (Van Audenrode 1994). When unemployment nearly doubled to 750,000 workers in France from May 1974 to May 1975, short time work attenuated the unemployment effect by quadrupling the number on short hours to 300,000 workers. During the same recession, the number of short-time workers expanded 10 times as fast as the number of unemployed persons in the Netherlands (Levitan and Belous 1977). Notwithstanding the success of STC across a variety of European countries, this section focuses on the German work-sharing programs as they represent some of the oldest, largest and most successful experiments with STC.

Germany was one of the earliest countries to implement work-sharing legislation on a national scale, dating back to the 1927 Placement and Unemployment Insurance Act. Although the program has been in place for decades, it was most prominent in the 1970s as a way to mitigate rising unemployment in Germany related to stagflation and globalization. At its height in 1975, some 12,548 firms and 773,334 workers participated in the STC program, preventing between 170,000 and 224,000 layoffs (Levitan and Belous 1977; Best 1988).

In order to qualify for the program in the 1970s, German employers had to demonstrate that an hours reduction was unavoidable and that work sharing would prevent the dismissal of workers. Employers also had to document a minimum 10 hours' reduction for one-third or more of their employees. The program was financed by a payroll tax of 3 percent split equally between workers and employers up to a certain earnings ceiling. An important characteristic of the German program was that the government also reimbursed participating firms for 50 percent of the public health insurance costs and 75 percent of retirement benefits paid on behalf of short-time workers. Although the STC legislation was amended in 1978 to include financial assistance extensions of up to 2 years, the program was temporary in nature, designed to attenuate short-term unemployment effects. Generally, most participants had their work time shortened by 40 percent for less than 3 months.[6] During this time, take-home income was almost always maintained at 80 to 90 percent of regular full-time earnings (Best 1988).

STC in North America

Critics of STC argued that the success of the German program was not transferable to the United States and Canada where the fixed costs of labor were higher (due to private provision of pensions and healthcare) and where there has been a tendency to use seniority as a guide to layoffs. Despite these very real obstacles, unemployment insurance-supported work sharing has been used as a successful way of avoiding layoffs and sharing the burden of temporary economic contractions in North America. In the United States, experimentation with STC has taken place at the state level. The first serious consideration of using unemployment compensation insurance to encourage work sharing resulted from Lillian Poses' plan to address the severe unemployment levels of New York City during the stagflation of the 1970s. Although the "Poses Plan" received general support from a coalition of representatives from business, organized labor and academia at a conference in April 1975, a 1976 bill to create a STC program in New York failed to emerge from a political subcommittee.

Due in part to the interest generated among policy experts by the Poses plan, California passed the first American STC program in June 1978, under the initiative of State Senator Bill Greene. Arizona and Oregon soon followed suit, implementing STC programs in 1982. Also in 1982, the federal Short Time Compensation Act, co-authored by US Representatives Patricia Schroeder and Robert Matsui, was passed by the US congress. The bill provided funding and direction to the US Department of Labor to facilitate and support the development of STC programs at the state level. In the same year, the Tax Equity and Fiscal Responsibility Act of 1982 permitted states to voluntarily enact work-sharing schemes as part of their unemployment compensation program. By 1986, 11 states had initiated STC programs. Presently, there are 17 states in America that allow workers to access federal unemployment benefits on a proportional basis as part of a work-sharing arrangement with their employers (Balducchi and Wandner 2007).

Since STC programs in the United States need to be developed at the state level and within the constraints of the federal unemployment insurance statutes, they tend to possess similar characteristics. For this reason, and because it is the largest of the STC states, California is featured as an illustrative example of the US programs. California's STC program was designed to allow employers to maintain an employment relationship with trained employees at near full pay, reduce employment loss among minorities and marginalized workers that tended to be the last hired and first fired, and provide a temporary adjustment mechanism for those looking for new jobs. The California program stipulated that at least 10 percent of the regular permanent work force in the affected work unit must experience a work time reduction. Moreover, the hours and wages of the participants had to be reduced by at least 10 percent. Work-sharing benefits were allowed for up to 20 weeks during a 52-week period for each participating employee.

In contrast with the more bureaucratic German program, California employers simply needed to complete a two-page application, provide basic information on employees, report the amount of the wage and hours reductions, and state that the reductions were economically necessary. Once approved, employers provided their participating employees with a weekly statement of reduced hours and wages, which the employees used to claim STC benefits. Best (1988: 21) calculates that, "workers eligible for maximum weekly benefits would have received $24 for each day lost in 1980 and $33 for each day lost in 1983." The California program was entirely voluntary and unionized employees had to receive a formal agreement from their union before deviating from their collectively bargained agreement. No personnel restrictions were placed on firms relating to transfers, termination, or new hiring. Continuation of fringe benefits (health insurance and retirement) was not addressed in the legislation. Firms were not required to make additional unemployment insurance contributions unless their benefit charges exceeded their existing contributions, at which time they were required to pay additional taxes ranging from 0.5 to 3.0 percent on the first $7,000 of every employee's wages in the following year. This "surcharge" was a way to keep seasonal firms and other rogue enterprises from abusing the program.

In response to the economic recession of 1981, the Canadian Minister of Employment and Immigration authorized the temporary establishment of a national STC program. The unexpected popularity of the program led to an increase of the original $10 million budget to more than $440 million by 1983. Eligibility for the Canadian program was modeled after the German program. It therefore required an initial workweek reduction of 20 percent, and the reductions could not go below 10 percent or higher than 60 percent for the length of the agreement. Moreover, firms needed to avoid industrial disputes during the reductions, provide evidence of future economic prospects, document previous work hours, attest that workweek reductions were both necessary and temporary, maintain at least 40 percent of the work force during the hours reduction, and provide the written consent of a collective bargaining agent or employee representative. Given the Canadian unemployment insurance replacement rate of 60 percent, the 1982 ceiling for benefits was US$210 a week or US$42 per day. Benefits were paid for a 26-week period and could be extended for 12 weeks if firms could convincingly argue that a return to full-time employment was likely. Two important aspects of the financing of the Canadian STC system were that past employment history did not affect contributions and that roughly one-fifth of the program costs were covered from the general revenues of the federal government. Thus, the Canadian program illustrates that a national work-sharing program does not have to be financed via payroll taxes and could be financed by a variety of federal fiscal arrangements. Although a state government, such as California, would have to be somewhat concerned with revenue neutrality when spending on payroll expansion incentives, a federal program would not have to be self-funding or revenue-neutral. Since a sovereign issuer of a currency can make near limitless amounts of money available to achieve a full utilization of labor, the US government could easily finance a broad-based STC program as the German, Canadian, and French governments have done from time to time on a limited scale.

Assessment of the STC programs

Most STC programs have been voluntary in nature and dependent on economic conditions—requiring employers to prove that the work-sharing was unavoidable. Given this limited and "defensive" role, it is unreasonable to expect the programs to significantly ameliorate unemployment in the aggregate. Nevertheless, the evidence reveals a rather significant rate of participation in the STC programs and a consequent mitigation of unemployment, particularly during times of economic difficulties. In the recession of 1982, for instance, the number of California STC agreements swelled by 3,371. By the middle of 1984, over 6,000 firms had been approved for STC arrangements, covering 232,700 workers. More recently, research by Balducchi and Wandner (2007) shows that participation in STC programs swelled in 13 American states during the 2001 recession and then contracted by 2005. For the United States as a whole the number of workers receiving STC benefits increased from 32,500 in 1997 to 111,200 during the recession of 2001. By 2005, the number of workers receiving partial unemployment benefits had fallen to 40,200. The rapid growth in number of workers accessing partial unemployment benefits during the economic contraction of 2001 suggests that STC can serve as a viable employment stabilization mechanism.

During the first year of Canada's STC program some 7,688 firms and 196,539 workers were approved to participate, and within 3 years participation had grown to 18,504 firms and 343,884 employees (Best 1988). Although the Canadian economy had roughly the same size workforce as California, participation in its STC program was substantially higher. Despite the relatively bureaucratic burden of the Canadian program, STC became a popular option for firms as an alternative to layoffs. The greater popularity of the Canadian program was likely related to the fact that it paid benefits that were more generous (almost twice) and lasted longer (at least 6 weeks) than the California scheme.

Van Audenrode (1994) has identified a link between the generosity of STC programs and the responsiveness of hours to fluctuations in labor demand. Analyzing the effectiveness of work time variations in achieving labor market adjustments in 10 OECD countries with STC programs Van Auden-rode (1994: 97) concludes that, "countries with the most generous STC programs have large and quick working time responses to variations in the need for labor. In those countries, overall labor adjustments end up being as flexible as in the United States because working time adjustments compensate for restrictions on firings." In other words, hours flexibility has tended to offset the greater rigidity that European firms face in expanding and contracting their payrolls. This suggests that a more solidaristic method of labor market adjustment is possible. Indeed, the greater participation in the Canadian and European STC programs could be related to a stronger culture of solidarity than prevails in the United States.

In Germany, California and Canada, STC compensation was disproportionately utilized by large manufacturing firms in the 1970s and 1980s. The manufacturing industry was not only experiencing rapid job loss at the time, but also had many workers with firm-specific skills who could be retained through work sharing. Best (1988: 54) reports that in California, "the vast majority of employees using UI-supported work-sharing programs are in skilled manual and operative occupations – 76 percent, compared to 56 percent of those using regular UI [programs]." Large firms were more likely to utilize the program due to the fact that they have personnel managers who are more likely to be aware of the STC program and to handle the administrative tasks. One California survey conducted in the second year of the program found that 58 percent of employers had no awareness of the STC program and 33 percentage claimed "vague" or "uncertain" awareness (Best 1988).

Given the individual's limited influence in work time determination, it is not surprising that the initiation of STC agreements has been a unilateral process, especially within the Californian and German plans. Compounded by its conception as a short-term stabilization program, work sharing almost always emerged as an initiative of the employer rather than the employees. A survey of the Californian program found that only half of employers involved workers in the decision to implement STC and only 8 percent included a formal vote or union decision (Best 1988). Nevertheless, there have been very few cases where employees have refused employer initiatives and most surveys of participants' impressions reveal that workers and employers alike prefer work sharing to layoffs. Best (1998: 183) reports that "77 percent of surveyed California employers and 60 percent of their Canadian counterparts perceived morale to be higher with work-sharing than would have been the case with layoffs." The increased morale translated into lower employee turnover costs than would have materialized with layoffs, resulting in labor productivity improvements for many of the participating firms. Forty percent of California employers reported that productivity was higher under work sharing than layoffs, while only 11 percent said it was lower (Best 1988). Most cited greater cooperation and motivation among the workforce as the source of the productivity boon.

Employers can benefit in manifold ways from work-sharing arrangements. If solidarity improves morale within the firm, it can lead to productivity improvements across a variety of work groups. Employers may also prefer work sharing to dismissals because it allows them to maintain a working relationship with employees who often possess expensive firm-specific skills and thereby reduce their personnel expenses relating to retention and recruitment of workers. Best (1998) argues that lower recruitment and training cost are the main source of labor productivity improvements for STC programs. Work sharing can also be easier for firms to implement, as layoffs often trigger formal grievances related to union contracts or discrimination protections. Given the various virtues of STC, it is not surprising that a high percentage of participating employers would use the program again. The fact that some 93 percent of California employers and 82 percent of Canadian employers said they would be willing to use STC again suggests that a program of work sharing can be implemented to the benefit of the various social partners involved in the employment relationship.

Although past STC schemes were a way for governments to attenuate unemployment during economic fluctuations, a society that placed less importance on the maximization of work hours could utilize government-financed work sharing as a permanent method of distributing future productivity benefits. That is, firms would not need to demonstrate that a reduction in hours is unavoidable and related to economic challenges in order to qualify for financial assistance. They would simply have to show that a certain percentage of their workforce reduced their hours below a threshold amount (e.g. 10 to 20 percent). Unlike temporary plans that typically terminate benefits after 6 months, a permanent program might offer benefits for a longer time period to ensure that productivity gains are available to maintain income levels, especially for low-paid workers, upon the expiration of financial benefits. (Many French firms qualified for up to 5 years of financial assistance during the implementation of the 35-hour week.) An important facet of work-sharing arrangements is that workers are able to display solidarity to one another by avoiding the burden of outright unemployment. In California, 92.1 percent of work-sharing participants—even those with 4 years' seniority and having "no chance of being laid-off"—felt that spreading the unemployment was more equitable than layoffs (Best 1988: 120). Rather than the costs of unemployment falling on a small group of individuals, work sharing allows a larger group to shoulder the costs of output reductions with only a marginal reduction in their total income, thereby stabilizing economic activity.[6]

Europe: the vanguard of work time experimentation

The French struggle for a 35-hour week

The intent and initial legislation of France's 35-hour workweek law shared many characteristics with STC plans. Although it has attracted a significant amount of attention in the Western political press of late, the modern history of work time reduction in France dates back to the early 1980s. In 1982 the Socialist government under the leadership of Francois Mitterrand reduced the statutory workweek from 40 to 39 and added a fifth week of paid vacation. Despite campaign promises of further reductions, the issue of work time reduction was abandoned for the next decade. It was then resurrected in the early 1990s as a way of addressing stubbornly high unemployment rates. Like the work-sharing experiments of the 1980s, French proponents of work time reduction envisioned an activist role for government by using cost savings from unemployment compensation to reduce the payroll taxes of firms that reduced average hours and hired more workers. In 1996, the Robien Law provided significant reductions in social security payroll taxes for companies that voluntarily reduced average work hours and increased employment by 10 percent. In less than 2 years, 1500 firms utilized the Robien incentives to introduce a 35-hour workweek, while 500 moved to 32-hour workweeks. The French Democratic Labor Confederation (CFDT) estimated that the work time reduction of 355,000 employees resulted in the creation of 25,000 new jobs and the elimination of 17,000 layoffs (Syndicalisme Hebdo 1988). The Robien Act was completely voluntary and left the issue of wage levels open to negotiation. In addition to accessing payroll tax benefits, 83 percent firms reorganized their production schedules to improve productivity, making it possible for many workers to reduce their work hours with no loss of pay. According to the French labor confederation CFDT, 62 percent of the first 1500 Robien agreements resulted in shorter hours with no loss of pay, while 37 percent entailed a less than proportional loss of pay. The loss of pay was proportional to the reduction in work hours in only 1 percent of accords. The success of the Robien Act in creating employment at little cost to employees and employers under voluntary conditions and in a variety of industries and occupations helped create a political climate conducive to a mandated work time reduction law.

In October 1997, Prime Minister Lionel Jospin fulfilled a campaign promise by working with the Communist Party and the Greens to pass a two-stage 35-hour law in June 1998. The first stage of the Aubry Laws, named after Employment and Solidarity Minister Martime Aubry, required all firms with more than 20 employees to pay overtime on hours above 35 per week after January 1, 2000. In order to minimize the effects on firm profitability, the law provided financial assistance akin to the Robien Act, with additional rewards for firms that moved to a 35-hour week before the deadline. The government offered rebates on social security contributions that reached a maximum for those receiving the minimum wage and declined the higher an employee's monthly income. To qualify for up to 5 years of assistance, companies had to reduce working time by at least 10 percent while increasing their workforce by 6 percent in the case of job creation or to maintain the same sized workforce for 2 years in the case of job retention. Greater financial assistance per new worker was available to firms that reduced hours by 15 percent and hired at least 9 percent more workers. Additional assistance was made available for firms that were labor intensive, in low-wage industries, or hired a high percentage of young, disabled, or chronically unemployed workers. Social security rebates averaged around 1,300 Euros per year per employee over 5 years. Employment contracts had to be negotiated collectively with a majority union or certified by an elected employee representative to qualify for financial assistance and flexibility exemptions (i.e. the use of overtime accrual accounts).[7]

The manner in which work time would be spread across the week, month, or year and the related impact on wages was left open for negotiation in an effort to spur productivity-enhancing work time reorganizations. The law granted employers more flexibility in overtime use, switching from a weekly to an annual accounting period. Linking shorter, but more flexible, work hours to longer operating hours for firms, work time reform in France sought productivity gains from making machines work longer, while individuals worked less. More extensive use of capital could enhance productive capacity and increase the return on capital, while reducing individual work times could minimize the social impact of protracted economic activity. Indeed, the intention of the temporary social security rebates was to encourage firms to restructure their operating and working hours in a manner that would improve long-run productivity, thereby reducing per unit labor costs. Generally, the cost to firms of introducing the 35-hour week was to be absorbed by productivity gains resulting from reorganization of the work, financial aid from the state and wage growth restraint.

The first Aubry Law incorporated a second law that could address any unforeseen consequences of the initial legislation. Intense lobbying by employers prior to the second round of legislation afforded them some concessions in the second Aubry Law of February 2000. These concessions would significantly reduce the number of jobs that would ultimately be created by the 35-hour legislation (Hayden 2006). Whereas the first law required a 10 percent work time reduction, based on a constant method of counting work hours, in order to receive payroll tax reductions, the second law simply required firms to reach a 35-hour agreement to qualify for relief. This allowed firms to exclude some breaks, days off, and certain types of training from their work time calculations, limiting the hours' reduction needed to get to a 35-hour threshold. The requirement to increase employment by 6 percent in order to receive financial assistance was also abandoned in the second law. Simply achieving 35 hours and expressing a commitment to creating or saving jobs was sufficient to attract government assistance.

Other key concessions of the second law related to the calculation of overtime and its costs to employers. Aubry II allowed the 35-hour target to be achieved on an annual basis of 1,600 hours, so long as weekly hours did not exceed 48 or average 44 over 12 weeks. Since the law provided workers with scarce protection from unilateral variations in hours, firms were able to exploit hours' flexibility to avoid hiring new workers. In addition to the flexibility of an annual overtime calculation, employers were also granted a transition period prior to the imposition of overtime limits and penalties. The second stage of the 35-hour legislation stipulated that the full 25 percent overtime premium would be postponed until 2001 and that only a 10 percent overtime penalty would be in force in 2000. Although the annual overtime limit remained at 130 hours per worker, the government gave all firms an additional 2 years before all hours in excess of 35 hours per week would count towards the annual limit. Delaying the imposition of overtime penalties effectively allowed firms to avoid payroll expansion by waiting for productivity gains to offset the wage costs associated with the lower overtime threshold. Since rapid and significant reductions are needed if work time reduction is going to have a sizeable employment effect, delaying the overtime penalties clearly diminished the potential employment effects of the 35-hour law.

All French employers, large and small, now face a weekly limit of 35 hours.[8] The second law granted overtime exemptions for executives but not managers. Importantly, the second stage of the law granted pay protections to minimum wage workers converted to 35-hour weeks, guaranteeing no reduction in their monthly income. The second stage of the Aubry Laws merged the social security rebates with a sliding scale rebate on low pay created by the Juppé government in 1995. The annual payroll tax relief ranged from 3,282 Euros per employee at the minimum wage (SMIC) level to 610 Euros for employees earning 1.8 times the minimum wage and over (Gubian 2000).

Although there has been a rigorous debate over the scale of employment effects of the 35-hour law, most studies reveal a positive employment effect. France's unemployment rate fell from 12.2 percent when the 35-hour law was announced in 1997 to an 18-year low of 8.6 percent in the spring of 2001. Moreover, growth in new jobs—which is not always apparent in declining unemployment statistics due to variations in labor force participation—increased 10 times more quickly than it did from 1974 to 1996 (Economist 2001). The 7.2 percent growth in employment between 1997 and 2001 represents the largest job growth of any 4-year period in France in the twentieth century (Husson 2002). Obviously, not all of the job growth was related to work time reduction, but as Hayden (2006: 512) points out the robust economic growth "contradicts critics' predictions of hobbled businesses, investment flight, and a damaged economy."

As with any macroeconomic analysis, the difficulty in assessing the success of France's 35-hour laws involves isolating the job growth related to work time reduction. Beffy and Fourcade (2005) identify work time reduction as one of three reasons why economic growth from 1993 to 2002 was more job intensive than similar growth in the past. Husson (2002) also argues that the 1997–2001 economic expansion created more jobs than the 1986–1990 expansion as a result of work time reduction. While annual job growth was only 1.5 percent in the late 1980s, it grew much more rapidly, at 2.7 percent, from mid-1997 to mid-2001. Likewise, Logeay and Schrieber (2006: 2068) compare macroeconomic forecasts of unemployment without the 35-hour law to the actual outcomes between 1999 and mid-2001 and conclude that work time reduction yielded "significant beneficial employment effects." The fact that job growth during the implementation of the 35-hour week was more robust than in any period of comparable growth in France suggests that work time reduction made a significant contribution to employment growth.

In July 2001, the National Planning Committee (*Commissariat Général du Plan*; CGP) published a report providing a midpoint evaluation of the implementation of the work time reduction laws. By the end of 2000, 62 percent of full-time employees in companies with over 20 staff were working the 35-hour week (as opposed to 1.6 percent in 1996). The average weekly working time for full-time employees in firms with 10 or more employees stood at 36.6 hours at the end of 2000, compared with 38.6 hours at the end of 1997. The report estimated that more than 250,000 jobs had been created as a direct result of agreements on the reduction of work time signed since 1996 (including those covered by the Robien Act).

Husson (2002) performed macroeconomic simulations for a slightly longer period (1997–2001) in order the isolate the job creation related to the 35-hour workweek versus macroeconomic and autonomous growth. Three different simulation models were used to deconstruct the historically robust job growth of 7.2 percent between 1997 and 2001. Husson (2002: 140) concludes that, "the overall econometric approach used here points to an estimated 500,000 additional jobs resulting from reduced working hours between 1997 and 2001." Artus (2002) uses a similar econometric approach to show that work time reduction generated 400,000 new jobs over the shorter period between 1999 and 2001. Since the average weekly work hour reduction from 38.89 to 36.15 (7 percent) between 1997 and 2001 equates to 1 million potential new jobs, roughly half of the "job-creating" potential of work time reduction can be viewed as being offset by greater labor productivity.

Another positive employment effect was manifest in the reduction of labor underutilization. Although it is difficult to capture in traditional job growth statistics, declining rates of involuntary part-time work suggest a favorable sharing of work hours. The rate of involuntary part-time work fell from 44 percent in 1997 to 35 percent in 2002 (EIROnline 2001). Furthermore, Oliveira and Ulrich (2002) find that more frequent transitions from part time to full time have taken place since the passage of the 35-hour law. The transition to full time has largely taken place among those previously working between 20 and 29 hours a week. Although this redistribution of hours diminishes the effect of work time reduction on unemployment and "net" job creation, it represents a benevolent reduction in labor underutilization that will foster more equitable labor market outcomes.

The variability of the employment estimates is not surprising given the difficulty in isolating the job creation related to work time reduction alone. A consensus has emerged around the French Labor Ministry's research and statistical agency (DARES) job-creation figure of 350,000. This figure is widely cited as the best available estimate given the agency's compilation of microeconomic data and macroeconomic controls for job creation that would have occurred without work time reduction. Given the variety of studies that manifest a positive employment effect in the range of 300,000 to 500,000 jobs, it is clear that work time reduction can have a positive employment impact. Hayden (2006: 514) argues that "although none of these individual estimates is beyond questioning, the fact that several methods converge on broadly similar results gives greater confidence in this range."

One clear implication of the 35-hour law is the importance of design in achieving the stipulated policy objectives. The evidence suggests that the Aubry Laws prompted firms to experiment with their work time organization in an effort to improve productivity. The National Planning Committee Report found that, "in 80 percent of cases, the reduction of working time has generated a reorganization of work, including, in 59 percent of companies, an adjustment to fluctuations in activity, in 26 percent, an increased scope for opening hours, and, in 20 percent, an extension in the period for which facilities and equipment can be utilized." The 35-hour law prompted the various social partners to re-negotiate wages, work organization, and the scale, scope, and flexibility of work time. For the vast majority of both managers and workers, work time reduction took the form of additional days off per year. Askenazy (2004) concluded that the most common outcome of France's 35-hour law was an "annualization" of work time.

For some workers this annualization of hours imposed unilateral flexibility on them and increased the intensity of their work. Jean-Louis Dayan (2002) reports that 42 percent of French workers experienced work intensification in the wake of the 35-hour law. If work time reorganization simply results in "speed-up," the productivity benefits of shorter work hours will be ephemeral as workers will eventually adjust their effort levels to offset the greater work intensity. Surveys of workers' attitudes subsequent to the 35-hour law suggest that a minority of French workers (28 percent) have experienced a deterioration in their working lives and that employers where given too much flexibility in implementing the details of work time reduction under the Aubry Laws. Unskilled female workers, who presumably have little control over their work hours, were the least happy with working arrangements, with 35 percent of them describing a deterioration of conditions. Askenazy (2004: 603) concludes that:

> Evidence suggests that in recent years reduction of working time has been associated with hours flexibilization and no clear improvement of

well-being at work ... this kind of [unilateral] flexibility implies increased uncertainty and greater difficulties in coordinating working lives and private lives. It may also induce an intensification of work and have potential adverse impacts on health and safety.

Ideally, work time reform should be designed to constrain undue work intensifications and render workers more content with both their working and non-working lives.

Although surveys suggest some uneasiness with the workplace adjustments made in the wake of the 35-hour law, the majority of workers are more satisfied with their daily lives subsequent to the work time reduction. As a result of work time changes prompted by the Aubry I Law, Estrade *et al.* (2001) found that, "employees are more satisfied with their daily lives and with their working conditions: 59.2 percent of those polled stated that their daily lives had improved thanks to the reduction of working time." Only 13 percent of surveyed workers said that their quality of life had deteriorated under the 35-hour regime. Sixty-six percent of working parents who negotiate their hours with their employers felt that the 35-hour law helped them balance work and family issues, while just over 50 percent of workers with imposed hours felt the same (Fagnani 2004). The 35-hour law has given many workers more time for parenting; 63 percent of women and 52 percent of men with children under 12 report spending more time with their kids (Méda and Orian 2001). French women have been particularly pleased with work time reduction: 71 percent report improvement in their daily life, while only 4.8 percent claim that it has deteriorated (Cette *et al.* 2005). Given that the 35-hour law amounted to a modest 8 percent reduction in average hours, there has not been a revolution in time use in France, but there has been some redistribution of domestic labors. The marginal increase in household assistance from men and the extra time off during the week has afforded many women more leisure time on the weekends.

In order to foster lasting productivity improvements, the problematic aspects of the work time adjustments related to work intensification need to be abated so that the greater satisfaction workers have enjoyed in their personal lives can spill over into their working lives. As the efficiency week theory suggests, employees who are more satisfied with their work–family balance in the wake of shorter hours will become more productive at work (Evans 1975; LaJeunesse 1998). Unfortunately, the 2003 revisions of the Aubry Law granted employers even more unilateral flexibility in avoiding the 35-hour work week target. Prior to the conservative reform of the Aubry Laws there was reason to be sanguine that working conditions might improve as the original legislation contained several clauses encouraging collective bargaining. For example, firms seeking flexibility from the traditional workweek needed to achieve that flexibility through a collectively-bargained contract, which could have addressed work intensification. Since the reform of the Aubry Laws granted employers other mechanisms to avoid overtime premiums, they are under less pressure to negotiate with unions over flexible work time.

Although every stage of the 35-hour workweek in France led to job creation, many observers claim that the employment effects were muted by design flaws and the timidity of government in setting the work time thresholds low enough. Proponents of a 32-hour workweek contend that larger hour reductions have a greater employment impact because they are less likely to be offset by productivity increases. Larrouturou, an advocate of the 4-day week in France, estimated that the 35-hour threshold should have only been expected to create between 200,000 and 250,000 jobs, whereas a 32-hour week would have created around 1.6 million jobs. He also argued that France could have achieved a 32-hour workweek with little loss of pay. By his 1998 estimates, the 18 percent reduction in work hours needed to achieve a 32-hour week could have been implemented with an average 3 percent reduction in pay (Larrouturou and Rocard 1998). There would have been no loss of pay for those earning less than 8500 Francs (US$1400) per month in 1998 and a maximum 5 percent reduction in pay for high-income earners.

Bloch-London *et al.* (2004) also contend that the reduction in hours was too modest, noting that workweeks were only reduced by 8.5 percent on average. Average weekly hours for full-time workers in France stood at just 38.9 hours in 1996, falling to 35.6 by the end of 2003 as a result of the 35-hour legislation. Many firms were able to define previous hours or days, which should have been free time, as working time under the 35-hour law, softening the impact of the law. Peugeot-Citroen (PSA Group) is a case in point. Peugeot-Citroen was already operating under an agreed standard metallurgy industry working week of 38.5 hours. By considering a 1-hour and 45-minute break as non-working time, the Peugeot-Citroen agreement stated that its weekly hours were 36.75. The company then only had to reduce weekly hours by 1 hour and 45 minutes to conform with the 35-hour law. When combined with the flexibility of an annual calculation of hours, autoworkers at Peugeot-Citroen frequently found themselves working Saturdays at no premium pay.

The flexibility granted to firms in achieving work time reduction on an annual basis also reduced the need for firms to expand their payrolls. By using flextime, employers where able to coordinate working hours with the most active production periods throughout the year, thereby avoiding significant payroll expansions and the payment of overtime. Although flextime may have eased the financial burden of work time reduction for employers by enhancing productivity, it restrained job growth and fostered a greater intensification of work, or "speed up." From a job creation standpoint, it would have been preferable to strictly regulate daily and weekly hours, but the French plan attempted to balance the goal of job creation against the objective of increasing productivity through improved scheduling.

Perhaps the biggest reason why greater long-term employment effects did not result from the Aubry Laws is because they were relaxed by the Raffarin government in 2003. The moderation of the Aubry Laws raised the annual overtime limit by 50 hours. This increased annualization now affords firms greater flexibility in responding to seasonal and cyclical fluctuations in production and more time to avoid the payment of overtime. Meanwhile the worker is left at the behest of the employer's daily, weekly, monthly and annual scheduling needs. The firm can require long hours from workers in the short run and then drastically reduce, or shut down, operations to offset the hours within the year. Indeed, 30 percent of firms that reduced hours to 35 in the year 2000 planned to vary the length of the workweek for some of their employees (Pham 2002). Annualization of overtime allows a construction firm, for example, to require long hours with no overtime when the weather and demand are conducive to building, and to shut down operations during bad weather or slow demand. The worker is then forced to realize their leisure time in a form or timeframe beneficial to the employer. Another drawback of an annual accounting of overtime is that if the comp-time is never forthcoming and the employer is obliged to pay the overtime premiums upon the expiration of 1 year, the employer effectively receives a no-interest loan on the overtime wages owed. If the firm is afforded too much flexibility in the calculation of overtime, they may be able to avoid annual overtime payments altogether. Meanwhile, workers are left to bear the private costs of long weekly hours while society bears the social costs. The revision of the Aubry Laws also reduced the overtime premium that small and medium-sized firms have to pay for the 36th through 39th hours from 25 to 10 percent (it remains 25 per cent for larger firms and for overtime hours in excess of the 39th weekly hour). By changing the statutory quota for annual overtime hours to 180 from 130 and reducing the penalty rates of overtime, the law of January 17, 2003 allowed companies to return to a 39-hour week for a small marginal cost. This may have even reversed some of the early employment gains related to the Aubry Laws.

With its experimental approach to work time reduction, the French government displayed a willingness to run larger budget deficits to help finance the expansion of private payrolls. The present work time experiment in France incorporates a Functional Finance approach (wittingly or not) by using the federal treasury to encourage payroll expansion as the preferred response to the legislated reduction in work time. In this manner, the French government has been able to financially encourage the additional employment of up to a half million individuals without having to directly employ those workers. Although the 35-hour law did not generate the number of jobs that some economists anticipated, employment growth was substantial and productivity growth accelerated more than anticipated. The virtues of the 35-hour law have even been acknowledged by French business leaders. Although initially opposed to the legislation, the French National Employers' Confederation (CNPF) eventually saw some benefits in the movement to the 35-hour week. CNPF President Selliere (1998) conceded that "there can even be cases, I don't deny it, where, thanks to the 35-hour week, the organization of work, working conditions or productivity will improve." The by-product of greater labor productivity cannot be classified as a policy failure since productivity growth affords society a higher standard of living and the potential for larger work time reductions in the future. The salient lesson from the French experiment is that the design of work time regulation is critically important to achieving the objectives of the policy, be they job creation, productivity growth or a social regulation of workaholism and consumerism.

Alternative approaches in Germany, Netherlands, and Denmark

Although France's 35-hour workweek has garnered the lion's share of media attention of late, there has been a gradual movement towards shorter work hours on multiple fronts in Europe for many decades now. Arguably, many of France's neighboring countries have been more progressive in reducing work hours and granting employees genuine choice in their attachment to paid work. Germany, the Netherlands, and Denmark have all achieved significant reductions in average annual work hours. In many cases, particularly for the Dutch economy, the reduction in working hours has been central to reducing unemployment and improving well-being.

German workers have been the beneficiaries of work time reductions achieved primarily through collective bargaining. The pioneer in Germany's contemporary short hours movement was the metalworkers' union IG Metall. In 1984, IG Metall ended a 7-week strike with an agreement to cut weekly work hours from 40 to 38.5 in 1985 and to 35 hours in 1995 without loss of pay, but with slower wage increases. As the largest independent trade union in the world, IG Metall set an important precedent for the German economy and by 1996 the 35-hour workweek was common in collectively bargained agreements. Despite there being no change in the legislated workweek of 48 hours, average annual hours worked in West Germany fell from 1,732 to 1,644 between 1987 and 1997.[9]

Partly due to the experience with short time compensation, German unions were aware of the virtues of work time reduction as an alternative to layoffs and unemployment caused by economic fluctuations. Employers had also warmed to work sharing as a way of retaining employees with firm-specific skills. In one popular example the standard workweek was drastically reduced while production shifts and days were added to improve productivity. In 1993, an agreement negotiated between union workers and Volkswagen AG Germany reduced work hours from 36 to 28.8 (a 20 percent reduction), while wages were cut by 11 to 15 percent. The agreement—which allowed the company to align work time with fluctuating product demand—is estimated to have saved around 30,000 jobs (Seifert and Trinczek 2000). The reorganization of work and production time at Volkswagen allowed the company to establish a comparative advantage in production and demonstrates how creative work time arrangements can lead to situations that benefit both workers and the bottom line.

The Volkswagen agreement fueled a debate over whether unions should hold out for work time reduction with no loss of pay or to embrace a "solidaristic wage policy" that amounts to modest wage cuts for well-paid workers in return for job security and creation. Given the proven productivity benefits of work time reduction and the federal government's fiscal ability to fund a full-employment economy, there is certainly no need for workers to suffer pay losses commensurate with work time reductions. However, the working class may deem a solidaristic wage cut by higher-income workers as an expedient way of achieving the employment, social, and environmental benefits related to work time reduction. Importantly, there would need to be a concrete quid pro quo of job creation or other social benefit in return for the pay reduction to ensure continued worker support for the policy. If pay cuts simply amount to greater firm profitability, workers will quickly lose their zeal for work time reduction policies. Union leaders contend that there is plenty of opportunity for such work sharing in Germany, since 1.8 billion hours of overtime were worked in 1998 at a time when four million people were unemployed (EUROnline 1999).

The lack of a concerted national effort to reduce work time in Germany has meant that the employment effects of shorter hours have not been as robust as they might have been with a legislated reduction in hours. Since German firms faced no regulatory pressure to reduce working time, it was not expected that the industry- and enterprise-level work time reductions, which were generally defensive in nature (minimizing job loss), would create many new jobs. Yet, it is important to recognize that when work time reduction was implemented in flagship industry agreements the employment impact was solidly positive. Rubin and Richardson (1997) conducted a meta-analysis of 12 studies of the 1985 workweek reduction to 38.5 hours and concluded that every study shows positive employment effects. Studying the German manufacturing industry between 1984 and 1989, Hunt (1999) found that a 1-hour decrease in weekly working time raised employment of hourly workers by 0.3 to 0.7 percent and of salaried workers by 0.2 to 0.3 percent. IG Metall's internal calculations show that the final reduction to 35 hours by 1995 saved or created 294,700 jobs in the metalworking industry over the decade (Hayden 1999: 146). At the macro level, Lehndorff (1995) suggests that work time reduction was responsible for 43 percent of all full-time jobs created in West Germany between 1983 and 1992.

Although work time reduction in Germany generated positive employment effects, relying on collective bargaining to reduce hours has not achieved widespread macroeconomic effects. Germany has been looking to its neighbors for additional ways to address unemployment and has recently adopted legislation modeled after a Dutch policy that protects the rights of all full-time workers to switch to part-time work. The success of the part-time protections in the Netherlands suggests that under the proper social conditions empowering all workers with the right to choose work time reduction can significantly impact unemployment. The Netherlands example illustrates the potential macroeconomic benefits that can flow from voluntary work time reduction when labor market legislation is designed to strengthen workers' choices over work hours.

The Netherlands was a pioneer in encouraging part-time work with a tri-partite consensus among employers, unions and the government that the promotion of part-time work was an effective way to reduce unemployment, encourage the labor force participation of women and elder workers, and provide greater scheduling flexibility to firms (MuConsult 2003). Although the growth in part-time employment in the 1970s was largely due to social pressures (related to the feminization of the workforce) rather than govern-ment policies, towards the end of the 1970s the Dutch government began to view part-time work as a means of combating unemployment (e.g. in the Wassenaar Agreement, 1982). The merits of part-time work have gained recognition since then and in November 1996 the Netherlands passed the Equal Treatment (Full-time and Part-time Workers) Act, prohibiting the distinction between employees based on working hours when entering, extending, or terminating employment contracts. Discrimination on the basis of working hours is often held to the same standard that the High Court has established for gender discrimination. In July 2000, the Netherlands further strengthened the ability of workers to influence their working hours by pas-sing the Working Hours (Adjustment) Act. The legislation provides employees in the private and public sectors with a legal right to change their working hours. Under the Working Hours Act, every employee who has worked for an employer with more than 10 employees for at least 1 year has the right to work more or fewer hours in the same position. In the case of increasing hours, a written agreement must be approved by a collective labor organization or personnel representative. Given the culture of part-time time work in the Netherlands and the general desire to reduce hours further, the facility to increase hours has not been used widely. In a survey of 122 col-lective labor agreements, only seven included additional provisions for an increase in work hours (MuConsult 2003). Nevertheless, the right to increase hours is a very important protection for those working very short hours and in need of greater income. It also provides some flexibility to firms in accommodating the requests for hours reductions.

An assessment of the first 3 years of the Working Hours Act reveals some intriguing findings regarding worker preferences and negotiated outcomes (MuConsult 2003):

> In the period since the introduction of the WAA (July 2000 – May 2003), men (27 percent) have indicated slightly more often than women (24 percent) that they wished to work fewer hours. The main reasons for both men and women to work less are to have more time for family or household duties in their private lives (34 percent) or to pursue hobbies and other private activities (30 percent). Most employees wish to work either eight hours (37 percent) or four hours (48 percent) less per week.

In 80percent of cases the desire to work fewer hours was combined with wishes concerning how the hours are spread over the days of the week. Over the last two and a half years, women (19 percent), more often than men (12 percent), wanted to work more hours per week. In almost 60 percent of cases these employees wanted to work more hours for financial reasons. Among those wishing to increase their working hours, in most cases this related to a small number of hours (38 percent wanted to work four hours a week more and 33 percent one day a week extra) ... Approximately half (53 percent) of the employees who had wished to reduce their working hours over the last two and a half years had also informed their employer of this ... More than half of the employees (54 percent) who had requested a reduction of their working hours from their employer had had their request granted. 10 percent of the requests were partially honoured and 23 percent of the requests were refused by the employer. 12 percent of the employees had still not received any response from the employer.

Contrary to the initial concerns of employer organizations, very few cases have been referred to the legal system for resolution—only 23 cases through 2003. Despite the majority of time requests being approved by the employer or overturned in favor of the worker upon appeal, the number of work time requests is far below what would be anticipated by surveys of worker preferences. Much of this may be due to a lack of familiarity with part-time laws and their ability to empower workers to tailor their work hours to their needs and desires. If the laws continue to establish a precedence of protecting workers' rights in work time negotiations, more employees may become embolden to approach their employers with requests and the Dutch economy may achieve a target of previous governments of an average workweek of 32 hours for both men and women by 2010.

The reduction of hours and voluntary switching to part-time work in the Netherlands has contributed immensely to the metamorphosis of the "miracle" Dutch economy. Unemployment in the Netherlands fell from 12 percent in the early 1980s to 3.4 percent in 1999. Despite a 12.6 percent growth rate of the labor force from 1995 to 2005, unemployment has remained low in the Netherlands, averaging 3.2 percent between 2000 and 2004 (3.1 percent in 2007). The employment reversal is even more impressive when one considers that the labor-force-participation rate has risen from 52 percent in 1982 to 66 percent in the mid-1990s. Smith (2004: 129) concludes that the turnaround, "prove[s] that work is not an infinite thing, that it can be 'shared' out by politicians in order to reduce unemployment." Nickell and van Ours (2000: 219) investigate the success of the Netherlands in reducing unemployment and arrive at a conclusion that contradicts the lump-of-labor/output fallacy, "combinations of *supply-oriented policies* are responsible ... [for] a significant reduction of the equilibrium unemployment rate since the early 1980s [emphasis added]." It should be noted that this conclusion sharply contradicts Nickell's earlier subscription to the lump-of-labor/output fallacy (Layard *et al.* 1991). By protecting the choice to work shorter hours as a basic social right, average annual work hours in the Netherlands have fallen to among the shortest in the world during the same decade in which one million new jobs were created. In 1970 the average Dutch worker worked 1,800 hours per year. By 1983 the number had fallen to 1,530 hours per year, decreasing further to 1,397 in 1995.

Much of the Dutch employment gains are related to a growth in part-time work. From 1983 to 1996 the fraction of employees working part time (less than 35 hours per week) increased from 21 percent to 36.5 percent, with 75 percent of part-time jobs being held by women. From 2000 to 2004 part-time employment averaged 43.6 percent of total employment in the Netherlands. Using a lower threshold of 30 hours per week shows that 35.5 percent of Dutch employees worked part time in 2006—still the highest percentage in Europe (OECD 2007: 32). A crucial difference in the Netherlands, however, is that part-time work is desired and viewed as providing a sufficient means of existence. Due in part to protections like the 1990 Pensions and Savings Act—which prohibited the use of an hour limit for entry into occupational pension funds—less than 5 percent of part-time work arrangements in the Netherlands can be described as involuntary (Lee 2004). The egalitarian sharing of hours in the Netherlands has allowed part-time workers to avoid the impoverished conditions of their "short hours" counterparts in the United States. Visser and Hemerijck (1997) find that the gap between part-time and full-time wages in the Netherlands was only 5 percent in the mid-1990s, due to 80 percent of collective agreements providing pro rata wages and fringe benefits for part-time workers and the government extending social benefits to part-time workers. Commenting on the equitable outcomes of the Dutch labor market reform, Smith (2004: 120, 128) writes, "the Netherlands was a *more solidaristic [sic]* nation in 1995 than it had been in 1980, when more people were in receipt of some form of government payment and when 'social' spending had been much higher." Another feature of the Dutch economy that makes part-time work attractive is the great variety of working time arrangements on offer in the Netherlands. Work regime options range from the 2-, 3- or 4-day week to the 4-, 6- or 9-month year.

Work time redistribution in the Netherlands has been achieved largely through voluntary measures with few mandates or restrictions (such as hours limits) from the state. This suggests that simply giving workers the legal and financial means to make bona fide choices about their work time allocations could go a long way in relieving current levels of labor under-utilization in the developed world. Government intervention in the labor market could then be reserved for fine-tuning macroeconomic objectives through work time regulation. Relative to other industrialized democracies, Dutch workers are at great liberty to "choose" their work hours, which might account for the high well-being rankings that they perennially achieve as a nation.

Due in part to success of the part-time protection legislation in the Netherlands, Germany has also adopted the right-to-request short hours by enacting the Part-Time and Fixed-Term Employment Act (Teilzeit-und Befristungsgesetz) in 2001. The protection of part-time workers has yet to generate the same macroeconomic benefits as the Dutch Law due to its later implementation and the greater latitude it gives employers to deny requests. Moreover, Burri *et al.* (2003) argue that German employers have traditionally been more hostile toward part-time work than Dutch employers.

Perceiving the virtues of the short hours movement in Central Europe and Scandinavia, the European Union has adopted a directive (97/81) to promote employee-oriented part-time work and to prevent discrimination of part-timers throughout the European nations. The UK also passed a "right-to-request" law in 2003, but it is limited to parents of school-aged children. Since July 2008, New Zealand has granted employees with children under 5 years old or dependent relatives the right to request a variation to their hours. Although granting working parents the right to request shorter hours may alleviate some work-life time pressures, a universal right to short hours will have a greater impact on socioeconomic participation and reduce the perception that short hours are a non-standard "exclusion" reserved for working mothers.

In Denmark, a 1993 law granted employees work time flexibility in a slightly different manner. The law effectively made social policy of the "one-in-five" system initiated by the French civil engineering company Rabot Dutilleul. The "one-in-five" program allowed workers to reduce their work time by 1 day, week, or month in every five. The Danish law likewise encourages regimes of "one-in-four," "one-in-seven" or "one-in-ten," with a proportionate increase in permanent staff (Gorz 1999). The law affords workers the right to take up to 1 year's leave divvied up over any period they wish. Since the worker is supposed to be replaced by an unemployed individual, the original worker receives 70 percent of the unemployment benefit that they would have drawn through a layoff (approximately 90 percent of salary); so the worker on leave receives around 60 percent of their salary.

The evidence emerging from work-time reduction experiments suggest positive employment effects. Although most work time experiments have been designed to preserve jobs, the employment effects suggest that a more ambitious and sustained program of work time regulation could generate robust job creation.

There is a growing body of evidence that suggests that reducing average working time can yield positive employment effects. Whether the analysis examines a particular policy shift in a single country or the long-run trend toward shorter hours across a collection of countries, there is ample evidence of employment gains (Booth and Ravillion 1993; Holm and Kiander 1993; Houpis 1993; Ilmakunnas 1995; Bockerman and Kiander 2002; Kapteyn *et al.* 2004). Even when the researchers attempt to reveal the "myth of work-sharing" by examining long-term employment growth across 16 OECD countries, they find that a 1 percent reduction in working hours results in a 0.34 percent increase in the employment rate (Kapteyn *et al.* 2004). Since most of the movement toward short hours can be described as modest or defensive in nature, the scope for large employment gains under an aggressive work time reduction policy remains intact. In short, there is very little evidence from the work time experiments conducted to date to suggest that greater experimentation should be abandoned.

In its *1998 Employment Outlook* (183), even the typically circumspect OECD has acknowledged that under the right conditions work time reduction can successfully create jobs and halt layoffs. Thus the key to job creation is designing a work time regulation program that fosters the "right conditions" for employment growth. The next chapter outlines which policies and programs are critical to cultivating more jobs in the developed world, without necessarily creating more aggregate work hours.

Skills shortages: are workers fungible?

As is the case with any full-employment policy, a potential challenge to job creation through shorter hours is the limited availability of skilled workers. Although there certainly could be a short-term shortage of highly qualified workers, education and training investment would ease the pressure in the long run. If skill levels are worker based and not job based, than a skills shortage might lead to increased overtime rather than payroll expansion. If this is the case, a short-run scarcity premium could accrue to highly skilled workers. Yet, the government could offset the added costs to employers by providing training assistance or similar subsidies.

It is important to note, however, that in many positions skills are primarily a function of the job, not the individual worker. De Foucauld (1988) comments:

> Except in the rare case of the "creative genius", a person who is irreplaceable is so only for a limited period. Someone considered irreplaceable at a particular moment can normally be replaced by another after a period of training and familiarization. Indeed, it is the duty of a coherent democracy to expedite such possibilities of substitution by encouraging access to skills for all, and thus to reject rigidities and fixed patterns in the division of social tasks.

When one acknowledges that skills are primarily a function of the job rather than the individual worker, labor supply bottlenecks do not represent a significant obstacle to a policy of gradual work time reduction. Moreover, since work sharing promotes longer employment relationships, employers will have an added incentive to invest in the human capital development of their staff. Similarly, the return on social investments in education and training will be higher in a fully employed economy, compelling the government to devote more resources to skills enhancement.

The German economy showed little evidence of skill shortages during the period of rapid work time reductions (Lehndorff 1995b). Even in the boom year of 1990, only 10 percent of firms indicated they were frustrated by labor shortages (Spitznagel and Kohler 1996). Likewise, the Dutch experiment with work time reform is not suggestive of acute skill shortages. Moreover, a *regulation* of work hours that was mindful of macroeconomic objectives and implications could always ease its long-term trend towards work time reduction in order to address a bona fide shortage of skills in the short run.

Distributive neutrality: balancing productivity gains between time, wages, output, and profits.

The evidence from work time experiments suggests that the employment effect is heavily influenced by the manner in which productivity gains are both fostered and distributed. Indeed, the issue of allocating productivity dividends is an important social task that requires policymakers to balance the demands of the various stakeholders. The issue of job growth, for instance, has to be balanced with other socioeconomic goals such as long-run productivity growth or environmental stewardship. If job creation emerges as the sine qua non of work time reform, then the social effort bargain has to create enough distributive neutrality for employers to allow them to expand their payrolls. The French experience suggests that governments can achieve a distributive outcome conducive to job creation by combining some short-run productivity offset with financial incentives tied to payroll expansion. If the short-run productivity offset is rather low, job creation will be more robust but may cause temporary financial hardships for employers. If the productivity offset is too high, employers will face little pressure to hire more workers. Although productivity improvements may forestall job creation, such an outcome should not jeopardize future work time reductions, as greater productivity ultimately makes it easier to reduce aggregate work hours over the long run and raise the standard of living of the employed and unemployed alike. Thus, if initial productivity allocations were not ideal, governments could continue to target job creation through work time reduction combined with alternative productivity distributions. So long as productivity improves with the secular reduction in hours, there is some room for error in the regulation of hours as policymakers continually perfect their management of the social effort bargain.

Recent experience corroborates the time-honored observation that per unit costs do not rise with shorter hours, particularly in the long run. During rapid work time reduction in Germany in the 1980s, unit wage costs fell even relative to those countries that did not change work time. The balance of the productivity distribution (between time or wages and profits) may have even shifted in favor of company profits (Bosch and Lehndorff 2001). Wage concessions, government subsidies (such as those implemented in France), and reorganization of operating hours have been used to ease the pressure placed on per unit labor costs. A variety of French studies, the OECD, and France's national planning office (OFCE) conclude that unit labor cost fell during the phase-in of the 35-hour law, which improved international competitiveness.[10] In their study of work time reductions in Europe, Cette and Taddei (1994: 45) conclude that, "all the compromises achieved have ultimately ended in the same financing mechanism: over the long run term, the bill is always paid for by productivity gains."

Many observers of the 35-hour law in France felt that employers received too great a productivity offset from worker and government concessions. Bulard (1999: 5) laments the inequities of the productivity bargain surrounding the 35-hour week, "everyone pays except the employer." Such sentiment is consistent with Bruce Philp's (2005) model of Marxian class relations that shows how an hours reduction at constant hourly wages can increase the employer's per unit income through a reduced incidence of taxation for social spending. Since firms can benefit in many ways from an hours reduction, governments should guard against employers receiving an excessive productivity dividend during the social effort bargain.

It is imperative to recognize that work time reduction can be an independent form of productivity gains. Shorter hours can shock employers into using both labor and capital more effectively. Max Weber (1922) suggested that firms and other economic agents are often ruled by tradition and habituation and only make changes when inveighed to do so by regulatory or competitive pressures. As such, a firm may obstinately adhere to a pattern of producing for no other reason than "this is the way it has always been done." A Calvinistic mentality that captive, idle workers are more disciplined and productive than emancipated workers still persists among many employers. Keeping individuals idle in the workplace is viewed as superior to having them subjected to their odious whims and cravings while away from their jobs. Even though the workday may continue to be highly porous, there is still a penchant among employers to lord over the work hours of their employees.[12] The regulatory or bargaining threat of higher labor costs (e.g. through higher overtime premiums) can serve to shock these firms into organizational innovations that enhance long-run productivity. Since reorganizing operating hours can have initial costs for employers, there is a reasonable case to be made for temporary government subsidies for firms that expand their payrolls through the reduction of average work times. This was part of the rationale behind the French government granting financial assistance to firms that could document payroll expansion under the first phase of 35-hour law.

The impact of individual hours reduction coupled with a reorganization of operating hours can have a prodigious impact on productivity in capital-intensive plants since large capital costs can then be spread out over more throughput. Bosch and Lehndorff (2001) argue that historically work time reduction has stimulated growth as it has forced firms into organizational innovations around the shorter 8-hour day and 40-hour week, resulting in as many as five or six shift systems of production rather than just one or two. Working time flexibility has been a common and crucial trade-off in work time reduction experiments. In Germany, weekly operating hours rose between 1984 and 1996 from 60.6 to 71.8. As long as individual work hours are decoupled from operating hours, extended operating hours to increase output can be a source of lower per unit costs.

Many industries have yet to exploit the severability of individual working times from operating times, which was at the heart of the debate over the 10-hour day in the nineteenth century. Over a century later, few establishments show interest in optimizing the use of their plant and machinery in terms of maximizing physical output. Pioneering firms offer some proof of the productivity improvements that are possible when more attention is directed to maximizing output rather than restricting it to boost profits. The reorganization implemented in the Volkswagen plants across Germany in the early 1990s held improved productivity as an end-goal. Switching to a 28.8 workweek allowed the company to operate its plants at three or four shifts a day, increasing annual operating hours for some models from 3,700 to 5,300 per year. Hewlett Packard's implementation of a 32-hour workweek and near 24-hour operation in Grenoble, France represents another firm-level experiment that was successful in both preserving jobs and increasing productivity. Often the success in achieving productivity gains is dependent upon a production flexibility that allows firms to adjust operating hours to variations in demand. As the French experience illustrates, hours' variability can cause some stress for workers but with adequate protections those burdens may become dust in the balance when compared with the personal and social benefits of reduced work time. Indeed, many overworked individuals may view some flexibility in work time schedules as a fair price to pay for fewer work hours.

In addition to the social productivity improvements mentioned hitherto, work time reduction may lead to a more efficient use of public infrastructure, or the "social capital stock." Shorter and more flexible hours can lead to improvements in *social* productivity as the entire infrastructure of society can then be used more effectively. Why should offices, classrooms, universities, computers, laboratories recreational facilities, campgrounds, retail outlets, etc. sit idle or empty for one-quarter to one-third (40–55 hours/168 hours) of the week? Retailers in 24-hour cities, such as New York, already benefit from longer operating hours or "production runs," but many workplaces and public facilities still operate on only one or two shifts per week. This creates added difficulties for those individuals working non-standard hours as they are excluded from engaging in certain activities at times that might otherwise fit their work and family schedule. The limited and inefficient use of the social capital stock may help explain why working non-social hours is sometimes linked to poor physical and mental health. Much of what currently makes weekend and evening hours "antisocial" is a culture of long work hours and the social burdens of the transition to longer, more flexible, operating hours. It should be noted, however, that long work hours and unemployment are also antisocial. A policy of shorter workweeks could ease the temporary anxieties arising from the transition to a 24-hour society. If properly devised and combined with other social reforms, shorter, more flexible, hours could address the social ills of long hours and under-employment and still tap into the efficiency gains of longer operating hours without creating undue social duress.

With a wider societal embrace of non-standard operating hours for public and private facilities, workers may be willing to work non-standard hours in exchange for shorter hours. The reward for accepting non-standard hours (i.e. the "graveyard" shift) could take the form of shorter hours rather than premium pay. Although non-standard hours pose potential costs and bur-dens on workers and families under current societal conditions, work time reduction that was coupled with an expanded use of both public and private infrastructure could result in many beneficial arrangements for workers. For example, parents seeking more time with their families could be in a position to realize shorter hours as well as mornings or afternoons with their chil-dren. When combined with work time reduction, flexible and non-standard hours can become much more manageable and beneficial to workers and their families.

Conclusion

History and experience suggest that productivity improvements have been, and will be, high enough to afford shorter hours at constant or even moder-ately higher income levels. The evidence also suggests that an "offensive" reduction of hours could generate substantial job creation if it was properly designed and implemented. Industrialized countries have realized a nine- to tenfold increase in real income over the last 120 years. Historically there has been plenty of productivity growth to go around. Moreover, work time reduction will itself provide productivity improvements though flex-time, reorganization of operating hours, and the efficiency week effects that draw heavily on higher levels of social productivity.

What has been missing is a mechanism to influence the social effort bargain over the distribution of those productivity dividends in the best interest of society and the planet. How society uses its greater productivity is an important social question that should be resolved in an open and democratic fashion.

The benevolent productivity effects of work time reduction suggest that there is little need to fear capital flight or deleterious effects on international competitiveness. Since most European countries have already ventured down the short hours path, the challenge is simplified for the laggards of work time reduction. Essentially, long-hours countries have benefited from "beggar thy neighbor" work time regimes that fail to share productivity gains with workers in the form of short hours. Long-hours countries, such as the United States, the UK, and Australia, should seriously question why they cannot afford workers the same humane work time regimes that European workers receive. If the only way that foreign markets can be captured is through long work hours and abject labor market segmentation, then serious economic reform is needed, and it should start with a productivity-enhancing reduction in workweeks. Indeed long-hours countries should heed the advice offered by Commons (1921: 816), "If foreign markets cannot be captured unless laborers are forced to work twelve hours in continuous industries, then they are not worth capturing."

6   A Proposal for Reform

Let private industry do as much as it can, but when it cannot provide jobs, it is the responsability of the government to meet that deficit. The only way that we can be certain that we allocate responsibly our resources and our capabilities is to have a mechanism that deals with this in some kind of a national planning agency.

UAW President Walter Reuther (1961: 377)

It is an essential part of any such social system that education should be carried further than it usually is at present, and should aim, in part, at providing tastes which would enable a man to use leisure intelligently.

Bertand Russell (1935: 22)

Given the potential of work time reform to achieve broad-based socioeconomic objectives, it is important that a work time regulation program be comprehensively and collectively designed. Our desideratum thus far has incorporated the "first principles" of improving socioeconomic participation in a stable and sustainable manner. The evidence from work time reduction experiments indicates that program design has a tremendous impact on the outcome of hours regulation. Thus, a process of work time regulation should entail an initial and ongoing identification of central policy objectives. Ideally, this identification process would be conducted in a democratic manner, considering the collective interests of the stakeholders involved in the social effort bargain. Thus, any reformation of work time needs to be mindful of its intended outcomes. Ad hoc reductions in work hours intended to accomplish narrow, short-term goals can have unintended consequences (such as work intensification) that can sour attitudes regarding a wider regulation of work hours. No policy is immune to the damaging public image effects of poor implementation and failed objectives. Lackluster or failed experiments can taint the opinions of leaders and the general public to the point of abandonment of future work time experimentation. This chapter therefore offers a suite of policy proposals that policymakers can use to influence the social effort bargain to achieve the macroeconomic objectives of employment growth and price stability without relying on more material throughput. Redistributing and reducing work hours through the mechanisms proposed here will bring more transparency, equity, and accountability to the social effort bargain. Democratizing the social effort bargain will enhance socioeconomic participation, improving both economic performance and subjective well-being.

The imperative of government initiative

In 1832, John Stuart Mill defended state intervention by arguing that "classes of persons may need the assistance of law, to give effect to their deliberate collective opinion of their own interests." Given the disconnect between desired and actual working hours and the growing polarization of work hours, legislative assistance is still needed today. The pressures placed on individuals by the existing social structure of production and accumulation outlined in earlier chapters create a serious hurdle for the achievement of work time reduction through individual choice. An over-reliance on individual choice to achieve a socially acceptable work time distribution is likely to exacerbate existing labor market inequities between men and women and full- and part-time workers. Allowing existing power balances under the guise of choice to achieve work time reduction will likely lead to a further polarization of work hours along educational, gender and wealth lines. Without collective action, progressive firms and individuals may face a prisoner's dilemma that penalizes work-sharing pioneers by allowing for greater income in the aggregate, but at a reduced rate per hour of work for those few that do achieve short hours. When work time bargaining is decentralized, those choosing shorter hours of their own volition will be less likely to reap the financial, social and economic (employment security) benefits offered by a collective regulation of social effort bargain (Eastman 1998). Those working long hours will be able to "free-ride" by deriving economic rents and relative social position from a tighter labor market and greater socioeconomic equality, while failing to engage in the social tradeoffs related to lower throughput, income and spending. Moreover, the ecological implications of our social distribution of labor militate towards the collective determination of work time parameters. Although free will should be given some discretion, it is unlikely individual choice will yield a reformation of production and consumption that is ecologically sound. Gorz (1983) argues that a commonly accepted norm of sufficiency has to be re-created collectively, making self-restraint a social endeavor rather than an enlightened individual choice.

If we cannot rely on individual choice, does collective action offer any prospect of work time reform? In the face of powerful influences promoting a work and spend lifestyle and the emasculated state of the union movement, it is unclear how much solidarity and initiative the working class will muster in embracing shorter hours. Historically, unionized workers have been more willing to agitate for social legislation that improved the lot of all workers when general employment conditions have been at their worst. In the past, high levels of unemployment and low job security have encouraged unions to fight for improved working conditions in general. Thus, renewed interest in work sharing may only come about if the inequities caused by the growing polarization of work hours become severe enough to prompt action by the union movement. Gorz (1989) suggests that work time reduction is the ideal battle ground for unions. If unions fail to address the polarization of work time, they risk being marginalized into a special interest group that protects a privileged, yet diminishing, gentry of workers. To reverse the marginalization of the underemployed, Gorz (1989: 233) argues that "an ambitious policy for a continual, programmed reduction in working hours is indispensable." Since work time reduction offers genuine social and ecological benefits, it could be an effective catalyst in mobilizing union members in solidarity with the unemployed, women's organizations, environmentalists, and other social reformers. Yet, as unions are only one group of stakeholders in the social effort bargain, governments cannot watch idly for working conditions to deteriorate to the point that weakened labor unions are revived and goaded into action. Since work time regulation will be most successful when coupled with other social reforms, government should initiate the movement toward an alternative distribution of social labors and allow room at the bargaining table for labor unions and other organizations with a vested interest.

Policy intervention is also justified on the grounds that it would remove the prisoner's dilemma that pressures individual firms to wait for other firms to reduce their work hours before following suit. Government intervention can reduce the reward to beggar thy neighbor work time regimes that allow laggard firms to benefit from the progressive efforts of their competitors. Regulation or incentives can be designed to give the firm some flexibility and scope for negotiation within over-arching goals of average and maximum work hours regimes.

Policy prescriptions

Work time reform should seek to improve societal relations by reducing the regulatory role of the market and money and increasing the influence of redistribution, reciprocity and mutuality in our social system of accumulation. Much of this shift is achieved by default as activities move from the paid labor market to the third sector. In such a society, individuals can transparently interact with others, gain their esteem and demonstrate their value not as workers but participants in the public sphere. This societal blueprint better prepares humanity to deal with the eminent technological and cultural changes of the post-industrial, climate-constrained world than lame attempts to shore up work-based society by extending the wage relation to non-market activities. Based on the evidence gleaned from the long history of work time regulation, this section delineates the policy steps that should be taken to improve the transparency, equity and accountability of the social effort bargain over working time.

A principal obstacle to payroll expansion in many countries is the level of per worker benefits paid by firms. In the United States, for example, per worker (rather than per hour) benefit costs paid by firms make the use of overtime hours financially attractive. Therefore, any policy (such as health-care reform) in the United States that reduces the fixed costs of labor will dramatically improve the attractiveness of payroll expansion. Short of the government assuming a larger portion of the fixed costs of labor, policy changes that allow firms to pay non-wage benefits on an hourly basis are likely to increase the willingness of firms to redistribute work hours and experiment with the size of their payrolls. Payroll taxes should be trans-formed therefore from a quasi-fixed expense to a variable cost of labor for employers (Frank 1999; Hamermesh and Slemrod 2008)

In addition to decreasing the fixed costs of labor, employees should be empowered to choose shorter hours. Work time reform should include the enactment of a work time bill of rights that prohibits discrimination on the basis of work hours. Modeled on the Dutch and Germany right-to-request laws, such legislation should protect part-time workers from discrimination in wages, promotions, scheduling, healthcare, retirement and other forms of compensation and working conditions. The right to request shorter hours (and refuse long hours) may eliminate the bulk of labor underutilization in a manner that is largely voluntary, especially in those long-hours countries that also experience low levels of involuntary part-time work. If large numbers of over-worked individuals voluntarily switch to shorter hours, very little com-pulsory government intervention may be needed to achieve full employment. Freeing up more hours of work for the underemployed could alleviate the financial pressures faced by low-income individuals, reducing the incidence of involuntary part-time work and "moon-lighting." The evidence from the Dutch experiment as well as surveys of actual working time relative to desired work hours suggests that granting workers a bona fide choice over work hours would go a long way towards eliminating unemployment in a manner that is beneficial to individual and social productivity. However, since the outcome of a work time request law is dependent on employees first asking for a change and employers then agreeing to it, the right to request still needs to be bolstered by a set of comprehensive non-negotiable labor regulations covering daily, weekly and overtime hours (Charlesworth and Campbell 2008).

Since the labor force in advanced industrial economies is increasingly comprised of professional workers, another essential policy modification is the expansion of hours regulation coverage to include greater numbers of white-collar workers. Particularly in the United States, broader working time coverage could reduce the severe polarization of work hours that has emerged in wake of labor market "flexibility." Simply bringing more workers under work time regulation at the current workweek threshold may reallo-cate enough hours to make a substantial impact on labor underutilization in long-hours countries. Mandating overtime payments for the approximately

2 million Australians that work 50 hours or more per week could free up nearly enough hours for the estimated 477,000 people who were unemployed and the 668,500 people who were seeking more hours in May 2008 (ABS 2008a, 2008b). Increasing the discretion of workers to choose their hours and eliminating unpaid overtime could yield extremely low unemployment rates in a largely voluntary manner in many advanced economies around the globe.

Another policy that could be highly effective in reducing the polarization of work hours is a statutory work time limit (i.e. maximum allowable hours). The United States is one of few developed nations without a statutory limit on weekly hours. Weekly work time limits could strengthen new work time rights and inclusions. Since excessive work hours entail social and environmental externalities a workweek limit akin to the European Directive on Work Time of 48 hours should be implemented in all advanced countries with as few exclusions as possible. The implementation of a work time limit in the United States and a tightening of the limit in other countries could curtail the use of excessive hours that currently affects 1 of every 5 workers worldwide (Lee *et al.* 2007).

If unacceptable levels of unemployment persist after workers have been granted additional powers in choosing their work hours and protected from work time extremes by hours limits and greater occupational inclusion, the weekly overtime threshold should be lowered and the overtime pay premium increased. In regulating the social effort bargain, policymakers will need to alter overtime thresholds on a regular basis. Regulating hours as an income policy will require the manipulation of the overtime threshold with the secular trend being towards a reduction in the workweek as productivity increases are devoted to work time reduction. Regulators may also choose to raise overtime penalty rates from time to time to increase compliance at a particular workweek threshold. Research has shown that changes in standard work hours (either through legislation or collective bargaining) have a very strong influence on actual work hours. A 1 percent reduction in standard work hours reduced actual hours worked by 0.82 percent in the Netherlands and by 0.92 percent in the UK (Hart and Sharot 1978; De Regt 1988). There is a broad consensus in the work time literature that policymakers can influence actual hours through legislation (Jacobson and Ohlsson 2000; Kapteyn *et al.* 2004).

An important political advantage of work time regulation is that very little new legislation would be required to implement a policy of improved work time regulation. Reducing the fixed costs of labor and implementing fiscal incentives for employers to hire more people rather than paying overtime would require new legislation, but much could be accomplished within the existing regulatory framework in many countries. Since hours regulation is already in effect in most countries, authorities could begin by expanding regulatory coverage (e.g. to salaried, white-collar workers), recalibrating overtime thresholds, and increasing overtime penalties. Moreover, protecting workers from hours discrimination may be as straightforward as expanding existing anti-discrimination legislation that already governs labor market activity.

Given the individual and social costs of excessive work hours that are often neglected in the social effort bargain, the overtime penalty should be at least twice the normal hourly wage. In 1975, US Representative John H. Dent introduced legislation (H.R. 1013) that would have increased the over-time penalty rate to two-and-a-half times the basic wage rate. Despite the fact that 13.2 million manufacturing workers were working 35.6 million overtime hours (the equivalent of 900,000 full-time jobs) at a time of high unemployment, the Dent Bill was never considered beyond the sub-committee hearings. To avoid higher overtime wages flowing to a privileged class of workers and exacerbating income inequality, half of the overtime penalty should be paid to the government as a workaholic excise tax that could be used to abate the social costs of long hours.

The government could also devote some of the overtime tax revenues to the payment of short time (unemployment insurance) compensation linked to hours reduction and payroll expansion. Using the workaholic tax revenue to promote short hours is largely symbolic, of course, as the government is quite capable of replacing the income lost by those workers that mutually agree with their employers to reduce work hours. Since productivity gains will ease any long-term financial burdens for firms, payroll expansion incentives could be temporary in nature—say, 2 to 5 years. Since small firms have a narrow range of options for dividing up tasks and reorganizing production, it may be prudent to offer small businesses greater payroll assistance (and for longer durations) than larger firms. Yet the additional assistance must be careful not to encourage small businesses to avoid payroll expansion entirely. In its second and more substantial work time reduction experiment the French government was able to encourage many small business to profitably take advantage of incentives to reduce average work hours, reorganize production, and hire more workers through a more generous and targeted payroll tax incentive scheme.

If it is determined that a one-time income reduction should accompany an hours redistribution in order to achieve certain social or ecological goals, policy should be designed to visit the income loss on those most capable of coping with a solidaristic reduction of hours. Policymakers could ensure no loss of pay up to the median wage and progressive losses above that level. Upon the expiration of government assistance, employers would be mandated to use productivity gains to maintain pay levels. As emphasized above, there is no need for a proportional reduction in hours and pay as firms will be able to offset most of the pressure on per unit labor costs by combining productivity improvements and government assistance with payroll expansion.

Governments can also influence work hours through their own workplace practices and the standards they establish for government contractors. Many European nations and American state governments have shown leadership in reducing work hours in the public sector, thereby placing pressure on the private sector to follow suit. Implementing a 4-day, 32-hour week for all public employees may marginally constrain the ability of private sector employers to demand long hours, particularly in those occupations in which the public and private sector compete. The effect would be even more pressing if reduced hours applied to all contracted employees on government-funded projects akin to prevailing and living wage campaigns. In the United States, the regulation of work hours for federal employees and contractors could be accomplished by the issuance of executive orders as the precedent for such was established as long ago as 1840 when President Van Buren established the 10-hour day on all government works. Implementing such a "prevailing hours system" would further strengthen the government's ability to influence the social effort bargain.

The benefits of shorter regulatory periods

Many advocates of reduced work time do not distinguish between shorter days, workweeks, or work years. Although longer annual leave periods will have some positive impact on productivity for individuals and grant firms more flexibility in accommodating shorter hours, a reduced workweek offers broader social and ecological benefits than regulating hours over a month, year or lifetime. The health and other social costs related to excessive hours explored in Chapter 4 offer compelling evidence in favor of weekly work time restrictions rather than periods that allow for the short-run "overworking" of employees. The advantage of shorter regulatory periods is analogous to the issue of minimum wage regulation. Setting minimum wages at the shorter durations of an hour, day or week and not bi-weekly, monthly or yearly, provides the employer with less opportunity to extract surplus labor from the worker in the form of longer hours. A monthly or annual minimum wage could simply result in longer hours for workers. The same principle applies to work time regulation as the more time flexibility employers have to comply with hour restrictions the greater latitude they have to increase work intensity. Thus, longer regulatory periods are more likely to result in work intensification and labor market segmentation than shorter periods.

If employers only face an annual hours limit, they can still extract long hours from their workers in the short run, causing significant social disruption and costs. The same criticism holds for regulating hours over a lifetime as there are obvious health and social implications of allowing individuals to work highly intensive work hours over a long period of years in anticipation of an earlier retirement. A weekly reduction in hours is also more likely to yield a scheduled block of time that workers can use on a regular basis to conduct important social functions. A survey conducted by Working Mother found that only 15 percent of working mothers in America took 2 weeks of vacation in a row in 2007. This suggests that families have used vacation time to cover the need for time off throughout the year. Rather than requiring workers to make judicious use of vacation time to fulfill ongoing personal and family needs, a policy of workweek reductions would make it easier to plan and conduct the many non-work activities that workers provide to their families and communities. Workers will find greater engagement in the community easier to organize when they have a specific block of time available on a weekly basis rather than at sporadic times throughout the year. Gorz comments on the advantages of weekly work hour reductions vis-á-vis more vacation leave,

> The demand for reduced working hours has always been the one most bitterly resisted by bosses. They have preferred to grant longer paid holidays. For holidays are a perfect example of a programmed *interruption* to active life, a period of pure consumption, unintegrated with everyday existence, doing nothing to enrich normal life with new dimensions, to give it an expanded autonomy or a content distinct from the professional role.

There are also gender equity and environmental concerns that should be considered in choosing the appropriate duration for hours regulation. Unlike longer vacation time, a weekly day off for men is more likely to result in them performing more unpaid work in the third sector, relieving the double burden faced by contemporary female workers. From an environmental standpoint commuting to work less often on a weekly basis can ease traffic congestion and pollution throughout the year and reduce work-related expenditures on items such as dry-cleaning, fast-food, daycare, and after-school care. Thus, if we are concerned with creating autonomous space outside the market in order to improve the social and ecological functioning of society we should opt for workweek reductions over more vacations and early retirements.

Compatible tax policy

Given the psychological research suggesting that societal engagement and personal relationships are the most influential predictors of happiness, a growing number of social scientists now contend that legislation should be assessed by how well it promotes greater social interaction and integration. Applying the policy touchstone of greater socioeconomic participation to the labor market militates for a much more active regulation of the distribution of work hours and tax structures that attenuate income inequalities and curtail work and spend pressures. Layard (2005) equates the social costs arising from an individual's quest for relative income advantage to the negative externality of pollution. He argues that the externality should be redressed by a progressive income tax designed to restrain acquisitive behavior. Relative income gains are a zero-sum game at the societal level. If a person works harder and earns more, they may gain by increasing their personal income compared with other people. But the other people lose because their income falls relative to the more successful individual. Bowles and Park (2005: 407–8) write that "Veblen effects cascade downward through the income distribution, with the richest group inflicting subjective costs on the next group, whose emulation of the consumption of the rich then augments its own consumption level, thus passing additional subjective costs to the groups further down." The winner does not care that they are polluting other people in this way, so society must alter the attractiveness of longer hours as a means of displaying an invidious distinction.

Progressive taxation provides exactly this incentive. If we make taxes commensurate to the damage that an individual does to others when they earn more, then they will only work harder if there is a true benefit to society as a whole. Bowles and Park (2005: 410) contend that "the consumption of those who, like the well-to-do, are directly or indirectly reference models for many would ideally be taxed at a higher rate than the consumption of those who are models to none or to few." Although a progressive *consumption* tax may curtail some of the conspicuous waste related to consumption, there may well remain a desire to invidiously distinguish oneself on the basis of earnings or net worth. In other words, taxing consumption only indirectly influences any choice workers may have over the allocation of their labor and leisure time. The possibility of deferring consumption (saving) can still yield pressures toward long hours. A progressive *income* tax then becomes a more effective means of influencing labor market outcomes that are only partially driven by consumption desires.

Dismissing a more targeted but less tractable tax on hours, Hamermesh and Slemrod (2008: 20) espouse a progressive income tax that, "not only features higher marginal tax rates than otherwise, but also marginal rates that rise with income more rapidly than otherwise." Hamermesh and Slemrod (2008) point out the class bias in the relatively little attention given to workaholism by behavioral economists. Sin taxes on activities such as smoking, drinking, and gambling, which tend to afflict the poor, have become a significant source of funding for governments, while the addiction to long hours—largely concentrated among wealthy, highly educated individuals—is only taxed indirectly through income taxes. A progress tax on income offers a more direct means of altering the labor/leisure calculus for workaholics than a consumption tax and is consistent with the sin taxes applied to other types of addictions. Finally, only taxing consumption, irrespective of the progressiveness of the tax, is more regressive than an income tax, which can be designed to have similar effects on the consumption patterns of the wealthy. Layard (2005: 228) writes, "taxation is a way of containing the rat race, and we should stop apologizing for its 'dreadful' disincentive effects. If tax-cutters think people should work still harder, they need to explain why."

Although progressive income taxes would have a general impact on the marginal attractiveness of working longer hours, a direct tax on excessive hours (a workaholic tax) would have a more expedient effect on the labor market without disrupting the many other types of activities related to income taxes (i.e. capital investments). An overtime tax, in the form of a double-time pay premium in which 50 percent of the premium went to the worker and 50 percent went to the government, could directly address a maldistribution of work hours and allow income taxes to be less progressive than they would have to be without a workaholic tax. Despite the minor administrative burden of collecting an overtime tax, its precision in modifying labor market behavior makes it more efficient than increasing the progressivity of taxes on multiple forms of income. If successfully designed, a workaholic tax would generate very little revenue as labor market behavior would adapt quickly to the new financial incentive structure. It bears repeating that the primary function of specific excise (or sin) taxes is to prompt behavioral changes, with revenue generation being a secondary concern. Therefore the success of a workaholic tax should not be judged by the revenue it produces or the impact it has on the public budget, but rather its effectiveness in reducing the incidence of long work hours.

Compatible education policy

The debate over the role of education in improving the human condition in the wake of abundance dates back to the classical thinkers. Mill used Malthus's concession—in the second edition (1803) of his *Essay on the Principle of Population*—that "moral restraint" and other normative checks could be used to keep population growth in line with the food supply to improve the human condition as a theoretical springboard to a "social" process of enlightenment. Society was no longer prostrate to natural laws, but could pursue a vision of social progress through education and social refinement. Mill (1873: 69) writes of the epiphany among social reformers of the classical period:

> Malthus's population principle was quite as much a banner, and point of union among us, as any opinion specially belonging to Bentham. This great doctrine, originally brought forward as an argument against the indefinite improvability of human affairs, we took up with ardent zeal in the contrary case, as indicating the sole means of realizing that improvability by securing full employment at high wages to the whole of the labouring population through a voluntary restriction of the increase of their numbers.

The social process of education held the promise of freeing mankind from the niggardliness of nature and the burden of scarcity. Just as the informed and prudent management of procreation offered the prospect of societal improvement in the classical period, the sublimation of emulative desires and "enlightened" consumption holds the prospect of improving the state of human affairs in contemporary society.

Another Classical economist, Alfred Marshall (1890: 719) wrote of the challenge and importance of learning to adapt our social psyche to a condition of abundance:

Unfortunately human nature improves slowly, and in nothing more slowly than in the hard task of learning to use leisure well. In every age, in every nation, and in every rank of society, those who have known how to work well have been far more numerous than those who have known how to use leisure well. But on the other hand it is only through freedom to use leisure as they will that people can learn to use leisure well; and no class of manual workers who are devoid of leisure can have much self-respect and become full citizens. Some free time from the fatigue of work that tires without educating is a necessary condition of a high standard of life.

Thus even in the embryonic stages of industrialism in Great Britain, social theorists were contemplating how education could be used to encourage human flourishing in an age of abundance.

Writing in America in the late 1800s, Simon Patten also argued that only through the "concerted action of society" could mankind complete the transition from the age of scarcity to the age of abundance. For Patten (1924: 97), the apex of human society could not be reached until the fruits of abundance were distributed to attain a *psychologically* classless society, in which the "feelings developed by the opposition of class interests" disappeared. Patten (1892: 102) hoped that in an age of abundance men would be more willing to allow the State to "retain their surplus for educational purposes." A new curriculum could then be developed that employed the emerging experimental psychology to instill habits suitable for an age of plenty. Patten (1892) felt that education should teach children and adults the habits that would create abundance and restraints which would prevent the squandering of human and natural resources on artificial desires. Modern society may have achieved a state of sufficiency had it been more successful in curtailing the emulative desires that constantly alter our definition of abundance.

Patten (1892: 20) also presciently argued that elementary and secondary schools should teach the implications of abundance rather than the "nobility of hardship." Children were to be taught that the dividends of abundance should not be socially exclusive. Patten (1895: 480) writes, "as the standard of the community rises, the minimum standard demanded of every free citizen should rise also." Students should also be taught to use social power to curtail social ills such as conspicuous consumption, egregious advertising, drunkenness, and persons with "defective mental powers" that were overly acquisitive. Patten (1895: 482) criticized the old curriculum for lionizing "historic heroes"—men who tried to attain a "golden age" by holding a "frail humanity above its natural level." A new curriculum would make heroes of social scientists who sought to "elevate mankind through the growth of common qualities and the ejection of discordant elements (Patten 1911: 468)." To Patten's mind, colleges should inculcate the restraints that preserve abundance and improve human welfare. This meant an emphasis on self-control, efficiency, economy, and generosity and service to others. Patten (1911) correctly predicted that in the age of abundance most adolescents would be consuming a wide variety and increasing quantity of goods. College curriculum then had to assume a new role, preventing the denigration of societal welfare through an over-consumption of material goods. Young men and women could be trained to take satisfaction in intellectual pursuits and in the creation of values appropriate to an affluent society rather than the gluttonous and invidious vices of physical gratification (eating, drinking, and sexual indulgences) and conspicuous consumption. In general, Patten argued that educational institutions needed to perform "social work" to train citizens to live in an age of abundance. Welfare capitalists also had a role in the reformation of values. Rather than praising the disciplinary virtues of hardship and a "work ethic," Patten (1892) encouraged philanthropists to channel money to social workers who would teach the lower classes how moderation of consumption (through restraint and variety) could relieve the monotony of work. Good citizenship was a result of habits, feelings, and ideals for Patten, not merely a hedonistic calculation of material interests.

The psychological evidence presented in Chapter 2 speaks to the prophetic nature of Patten's educational vision. The failure of economic growth to improve our social well-being underscores the need for a new approach to education that places more emphasis on social and emotional intelligence. One universal finding of the well-being research is that social support—feeling liked, affirmed, needed, and encouraged by friends, family, and community—promotes both health and happiness (Myers 1992). Survey respondents regularly claim that family, friends, and community are the most important aspect of their happiness (Warr and Payne 1982; Relationship Forum 2007). As Baumeister and Leary (1995: 522) put it, "human beings are fundamentally and pervasively motivated by a need to belong." Consequently, educational curriculums at all levels should be revamped to serve the "social needs" of individuals in an affluent society rather than the needs of commerce in a period of competitive scarcity. We should concern ourselves, first and foremost, with rearing good citizens rather than preparing young people for the competitive trenches of the labor market. Under proper guidance, non-hedonistic pleasures—such as spiritual and intellectual activities—can become increasingly important in a society of abundance.

Patten's view of education as "social work" clearly anticipated the resistance that would emerge against a social psyche of abundance. A long-standing objection to less remunerative work has been the argument that individuals will not be able to occupy their newfound time in a socially-benevolent manner. Such thinking, it should be noted, is based on the belief that working and spending somehow results in superior outcomes than individuals could achieve without the guiding influence of starvation wages, acquisitive behavior, or relative prices. The conclusion that less work time will result in truancy, alcoholism and other "at-risk" behavior evokes a very pessimistic view of humanity. Certainly, work time reduction does present the opportunity for more debauchery, but it is not clear that socially disruptive behavior would be more prevalent than under the contemporary practice of maintaining labor market frustrations for a large and growing fraction of workers. The evidence that emerged from the last widespread reduction in working hours from the end of the Industrial Revolution until the late 1960s is not suggestive of individuals engaging in widespread disruptive behavior. Rather the travel, recreation and entertainment industries expanded rapidly as a direct result of people working fewer hours than they did during the Industrial Revolution. Some may question the worth of these activities, but they are certainly an improvement over the anticipated criminal, intoxicated and indolent activities predicted by those possessing a pessimistic view of human nature.

Encouraging an expansion and socially judicious use of free time would challenge the traditional life-course of school-work-retirement, where each stage occupies one distinct phase of a person's life. The notion of having one employer and even one occupation for an entire working life is increasingly anachronistic. Young workers today can expect to change their careers multiple times, necessitating a continual upgrading of skills. Moreover, with the structural changes wrought by technological change, many workers facing retrenchment will need to be re-skilled for completely new lines of work. Work time reduction (or job sharing) could be viewed as a critical component of government re-employment programs since it affords workers the "transitional time" to partake in the education and training opportunities that responsive governments would offer to all adults. To both compete in the post-industrial economy and to contribute to a post-modern society, education will need to become a life-long process. In many respects, societies have made great advances in extending education to adults, but governments will need to redouble their efforts to bring about a more virtuous use of free time.

Without stipulating specific structural reforms, there is much that a curriculum overhaul could include: improving psychological management (of anger, envy, and depression); promoting altruistic activities (including the mutual benefits of loving and serving others); cultivating an appreciation of cultural art, architecture and esthetic beauty; enhancing knowledge of society's historical place; increasing political participation; honing parenting skills; increasing philosophical and religious literacy and tolerance; and elevating general civility. Clearly, such a curriculum introduces principles of morality as matters of discussion and deliberation. It is an extension of Aristotle's admonishment that the "unexamined life is not worth living." Reforming work time requires action to influence the content of leisure if certain social and ecological objectives are to be met. The goal of increased socioeconomic participation relies on individuals becoming more active in their families, communities, and societies when relieved from long or insufficient hours. This contrasts with leisure time in the productivist (work fetish) vision which views free time as a source of more consumption. If free time is to serve a higher purpose than the accretion of material goals, there will be a role for education, instruction, and access to aid in the acquisition of skills and interests related to non-market activities. As preceding chapters have highlighted, individuals in market societies have been taught from mother's knee that hard work is virtuous and fertile in a meritorious society. We have been socialized to think that we can "work" our way out of any problem or predicament. Yet, if overwork is the source of the problem it may require challenging societal adjustments. Any move to a "postmaterialist" existence will therefore require significant intellectual, psychological, and moral transformations. But there is no reason why these profound changes should not be prompted by a gradual and measured reduction in work hours that balances economic, social and ecological concerns.

As it serves to alter the deeply engrained social psychology of market capitalism, education plays a vital role in a social reform. Stanfield (1987: 149) argues that:

> Planning cannot be made to work if it is merely superimposed on the market society with the personality structures of individuals of that society. The social psychology of planning is of crucial importance. The new order of planning must include institutions leading to a revivified *civitas* and *philia;* it must pave the way for values articulation and clarification as well as resolution of values conflicts.

A new institutional arrangement devoted to regulating work time could satisfy many of the requirements of such a new order of planning. By halting the hedonic treadmill, work time regulation sows the seeds for a new value system and social psychology that is less dependent on economic gain.

7 Conclusion

Distinguishing between ends and means to an end is an important responsibility of policymakers. In the case of work time regulation, however, the two become fused. Since it promotes a societal transformation, the short-term objective of achieving equitable labor market outcomes through hours redistribution and reduction also brings society closer to the long-term of goal of more autonomous time outside the marketplace. Work time regulation can provide instant relief of working class anxieties; but since it goes to the heart of labor exploitation, it also initiates a process that transforms society. The acknowledgement that work time negotiation is effectively a social effort bargain presents the opportunity to ameliorate labor market inequities while simultaneously placing society on a path to a fuller human existence. Promoting a more democratic management of the social effort bargain offers the very real possibility of fashioning a social system of accumulation that is no longer prostrate to the idolatry of paid work and economic growth. The aim is not just a marginally better world, but a different one, where the values of community, democracy, equality and solidarity, and therefore true freedom, receive greater importance than economic throughput.

As industrial economies increasingly struggle with the "progress paradox" and the challenges of global warming, traditional full-employment policies conceived under a fetish for work and growth will fail to improve socio-economic participation and human welfare. Not only are such conventional policies unsustainable from a social and environmental standpoint, but their inflationary tendencies will spark significant political opposition to their implementation. Since work time regulation does not depend on greater output to tighten labor markets, it offers distinct advantages over competing full-employment policies that rely on neurotic work and spend behaviors. In addition to increasing socioeconomic participation and, as a consequence, social productivity, work time regulation that links hours reduction to future productivity increases could achieve significant price stability as it represents an incomes policy that prevents both excessive spending and wage claims. The flexibility of work time regulation also creates the possibility to reduce price pressures by increasing average working times in periods of extraordinary economic circumstances. In a climate-constrained world of growing abundance, it is only logical for wealthy societies to contemplate a redistribution and continual regulation of social labors. Redistributing hours of work and democratically regulating future work time regimes through a social effort bargain is the single most sustainable, non-inflationary and equitable method of achieving greater socioeconomic participation.

On par with the many economic benefits, work time regulation offers the capability for citizens living in an age of abundance to define themselves as something other than paid employees. The redistribution of hours resulting from work time regulation represents a first step in a process of enlightenment in which workers will create an identity through the whole of their relationships at work, home, community, and play. Work time regulation that minimizes the importance of remunerative work for harried workers and expands earned income for underemployed workers can provide the time or money needed to perform more activities in the third sector. Having such an alternative to the private sector is crucial for a social movement intent on abandoning "economic gain" as a guiding social principle. There is certainly a role for government in fostering the pursuit of "loftier ideals" subsequent to a redistribution of work time, but the first precondition for enhanced human development is greater socioeconomic participation, which means more paid work for some and less for others.

Modern society, as Veblen averred, is rife with ceremonial adequacies—activities we partake in for their own sake. It is the challenge of advanced societies to recognize such fanaticism and redirect it in a benevolent manner. Increasingly, post-industrial societies will have to address the deeply engrained veneration of paid work and sever its umbilical connection to socioeconomic involvement. History will judge our ingenuity and capacity to adapt to the winds of technological change in a climate-constrained, post-industrial world. Social scientists and political leaders committed to alleviating unemployment should ask themselves if they want to be remembered by their grandchildren as a proponent of more work, more spending, more ecological damage, and more of the neurosis related to life on the hedonic treadmill. If they are uneasy with such a legacy, they should embrace a social effort bargain that fosters an alternative social distribution of work hours as way of forging a participatory society that is more equitable and rewarding for the vast majority of citizens in the developed world and more sustainable for all inhabitants of the world, present and future.

Notes

Introduction

1 Recommendations of hybrid policies date back at least to the 1966 National Commission on Technology, Automation, and Economic Progress created by the US Congress and appointed by the President. The commission of business executives and labor leaders espoused a guaranteed income of $3000 to every family, fourteen years of public education for every qualified person, and to use the US government as a residual employer of all those unable to find employment in the private sphere.

1 The Origins of the Work and Growth Fetish

1 The usefulness of work in this regard was not shared by divergent theories that anticipated a more apocalyptic coming of the Kingdom of God. In such theories, work and other worldly distractions wasted time that belonged to spiritual pursuits in the interim before the coming divine intervention that would redeem the earth. (See Tilgher 1977 for these divergent views.)
2 Perhaps the most conflicted role has been played by the American labor unions. Contrary to the early history of the American labor movement and to the cooperative work time reductions recently achieved in Europe, organized labor in the United States has largely abandoned work time restrictions as a bargaining imperative since World War I and, in many cases, has pursued overtime hours and premiums as income maintenance for workers with otherwise stagnant real earnings.
3 Feagin (1975: 164) similarly summarizes the later War on Poverty "as an attempt to meet poverty problems that focused heavily on employment-related or educational services and on integrating the unemployed poor into the economy. The payoff for capitalism, however, may have been greater than for the poor."
4 David Spencer (2003: 236) argues that the sources of work resistance have "been variously identified with the irksomeness of work effort, the allure of leisure time, and the slothfulness of workers."
5 This view of the worker leads Williamson to a rather disingenuous application of opportunism (Spencer 2003). While workers have an unwavering desire to shirk, employers are held to be the stewards of the common good by collectively maximizing efficiency. Despite the innate opportunism of human nature, continuous operation in a competitive labor market is the only institutional restraint required to keep firms from exploiting workers. Production inefficiencies are then the result of shirking workers rather than abusive bosses; and institutional measures designed to modify worker motives and behavior become imperative.

2 Rethinking the Work Fetish and the Growth Consensus

1 Stanfield (1996) identifies a methodical paradox in the fact that John K. Galbraith is one of the most widely cited economists of the last five decades, while few people are able to recognize the Institutionalist tradition that underlies his thinking.

2 Galbraith (1952: 4) also wrote of the limited options regarding the organization of society, "It is part of man's pride that he makes economic policy; in fact, in economic affairs, he normally adjusts his actions, within a comparatively narrow range of choice, to circumstances."

3 The instincts that motivate humans might be better described as "impulses" as they are not entirely congenital (Veblen 1964).

4 A recent and rather unprecedented public announcement by the Ford Motor Company validates Galbraith's claim that producers will offer "that which can be sold" over "that which is socially useful." In its first *Corporate Citizen Report*, issued at the company's annual shareholders meeting in May 2000, Ford Motor Company said that its highly profitable sport utility vehicles contributed more than cars to global warming, emitted more smog-causing pollution, and endangered other motorists. The company said that it will continue producing the vehicles because they are so profitable but would seek technological solutions and consumer alternatives to sport utility vehicles.

5 There is also greater dispersion around the average lifespan in some countries such as the United States, suggesting that growing economic inequality is manifest in health disparities.

6 The social costs of urban sprawl and gated communities are readily apparent in many blighted inner cities and under-funded school districts across America.

7 There is some contention that our well-being is primarily determined by our hedonic endowments (see Wilkinson 2007), but the research on the biology of moods suggests that genetic make-up is only a minor factor in determining well-being, especially trends in well-being. Lane (2000: 42) writes, "[An] illustrative review of cases of apparent biological fixity is impressive but not determinative. It does not explain why people are happier when they marry rather than live with an unmarried partner, why certain kinds of precipitating events should plunge people into depression, why the death of a daughter's mother before but not after age eleven should predict depression, of why happy childhoods do not predict happy adulthoods ... Biology is not destiny."

8 The psychological research also suggests that the *causation* between individual wealth and well-being is nebulous. Diener *et al.* (2002) found that cheerfulness in the first year of college was associated with higher income when respondents reached their 30s. In their review of the literature on the subject, Diener and Seligman (2004: 8) conclude that, "longitudinal findings indicate that some part of the association between income and happiness is likely due to happy people going on to earn more money than unhappy people."

9 Their analysis of Eurobarometer Surveys for a similar time period (1973–98), in which British respondents were asked to rate their "life satisfaction" rather than "happiness," finds that well-being has not risen systematically in Great Britain either.

10 Sachs (1998: 125) notes that while an average Navajo household held only 236 possessions, modern households contain over 10,000 objects on average.

11 Some employment growth is likely in the knowledge sector, consisting of an elite group of professionals in science, engineering, management, consultancy, teaching, marketing, media, and entertainment. Although further growth of the knowledge sector is entirely feasible, its fruition is largely at the discretion of the sector itself. Holding their own interests paramount, it is unlikely that knowledge

sector workers will create employment space adequate to absorb the mass of workers displaced by "smart technology."

12 Urban planning has an important role to play in fashioning the proper social arrangements as the design of cities, the architecture, the public amenities and public transportation can encourage self-directed activity, cooperation, volunteerism, and interaction. Marcuse (1979) advised, "after the revolution, we shall tear down the cities and rebuild them."

13 Thirty-eight percent of the paid workers in the non-profit sector work part time, with average hours work rising from 16.5 in 1998 to 20 in 2004 (Haugh and Kitson 2007).

3 Work Time Regulation as a Macroeconomic Policy Tool

1 Many critiques of the NAIRU, such as Pollin (1998), rely on Marx's "surplus army" approach.

2 On many macroeconomic issues, such as inflation, the business class has formed a powerful political alliance with the bondholding class to protect their kindred interests. (See Kalecki 1943 and Canterbery 2002.)

3 Policy examples abound in the United States including, the 1996 Welfare to Work Act, Earned Income Tax Credits, unemployment compensation, and a variety of Social Security disability and survivor benefits that are tied to work credits and income levels.

4 Dankert *et al.* (1965) claim that Walter Reuther, President of the United Auto Workers union, outlined a plan for a "flexible adjustment of the workweek," which would relate reductions in the workweek to the unemployment rate. Yet, nothing could be found on the topic in the *UAW Report of Walter P. Reuther to the 19th UAW Constitutional Convention* cited by the authors.

5 John Commons may have been ahead of his time in espousing work time regulation, and felt daunted by the career risks involved with the advocacy of work time reductions. There is some speculation that Commons may have lost his endowed chair at Syracuse University for advocating a work time reduction to a five-and-a-half-day week. Parsons (1985: 757) chronicles how funding for his faculty position suddenly disappeared after Commons spoke out at a church meeting called to protest the playing of baseball on Sunday by factory workers. Commons made the relatively mild remark, "I agree with you that this is pretty bad and I have a suggestion. Instead of having them work six days a week, I suggest that you give the workers Saturday afternoon off, so they can play ball then."

6 The Youth Employment Programme (*emplois jeunes*), which employed 213,000 young French workers (12 percent of all jobs held by 15–24 year olds) proved disappointing as a transition towards permanent private-sector employment. Despite concentrating assistance on individuals with relatively high educational qualifications, it failed to provide the kind of job experience that improved their chances of finding private-sector work. Only one in three participants found work before their contract ended and only one in twenty did so in the private sector (OECD 2003). Iturriza *et al.* (2008: 32) offer a similar assessment of Argentina's job guarantee (Jefes) program finding that "individuals enrolled in the Plan are between 12 to 19 percentage points less likely to transit to employment as compared to individuals who applied but did not join the Plan. The negative effect of the program tends to be larger for females and as a consequence, over time, the program becomes increasingly feminized." The permanency of public sector work is not necessarily undesirable, particularly in a developing country context where the alternative is unemployment, but its prevalence challenges the efficacy of a buffer stock mechanism flexibly adapting to private sector employment oscillations.

7 Economists of many persuasions have offered evidence of the "efficiency week" over the last two centuries, including Smith, Marx, Mill, Bienfield, Nyland, Chapman, Bosch and Lehndorf, and Rubin and Richardson. (See LaJeunesse 1998 for a brief description.)

8 Although the proposals assume multiple appellations, such as a guaranteed annual income, basic income guarantee (BIG) or a negative income tax, they are effectively equivalent in spirit and object. Proponents of the separate proposals would contend, however, that the *functional* efficiency of each plan varies and therefore carries economic and political importance.

9 The history of work time reduction, including the hasty 2003 reform of the 35-hour law in France, suggests that there would also be truculent opposition to work time reduction from the "business" or "enterprising" class, but with inflation in check the threats to the bond-holding (Rentier) class are less immediate.

10 Some advocates of a participation income acknowledge that the costly and bureaucrat task of validating socially useful activities could threaten the long-run existence of the scheme (Van Parijs *et al.* 2001).

11 Income guarantee proponents are likely to retort that much of the spending could be taxed back by the government to avoid undue economic growth. This simply results in greater tax churning and inefficiency. It would be more efficient to simply expand government assistance for those in need.

4 The Ecological and Social Sustainability of Work Time Regulation

1 Many researchers have shown that the adverse effects of long work hours tend to be exacerbated by a worker's lack of control over hours (Fenwick and Taussig 2001). Golden and Wiens-Tuers (2006) find that when overtime hours are required by the employer, workers report more frequent interference with family and somewhat more frequent fatigue.

2 American trucking companies operate on thin profit margins and face competitive pressure from other transportation sources. Additionally, under the Bush Administration's management of the North American Free Trade Agreement, truckers now face competition from their Mexican counterparts in certain areas of the United States. With the transport of perishable goods and the implementation of just-in-time inventories, punctual deliveries command such a premium that trucking companies employ dispatchers to prod, plead and threaten drivers to drive as long as possible to arrive on time. Drivers are financially responsible for being on time, which often represents a penalty for getting a good's night sleep (Hecker 1998; Belman and Monaco 2001).

3 The incidence of part-time work as an ideal work arrangement did not vary much by income or education level, but there were minor differences by race. Black mothers were more likely than white mothers to cite full-time work as an ideal, but both races had similar preferences for "no outside employment" as an ideal.

4 "Employment status of the population by sex, marital status, and presence and age of own children under 18, 2005–6 annual averages." Table 5, Bureau of Labor Statistics.

5 It is important that the right to part-time scheduling extends to all classes of workers in order to avoid resentment towards a protected class (of parents) and to afford employers more options in dealing with work time requests. Since the Right to Request Law in the UK only applied to parents, employers often received similar work time requests that were difficult to accommodate.

6 Yankelovich, Young Adult Europe (1994) in *Yankelovich Monitor* 1971–95 (cited in Gorz 1999: 63).

7 Golden and Gebreselassies' (2007) analysis of 2001 Current Population Survey data suggest that the percentage of "overemployed" full-time workers is only

7.5 percent of the US labor force. However, the survey question used is a prime example of the false choice offered to workers as they investigate the "extent one may be willing to reduce hours of work at one's current job for less income." Specifically, the May 2001 CPS Supplement survey asks, "If you had a choice would you prefer to: work fewer hours but earn less money. Work more hours but earn more money. Work the same number of hours and earn the same money?" The authors recognize the difficulty arising from the all-or-nothing nature of the CPS question and the likelihood that the results have a downward bias. Golden and Gebreselassie (2007: 19) acknowledge that "if workers are presented exclusively with various hours and pay reduction options, the proportions indicating overemployment are higher; [that] respondent openness to hours reduction is greatest when surveys do not explicitly state any direct tradeoff of lower income; [and that] workers' inclination to forgo current income is considerably less than the willingness to forgo future income or raises."

8 For British trends see, "European Foundation for Improvement of Living and Working Conditions (2003): A new organisation of time over working life." Available at www.eurofound.ie

9 This is broadly consistent with Kattenbach (2007) who reports a desire by all European workers (male and female) to reduce working time by 4.5 hours a week.

10 Desires for shorter hours are rarely put to employers for fear of discrimination or retaliation. Even in Germany where the right for shorter hours is legally protected, Wanger (2004) finds that staff members who want to reduce working time are not expecting to reach an agreement with their employer and, consequently, do not even ask for it.

5 The Employment Effects of Work Time Reduction

1 Blaug (1958: 224) also comments on the lack of sophistication in the economic arguments surrounding the Factory Acts, "to be sure, economic theory added very little in the way of theoretical analysis to popular thinking about the Factory Acts. The level of formal analysis barely rose above the commonplace: no effort was made to distinguish the short-run and long-run effects of a change in hours, without which distinction of any analysis was bound to be naïve."

2 This argument is largely analogous to the neoclassical assessment of the employment effects of minimum wage increases.

3 In the United States, the virtues of STC include lower unemployment compensation insurance costs since firms will not have to rely on layoffs that attract higher premiums.

4 Best and Mattesich (1980) demonstrate the stabilizing effect of the design of the California STC program. They examine a hypothetical firm employing workers under the prevailing US earnings structure to show that the top fifth of income earners receives a take-home pay of 91 percent of their previous earnings under STC, while the average worker takes home 92 percent of their pay. Yet, the bottom fifth of wage earners receives an STC benefit of $128 per week versus the $74 payment they would receive with a full-time layoff. Thus, the California STC program serves as a useful example of how a progressive benefit scheme can stabilize consumption during an economic contraction by shifting income to low-income workers who generally have a higher marginal propensity to consume than higher paid employees. STC can therefore serve an effective automatic stabilizer, particularly when a poor distribution of income is chiefly responsible for the economic slump (Ayres 1943).

5 Between 1977 and 1978, most participating firms and workers used the STC program for 3 months or less, and in 1981, 61 percent of participants used the program between 3 and 6 months (Best 1988).

6 The average employee in California received a 21 percent reduction in hours with only an 8 percent fall in weekly take-home pay. A reduced payroll and income tax liability accounts for some of the difference.

7 In the case of a minority union, the contract terms had to be passed by a majority vote in a referendum in order to attract financial assistance.

8 The new laws define actual working time as "time during which the employee is at the employer's disposal, must comply with the latter's instructions, and is not free to go about his/her business."

9 www.eiro.eurofound.ie/servlet/ptconvert?de9803255f

10 See Gubian *et al.* (2005); Crépon *et al.* (2005); Heyer (2005); OECD Economic Outlook (2005).

11 Employers are not solely responsible as the mentality of control and the socialization of work habits are manifest in much of our modern culture. Even our school systems seem to be organized around inculcating good "factory habits" rather than innovative or independent thinking. However, the recent popularity of home schooling shows promise for work time reform. The liberation that comes with home schooling will hopefully broaden students' academic exposure and introduce them to a less regimented way of life—planting the seeds for a similar revolution in work time.

References

ABS [Australian Bureau of Statistics] (2002) *Forms of Employment*, November 2001, Catalogue No. 6359.0, Canberra.

——(2003) *Australian Social Trends*, Online. Available http://www.abs.gov.au/Aussta ts/abs/abs@.nsf/7d12b0f6763c78caca257061001cc588/923ec292aba44932ca2570ec00006 ee7!OpenDocument (accessed 25 August 2008).

——(2008a) *Australian Labour Market Statistics*, July 2008, Online. Available http://www.abs.gov.au/AUSSTATS/abs@.nsf/DetailsPage/6105.0Jul percent202008?Open-Document (accessed 4 September 2008).

——(2008b) *Australian Social Trends, 2008*, Online. Available http://www.abs.gov.au/AUSSTATS/abs@.nsf/Lookup/4102.0Chapter7102008 (accessed 4 September 2008).

Ackerman, F. and Stanton, A. (2008) *The Costs of Climate Change: What We'll Pay if Global Warming Continues Unchecked*, New York: National Resources Defense Council.

Advisory Group on Working Time and the Distribution of Work (1994) *Report of the Advisory Group on Working Time and the Distribution of Work*, Ottawa: Human Resources Development Canada.

Alesina, A., DiTella, R. and MacCulloch, R. (2004) "Inequality and Happiness: are Europeans and Americans Different?" *Journal of Public Economics* 88: 2009–42.

Amagasa, T., Nakayama, T. and Takahshi, Y. (2005) "Karojisatsu in Japan: Characteristics of 22 Cases of Work-related Suicide," *Journal of Occupational Health* 47: 157–64.

An Unexpected Tragedy: Evidence for the connection between working hours and family breakdown in Australia. (2007) *The Relationships Forum*. Online. Available http://www.relationshipsforum.org.au/assets/downloads/rfa_an_unexpected_tragedy _executive_summary.pdf (accessed 5 January 2008).

Anderson, N. (1938) *The Right to Work*, Westport, CT: Greenwood Press (1973 Reprint), New York: Modern Age Books.

Anthony, P.D. (1977) *The Ideology of Work*, London: Tavistock.

Applebaum, H. (1984) *Work in Market and Industrial Societies*, Albany, NY: State University of New York Press.

Arditti, J.A. (1997) "Women, Divorce and Economic Risk," *Family Court Review* 35 (1): 79–89.

Artus P. (2002) "Réduction de la durée du travail, une analyse simple des faits," *Flash de la CDC IXIS*, no. 2002-8: 4–10.

Askenazy, P. (2004) "Shorter Work Time, Hours Flexibility, and Labor Intensification," *Eastern Economic Journal* 30 (4): 603–15.

Ayres, C.E. (1935) "Moral Confusion in Economics," *International Journal of Ethics* 45 (2): 170–99.

——(1938) *The Problem of Economic Order*, New York: Farrar and Rinehart.

——(1943) "The Significance of Economic Planning," in S. Eldridge (ed.) *Development of Collective Enterprise*, Lawrence, KS: University of Kansas Press.

——(1944) *The Theory of Economic Progress*, Chapel Hill, NC: The University of North Carolina Press.

——(1946) *The Divine Right of Capital*, Boston, MA: Houghton Mifflin Company.

——(1952) *The Industrial Economy: Its Technological Basis and Institutional Destiny*, Boston, MA: Houghton-Mifflin.

——(1961) *Toward a Reasonable Society: The Value of Industrial Civilization*, Austin, TX: University of Texas Press.

Aznar, G. (1988) "Revenu minimum garante et deuxième cheque," *Futuribles*, April: 61.

——(1993) *Travailler Moins pour Travailler Tous*, Paris: Syros.

Balducchi, D. and Wandner, S. (2007) "Work Sharing Policy: Power Sharing and Stalemate in American Federalism," *The Journal of Federalism* 30: 1–26.

Bascom, W. (1948) "Ponapean Prestige Economy," *Southwestern Journal of Anthropology* 4: 211–221.

Baumeister, R.F. and Leary, M.R. (1995) "The Need to Belong: Desire for Interpersonal Attachment as a Fundamental Human Motivation," *Psychological Bulletin*, 117: 497–529.

Beder, S. (2000) *Selling the Work Ethic: From Puritan Pulpit to Corporate PR*, New York: Zed Books Ltd.

——(2005) "Digging your own grave," in L. Carroli (ed.) *The Ideas Book*, St. Lucia, Queensland: University of Queensland Press: 30–39.

Beffy, P.O. and Fourcade, N. (2005) "Le ralentissement de la productivité du travail au cours de années 1990: l'impact des politiques d'emploi," *Economie et Statistique* 3–23: 376–377.

Beilinski, H., Bosch, G. and Wagner, A. (2002) *Europeans Work Time Preferences*, Dublin: European Foundation for the Improvement of Living and Working Conditions.

Bell, L. and Freeman, R. (1995) "Why do Americans and Germans Work Different Hours?" in F. Buttler, W. Franz, R. Schettkat and D. Soskice (eds) *Institutional Frameworks and Labor Market Performance*, London: Routledge.

Belman, D. and Monaco, K. (2001) "The Effects of Deregulation, Deunionization, Technology and Human Capital on the Work and Work Lives of Truck Drivers," *Industrial and Labor Relations Review*, 54 (2): 502–524.

Benimadhu, P. (1987) *Hours of Work: Trends and Attitudes in Canada*, A Conference Board Report, Report 18–87.

Bernstein, P. (1997) *American Work Values: Their Origin and Development*, Albany, NY: SUNY Press.

Berscheid, E. (1985) "Interpersonal Attraction," in G. Lindzey and E. Aronson (eds) *The Handbook of Social Psychology*, New York: Random House.

Best, F. (1988) *Reducing Workweeks to Prevent Layoffs: The Economics and Social Impacts of Unemployment Insurance-Supported Work Sharing*, Philadelphia, PA: Temple University Press.

Best, F. and Mattesich, J. (1980) "Short-Time Compensation Systems in California and Europe," *Monthly Labor Review*, July: 13–22.

Blanchard, O. and Summers, L. (1987) "Hysteresis in Unemployment," *European Economic Review*, 31: 288–295.

Blanchflower, D.G. and Oswald, A.J. (2004) "Well-being Over Time in Britain and the USA," *Journal of Public Economics*, 88 (7–8): 1359–1386.

——(2008) "Hypertension and happiness across nations," *Journal of Health Economics*, 27 (2): 218–233.

Blaug, M. (1958) "The Classical Economics and the Factory Acts – A Re-examination," *Quarterly Journal of Economics*, 72: 211–226.

——(1985) *Economic Theory in Retrospect*, 4th ed., Cambridge: Cambridge University Press.

Bleakley, D. (1981) *In Place of Work, the Sufficient Society: a Study of Technology from the Point of View of People*, London: SCM Press.

——(1983) *Work: the Shadow and the Substance: a Reappraisal of Life and Labour*, London: SCM Press.

Bloch-London, C., Askenazy, P. and Roger, M. (2004) "La France et le temps de travail, 1804–2004," in P. Fridenson and B. Reynaud (eds) *France and Working Time, 1804–2004*, Paris: Odile Jacob.

Block, F. and Somers, M. (2005) "In the Shadow of Speenhamland: Social Policy and the Old Poor Law," in K. Widerquist, M. Lewis and S. Pressman (eds) *The Ethics and Economics of the Basic Income Guarantee*, Burlington, VT: Ashgate.

Bluestone, B. and Rose, S. (1997) "Overworked and Underemployed: Unravelling the Economic Enigma," *The American Prospect* 31: 58–69.

Blyton, P. and Noon, M. (2002) *The Realities of Work*, New York: Palgrave.

Borjas, G., Freeman, R., Katz, L., DiNardo, J. and Abowd, J. (1997) "How Much Do Immigration and Trade Affect Labor Market Outcomes?" *Brookings Papers on Economic Activity*, 1997 (1): 1–90.

Bockerman, P. and Kiander, J. (2002) "Has Work-Sharing Worked in Finland?" *Applied Economics Letters*, 9: 39–41.

Bologna, S. (1996) "Durée du travail et postfordisme," Futur Antèrieur 35/36: 19–28.

Booth, A. and Ravallion, M. (1993) "Employment and the Length of the Working Week in a Unionised Economy in Which Hours of Work Influence Productivity," *Economic Record*, 69: 428–436.

Bosch, G. and Lehndorff, S. (2001) "Working-Time Reduction and Employment: Experiences in Europe and Economic Policy Recommendations," *Cambridge Journal of Economics*, March (2): 209–243.

Boules, R. and Cette, G. (2005) "A Comparison of Structural Productivity Levels in the Major Industrial Countries," *OECD Economic Studies* No. 41/2: 75–108.

Böheim, R. and Taylor, M. "Actual and Preferred Working Hours," *British Journal of Industrial Relations*, 42 (1): 149–166.

Bowles, S. and Park, Y. (2005) "Emulation, Inequality, and Work Hours: Was Thorstein Veblen Right?" *The Economic Journal* 115 (November): F397–F412.

Braverman, H. (1974) *Labor and Monopoly Capital: The Degradation of Work in the Twentieth Century*, New York: Monthly Review Press.

Bremner, R. (1956) *From the Depths*, New York: New York University Press.

Brundtland, G.H. (1987) *World Commission on Environment and Development, Our Common Future (The Brundtland Report)*, Oxford: Oxford University Press.

Brickman, P., Coates, D. and Janoff-Bulman, R. (1978) "Lottery Winners and Accident Victims: is Happiness Relative?" *Journal of Personality and Social Psychology*, No. 36: 917–27.

Brown, L. (1999) *State of the World: A Worldwatch Institute Report on Progress Toward a Sustainable Society*, New York: W.W. Norton and Company.

Buell, P. and Breslow, L. (1960) "Mortality from Coronary Heart Disease in California Men Who Work Long Hours," *Journal of Chronic Diseases*, 11: 615–626.

Bulard, M. (1999) "What Price the 35-hour Week?" *Le Monde Diplomatique* September. Online. Available http://mondediplo.com/1999/09/12hours (accessed 2 September 2008).

Burkett, P. (1998) "Insiders and Outsiders, Unemployment and Worktime: Rothschild's Analysis Extended," *Review of Radical Political Economics*, 30 (3): 64–113.

Burri, S., Opitz, H. and Veldman, A. (2003) "Work-Family Policies in Working Time Put into Practice: A Comparison of Dutch and German Case Law on Working Time Adjustment," *International Journal of Comparative Labour Law & Industrial Relations*, 19: 321–355.

Campbell, I. (2002) "Snatching at the Wind? Unpaid Overtime and Trade Unions in Australia," *International Journal of Employment Studies* 10 (2): 109–156.

Canterbery, R. (2002) "Theory of the Bondholding Class", *Journal of Economic Issues*, Vol. XXXVI (2): 365–372.

Carlyle, T. (1849) "The Nigger Question" reprinted in *Thomas Carlyle: Critical and Miscellaneous Essays* (1899), vol. 4, London: Chapman and Hall: 348–83.

Carnegie, A. (1933) *The Gospel of Wealth and Other Timely Essays*, Garden City, NY: Doubleday and Doran.

Cette, G., Dromel, N. and Méda, D. (2005) "Les déterminants du jugement des salariés sur la RTT," *Économie et Statistique* 119: 376–377.

Cette, G. and Gubian, A. (1998) "Les evaluations de effets sur l'emploi d'une reduction de la duree du travail: quelques remarques," *Travail and Emploi*, No. 74: 91–109.

Cette, G. and Taddei, D. (1994) *Temps du travail-modes d'emploi. Vers la semaine de quatre jours?* Paris: Librairie Générale Française.

Chandler, A. (1977) *The Visible Hand: The Managerial Revolution in American Business*, Cambridge, MA: Belknap Press.

Chapman, S.J. (1909) "Hours of Labour," *The Economic Journal*, 19 (75): 353–373.

Charlesworth, S. and Campbell, I. (2008) "Right to Request Regulation: Two New Australian Models," *Australian Journal of Labour Law*, 21: 116–136.

Churchill, W.S. (1908) *Liberalism and the Social Problem*, London: BiblioBazaar, LLC.

Clark, A.E. (2001) "What Really Matters in a Job? Hedonic Measurement Using Quit Data," *Labour Economics* 8: 223–242.

Clark, A.E., Frijters, P. and Shields, M.A. (2008) "Relative Income, Happiness and Utility: An Explanation of the Easterlin Paradox and Other Puzzles," *Journal of Economic Literature*, 46 (1): 95–144.

Clark, A.E. and Oswald, A.J. (1994) "Unhappiness and Unemployment," *Economic Journal*, 104: 648–659.

——(1996) "Satisfaction and Comparison Income," *Journal of Public Economics,* 61 (3): 359–381.

——2006 "Unhappiness and Unemployment Duration," *Applied Economics Quarterly*, 52 (4): 291–308.

Clark, A., Oswald, A. and Warr, P. (1996) "Is Job Satisfaction U-shaped in Age," *Journal of Occupational and Organizational Psychology*, 69: 57–81.

Clarkberg, M. and Moen, P. (2001) "Understanding the Time-Squeeze: Married Couples' Preferred and Actual Work-Hour Strategies," *American Behavioral Scientist*, 44: 1115–1136.

Cobb, C., Halstead, T. and Rowe, J. (1995) "If the GDP is Up Why is America Down?" *Atlantic Monthly*, 276 (4): 59–78.

Cohen, G.A. (1978) *Karl Marx's Theory of History: A Defence*, Princeton, NJ: Princeton University Press.

Committee on Recent Economic Changes (1929) *Recent Economic Changes in the United States*, New York: McGraw-Hill.

Commons, J. (1921) "Eight-hour Shifts by Federal Legislation," in J. Commons (ed.) *Trade Unionism and Labor Problems, Second Series*, Boston, MA: Athenaeum Press: 807–23.

——(1969) *Industrial Goodwill*, New York: Arno, 1969.

Compass (2006) "Direction for the Democratic Left", *A New Political Economy: Compass Program for Renewal*, London: Lawrence and Wishart Limited.

Cooke, M. (1920) "Letter to Sidney Hillman-April 15, 1920," *Morris Cooke Papers*, Box 9, Files 73-90. Franklin Delano Roosevelt Library, Hyde Park.

Copeland, M. (1931) "Economic Theory and the Natural Science Point of View," *American Economic Review* 21: 67–79.

Cordes, C. (2005) "Veblen's 'Instinct of Workmanship,' Its Cognitive Foundations, and Some Implications for Economic Theory," *Journal of Economic Issues*, XXXIX (1): 1–20.

Cowdrick, E. (1927) "The New Economic Gospel of Consumption," *Industrial Management*, LXXIV (4): 208–231.

Cowling, S., Mitchell, W. and Watts, M. (2003) *"The Right to Work versus the Right to Income,"* Working Paper No. 03–08 Centre of Full Employment and Equity: Newcastle, AU. Online. Available http://e1.newcastle.edu.au/coffee/ (accessed 14 July 2005).

Crépon, B., Leclair, M. and Roux, S. (2005) "RTT, productivité et employ: nouvelles estimations sur données d'entreprises," *Economie et Statistique* 376–377: 55–89.

Cross, G. (1993) *Time and Money: the Making of Consumer Culture*, London: Routledge.

Csikszentmihalyi, M. (1990) *Flow: The Psychology of Optimal Experience*, New York: Harper and Row.

Daly, H. (1996) "Sustainable Growth? No Thank You," in J. Mander and E. Goldsmith (eds) *The Case Against the Global Economy*, San Francisco: Sierra Club Books: 190–210.

Daly, H. and Cobb, J. (1994) *For the Common Good: Redirecting the Economy Toward Community, the Environment, and a Sustainable Future*, Boston, MA: Beacon Press.

Dankert, C., Mann, F. and Northrup, H. (1965) *Hours of Work*, New York: Harper & Row.

Dayan, J.L. (2002) *"35 heures, des ambitions aux réalités,"* Paris: La Découverte.

Deci, E.L. and Ryan, R.M. (1985) *Intrinsic Motivation and Self-Determination in Human Behavior*, New York: Plenum Press.

De Foucauld, J.B. (1988) *La fin du social-colbertisme*, Paris: P. Belfond.

DeGregori, T. (1973) "Prodigality or Parsimony: The False Dilemma in Economic Development Theory," *Journal of Economic Issues*, 7: 259–266.

Dembe, A.E., Erickson, J.B., Delbos, R.G. and Banks, S.M. (2005) "The Impact of Overtime and Long Hours on Occupational Injuries and Illnesses: New Evidence from the United States," *Occupational and Environmental Medicine* 62: 588–597.

Dement, W. and Vaughan, C. (1999) *The Promise of Sleep*, New York: Delacorte Press.

Denniss, R. (2003) "Annual Leave in Australia: An Analysis of Entitlements, Usage, and Preferences, Discussion Paper 56, *The Australian Institute*. Online. Available https://www.tai.org.au/?q = node/8&offset = 5 (accessed 15 December 2008).

De Regt, E. (1988) "Labor Demand and Standard Working Time in Dutch Manufacturing, 1945-82," in R. Hart (ed.) *Employment, Unemployment and Labour Utilization*, Boston, MA: Unwin Hyman.

DeVroey, M. (1998) "Accounting for Involuntary Unemployment in Neoclassical Theory: Some Lessons from Sixty Years of Uphill Struggle," in R. Backhouse, D. Hausman, U. Maki and A. Salanti (eds) *Economics and Methodology: Crossing Boundaries*, London: Macmillan.

Diener, E. and Biswas-Diener, R. (2001) "Making the Best of a Bad Situation: Satisfaction in the Slums of Calcutta," *Social Indicators Research*, 55: 329–352.

Diener, E. and Biswas-Diener, R. (2002) "Will Money Increase Subjective Well-being?" *Social Indicators Research* 57: 119–169.

Diener, E., Nickerson, C., Lucas, R.E. and Sandvick, E. (2002) "Dispositional Affect and Job Outcomes," *Social Indicators Research*, 59: 229–259.

Diener, E. and Oishi, S. (2000) "Money and Happiness: Income and Subjective Well-Being across Nations," in E. Diener and E.M. Suh (eds) *Subjective Well-Being across Cultures*, Cambridge, MA: MIT Press.

Diener, E., Sandvik, L. and Diener, M. (1993) "The Relationship between Income and Subjective Well-Being: Relative or Absolute?" *Social Indicators Research*, 28: 195–223.

Diener, E. and Seligman, M. (2004) "Beyond Money: Toward an Economy of Well-being," *Psychological Science in the Public Interest*, 5 (1): 1–31.

Duesenberry, J.S. (1949) *Income, Saving and the Theory of Consumer Behavior*. Harvard Economic Studies, Vol. LXXXVII. Cambridge, MA: Harvard University Press.

Dunn, R. (1984) "Servants and Slaves. The Recruitment and Employment of Labor," in J. Greene and J.R. Pole (eds) *Colonial British America. Essays in the New History of the Early Modern Era*, Baltimore, MD: John Hopkins University Press: 157–194.

Easterbrook, G. (2004) *The Progress Paradox*, New York: Random House.

Easterlin, R. (1974) "Does Economic Growth Improve the Human Lot? Some Empirical Evidence," in P. David and M. Reder (eds) *Nations and Households in Economic Growth: Essays in Honor of Moses Abramowitz*, New York: Academic Press: 89–125.

——(1995) "Will Rising the Income of All Increase the Happiness of All?" *Journal of Economic Behavior and Organization*, 27 (1): 35–48.

Easterlin, R.A. (2001) "Income and Happiness: Towards a Unified Theory," *Economic Journal*, 111 (473): 465–484.

Eastman, W. (1998) "Working for Position: Women, Men and Managerial Work Hours," *Industrial Relations*, 37 (1): 51–66.

Eckersley, R. (2004) *Well & Good: How We Feel & Why it Matters*, Melbourne, AU: Text Publishing.

—(2007) "The Politics of Happiness," *Living Now*, March (93): 6–7.

Economist (1999) "The Perils of Pork and Gravy: A Backlash Builds against Japan's Big Public Spending Plans," June 12: 38.

—— (2001) "Its Perky for Now," January 4.

Egeland, J. and Hostetter, A. (1983) "Amish Study: I. Affective Disorders among the Amish," *American Journal of Psychiatry*, 140: 56–61.

Eichner, A. (1985) *Toward a New Economics: Essays in Post-Keynesian and Institutionalist Theory*, Armonk, NY: ME Sharpe.

EIROnline (1999) "Unions Demand Creation of New Jobs through Reduction of Overtime," *European Industrial Relations Observatory On-line*. Available www.eiro.eurofound.ie/servlet/ptconvert?de9901289n (accessed 5 February 2006).

—— (2001) "Involuntary Part-Time Work Declines," *European Industrial Relations Observatory On-line.* November. Online. Available www.eiro.eurofound.eu.int (accessed 25 January 2007).

Ekins, P. (1993) "Making Development Sustainable," in W. Sachs (ed.) *Global Ecology: A New Arena of Political Conflict,* London: Zed Books: 90–113.

Estrade, M., Méda, D. and Orain, R. (2001) "Les effets de la réduction du temps de travail sur les modes de vie: qu'en pensent les salariés un an aprés?" ['The Effects of Working Time on Lifestyles: Employees Speak, One Year On'] *Premières informations et premières synthèses,* MES-DARES: No. 21.1.

Evans, A. (1975) *Hours of Work in Industrialised Countries,* Geneva: International Labour Office.

Fagan, C. (2004). In J.C. Messenger (ed.) *Working Time and Workers' Preferences in Industrialized Countries: Finding the Balance, Routledge Studies in Modern World Economy,* New York: Routledge.

Fagnani, J. (2004) "The 35-Hour Laws and the Work and Family Life Balance in France," *Working Time for Working Families: Europe and the United States,* WorkLife Law Program, American University Washington College of Law.

Fanfani, A. (1934) *Capitalism, Protestantism, and Catholicism,* Norfolk, VA: HIS Press (2003 Reprint).

Feagin, J. (1975) *Subordinating the Poor: Welfare and American Beliefs,* Englewood Cliffs, NJ: Prentice-Hall.

Feis, H. (1924) "The Attempt to Establish the Eight-Hour Day by International Action," *Political Science Quarterly,* 39 (4): 624–649.

Fenwick, R., and Tausig, M. (2001) "Scheduling Stress: Family and Health Outcomes of Shift Work and Schedule Control," *American Behavioral Scientist,* 44 (7): 1179–1198.

Fetscher, I. (1971) *Marx and Marxism,* New York: Herder and Herder.

Ford, H. (1926) "The 5-Day Week in the Ford Plants," *Monthly Labor Review,* December: 10–14.

Foster, J.F. (1981) "The Reality of the Present and the Challenge of the Future," *Journal of Economic Issues,* XV (4): 963–968.

Fox, D. (1967) *The Discovery of Abundance: Simon N. Patten and the Transformation of Social Theory,* Ithaca, NY: Cornell University Press.

Francois-Poncet, A. (1922) *La France et les huit heures,* Paris: Librairie Marcel Riviere.

Frank, R. (1999) *Luxury Fever: Money and Happiness in an Era of Excess,* Princeton, NJ: Princeton University Press.

Franklin, B. (1932) *Autobiography,* New York: Library of America (2005 Reprint).

Frey, B.S. and Oberholzer-Gee, F. (1997) "The Cost of Price Incentives: An Empirical Analysis of Motivation Crowding-Out," *American Economic Review,* 87: 746–755.

Frey, B.S. and Stutzer, A. (2002) *Happiness and Economics: How the Economy and Institutions Affect Human Well-Being,* Princeton, NJ: Princeton University Press.

Frey, W. (1994) "The New White Flight," *American Demographics,* 16 (4): 40–48.

Friedman, M. (1962) *Capitalism and Freedom,* Chicago: University of Chicago Press.

Friedman, W. and Casner-Lotto, J. (2003) *Time is of the Essence: New Scheduling Options for Unionized Employees,* New York: Work in America Institute.

Frijters, P., Haisken-DeNew, J.P. and Shields, M.A. (2004) "Money Does it Matter! Evidence from Increasing Real Income and Life Satisfaction in East Germany Following Unification," *American Economic Review,* 94: 730–740.

Galbraith, J.K. (1952) *American Capitalism*, Boston, MA: Houghton Mifflin Company.
——(1958) *The Affluent Society*, Boston, MA: Houghton Mifflin (4th Edition 1984).
——(1973) *Economics and the Public Purpose*, New York: New American Library.
Galbraith, James K., Conceição, P. and Ferreira, P. (1999) "Inequality and Unemployment in Europe: The American Cure," UTIP Working Paper No. 11. Online. Available http://ssrn.com/abstract = 228689 (accessed 8 September 2008).
Gallup Poll Monthly (1991) September.
Gardner, J. and Oswald, A.J. (2001) "Does Money Buy Happiness? A Longitudinal Study Using Data on Windfalls," *mimeo*, Warwick University.
—— (2007) "Money and Mental Wellbeing: A Longitudinal Study of Medium-Sized Lottery Wins," *Journal of Health Economics*, 26: 49–60.
Garraty, J. (1978) *Unemployment in History. Economic Thought and Public Policy*, New York: Harper and Row.
George, C. and George, K. (1961) "Protestantism and Capitalism in Pre-Revolutionary England," in S.N. Eisenstadt (ed.) *The Protestant Ethic and Modernization*, New York: Basic Books: 156–176.
Gibson, T. (1990) "Who Will do the Dirty Work?" in V. Richards (ed.) *Why Work? Arguments for the Leisure Society*, London: Freedom Press: 108–14.
Gillman, J. (1965) *Prosperity in Crisis*, New York: Marzani & Munsell.
Gini, A. and Sullivan, T. (1989) "A Critical Overview," in A. Gini and T. Sullivan (eds) *It Comes with the Territory: an Inquiry Concerning Work and the Person*, New York: Random House.
Gneezy, U. and Rustichini, A. (2000) "A Fine is a Price," *Journal of Legal Studies*, 29: 1–18.
Golden, L. and Altman, M. (2008) "Why to People Overwork? Over-Supply of Hours of Labor, Labor Market Forces and Adaptive Preferences," in R. Burke and G. Cooper (eds) *Effects of Work Hours and Work Addiction: Strategies for Dealing with Them*, Amsterdam: Elsevier.
Golden, L. and Gebreselassie, T. (2007). "Overemployment Mismatches: the Preference for Fewer Work Hours," *Monthly Labor Review* April: 18–37.
Golden, L. and Wiens-Tuers, B. (2006) "To Your Happiness? Extra Hours of Labor Supply and Worker Well-Being," *Journal of Socio-Economics*, 35 (2): 382–397.
Goldthorpe, J.H. (1978) "The Current Inflation: Towards a Sociological Account," in F. Hirsch and J.H. Goldthorpe (eds) *The Political Economy of Inflation*, London: Martin Roberson.
Gorres, P.A. (1984) Die Umverteilung der Arbeit, Beschaftigungs-, Wachstums-und Wohlfahrtseffekte einer Arbeitzeitverkurzang, Frankfurt/New York: Campus.
Gorz, A. (1980) *Ecology as Politics*, Boston, MA: South End Press.
—— (1983) *Farewell to the Working Class: An Essay on Post-Industrial Socialism*, Boston, MA: South End Press.
—— (1989) *Critique of Economic Reason*, London: Verso.
——(1992) "On the Difference between Society and Community and Why Basic Income Cannot by Itself Confer Full Membership," in P. Van Parijs (ed.) *Arguing for Basic Income*, London: Verso.
——(1994) *Capitalism, Socialism, Ecology*, London: Verso.
——(1999) *Reclaiming Work*, Malden, MA: Polity Press in association with Blackwell Publishers Ltd.
Gottschalk, S. (1973) "The Community-Based Welfare System: An Alternative to Public Welfare," *The Journal of Applied Behavioral Science*, 9: 230–255.

Greider, W. (1987) *Secrets of the Temple: How the Federal Reserve Runs the Country*, New York: Simon and Schuster.

——(2003) *The Soul of Capitalism: Opening Paths to a Moral Economy*, New York: Simon and Schuster.

Gross, B. (1971) "Planning in an Era of Social Revolution," *Public Administration Review*, 31 (3), Special Symposium Issue: Changing Styles of Planning in Post-Industrial America, May/June: 259–297.

Gubian, A. (2000) "La réduction du temps de travail á mi-parcours: premier bilan des effets sur l'emploi," *Travail et Emploi*, 83: 9–25.

Gubian, A., Jugnot, S., Lerais, F. and Passeron, V. (2005) "Les effets de la RTT sur l'emploi: des simulations ex ante au evaluations ex post," *Economie et Statistique* 376–77: 47–49.

Hagerty, M.R. (2000) "Social comparisons of income in one's community: Evidence from nation surveys of income and happiness," *Journal of Personality and Social Psychology*, 78: 746–771.

Hahnel, J. (1998) "Is Time Really Money?" *Dollars and Sense*, Economic Affairs Bureau (January/February), 43.

Hamermesh, D.S. and Slemrod, J.B. (2008) "The Economics of Workaholism: We Should Not Have Worked on This Paper," *The B.E. Journal of Economic Analysis & Policy*, 8 (1) (Contributions), Article 3. Online. Available http://www.bepress.com/bejeap/vol8/iss1/art3 (accessed 3 December 2008).

Hamilton, C. and Denniss, R. (2000) "Tracking Well-being in Australia. The Genuine Progress Indicator 2000," *The Australia Institute,* Discussion Paper Number 35. Online. Available https://www.tai.org.au/index.php?q = node/16&offset = 2 (accessed 12 December 2008).

Hamilton, D. (1970) *Evolutionary Economics: A Study of Change in Economic Thought*, Albuquerque: University of New Mexico Press.

Harpers Index (1998) *Harper's Magazine*, May: 15.

Hart, Peter and Associates. (2003) *Imagining the Future of Work*, New York: Alfred Sloan Foundation.

Hart, R.A. and Sharot, T. (1978) "The Short-Run Demand for Worker and Hours: a Recursive Model," *Review of Economic Studies*, 45: 299–309.

Haugh, H. and Kitson, M. (2007) "The Third Way and the Third Sector: New Labour's Economic Policy and the Social Economy," *Cambridge Journal of Economics*, 31 (6): 973–994.

Hayden, A. (1999) *Sharing the Work, Sparing the Planet*, Toronto: Between the Lines.

——(2006) "France's 35-Hour Week: Attack on Business? Win-Win Reform? Or Betrayal of Disadvantaged Workers?" *Politics and Society*, 34 (4): 503–542.

Heath, J. and Kiker, B. (1992) "Determinants of Spells of Poverty Following Divorce," *Review of Social Economy*, 50 (3): 305–316.

Hecker, D. (1998) "How Hours of Work Affect Occupational Earnings," *Monthly Labor Review*, October: 8–10.

Heilbroner, R. (1980) *Marxism: For and Against*, New York: WW Norton.

—— (1993) *Twenty-First Century Capitalism*, St. Leonards, Australia: Allen & Unwin Pty Ltd.

Heilbroner, R. and Singer, A. (1998) *The Economic Transformation of America: 1600 to Present*, New York: Harcourt Brace College Publishers.

Helliwell, J.F. (2003) "How's Life? Combining Individual and National Variables to Explain Subjective Well-Being," *Economic Modeling*, 20: 331–360.

Heyer, E. (2005) "L'assouplissement des 35 heures devrait rester marginal," (Interview in) *Le Journal du Management*, March 30.

Hill, C. (1991) *Society and Puritanism in Pre-Revolutionary England*, London: Penguin Books.

Hochschild, A. (1997) *The Time Bind: When Work Becomes Home and Home Becomes Work*, New York: Metropolitan.

Hofstadter, R. (1955) *The Age of Reform*, New York: Vintage Books.

Holm, P. and Kiander, J. (1993) "The Effects of Work-Sharing on Employment and Overtime in Finnish Manufacturing 1960-1987," *Applied Economics*, 25: 801–810.

Holst, E. and Schupp, J. (2002) "Arbeitszeitwünsche schwanken mit der onjunktur," *Wochenbericht* 69: 370–373.

Holt, R. and Pressman, S. (2001) "What is Post Keynesian Economics," in R. Holt and S. Pressman (eds) *A New Guide to Post Keynesian Economics*, New York: Routledge: 1–11.

Home Office (2004) *Home Office Citizenship Survey*, London: Home Office.

Houpis, G. (1993) *The Effect of Lower Hours of Work on Wages and Employment*, Center for Economic Performance, Discussion Paper no. 131, London School of Economics and Political Science.

Hume, D. (1978) *Treatise on Human Nature*, Oxford: Oxford University Press.

Hunnicutt, B. (1988) *Work Without End: Abandoning Shorter Hours for the Right to Work*, Philadelphia, PA: Temple University Press.

Hunt, J. (1999) "Has Work-Sharing Worked in Germany?" *Quarterly Journal of Economics*, 114 (1): 117–148.

Husson, M. (2002) "Réduction du temps de travail et employ: une nouvelle évaluation," *Revue de l'IRES* 38 (1): 4.

Ilmakunnas, P. (1995) "Working Time and Labour Demand in Finnish Manufacturing: Short-Run and Long-Run Effects," *Applied Economics*, 27: 995–1002.

Inglehart, R. (1990) *Culture Shift in Advanced Industrial Society*, Princeton, NJ: Princeton University Press.

Inglehart, R., Foa, R., Peterson, C. and Welzel, C. (2008) "Development, Freedom, and Rising Happiness: A Global Perspective (1981–2007), *Perspectives on Psychological Science*, 3 (4): 264–285.

Innes, S. (1988) *Work and Labor in Early America*, Chapel Hill, NC: University of North Carolina Press.

IPCC (2007) *Climate Change 2007: Synthesis Report*. Intergovernmental Panel on Climate Change. IPCC Plenary XXVII (Valencia, Spain, 12–17 November 2007). Online. Available http://www.ipcc.ch/ipccreports/ar4-syr.htm (accessed 14 December 2008).

Iturriza, A., Bedi, A. and Sparrow, R. (2008) "Unemployment Assistance and Transition to Employment in Argentina." Online. Available http://ssrn.com/abstract = 1152267 (accessed 10 July 2008).

Jacobs, J. and Gerson, K. (1998) "Who are the Overworked Americans?" *Review of Social Economy*, 56 (4): 442–459.

——(2000) "Do Americans Feel Overworked? Comparing Ideal and Actual Working Time," in T.L. Parcel and D.B. Cornfield (eds) *Work and Family: Research Informing Policy*, Thousand Oaks, CA: Sage: 71–95.

Jackson, T. "Chasing Progress: Beyond Measuring Economic Growth," *New Economics Foundation*. Online. Available http://portal.surrey.ac.uk/pls/portal/docs/PAGE/ENG/STAFF/STAFFAC/JACKSONT/PUBLICATIONS/MDP.PDF (accessed 12 December 2008).

Jacobson, T. and Ohlsson, H. (2000) "Working Time, Employment, and Work Sharing: Evidence from Sweden," *Empirical Economics*, 25: 169–187.

Jefferson, T. (1743–1826) *Notes on the State of Virginia, Query 19*, Electronic Text Center, University of Virginia Library. Online. Available http://etext.virginia.edu/toc/modeng/public/JefVirg.html (accessed 10 December 2008).

Jenkins, C. and Sherman, B. (1979) *The Collapse of Work*, London: Eyre Methuen.

Jones, B. (1995) *Sleepers Awake: Technology and the Future of Work*, Melbourne: Oxford University Press.

Kalecki, M. (1943) "Political Aspects of Full Employment," in J. Osiatyinski J (ed.) *Collected Works of Michael Kalecki*, Oxford: Oxford University Press: 347–356 (Reprinted in 1990).

Kahn, S. and Lang, K. (1987) "Constraints on the Choice of Work Hours: Agency vs. Specific-Capital," *NBER* Working Paper No. 2356.

Kahneman, D. (1999) "Objective Happiness," in D. Kahneman, E. Diener and N. Schwarz. (eds) *Well-Being: The Foundations of Hedonic Psychology*, New York: Russell Sage Foundation: 3–25.

Kapteyn, A., Kalwij, A. and Zaidi, A. (2004) "The Myth of Worksharing," *Labour Economics*, 11: 293–313.

Kapteyn, A. Praag, B.M. and van Herwaarden, F.G. (1976) "Individual Welfare Functions and Social Reference Spaces," *Economic Letters* 1: 173–178.

Kasser, T. and Ryan, R.M. (1993) "A Dark Side of the American Dream: Correlates of Financial Success as a Central Life Aspiration," *Journal of Personality and Social Psychology*, 65: 410–422.

—— (2001) "Be Careful What You Wish for: Optimal Functioning and the Relative Attainment of Intrinsic and Extrinsic Goals," in P. Schmuck and K.M. Sheldon (eds), *Life Goals and Well-Being: Towards a Positive Psychology of Human Striving*, Gottingen: Hogrefe & Huber Publishers: 116–131.

Kasser, T., Ryan, R.M., Couchman, C.E. and Sheldon, K.M. (2004) "Materialistic Values; Their Causes and Consequences," in T. Kasser and A.D. Kanner (eds) *Psychology and Consumer Culture: The Struggle for a Good Life in a Materialistic World*, Washington DC: American Psychological Association: 11–28.

Kattenbach, R. (2007) "The Right to Part-Time: Practical Implications from the Managerial Point of View," *Management Revue*, 18 (3): 350–366.

Katz, L. (1998) "Wage Subsidies for the Disadvantaged," in R. Freeman and P. Gottschalk (eds) *Generating Jobs: How to Increase Demand for Less-Skilled Workers*, Russell Sage: 21–53.

Kelso, L. and Hetter, P. (1968) "Equality of Economic Opportunity through Capital Ownership," in R. Theobald (ed.) *Social Policies for America in the Seventies: Nine Divergent Views*, Garden City, NY: Doubleday.

Kennedy, R. (1968) Address to the University of Kansas. March 18, Online. Available http://www.jfklibrary.org/Historical+Resources/Archives/Reference+Desk/Speeches/RFK/RFKSpeech68Mar18UKansas.htm (accessed 14 September 2008).

Keown, L.A. (2007) "Time Escapes Me: Workaholics and Time Perception," *Canadian Social Trends* (Summer). Statistics Canada, Catalogue No. 11–008: 28–32.

Keynes, J.M. (1923) *A Tract on Monetary Reform*, London: Macmillan.

—— (1932) "The World's Economic Outlook," *Atlantic Monthly*, 149: 521–526.

——(1936) *The General Theory of Employment, Interest and Money*, London: Macmillan (2007 Reprint).

——(1972) *The Collected Writings of John Maynard Keynes: Essays in Persuasion*, in D. Moggridge (ed.), London: MacMillan.

——(1980) *The Collected Writings of John Maynard Keynes*, in D. Moggridge (ed.), London: MacMillan.

King, J. (2001a) "Labor and Unemployment," in R. Holt and S. Pressman (eds) *A New Guide to Post Keynesian Economics*, New York: Routledge.

——(2001b) "The Last Resort? Some Critical Reflections on ELR," *Working Paper* LaTrobe University, February.

Klerman, G.L., Lavori, P.W., Rice, J., Reich, T., Endicott, J., Andreason, N.C., Kellor, M.B. and Hirschfield, R. (1985) "Birth Cohort Trends in Rates of Major Depressive Disorder among Relatives with Affective Disorder," *Archives of General Psychiatry*, 42: 689–693.

Kohler, H. and Spitznagel, E. (1996) *Überstunden in Deutschland*, Werkstattbericht, 4, IAB, NÜrnberg.

Kriesler, P. and Halevi, J. (2001) "Political Aspects of 'Buffer Stock' Employment" in E. Carlson and W.F. Mitchell (eds), *Achieving Full Employment, The Economic and Labour Relations Review*, Vol. 12 (supplement): 72–82.

Kuznets, S. (1934) *National Income, 1929-1932. Senate document no. 124*, Washington, DC: 73rd United States Congress, 2nd session.

Labaree, B. (1979) *Colonial Massachusetts. A History*, Millwood, NY: KTO Press.

Lafargue, P. (1883) *The Right to be Lazy*, Chicago, IL: Charles Kerr (Reprint 1989).

LaJeunesse, R. (1998) "Toward an Efficiency Week," Challenge January/February: 92–109.

Lane, R.E. (2000) *The Loss of Happiness in Market Democracies*, New Haven, CT: Yale University Press.

Larrouturou, P. and Rocard, M. (1998) "Un nouvel enthousiasme," *Le Monde*, May, 21.

Layard, R. (1996) "Subsiding Employment Rather than Unemployment," in M. Baldassarri, L. Pagenetto and E.S. Phelps (eds) *Equity, Efficiency, and Growth: the future of the Welfare State*, New York: St. Martin's Press.

—— (2005) *Happiness: Lessons from a New Science*, New York: The Penguin Press.

Layard, R., Nickell, S. and Jackman, R. (1991) *Unemployment: Macroeconomics Performance and the Labour Market*, Oxford: Oxford University Press.

Lebaube, A. (1991) "Taylor n'est pas mort" *Le Monde initiatives*, December 4.

Lee, S. (2004) "Working-hour Gaps: Trends and Issues," in J.C. Messenger (ed.) *Working Time and Workers' Preferences in Industrialized Countries: Finding the Balance, Routledge Studies in Modern World Economy*, New York: Routledge.

Lee, S., McCann, D. and Messenger, J.C. (2007) *Working Time Around the World: Trends in Working Hours, Laws and Policies in a Global Comparative Perspective*, London and Geneva: Routledge.

Lehndorff, S. (1995a) "Working Time and Operating Time in the European Car Industry, in D. Anxo, G. Bosch, D. Bosworth, G. Cette, T. Sterner and D. Taddei (eds) *Work Patterns and Capital Utilisation: an International Comparative Study*, Dordrecht: Kluwer: 311–337.

—— (1995b) "La rédistribution de l'emploi en Allemagne," *Futuribles* 195: 5–20.

——(2000) "Working Time Reduction in the European Union: a Diversity of Trends and Approaches," in L. Golden and D. Figart (eds), *Working Time: International Trends, Theory and Policy Perspectives*, London: Routledge: 38–56.

Leibenstein, H. (1980) *Inflation, Income Distribution and X-Efficiency Theory*, London: Croom Helm.

Leiss, W. (1976) *The Limits to Satisfaction*, Toronto, Ontario: University of Toronto.

Lerner, A. (1943) "Functional Finance and Federal Debt," *Social Research*, February: 38–51.

Leverhulme, W. (1919) *The Six-hour Day & Other Industrial Questions*, New York: Holt and Company.

Levine, R. and Renelt, D. (1992) "A Sensitivity Analysis of Cross Country Growth Regressions," *American Economic Review*, 82 (4): 942–963.

Levitan, S. (1964) *Reducing Work Time as a Means to Combat Unemployment*, Kalamazoo: UpJohn Institute.

Levitan, S.A. and Belous, R. (1977) *Shorter Hours, Shorter Weeks: Spreading the Work to Reduce Unemployment*, Baltimore, MD: Johns Hopkins University Press.

Lewis, T., Fari, A. and Lannon, R. (2000) *A General Theory of Love*, New York: Random House.

Linder, S. (1970) *The Harried Leisure Class*, New York: Columbia University Press.

Lipietz, A. (1995) *Green Hopes*, Cambridge: Polity Press.

Lipsey, R. and Steiner, P. (1972) *Economics*, New York: Harper &Row.

Logeay, C. and Schreiber, S. (2006) "Testing the Effectiveness of the French Work-Sharing Refrom; A Forecasting Approach," *Applied Economics*, 38: 2053–2068.

Lyubomirsky, S., King, L. and Diener, E. (2003) "Happiness as a Strength: A Theory of the Benefits of Positive Affect," *Mimeo*. University of California, Riverside.

Mander, J. (1991) *In the Absence of the Sacred: The Failure of Technology and the Survival of the Indian Nations*, San Francisco: Sierra Club Books.

Marcuse, H. (1979) *Eros and Civilization*, Frankfurt, Germany: Suhrkamp.

Marshall, A. (1890) *Principles of Economics*, London: Macmillan and Co., Ltd. (8th edition reprint 1920).

Marshall, G. (1982) *In Search of the Spirit of Capitalism: An Essay on Max Weber's Protestant Ethic*, New York: Columbia University Press.

Maruyama, S. and Morimoto, K. (1996) "Effects of Long Work Hours on Life-Style, Stress and Quality of Life among Intermediate Japanese Managers, *Scandinavian Journal of Work, Environment and Health*, 22: 353–359.

Marx, K. (1968) *Theories of Surplus Value, 3 volumes*, London: Lawrence and Wishart.

——(1970) *Wages, Price, and Profit*, Peking: Foreign Languages Press.

—— (1973) *Grundrisse*, Harmondsworth: Penguin.

——(1975) *Early Writings*, Harmondsworth: Penguin. (Translation by Rodney Livingstone and Gregor Bento.)

——(1977) *Capital* in *Karl Marx: Selected Writings*. In D. McLellan (ed.) Oxford: Oxford University Press.

—— (1991) *Capital, Vol. 3*, Harmondsworth: Penguin.

Maume, J.D. and Bellas M.L. (2001) "The Overworked American or the Time Bind? Assessing Competing Explanations for Time Spend in Paid Employment," *American Behavioral Scientist*, 44 (7): 1137–1156.

McCann, D. (1995) "Apology of the Hireling: a Work Ethic of the Global Marketplace," *The Christian Century*, 112 (17): 542–546.

McCarthy, M.E., Rosenberg, G.S and Lefkowitz, G. (1981) *Work Sharing Case Studies*, Kalamazoo, MI: W.E. Upjohn Institute for Employment Research.

McInnes, J. (2005) "Work-Life Balance and the Demand for Reduction in Working Hours: Evidence from the British Social Attitudes Survey 2002," *British Journal of Industrial Relations*. 43 (2): 273–295.

McNamara, C. (2004) "Workaholism." Online. Available http://www.manage-menthelp.org/prsn_wll/wrkholic.htm. (accessed 2 March 2008).

Meadows, D.H. (1997) "Places to Intervene in a System (in Increasing Order of Effectiveness)," *Whole Earth* 91: 78–84.

Meadows, D.H., Meadows, D.L., Randers, J. and Behrens, W. (1972) *Limits to Growth*, New York: Universe Books Publication.

Méda, D. and Renaud O. (2003) "Peu de modifications dans le partage de tàches au sein des couples," in C. Bloch-London and J. Pélisse (eds) *La reduction du temps de travail: Des politiques aux pratiques*, Paris: La Documentation Française: 30–32.

Mill, J.S. (1832) *The Collected Works of John Stuart Mill, Volume XII – The Earlier Letters of John Stuart Mill 1812–1848 Part I*, in F. Mineka (ed.) Toronto: University of Toronto Press (Reprint 1963).

——(1873) *Autobiography*, London: Penguin Books Ltd (Reprint 1989).

——(1929) *Principles of Political Economy with Some of Their Applications to Social Philosophy*, London: Longmans.

Minarik, J. (1980) *The Size Distribution of Income During Inflation*, Washington, DC: The Brookings Institution.

Minsky, H. (1986) *Stabilizing an Unstable Economy*, New Haven, CT: Yale University Press.

Mitchell, Wesley C. (1937) *The Backward Art of Spending Money: and Other Essays*, New York: McGraw-Hill.

Mitchell, W.F. (1998) "The Buffer Stock Employment Model and the NAIRU: The Path to Full Employment," *Journal of Economic Issues*, 32 (2): 547–555.

Mitchell, W.F. and Watts, M. (2004) "A Comparison of the Macroeconomic Consequences of Basic Income and Job Guarantee Schemes," Working Paper No. 04–05. *Centre of Full Employment and Equity*. Newcastle, AU. (July).

Mitchell, W.F. and Wray, L.R. (2004) "Full Employment through a Job Guarantee: a Response to Critics," Working Paper No. 04-13. Centre of Full Employment and Equity, University of Newcastle. Online. Available http://e1.newcastle.edu.au/coffee/templates/wp2.cfm?id = 74 (accessed 14 December 2008).

—— (2005) "In Defense of Employer of Last Resort: a Response to Malcolm Sawyer," *Journal of Economic Issues*, 39 (1): 235–245.

Morgenstern, H., Kelsh, M., Kraus, J. and Margolis, W. (1991) "A Cross-sectional Study of Hand/Wrist Symptoms in Female Grocery Checkers," *American Journal of Industrial Medicine*, 20: 209–218.

Moore, B. (1978) "Monetary Factors," in A.S. Eichner (ed.) *A Guide to Post Keynesian Economics*, Armonk, NY: M.E. Sharpe: 120–138.

Morris, R. (1946) *Government and Labor in Early America*, New York: Columbia University Press.

Muchmore, L.R. (1970) "A Note on Thomas Mun's 'England's Treasure by Foreign Trade'," *Economic History Review*, 23 (3): 498–503.

MuConsult (2003) *Onderzoek ten behoeve van evaluatie Waa en Woa. Eindrapport*. Amersfoort: MuConsult. Online. Available http://docs.szw.nl/pdf/129/2004/129_2004_3_5271.pdf (accessed 3 March 2008).

Mumford, L. (1934) *Technics and Civilization*, New York: Harcourt, Brace and World.

Myers, D. (1992) *The Pursuit of Happiness: Who is Happy- and Why*, New York: William Morrow and Company, Inc.

National Commission on Technology, Automation and Economic Progress, Technology and the American Economy (1966) Washington, DC: US Government Printing Office.

Negt, O. (1989) *Die Herausforderung der Gewerkschaften*, Frankfurt-am-Main and New York: Campus Verlag.

Nemirow, M. (1984) "Work-Sharing Approaches: Past and Present," *Monthly Labor Review*, September: 34–39.

Nickell, S. and van Ours, J. (2000) "Why has Unemployment in the Netherlands and the United Kingdom Fallen so Much?" *Canadian Public Policy*, XXVI (Supplement 1): S201–S220.

Nickerson, C., Schwarz, N., Diener, E. and Kahneman, D. (2003) "Zeroing in on the Dark Side of the American Dream: A Closer Look at the Negative Consequences of the Goal for Financial Success," *Psychological Science*, 14: 531–536.

Noon, M. and Blyton, P. (1997) *The Realities of Work*, Basingstoke: Macmillan Business.

Nyland, C. (1989) *Reduced Worktime and the Management of Production*, Cambridge: Cambridge University Press.

Oberholzer, E. Jr. (1959) "The Church in New England Society," in J. Smith (ed.) *Seventeenth-Century America. Essays in Colonial History*, Chapel Hill, NC: University of North Carolina Press: 143–165.

OECD (1998). *Employment Outlook*: June, Paris: Organization for Economic Cooperation and Development.

—— (2003) *OECE Economic Surveys, France 2002-2003*, Paris: Organization for Economic Cooperation and Development.

—— (2005) *Economic Outlook*, No. 78, Paris: Organization for Economic Cooperation and Development, Statistical Annex, table 43.

—— (2007) *OECD in Figures 2007*, Paris: Organization for Economic Cooperation and Development. Online. Available www.oecd.org/infigures

Oliveira A. and Ulrich V. (2002) "L'incidence des 35 heures sur le temps partiel," *Premières Synthèses*, no. 07.1, MES-Dares.

Orr, D. and Frank, E. (2003) "Focus on the Fed: The Bond Market versus the Rest of Us," in J. Miller and A. Offner (eds) *Real World Macro*, 17th edition. Cambridge, MA: Economic Affairs Bureau.

Oswald, A.J. (1997) "Happiness and Economic Performance," *Economic Journal*, 107: 1815–1831.

——(2006) "The Hippies Were Right All Along About Happiness," *Financial Times*, January 18: 28.

Ott, J. (2005) "Level and Inequality of Happiness in Nations: Does Greater Happiness of a Greater Number Imply Greater Inequality in Happiness," *Journal of Happiness Studies* 6: 397–420.

Ovaska, T. and Takashima, R. (2006) "Economic Policy and the Level of Self-Perceived Well-Being: An International Comparison," *Journal of Socio-Economics*, 35: 308–325.

Owen, J.D. (1989) *Reduced Working Hours-Cure for Unemployment or Economic Burden?* Baltimore, MD: The Johns Hopkins University Press.

Palley, T. (2001) "Government as Employer of Last Resort: Can it Work?" *Industrial Relations Research Association*, 53rd Annual Proceedings: 269–274.

Parsons, K.H. (1985) "John R. Commons: His Relevance to Contemporary Economics," *Journal of Economic Issues*, XIX (3): 755–778.

Pascarella, P. (1984) *The New Achievers: Creating a Modern Work Ethic*, New York: The Free Press.

Patten, S. (1885) *The Premises of Political Economy*, Philadelphia, PA.

——(1892) "The Importance of Economic Psychology to Teachers" *Sixty-Third Annual Meeting of the American Institute of Instruction*, Boston: 20–21.

——(1895) "Economics in Elementary Schools" *Annals*, V: 478–489.

——(1911) "An Economic Measure of School Efficiency" *Educational Review*, May: 467–477.

——(1924) *Essays in Economic Theory*, New York: A. Knopf.

Peach, J. (1987) "Distribution and Economic Progress," *Journal of Economic Issues*, XXI (4): 1495–1521.

Pettijohn, T.F. II and T.F. Pettijohn (1996) "Perceived Happiness of College Students Measured by Maslow's Hierarchy of Needs," *Psychology Reports*, 79: 759–762.

Pew (2007) "Fewer Mothers Prefer Full-time Work: From 1997 to 2007," *Pew Research Center: A Social & Demographic Trends Report*, July 12.

Pham, H. (2002) "Les mondalités de passage á 35 heures en 2000," *Premiéres informations et premiéres synthéses* 6 (3): 7–8.

Phelps, E.S. (1996) "On the damaging side effects of the welfare system: how, why and what to do?" in M. Baldassarri, L. Pagenetto and E.S. Phelps (eds), *Equity, Efficiency, and Growth: the Future of the Welfare State*, New York: St. Martin's Press.

——(1997) *Rewarding Work*, Cambridge, MA: Harvard University Press.

Philipps, L. (2008) "Silent Partners: The Role of Unpaid Market Labor in Families," *Feminist Economics*, 14 (2): 37–57.

Philp, B. (2001) "Marxism, Neoclassicism and the Length of the Working Day," *Review of Political Economy*, 13 (1): 27–39.

Philp, B., Slater, G. and Harvie, D. (2005) "Preferences, Power, and the Determination of Working Hours," *Journal of Economic Issues*, XXXIX (1): 75–89.

Polanyi, K. (1944) *The Great Transformation*, Boston: Beacon Press (1994 Reprint).

——(1971) "The Economy as Instituted Process," in K. Polanyi, C.M. Arensberg and H. Pearson (eds) *Trade and Market in the Early Empires*, Chicago, IL: Gateway Edition.

—— (1977) *The Livelihood of Man*, New York: Academic Press.

Pollin, R. (1998) "The 'Reserve Army of Labor' and the 'Natural Rate of Unemployment': Can Marx, Kalecki, Friedman, and Wall Street All Be Wrong?" *Review of Radical Political Economics*, 30 (3): 1–13.

Prasch, R. (2002) "What is Wrong with Wage Subsides?" *Journal of Economic Issues*, XXXVI (2): 357–364.

——(2004) "How is labor distinct from Broccoli?" in D. Champlin and J. Knoedler (eds) *The Institutionalist Tradition in Labor Economics*, Armonk, NY: M.E. Sharpe: 146–158.

Princen, T. (2005) *The Logic of Sufficiency*, Cambridge, MA: MIT Press.

Probert, B. (1995) "The Overworked and the Out-of-Work: Redistributing Paid Work, Unpaid Work and Free Time," in J. Inglis (ed.) *The Future of Work*, Darlinghurst, AU: Australian Council of Social Service Inc.

Proctor, S.P., White, R.F., Robins, T.G., Echiverria, D., and Rocskay, A.Z. (1996) "Effect of Overtime Work on Cognitive Function in Automotive Workers," *Scandinavian Journal of Work, Environment and Health*, 22: 124–132.

Prothro, J. (1954) *Dollar Decade: Business Ideas in the 1920s*, Baton Rouge, LA: Louisiana State University Press.

Putnam, R. (2001) *Bowling Alone: The Collapse and Revival of American Community*, New York: Simon and Schuster.

Rae, J. (1894) *Eight Hours for Work*, London: MacMillan and Co.

Raggatt, P.T. (1991) "Work Stress among Long-Distance Coach Drivers: a Survey and Correlational Study, *Journal of Organizational Behavior*, 12: 565–579.

Ranson, B. (1987) "The Institutionalist Theory of Capital Formation," *Journal of Economic Issues*, XXI (3): 1265–1277.

Reich, R. (1993) *The Work of Nations: Preparing Ourselves for 21st-Century Capitalism*, London: Simon & Schuster.

Reid, D. (1996) "Weddings, Weekdays, Work and Leisure in Urban England 1791–1911," *Past and Present*, 153: 135–163.

Relationship Forum (2007) *An Unexpected Tragedy: Evidence for the Connection between Working Patterns and Family Breakdown in Australia*, Sydney: Relationships Forum Australia Inc. Online. Available: http://www.relationshipsforum.org.au (accessed 16 December 2008).

Reuther, W. (1961) AFL-CIO Proceedings of the Fourth Constitutional Convention, Miami beach, FL, Dec. 7–113.

Reynolds, L. (1974) *Labor Economics and Labor Relations*, Englewood Cliffs, NJ: Prentice Hall.

Rifkin, J. (2000) *The End of Work: The Decline of the Global Labor Force and the Dawn of the Post-Market Era*, New York: Penguin Books.

Robinson, B. (1997) "Work Addiction and the Family: Conceptual and Research Considerations," *Early Child Development and Care*, 137 (1): 77–92.

Robinson, B., Carroll, J. and Flowers, C. (2001) "Marital Estrangement, Positive Affect, and Locus of Control Among Spouses of Workaholics and Spouses of Non-workaholics: A National Study," *American Journal of Family Therapy*, 29: 397–410.

Robinson, J. (1969) *Introduction to the Theory of Employment*, London: St. Martin's Press.

Roediger, D. and Foner, P. (1989) *Our Own Time: A History of American Labor and the Working Day*, New York: Verso.

Rothschild, K.W. (1991) "A Note on Insiders, Outsiders, and the Two-Thirds Society," *Kyklos*, 44 (2): 233–239.

Rousseau, J.J. (1986) *The First and Second Discourses*, New York: MacMillan.

Rowe, J. (1999) "The Growth Consensus Unravels," *Dollars and Sense*, No. 224 July–August. Online. Available http://www.dollarsandsense.org/archives/1999/0799rowe.htm (accessed 9 September 2008).

Rowthorn, R.E. (1977) "Conflict, Inflation and Money," *Cambridge Journal of Economics*, 1: 215–239.

Rubin, M. and Richardson, R. (1997) *The Microeconomics of the Shorter Working Week*, Brookfield, VT: Ashgate Publishing Co.

Russek, H.I. and Zohman, B.L. (1958) "Relative Significance of Heredity, Diet and Occupational Stress in Coronary Heart Disease of Young Adults," *American Journal of Medicine*, 325: 266–275.

Ruskin, J. (1860) *Unto this Last and Other Writings*, London: Penguin Classics (1985 Reprint).

Ruskin, J. (2008) "Unto this Last" Online. Available http://www.ruskinmuseum.com/Ruskin.html (accessed 15 July 2008)

Russell, B. (1935) *In Praise of Idleness*, London: Unwin Paperbacks (1976 Reprint).

Sachs, W. (1993) *Global Ecology: A New Arena of Political Conflict*, London: Zed Books.

Sachs, W., Loske, R. and Linz, M. (1998) *Greening the North: A Post-industrial Blueprint for Ecology and Equity*, London and New York: Zed Books.

Sahlins, M. (1972) *Stone Age Economics*, Chicago: Aldine Publishing.

Sampson, A. (1996) *Company Man: The Rise and Fall of Corporate Life*, London: HarperCollins Business.

Samuelson, P. (1971) *Chicago Tribune*, December 9. Section 1A: 7.

Sawyer, M. (2003) "Employer of Last Resort: Could it Deliver Full Employment and Price Stability?" *Journal of Economic Issues*, XXXVII (4): 881–907.

Schnapper, M.B. (1972) *American Labor*, Washington DC: Public Affairs Press.

Schor, J. (1991) *The Overworked America: The Unexpected Decline of Leisure*, New York: Basic Books.

——(1995). "Trading Income for Leisure Time, is There Public Support for Escaping Work-and-Spend?" in V. Bhaskar and A. Glyn (eds) *The North, the South and the Environment, Ecological Constraints and the Global Economy*, Tokyo: Earthscan Publications, United Nations University Press.

——(1998) *The Overspent American*, New York: Harper.

Schultz, D.P. (1978) *Psychology and Industry Today: an Introduction to Industrial and Organizational Psychology*, New York: Macmillan.

Schulze, G. (1993) "Soziologie des Wohlstands," in E.U. Huster (ed.) *Reichtum in Deutschland*, Frankfurt: Campus, 182–209.

Schumacher, E.F. (1974) *Small is Beautiful*, London: Sphere Books Ltd.

Seifert, H. and Trinczek, R. (2000) "New Approaches to Working Time Policy in Germany: The 28.8 Hour Working Week at Volkswagen Company," *WSI-Discussion Paper No. 80*. Düsseldorf/München: WSI.

Seligman, M. (1988) "Why is There So Much Depression Today?" in I.S. Cohen (ed.) *G. Stanley Hall Lectures*, Vol. 9, Washington DC: American Psychological Association.

Selliere, E.A. (1998) Interview in *Liberation*, September 7.

Senior, N.W. (1837) *Letters on the Factory Act, as it Affects the Cotton Manufacture, Addressed to the Right Honourable the President of the Board of Trade*, London: B. Fellowes.

Shah, M. and Marks, N. (2004) "A Well-being Manifesto for a Flourishing Society," *New Economics Foundation Brochure*, London: NEF.

Shapiro, C. and Stiglitz, J. (1984) "Equilibrium Unemployment as a Worker Discipline Device," *American Economic Review*, 74: 433–444.

Shields, M. (1999) "Long working hours and health," *Health Reports*, Statistics Canada 11: 2.

Shulman, S. and Smith, C. (2005) "Immigration and African Americans," in C. Conrad, J. Whitehead, D. Mason and J. Stewart (eds) *African Americans in the US Economy*, Lanham, MD: Rowan and Littlefield.

Simmons, R. (1976) *The American Colonies. From Settlement to Independence*, New York: W.W. Norton.

Skinner, N. and Pocock, B. (2008) "Work, Life and Workplace Culture: The Australian Work and Life Index 2008," *Centre for Work + Life, Hawke Research Institute*, University of South Australia.

Smith, T. (2004) *France in Crisis: Welfare Inequality and Globalization since 1980*, Cambridge, UK: Cambridge University Press.

Sparks, K., Cooper, C., Yitzhak, F. and Shirom, A. (1997) "The Effects of Hours of Work on Health: A Meta-analytic Review," *Journal of Occupational and Organizational Psychology*, 70: 391–408.

Smith, A. (1776) *The Wealth of Nations*, London: Random House Publishing Group (Modern Library Series 1994 Reprint).

Smith. S. and Razzell, P. (1975) *The Pools' Winners*, London: Calibon Books.

Sokejima, S. and Kagamimori, S. (1998) "Working Hours as a Risk Factor for Acute Myocardial Infarction in Japan: Case-Control Study," *British Medical Journal*, 317: 775–780.

Solberg, E.C., Diener, E. and Robinson, M. (2004) "Why are Materialists less Satisfied?" in T. Kasser and A.D. Kanner (eds), *Psychology and Consumer Culture: The Struggle for a Good Life in a Materialistic World*, Washington, DC: American Psychological Association: 29–48.

Solnick, S. and Hemenway, D. (1998) "Is more always better? A survey on positional concerns," *Journal of Economic Behavior and Organization*, 37: 373–383.

Souza-Poza, A. and Henneberger, F. (2000) "Work Attitudes, Work Conditions and Hours Constraints: An Explorative, Cross-national Analysis," *Labour*, 14 (3): 351–372.

Spencer, D. (2003) "Love's Labor's Lost? The Disutility of Work and Work Avoidance in the Economic Analysis of Labor Supply" *Review of Social Economy*, LXI (2): 235–250.

Spiegel, N.W. (1991) *The Growth of Economic Thought*, Durham, NC: Duke University Press.

Spurgeon, A. (2003) *Working Time: Its Impact on Safety and Health*, Seoul, Korea: International Labor Organization and Korean Occupational Safety and Health Research Institute.

Stabile, D. (1996) *Work and Welfare: The Social Costs of Labor in the History of Economic Thought*, Westport, CT: Greenwood Press.

Stanfield, J.R. (1986) *The Economic Thought of Karl Polanyi: Lives and Livelihood*, London: Palgrave MacMillan.

——(1992) "The Fund for Social Change," in J. Davis (ed.) *The Economic Surplus in Advanced Economies*, Brookfield, VT: Edward Elgar: 130–148.

——(1996) *John Kenneth Galbraith: Contemporary Economists Series*, London: Palgrave Macmillan.

——(1999) "The Scope, Method, and Significance of Original Institutional Economics," *Journal of Economic Issues*, 33: 231–255.

Stanfield, J.R. and J.B. Stanfield. (1980) "Consumption in Contemporary Capitalism: The Backward Art of Living," *Journal of Economic Issues*, 14 (2): 437–451.

—— (1997) "Where Has Love Gone? Reciprocity, Redistribution, and the Nurturance Gap," *Journal of Socio-Economics*, 26: 111–128.

Steinbeck, J. (1939) *The Grapes of Wrath*, New York: Viking Press.

Stern, N. (2007) *The Economics of Climate Change: The Stern Review*, Cabinet Office – HM Treasury, Cambridge: Cambridge University Press.

Stevenson, B. and Wolfers, J. (2007) "The Paradox of Declining Female Happiness," Online. Available http://bpp.wharton.upenn.edu/betseys (accessed 22 July 2008).

Stewart, M. and Swaffield, J. (1997) "Constraints on the Desired Hours of Work of British Men," *The Economic Journal*, 107: 520–535.

Stier, H. and Lewin-Epstein, N. (2003) "Time to Work: a Comparative Analysis of Preferences for Work Hours," *Work and Occupations*, 30 (3): 302–325.

Stutzer, A. (2004) "The Role of Income Aspirations in Individual Happiness" *Journal of Economic Behavior and Organization*, 54 (1): 89–109.

Sustainable Development Issues Network (2008) *Outreach Issues,* May. Online. Available http://sdin-ngo.net/publications/oi/080508–06.html (accessed 9 September 2008).

Syndicalisme Hebdo (1988) 22 May, Paris: CFDT: 29.

Taddei, D. (1997) *La Reduction du Temps de Travail*, Paris: La Documentation Française.

Talberth, J., Cobb, C. and Slattery, N. (2007) "The Genuine Progress Indicator 2006: A Tool for Sustainable Development," *Redefining Progress*. Online. Available www. rprogress.org (accessed 3 August 2008).

Tawney, R.H. (1937) *Religion and the Rise of Capitalism*, London: Harmondsworth: Penguin Books (1990 Reprint).

Taylor, F.W. (1947) *Scientific Management, Comprising Shop Management, the Principles of Scientific Management [and] Testimony before the Special House Committee*, New York: Harper.

Thiel, H.G., Parker, D. and Bruce, T.A. (1973) "Stress Factors and the Risk of Myocardial Infarction," *Journal of Psychosomatic Research* 17: 43–57.

Thompson, E.P. (1967) "Time, Work-Discipline, and Industrial Capitalism," *Past & Present*, 38 (1): 56–97.

Thompson, P. (1983) *The Nature of Work: An Introduction to Debates on the Labour Process*, Atlantic Highlands, NJ: Humanities Press International.

Thoreau, H.D. (1854) *Walden* (Collector's Library). London: CRW Publishing Limited (2004 Reprint).

Tilgher, A. (1977) *Work: What it has Meant to Men through the Ages.* Translated by Dorothy Fisher. New York: Arno Press.

Titmuss, R.H. (1970) *The Gift Relationship,* London: Allen and Unwin.

Tobin, J. (1968) "Raising the Income of the Poor," in K. Gordon (ed.) *Agenda for the Nation*, Washington DC: The Brookings Institution.

Tool, M. (1998) "Employment as a Human Right," in J. Michie and A. Reati (eds) *Employment Technology, and Economic Needs: Theory, Evidence, and Public Policy*, Cheltenham, UK: Edward Elgar.

Trinkoff, A.M., Le, R. Geiger-Brown, J. and Lipscomb, J. (2007) "Work Schedule, Needle Use and Needlestick Injuries Among Registered Nurses," *Infection Control and Hospital Epidemiology*, 28: 156–164.

Trout, C. (1973) "Welfare in the New Deal Era," *Current History*, 65: 11–14.

Tseng, Y. and M. Wooden (2005) *Preferred vs Actual Working Hours in Couple Households*, Melbourne Institute Working Paper No. 7/05. Melbourne.

Tugwell, R., Munro, T. and Stryker, R. (1927) *Industry's Coming of Age,* New York: Harcourt Brace and Company.

Uehata, T. (1991) "Long Working Hours and Occupational Stress-Related Cardiovascular Attacks Among Middle-Aged Workers in Japan," *Journal of Human Ergology*, 20: 147–153.

Ulmer, M. (1972) "Toward Public Employment and Economic Stability," *Journal of Economic Issues,* 6 (4): 149–170.

UNICEF, *Child Poverty in Perspective: An Overview of Child Well-Being in Rich Countries. Innocenti Report Card 7.* Innocenti Research Centre, Florence: The United Nations Children Fund, 2007.

United Nations (2006) "World Hunger Increasing" *FAONewsroom*, Food and Agriculture Organization, Rome, 30 October. Online. Available http://www.fao.org/ newsroom/en/news/2006/1000433/index.html (accessed 26 March 2008).

Van Audenrode, M. (1994) "Short-Time Compensation, Job Security and Employment Contracts: Evidence from Selected OECD Countries," *The Journal of Political Economy*, 102 (1): 76–102.

Van der Hulst, M. (2003) "Long workhours and health," *Scandinavian Journal of Work, Environment & Health*, 29 (3): 171–188.

Van Parijs, P. (1995) *Real Freedom for All: What (If Anything) Can Justify Capitalism?* Oxford: Clarendon Press.

Van Parijs, P., Rogers, J. and Cohen, J. (2001) *What's Wrong with a Free Lunch?* Boston: Beacon Press.

Van Praag, B. and Fritjers, P. (1999) "The Measurement of Welfare and Well-Being: The Leyden Approach," in D. Kahneman, E. Diener and N. Schwarz (eds) *Well Being: The Foundations of Hedonic Psychology*, New York: Russell Sage Foundation.

van Wanrooy, B. (2007) "A Desire for 9 to 5: Australians' Preference for a Standard Working Week," *Labour & Industry*, 17 (3): 71–95.

Veblen, T. (1898) "The Instinct of Workmanship and the Irksomeness of Labor," *The American Journal of Sociology*, 4 (2): 187–201.

——(1899) *The Theory of the Leisure Class*, New York: Macmillan.

——(1904) *The Theory of Business Enterprise*, New Bruinswick, NJ: Transaction Books (1978 Reprint).

——(1919) *The Vested Interests*, New Brunswick, NJ: Transaction Publishers (2002 Reprint).

——(1921) *The Engineers and the Price System*, New York: The Viking Press.

——(1964) *The Instinct of Workmanship and the State of the Industrial Arts*, New York: WW Norton.

Visser, J. and Hemerijck, A. (1997) *A Dutch Miracle: Job Growth, Welfare Reform and Corporatism in the Netherlands*, Amsterdam: Amsterdam University Press.

Walker, D. (1979) "The Institutionalist Economic Theories of Clarence Ayres," *Economic Inquiry*, XVII: 519–538.

Walker, T. (2004) "The 'Lump-of-Labor' Case against Work-Sharing," in L. Golden and D. Figart (eds) *Working Time: International Trends, Theory and Policy Perspectives*, New York: Routledge.

Wallace, M. (1989) "Brave New Workplace: Technology and Work in the New Economy," *Work and Occupations*, 16 (4): 363–392.

Wanger, S. (2004) Teilzeitarbeit – Ein Gesetz liegt im Trend (Rep. No.): Nürnberg: Institut für Arbeitsmarkt-und Berufsforschung der Bundesagentur für Arbeit.

Warr, P. and Payne, R. (1982) "Experiences of Strain and Pleasure Among British Adults," *Social Science and Medicine* 16: 1691–1697.

Webb, S. and Webb, G. (1963) *English Poor Law Policy*, Hamden, CT: Archon Books.

Weber, M. (1922) *Wirtschaft und Gesellschaft, bearbeitet von Max Weber*, Tubingen: JCB. Mohr.

Weintruab, S. (1961) *Classical Keynesian, Monetary Theory, and the Price Level*, Philadelphia, PA: Chilton Co.

Whaples, R. (2001) "Hours of Work in U.S. History," EH.Net Encyclopedia, August. Online. Available http://eh.net/encyclopedia/article/whaples.work.hours.us (accessed 15 July 2008).

White, W. (1960) *The Organization Man*, Harmondsworth: Penguin.

Whitley, J. and Wilson, R. (1986) "The Impact on Employment of a Reduction in the Length of the Working Week," *Cambridge Journal of Economics*, 10: 43–59.

Widerquist, K., Lewis, M. and Pressman, S. (2005) *The Ethics and Economics of the Basic Income Guarantee (Alternative Voices in Contemporary Economics)*, London: Ashgate Publishing.

Wilde, O. (1997) *Collected Works of Oscar Wilde: The Plays, the Poems, the Stories and the Essays, Including De Profundis*, London: Wordsworth Editions.

Wilding, K., Clark, J., Griffth, M., Jochum, V. and Wainwright, S. (2006) *The UK Voluntary Sector Almanac*, London: NCVO.

Wilkinson, W. (2007) "In Pursuit of Happiness Research: Is it Reliable? What Does it Imply for Policy?" Cato Institute Policy Analysis Series, The Cato Institute. Washington, DC. No. 590 April 11. Online. Available http://www.cato.org/pub_-display.php?pub_id = 8179

Williamson, O. (1985) *The Economic Institutions of Capitalism,* New York: Free Press.

Wolfe, A. (1973) *The Seamy Side of Democracy,* New York: David McKay Co.

"Working time developments and the quality of work: The case of France." European Industrial Relations Observatory (EIRO). Online. Available http://www.eiro.eurofound.ie (accessed 10 April 2008).

World Health Organization (2006) "Obesity and overweight" *Fact sheet N°311* September. Online. Available http://www.who.int/mediacentre/factsheets/fs311/en/print.html (accessed 26 March 2008).

Wray, L.R. (1998a)*Understanding Modern Money: The Key to Full Employment and Price Stability*, Cheltenham: Edward Elgar.

——(1998b) "Zero Unemployment and Stable Prices," *Journal of Economic Issues,* 32 (2): 539–545.

——(2001) "Money and Inflation," in R. Holt and S. Pressman (eds) *A New Guide to Post Keynesian Economics,* New York: Routledge.

Wray, L.R. and Forstater, M. (2004) "Full Employment and Social Justice," in J. Knoedler and D. Champlin (eds) *The Institutionalist Tradition in Labor Economics,* Armonk, NY: ME Sharpe: 253–272.

Wuthnow, R. (1996) *Poor Richard's Principle: Recovering the American Dream Through the Moral Dimension of Work, Business and Money*, Princeton, NJ: Princeton University Press.

Xenos, N. (1989) *Scarcity and Modernity*, New York: Routledge.

Yang, H., Schnall, P., Jauregui, M., Su, T. and Baker, D. (2006) "Work hours and Self-Reported Hypertension Among Working People in California," *Hypertension* 48: 744–750.

Zelinski, E. (1997) *The Joy of Not Working: a Book for the Retired, Unemployed, and Overworked*, Berkeley, CA: Ten Speed Press.

Zinn, H. (1999) *A People's History of the United States: 1942–Present,* New York: HarperCollins.

Index

284   *Index*

General Health Questionnaire 86
General Motors 205
General Social Survey 89
Genuine Progress Indicator *see* GPI
George, C. and George, K. 15
Georgia 16
German economy 221, 228
German employers 207, 222, 226
German Historical School 60
German Historicists 36, 60, 62
German origins of STC 207
German program 208–9
German unions 221
German workers 221
Germany 3, 16, 60–1, 80, 90, 95, 146,
   162, 181, 189, 207, 211, 221–2, 226,
   228, 230, 253
Gerson, K. 134, 180, 185
Gestalt theory 63
GHG emissions 165–6
Gibson,T. 109
Gilded Age 18, 20
Gilman, J. 111
Gini, A. 180
globalization 119, 207
Gneezy, U. 102
God 10–14, 18, 20, 28, 39
gold 24, 122
Golden, L. 87, 184, 252–3
Goldthorpe, J. 112, 141
Gompers, S. 193
goodwill 39–40
Gorres, P. 203
Gorz, A. 75, 98–101, 104, 108–9, 118,
   124, 136, 152, 165, 191–2, 226,
   234–5, 240, 252
Gottschalk, S. 151, 153
government assistance 214, 238, 252
government bonds 123
government contractors 158, 238
government debt 122–3, 125
government expenditures 28, 43–4, 77,
   106, 112, 114–15, 121–3, 125, 130–1,
   145, 164, 200–1
government intervention 6, 44, 105,
   112, 162, 191, 225, 235–6
GPI (Genuine Progress Indicator) 77–8
Great Britain 28, 243, 250
Great Depression 38, 42–4, 106, 124,
   204
Great Wall of China 18
greater socioeconomic participation 1,
   4, 6, 87, 104, 115–16, 125, 153,
   161–2, 179, 240, 248

Greek philosophers 8–9, 23, 50
Green GDP 77
Greene, B. 208
Greens 213
Greider, W. 140
Grenoble 230
Gresham's Law 69
Grimes 36
growth consensus 44, 49–50, 74–5, 77,
   94, 112, 159, 250
Gubian, A. 184, 215, 254
Gustav, A. 60

Hagerty, M. 84
Hahnel, J. 185
Halle University 60
Hamburg, Germany 60
Hamermesh, D. 169–70, 236, 241
Hamilton, D. 26, 28, 56–7, 63, 78
hand/wrist injuries characteristic 171
happiness
   aggregate 87
   collective 81, 103
   female 176
   gross national 81
   individual's 83, 90
   male 176
   personal 88
happiness levels 82
Happiness Rankings 82–3
happiness research 9, 26, 38, 63, 76, 78–
   9, 81–91, 93, 169, 188, 240, 244, 250
harmony 2, 4, 10–11, 158
Harpers Index 67
Hart and Associates 182, 237
Harvard students 86
Haugh, H 101, 251
Hayden, A. 101, 124, 152, 164, 168,
   191, 214–15, 217, 222
health 49, 77, 79–80, 83, 91, 126,
   147, 159, 168–70, 172–3, 175, 218,
   239, 244
   mental *see* diseases, mental (illnesses,
      mental)
   personal 169
   psychological 6, 172
health disparities 250
health insurance 77, 206, 209
healthcare 76, 79, 84, 153, 169, 208, 236
heart attack *see* cardiovascular
   disorders
heart attack fatalities *see* cardiovascular
   disorders (heart attack)
Heath, J. 117